KING GEORGE'S OWN
CENTRAL INDIA HORSE
The Story of a Local Corps

From a Miniature

Captain Henry Otway Mayne

KING GEORGE'S OWN
CENTRAL INDIA HORSE
The Story of a Local Corps

BY

MAJOR-GENERAL W. A. WATSON,
C.B., C.M.G., C.I.E.
HONORARY COLONEL OF THE REGIMENT

WITH A CHAPTER RELATIVE TO
THE SECOND AFGHAN WAR BY

COLONEL SIR NEVILLE CHAMBERLAIN, K.C.B.

WITH ILLUSTRATIONS AND MAPS

The Naval & Military Press Ltd

Reproduced by kind permission of the Central Library,
Royal Military Academy, Sandhurst

Published by
The Naval & Military Press Ltd
Unit 10, Ridgewood Industrial Park,
Uckfield, East Sussex,
TN22 5QE England
Tel: +44 (0) 1825 749494
Fax: +44 (0) 1825 765701
www.naval-military-press.com
© The Naval & Military Press Ltd 2005

In reprinting in facsimile from the original, any imperfections are inevitably reproduced and the quality may fall short of modern type and cartographic standards.

PREFACE.

To All Ranks of the Central India Horse.

Some years ago, at one of our regimental dinners in London, my friend Colonel Hewlett suggested that, since the Central India Horse had entered a new period of its existence, somebody should be called upon to write a history of the old; and I, being supposed to be imbued, more than most others present on that occasion, with the spirit of those old times, was entrusted with this laborious but very pleasant duty. I admit the qualification; but because it is the only qualification you will find that my effort, now at last accomplished, has resulted in a somewhat informal 'family record' rather than in a Regimental History of the official sort. I send it out to you nevertheless as a token of my love for the men whose doings, and the places whose charm, are recorded here; of my appreciation of my own good fortune in being one of you, and of my unfading recollection of an exceedingly happy life.

Much help has been given to me. My thanks are due, in the first place, to the Secretary in the Military

PREFACE

Department at the India Office, and to the Agent to the Governor-General at Indore, who have very kindly placed many old documents at my disposal. The Commandant of the regiment has sent me a box full of old Order Books and other records, without which the book could not have been written. Major Otway Mayne, until recently Chief Constable of Buckinghamshire, has provided me with information concerning early days, and has allowed me to produce that beautiful miniature of his father which forms the frontispiece. To Colonel C. H. Beatson am I indebted for the picture of Beatson of 'Beatson's Horse,' and to Mrs Caine for the early photograph of her father, Sir Richard Meade. Miss Bradford of Chawton has kindly lent me some of her father's papers. Many regimental officers, past and present, have supplied me with notes. Of these, Colonel Masters and General Edwards have told me stories of their own experiences; Generals Douglas and Birdwood have given me accounts of the incidents in Persia; Colonel Hewlett has reminded me of certain sporting details; and in regard to the Great War I am especially grateful to Sir Norman Leslie, Colonel Gourlie, General Hoare, and Major Rawdon Macnabb for the material which, with so much trouble, they have collated for me. Colonel John Pinney, Colonel A. P. Browne, Colonel Hutchison, Major Charles Daunt, Sir Thomas Lawson-Tancred, Captain T. Westmacott, and Captain W. W. K. Page have also sent me notes on this subject. To Sir Neville Chamberlain, who has written the chapter on the Second Afghan War, and to Colonel Donald Cameron am I indebted for

PREFACE

advice and encouragement throughout. I am grateful also to Captain Whitworth, the historian of the 2nd Lancers, and to Mr W. E. Massey, the author of 'Allenby's Final Triumph,' for permission to use their works; and finally, but not least, to Mr James Blackwood for the interest which he has taken in the book and for the excellent form in which he has brought it out.

May I hope that these records will, for the old, revive pleasant memories of the past, and, for the young, provide an incentive to emulate the deeds of their heroic predecessors. You are not an old regiment, but you have many great names on your rolls. To these names do you owe the traditions which have made you conspicuous. May you keep those old traditions alive.

THE AUTHOR.

TELSCOMBE, SUSSEX,
November 25, 1929.

CONTENTS.

CHAP.		PAGE
I.	THE BIRTH OF THE REGIMENT	1-18
II.	THE PURSUIT OF TANTIA TOPI	19-37
III.	MEADE'S HORSE, BEATSON'S HORSE, AND MAYNE'S HORSE	38-66
IV.	CENTRAL INDIA HORSE	67-81
V.	TRAVERS	82-92
VI.	THE SILLADAR SYSTEM	93-106
VII.	HENRY DALY	107-118
VIII.	OTHER MUTINY HEROES	119-141
IX.	THE SECOND AFGHAN WAR, BY SIR NEVILLE CHAMBERLAIN, K.C.B.	142-172
X.	MARTIN	173-194
XI.	BULLER	195-210
XII.	GERARD	211-223
XIII.	AGAR AND GOONAH	224-240
XIV.	THE TIRAH CAMPAIGN	241-255
XV.	BETWEEN TIRAH AND PERSIA	256-284
XVI.	THE REGIMENT IN PERSIA	285-304
XVII.	THE GREAT WAR—FRANCE	305-329
XVIII.	THE GREAT WAR—FRANCE (*continued*)	330-357
XIX.	THE GREAT WAR—FRANCE (*continued*)	358-380
XX.	THE GREAT WAR—PALESTINE	381-406
XXI.	WE LEAVE CENTRAL INDIA	407-414

CONTENTS

APPENDICES.

APPENDIX		PAGE
I.	MAKING A 'CAVALRY TRACK'	415-419
II.	LETTERS TO THE COMMANDING OFFICER ON THE DEPARTURE OF THE REGIMENT FROM FRANCE .	420-421
III.	BRITISH OFFICERS WHO SERVED WITH THE REGIMENT DURING THE GREAT WAR . . .	422-423
IV.	RECORDS OF EXTRA-REGIMENTAL SERVICES OF BRITISH OFFICERS DURING THE GREAT WAR .	424-455
V.	REWARDS GAINED DURING THE GREAT WAR .	456-459
VI.	BRITISH OFFICERS WHO WERE POSTED TO THE 39TH, OR SECOND REGIMENT, DURING THE GREAT WAR	460

INDEX 461

ILLUSTRATIONS.

CAPTAIN H. O. MAYNE		*Frontispiece*
CAPTAIN RICHARD JOHN MEADE		*Facing p.* 39
From a photograph by VANDYK.		
COLONEL WILLIAM FERGUSSON BEATSON		,, 46
From an engraving by D. J. POUND.		
DAFADAR HARSA SINGH		,, 182
DAFADAR KADIR BAKSH		,, 204

MAPS.

THE JUNGLES OF CENTRAL INDIA		*Facing p.* 18
SKETCH MAP OF NORTHERN FRANCE		,, 312
ACTION AT CAMBRAI		,, 371
PALESTINE AND SYRIA		,, 384

The Central India Horse.

CHAPTER I.

THE BIRTH OF THE REGIMENT.

WE were born in the jungles of Central India. These inaccessible regions, the haunt of the tiger and the dacoit,[1] were garrisoned during the forty years preceding the Mutiny by Contingents of all arms of the service, provided by the chiefs in whose territories they were quartered, but administered by the East India Company and led by British officers. These Contingents, or Sebandies as they were sometimes called, were raised for local service only. In their origin they were little more than Police. The men were enlisted locally, and lived with their families in permanent Lines. The risk of disloyalty was thus reduced to a minimum. Each corps preserved its own individuality, and knew little of its neighbours. The Rajah was its 'sirkar,'[2] with the 'Company Bahadur'[3] in the background, and his interests were its own. But there was not much soldiering. A little guard mounting and a little

[1] Armed robber. [2] Government. [3] East India Company.

drill, with good pay and comfortable quarters, sufficed to content the sepoy. It was not enough for the British officer. The monotony of inaction entered into his soul, and he set to work to improve things. He looked further afield for his recruits; he enlisted men from the fighting classes; he smartened their uniform; he polished up their equipment, and he trained them up to the level of the Regular Army. He was supported, and even encouraged, by the Political Agents, under whose direct orders the Contingents were originally placed. Especially was this the case in Bhopal, where the Agent, Captain Cunningham, favoured the Sikh element, and so founded that Sikh colony at Sehore which has given our regiment so many remarkable men. The higher political authorities viewed this development with some anxiety. Local distinctiveness was vanishing, and with it that security which local recruiting was intended to provide. The Contingents were becoming mere offshoots of the Bengal Army.

A few years before the Mutiny a change was made. All the Contingents in Central India were placed directly under the orders of the Agent to the Governor-General at Indore. This only made matters worse. The regiments became more and more assimilated to one another and to the Regular regiments. They even went to Camps of Exercise. As trained soldiers they were getting on very well. Would they be faithful warriors? They were learning too much; they had too many friends in the Bengal Army. The Politicals grew more anxious than ever. If unrest occurred in Bengal it might spread to Central India. And it did. Within a month of the outbreak at Meerut the spirit of insurrection descended upon the Contingents, and swept through them like flame before the wind.

Before the end of May 1857 the Maharajah of Gwalior, already suspicious of his men, had suggested that our women and children should be removed from the cantonment of Morar. Here were the Headquarters and the greater part of the Gwalior Contingent, a force of 8318 men, commanded by Brigadier-General Ramsay, comprising two cavalry regiments, four batteries, and seven battalions. One battalion, the third, was at Sipri; the fifth was at Agar; the sixth at Lalitpur, with a wing at Asirgarh; and the seventh at Neemuch. There were some Regular regiments at Neemuch. These broke out on the 4th of June, and carried the Gwalior men with them. The sixth mutinied at Lalitpur on the 13th. Between the 14th and 18th the battalion at Sipri and all the troops at Morar turned on their British officers, murdered many of them, and sacked and burnt the cantonments. The men of the fifth battalion, isolated as they were at Agar, remained steady for the moment; but they, too, joined the throng a few weeks later, and, after killing their Adjutant, Lieutenant O'Dowda, and Dr James and his wife, went shouting up the Grand Trunk road to Agra. Of all the units of this great Contingent a mere handful of men of the 2nd Cavalry were loyal throughout. The rest, for all their military efficiency, were worse than useless.

Meanwhile the clouds were gathering at Indore. Sir Robert Hamilton, the Agent to the Governor-

General, was at home on furlough, and Colonel Durand, afterwards Sir Henry Marion Durand, K.C.S.I., C.B., Lieutenant-Governor of the Panjab, one of the most brilliant military civilians of his day, was acting for him. The only European troops in Central India at the time were some gunners—one battery of artillery, in point of fact, under the command of Major Hungerford—at Mhow; and there, where Regular regiments of the Bengal Army were quartered, it was necessary for them to remain. Durand placed no dependence on these Regular regiments, but he believed that the Contingents and certain local corps which were at his disposal were not tainted with disloyalty. At the Residency was his escort, a troop of the Malwa Contingent Cavalry. At Mehidpur was the remainder of that Contingent, consisting of a regiment of cavalry, a battery of artillery, and a battalion of infantry, provided jointly by Holkar, Dewas, and Jaora. At Sehore was the Bhopal Contingent, a body of similar composition but smaller strength. At Sirdarpur was the Malwa Bhil Corps.

By the 20th of May 150 cavalry, three companies of infantry and two guns of the Bhopal Contingent, 200 men of the Malwa Contingent Infantry, and 270 men of the Malwa Bhil Corps were concentrated round the Residency. To these were added a few days later three companies of infantry, three guns, and a few troopers of Holkar's army, the whole under the command of Colonel James Travers of the Bhopal Contingent; and with these Durand hoped to maintain his position till help should come. He looked for succour to the south. Lord

Elphinstone, the Governor of Bombay, had lost no time in despatching an expedition under General Woodburn for the relief of Central India. If only the men would be true till this column drew near, the situation was safe. But there were already signs of disaffection. Early in June the cavalry of the Malwa Contingent, on the march from Mehidpur to Neemuch, mutinied and shot their British officers; so the troop of this regiment forming the escort was at once removed to Mehidpur. Then came the news of the revolt of the Gwalior troops. Other warnings were not wanting. Ghaus Mahomed, Nawab of Jaora, a very staunch friend who joined our avenging forces later in the year, informed Durand of an understanding between Holkar's troops and the rebels. Holkar himself became alarmed. His men were 'at one,' he reported, with the Malwa Cavalry. Before the end of the month the situation had become as bad as it could be. But Durand still hoped, as he calculated that the Bombay column could not be far off. And then he heard that Woodburn had been diverted to Aurangabad to quell an incipient rising in the Hyderabad Contingent. He could now only wait upon events. The Nawab of Jaora continued his warnings. The troops at Mhow were becoming uneasy. During the last days of June the Sikh sowars of the Bhopal Contingent observed that Holkar's guns were shifted about at night. Religious mendicants appeared in the Lines. The crisis was approaching.

Holkar's troops were posted on the west side of the Residency, not much more than 100 yards from it, watching the approaches from the city. The

Contingent troops and the Bhil Corps were on the northern side, around the Stables, the Post Office, and the Treasury. At 8 o'clock in the morning of the 1st of July a man of the name of Saadat Khan, a Risaldar of Holkar's army, followed by a few sowars and a rabble from the city, galloped down to the Residency and proclaimed to the Durbar troops a fabricated order that the Sahibs were to be killed. The infantry was immediately formed up, and the guns opened fire on the Stables.

Travers had just entered the Orderly Room. Durand, inside the Residency, was writing a letter. Travers hastened to the Stable Square, and attempted to form the Bhopal Cavalry for a charge. The men were unwilling. Their native officers had been tampered with. Feeling that persuasion was useless and delay intolerable Travers drew his sword, gave the order to gallop, and himself charged down upon the guns. He was followed by five Sikhs.[1] The guns were captured, and Travers engaged Saadat Khan, whom he wounded. But success was momentary. There was no support. This little band of heroes soon found themselves under heavy fire from the enemy's infantry at close range, and were obliged to retire to the Stable Square.

Meanwhile Durand had had time to make arrangements for defence and to write to Colonel Platt, commanding at Mhow, requesting him to send Hungerford's battery. The two guns of the Bhopal Contingent were brought into action, being served

---

[1] Their names are worthy of record: they are Lachman Singh, Ganda Singh, Gujar Singh, Indar Singh, and Garja Singh.

by Captain Cobbe, the Executive Engineer, two European sergeants, and fourteen native gunners, who remained faithful and did their duty well. Captain Magniac tried to form up the infantry of the Bhopal and Malwa Contingents, but, with the exception of twelve of the former, both these bodies refused to fight, and in fact went bodily over to the enemy. Captain Magniac then returned to the Residency at about the same time as Travers rode back from his charge. It was about 8.45. The rebels were being reinforced. Their guns were moved to a position whence they could fire on the Residency itself. Durand had left to him only 270 men of the Bhil Corps and two Bhopal guns. The Bhil Corps, useless in the open, were brought inside the Residency. Here were five Europeans of the Telegraph Department, eight ladies—including Mrs Durand,—and three children. The Bhopal Cavalry had taken shelter behind the building on the eastern side. The rebel infantry was creeping up, threatening to outflank them. Though unwilling to attack, they wished to save the lives of the officers and the ladies. They sent word to Durand that if he would retreat at once they would see him and his party out of danger. The Bhopal guns were still in action ; but Cobbe, who had been seriously ill, had fainted from exhaustion, and one of the sergeants had been severely wounded. The Bhils inside the Residency were panic-stricken. There was no sign of Hungerford's battery, nor could it indeed arrive in time to save the situation. Further resistance was useless. Durand decided to retire upon Simrole.

The Bhopal guns were brought behind the Residency. The women and children were placed on the wagons and in a couple of bullock carts; and a little after 10 o'clock, with the Sikh sowars leading and the Bhils bringing up the rear, the retreat began.

Soon after starting Travers was reminded of Hungerford's battery, which might at that moment be on the march from Mhow, and called for a volunteer to take a note to Hungerford informing him that Indore had been abandoned. A Sikh sowar came forward, took the letter, salaamed, and started on his journey. There were rebels all round him. Every village was up in arms. His horse was shot; but, avoiding the road and dodging from patch to patch of jungle, he eventually crept into Rao—half-way between Mhow and Indore,—where he met the battery and delivered his message. Hungerford gave him a spare horse to escape on, and himself went back to Mhow as fast as he could go. The sowar galloped off to the shelter of the Ghats[1] below Mhow, where, however, he managed to lose his second horse. Disguising himself as a fakir, he returned to Indore on foot, and, sitting by the roadside, was able to observe the movements of the rebels and to identify their leaders, against whom he gave valuable evidence some years later. Finally he made his way to Sehore. The name of this faithful soldier was Harsa Singh. Travers, who received the Victoria Cross for his conduct on this day, was afterwards the first Commandant of the Central India Horse, and Harsa Singh was our greatest shikari.

Hungerford returned to Mhow just in time. The troops there mutinied that evening; but they

---

[1] Hills—primarily a 'descent to water.'

were overawed by the battery, and took the road to
Agra without doing very much damage. The Europeans took shelter in the Fort. Three officers lost
their lives, and three had very narrow escapes.
They were pursued by sowars on to the glacis, and
were hauled up over the wall of one of the bastions.
One of these three was Lieutenant Cunliffe Martin
of the 1st Bengal Cavalry, who served for many
years afterwards, and retired as Commandant of the
Central India Horse in 1888.

Durand meanwhile had been obliged to change
his destination to Sehore, where he and his party
arrived on the 4th of July. They were hospitably
received by the Begum, who provided them with
carriages and escort, and sent them down to Hoshangabad. Durand's main object now was to communicate with the disappointing column under
General Woodburn. This column, consisting of two
squadrons of the 14th Light Dragoons, the 25th
Bombay Infantry, a battery of artillery, and some
Sappers and Miners, had set out from Bombay on
the 10th of June. At Ahmednagar news was received not only of the critical situation in Central
India, but of an insubordinate spirit amongst the
sowars of the 1st Cavalry Hyderabad Contingent at
Aurangabad. The march was continued towards
Mhow, but for a short distance only, for on the
19th of June a certain Captain Henry Otway Mayne
of the 1st Cavalry Hyderabad Contingent arrived
in camp with the women and children from Aurangabad; and Woodburn, whether with or without orders
from superior authority is uncertain, immediately
turned his face in that direction.

THE BIRTH OF THE REGIMENT [1857

Mayne, one of the founders of our regiment, was by no means the least remarkable of that band of intrepid cavalry leaders which the Mutiny brought forth, but he served on the outskirts of rebellion : the limelight of Delhi and Lucknow missed him, and so he failed to catch the public eye. Born in March 1819, he was, at the age of nineteen, appointed to the 6th Madras Cavalry, and two years later was transferred to the Hyderabad Contingent, of which he soon became Brigade-Major. In 1847 he went to the Second Sikh War as A.D.C. to Lord Gough, and was present at the battles of Chilianwalah and Gujerat, being twice mentioned in Despatches. At the close of the campaign he was made A.D.C. to the Viceroy, Lord Dalhousie. The latter's successor, Lord Canning, sent him in 1856 to reorganise the 1st Cavalry Hyderabad Contingent, which had shown signs of insubordination. Early in the following year the permanent Commandant returned from Europe. Mayne handed over the regiment in a perfect state of discipline, and reverted to the duties of Second-in-Command. It was the recurrence of trouble in this regiment that necessitated the removal of the ladies and brought the Bombay column to Aurangabad. Mayne was now attached to it as Intelligence Officer.

General Woodburn marched into Aurangabad on the 23rd of June, and proceeded to disarm the mutinous cavalry. The men were paraded on foot; but, becoming alarmed, they broke away, reached their horses, mounted, and fled, with the 14th Light Dragoons after them. The horses of the latter were overburdened and tired. Not more than a dozen of the mutineers were captured. The rest were dispersed. And that was the beginning and end of all mutiny south of the Nerbudda.

The Dekhan Field Force, as it was now called, remained halted at Aurangabad for more than a fortnight, doing very little. Durand, on his arrival at Hoshangabad, had written to the Government of India, to the Chief Commissioner of the Central Provinces, and to General Woodburn, urging the importance of preserving the Nerbudda line. Sensible of the danger of delay and the futility of correspondence, he set out himself for Aurangabad. His letters, however, had set the Dekhan Field Force in motion. Reinforced by a bullock battery of the Hyderabad Contingent and commanded by Brigadier-General Stuart, for General Woodburn had returned to Poona very ill, the column left Aurangabad on the 12th of July. On the 22nd it reached Asirgarh, and here Durand joined it. At Simrole it was augmented by the arrival of the 3rd Cavalry Hyderabad Contingent under Major Orr. Mhow was reached on the 2nd of August, and the Europeans were released from the Fort.

There ensued a short period of inactivity. The monsoon was now at its height. The rain was incessant. The black cotton soil we have known so well made movement absolutely impossible. But there was much to guard against, much to prepare. Twelve miles off was the city of Indore, full of enemies. The Residency had been looted. The buildings around it were a mass of ruins. Holkar's troops were in open rebellion. The Maharajah, loyal but helpless, was confined to the upper chambers of his palace. The firing of guns during the Dasera festival created frequent alarms. Farther north, in Western Malwa, disaffection had been brought to a head by the appearance of a miscreant styling himself the Shahzada Humayun or Firozeshah. Wearing the garb of a pilgrim, and stating that he had just returned from Mecca, this person, with a few followers, approached Mandesore on the 26th of August. He was immediately joined by a body of Mekranis and other ruffians, who escorted him to the palace and set him on the throne. Turbulent characters from all parts of Central India hastened to his standard. The faithful chiefs of Jaora, Ratlam, Sailana, and Sitamao were in jeopardy, and repeatedly applied to Durand for help; but the rains, besides being heavy, were unusually protracted, and it was not until the 20th of October that the column under General Stuart, now reorganised and newly equipped and accompanied by Durand, left Mhow on its avenging mission.

On the morning of the 22nd General Stuart approached Dhar. Mayne, who was riding with a few sowars at the head of the advanced guard, reported that he had been fired on from the Fort. The Rajah of Dhar was a minor, and the Durbar[1] had, contrary to the orders of Government, enlisted a number of Arabs, Mekranis, and other Wilaitis, who had taken possession of the place, and were prepared to stand a siege. It did not last long. The town was taken on the 25th, and the Fort fell six days later. The majority of the rebels escaped and made their way to Mehidpur. Here was the

---

[1] "The Durbar" here means the Governing Body.

Malwa Contingent, infantry and artillery, commanded by Major Timmins, who had with him also a small detachment of the 2nd Cavalry Gwalior Contingent under Risaldar Mir Amjad Ali. The rebels entered the cantonment on the 8th of November. Timmins had six guns, but his men feared the Wilaitis, and went over to them. Only the men of the Gwalior detachment were true. Amjad Ali was a well-known Risaldar of the Contingent. He had friends at the Court of Delhi who did much to persuade him to abandon his allegiance to the British Raj, but without avail. These fellows helped Lieutenant Dysart to work the guns, and then charged the approaching Wilaitis. Numbers, however, were against them. The Risaldar and two sowars, Inayat Ali and Mir Al Rasul, were severely wounded. Nothing more could be done. If the Sahibs were to be rescued, it was time to go. Major and Mrs Timmins and Lieutenant Dysart were the only Europeans left alive. The party were just able to mount and leave the station unobserved when a stray shot killed Mrs Timmins' horse. Her servants, who were making their final salaams, took her quickly away and concealed her until the rebels had completed their orgy of destruction and had marched off with their booty towards Mandesore.

Timmins and Dysart, with Amjad Ali and his faithful warriors, took the direction of Dhar, and came into Durand's camp at Noyla on the 10th. Major Orr was immediately despatched with his regiment to Mehidpur. Passing through the cantonment, which was empty, he came up with the rebels at the village of Rawal, killed a hundred of them, took seventy-four prisoners, and recovered all the guns and ammunition which they had taken away. Mir Amjad Ali's party was for the time being attached to Durand personally as his escort. A little later it became the nucleus of a new regiment which was to be raised by Captain Mayne, and is now the Central India Horse.

Amjad Ali became our first Risaldar Major, and four of his men, Mir Al Rasul,[1] Hidayat Ali, Khudiar Khan, and Singram, eventually reached commissioned rank.

Durand, after dismantling the Fort at Dhar, pushed northwards to strike a blow at the Mandesore rebels. General Stuart's force was not more than 1500 strong. The rebels numbered some 14,000, but they were divided. Firozeshah himself, with 2000 men, was in the Fort at Mandesore. The remainder were besieging Neemuch. At Unel, on the 14th of November, the news of Orr's victory at Rawal was received, and Orr himself marched into camp a few days later. At Tal the Nawab of Jaora, with a small retinue, joined Durand. His own brother and all his armed forces had gone over to the rebels a few days previously. The 19th and 20th were spent crossing the Chambal. On the 21st the troops went into camp within sight of the city of Mandesore. At 1 o'clock the outposts were attacked. Major Robertson of the 25th Bombay

---

[1] Mir Al Rasul was a delightful fellow. In later years he dyed his beard red and trimmed it very smartly. He had a keen sense of humour, and was a great favourite with the subalterns, whom he used to invite to go pig-sticking with him at his home near Delhi. Being a strict Mussulman, he would feel defiled by contact with the unclean beast, and after slaying one would, with a fine gesture, hurl away his spear.

Infantry, the Outpost Commander, opened fire with his guns, and ordered Lieutenant Drew of the 14th Light Dragoons and Major Orr of the Hyderabad Contingent to charge the enemy, who fled back into the town with the loss of one hundred killed and many wounded before the main body came into action.

It was now imperative to relieve Neemuch, for the besiegers were drawing very close. They had, in fact, on the same day that the above action took place, brought up their scaling ladders and commenced an assault, which, however, was unsuccessful. Skirting the city of Mandesore, Durand and Stuart marched northwards soon after mid-day on the 22nd. A little earlier than this the besiegers of Neemuch, hearing of the proximity of British troops, had marched southwards to meet them, and so it happened that the two armies came in contact at the village of Golaria, some five miles north of Mandesore. The 14th Light Dragoons and the Hyderabad Cavalry dashed to the front and got in amongst the enemy's infantry, but were unable to prevent them from occupying the village. It was late in the afternoon. The cavalry, without the support of infantry or guns, were obliged to return to the main body, and both sides went into camp. Early next morning Stuart went forward. To guard against an attack from Mandesore the rear-guard was composed of two companies of the 25th and a squadron of the 14th Light Dragoons with a couple of guns. The enemy's position was soon disclosed: his right in the village of Golaria, his centre along an open ridge, and his left covered by jowari crops and badly broken ground. His six guns were amongst some palm-trees near the centre. Hungerford's and Woolcombe's batteries, opposite the centre, opened fire at 900 yards; but Hungerford, whose battery escort consisted of thirty men of the 14th Light Dragoons under Lieutenant Cunliffe Martin, who had escaped from the mutineers at Mhow, presently moved to the right front, where he could enfilade the enemy's line. Meanwhile our infantry—the 86th "County Downs," the 25th Bombay Infantry, and a battalion of the Hyderabad Contingent—attacked the ridge. They were met by an advance of the enemy's infantry, who charged down with banners flying to within a few yards of the 25th, but were received with the bayonet and driven back to their trenches. Cunliffe Martin had taken the opportunity of this counter-attack to charge the battery in the palm-trees. Followed by the dragoons he galloped into it, sabred the gunners, and took the guns, but he was severely wounded on the knee: the musketry fire from some huts on the outskirts of the village was causing many casualties, and he was obliged to go back to Hungerford. At this juncture the rear was attacked by the rebels from Mandesore. A troop of the 14th and the whole of the Hyderabad Cavalry were sent to reinforce the rear-guard, and the attack was repulsed. The main action continued. The enemy was dislodged from the ridge, and most of his infantry left the field. Those who remained took refuge in the village of Golaria, where they were left for the night. On the following morning, the 24th, the village was taken, the rebels were completely routed, and Firozeshah and all his followers fled precipitately to the Rampura-Bhanpura jungles and the wild country about Jhalra Patan.

Neemuch was thus relieved, and Mayne, with a few sowars, rode in and brought out the garrison.

Durand's mission was now accomplished. He returned with Stuart's column to Indore, where he disarmed Holkar's troops and made over charge of the Residency to Sir Robert Hamilton. But before leaving Mandesore he wrote the following letter to Captain Mayne :—

"*From* Colonel H. M. DURAND, officiating Agent to the Governor-General in Central India,

"*To* Captain H. O. MAYNE.

"No. 45-A, dated the 27th November 1857.

"Brigadier-General Stuart, commanding Mhow Field Force, having at my request placed your services at my disposal, I have the honour to request that you take charge of the details of Cavalry noted in the margin. These detachments having proved loyal to the British Government will form the nucleus of a body of Irregular Cavalry which I am about to propose to the Government of India to have raised and formed, under your command, for employment in Central India.

"(2) Until further orders it will be advisable that you also take charge, temporarily, of the guns and Artillery details, which have accompanied the Sikh Cavalry to Mhow.

"(3) I shall, as soon as possible, furnish

(1) Troop of late 2nd Gwalior Contingent Cavalry at Khull.

(2) Half Troop of 2nd Gwalior Contingent Cavalry.

(3) Detachment of Sikh Cavalry of late Bhopal Contingent as per accompanying copy of Lieutenant-Colonel Stockley's letter.

(4) Detachment of Malwa Contingent Cavalry.

you with further instructions, but I shall feel obliged by your at once examining the condition of Risaldar Amjad Ali's Half Troop, now forming my Escort. The losses, sufferings, and loyal conduct of Amjad Ali and his men will form the subject of a separate representation to The Right Honourable the Governor - General in Council, but it is necessary to have a report upon the present state of these meritorious men as to arms, horses, etcetera."

Mayne reached Indore on the 15th December. On this day the regiment began its career. Lieutenant Cunliffe Martin was appointed Second-in-Command and Adjutant. Assistant Surgeon H. C. Brodrick of the Madras Establishment was appointed in medical charge. Amjad Ali and his men, as well as the few remains of the Malwa Contingent Cavalry, were enrolled, and the detachment of the 2nd Gwalior Cavalry was called up from Khull on the Nerbudda. On the 28th the regiment marched to Sehore, where Naeb Risaldar Indar Singh, Jemadars Narain Singh [1] and Garja Singh,[2] and thirty-two sowars of the Bhopal Contingent were brought on the strength. On the 5th February 1858 Mayne arrived at Goonah, and settled down to the business of training his new corps.

[1] The English equivalents for the various Indian ranks are:—
    Risaldar = Major.   Dafadar = Sergeant.
    Rissaidar = Captain.   Naeb Dafadar = Corporal.
    Jemadar = Lieutenant.   Sowar = Private.
[2] The same Garja Singh who, with four others, followed Travers into Holkar's battery. All five were enrolled in the new corps.

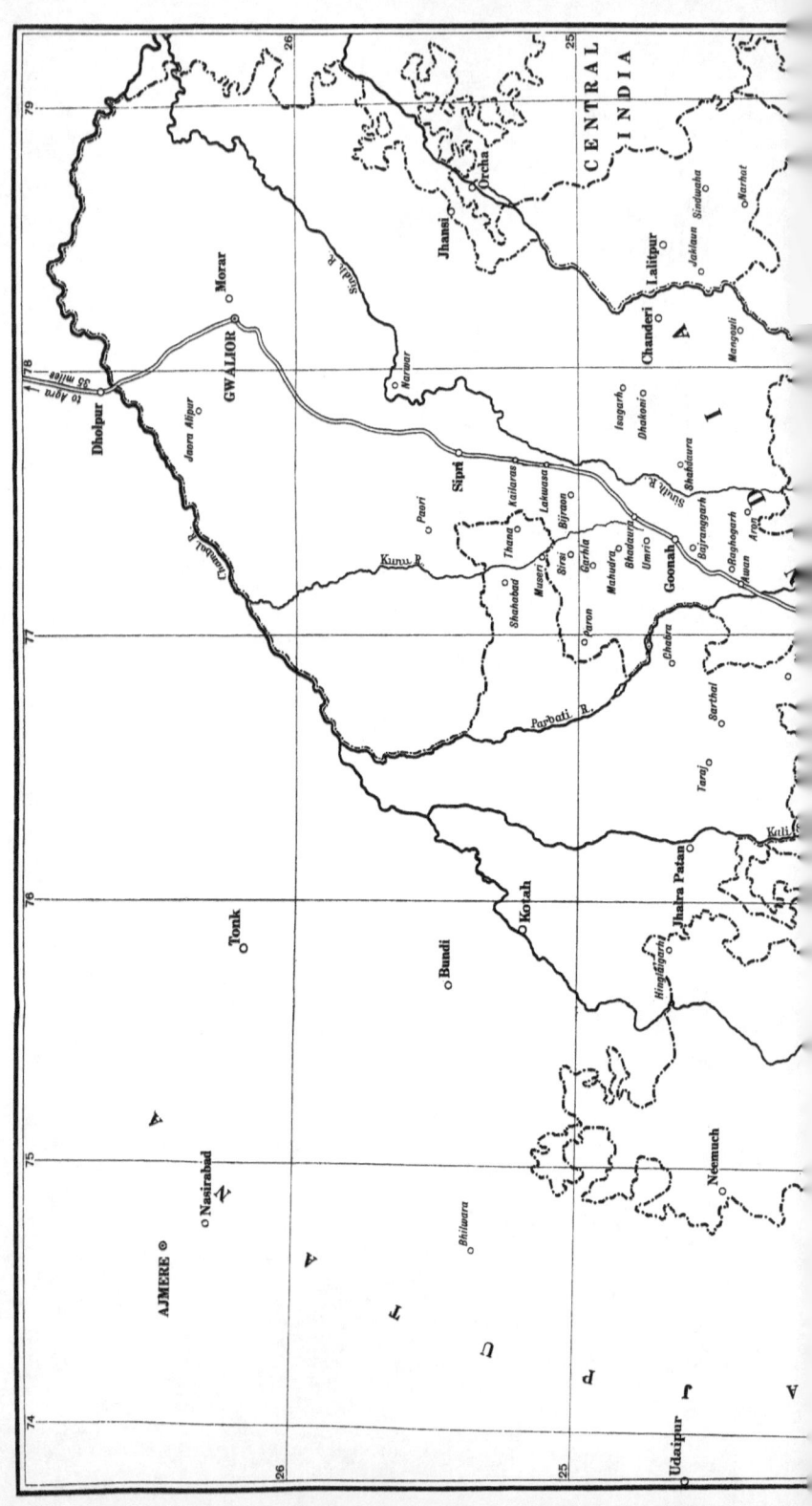

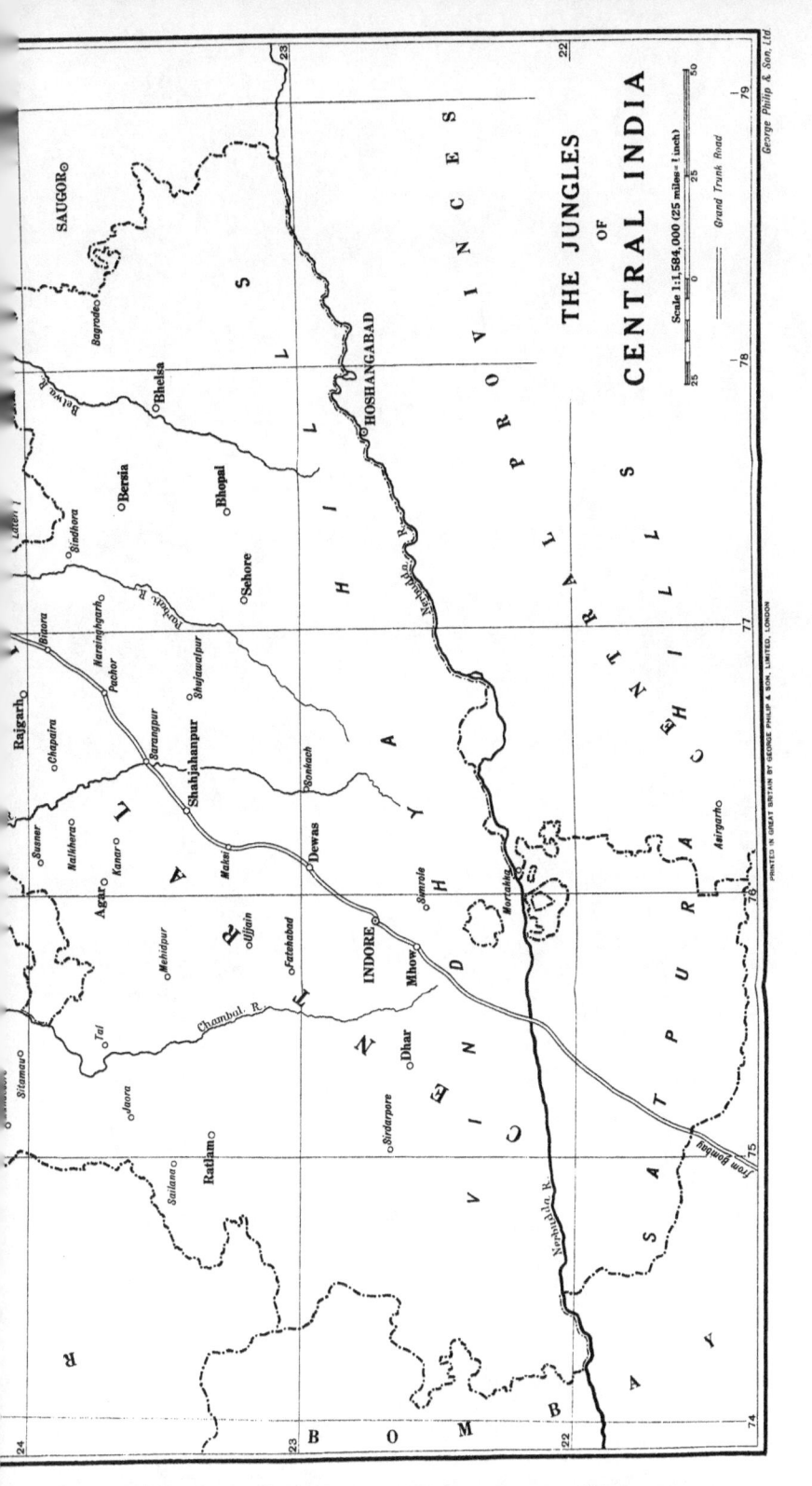

CHAPTER II.

THE PURSUIT OF TANTIA TOPI.

LEAVING Mayne at Goonah, engaged in his task of organisation, we must now follow the closing events of the Mutiny in Central India in order to bring upon the scene two other regiments which were raised about the same time as Mayne's, and were eventually incorporated in his to become, when the crisis was over and Mayne had departed, the Central India Horse.

Stuart's column after refitting at Indore, became the Second Brigade of the Central India Field Force under Sir Hugh Rose. How that force swept through Central India, relieving Saugor, taking Chanderi, Jhansi, and Kalpi, and how, after "marching a thousand miles and taking a hundred guns," it defeated Tantia Topi and the Rani of Jhansi at Gwalior, is told in history. No detachment of our regiment took part in that campaign. But on the 1st June 1858, when the Maharajah of Gwalior was driven from his capital by the arrival of Tantia and the defection of his own troops, he was met at Dholpur and escorted thence into Agra by a squadron of a newly formed regiment known as 'Meade's Horse.'

Captain R. J. Meade[1] had already a distinguished reputation as a Staff Officer. Originally in the 65th Bengal Infantry, he had been for some years D.A.A.G. at Pegu. At the outbreak of the Mutiny he was Brigade-Major of the Gwalior Contingent, and when that Contingent revolted he had escaped, with others, to Agra. Here, since the relief of the place by Greathed's column in October 1857, there had been comparative tranquillity; but there was little military organisation within the Fort, there were no mounted troops to deal with marauding bands which still infested the neighbourhood, nor even a few sowars for orderly duty. Towards the end of 1857 Meade was therefore entrusted with the task of raising a body of Horse. Selecting as his Second-in-Command Lieutenant Cockburn of the 1st Cavalry Gwalior Contingent, who had already distinguished himself, and assisted by Sergeant Hartigan, V.C., of the 9th Lancers, he soon had a regiment in being which, during the first week of March 1858, was inspected by General Showers and pronounced fit for service. From this time until the flight of Scindia, Meade was employed in keeping order in the District. A fortnight of intense anxiety followed the Maharajah's arrival at Agra; but on the 13th June news was received of Rose's advance from Kalpi on Gwalior, coupled with an order from the Commander-in-Chief to send a detachment to reinforce him. A wing of Meade's Horse formed part of this detachment, but was again employed to escort the Maharajah, who decided that he could now safely return to his own territories. His High-

[1] Afterwards Colonel Sir Richard Meade, K.C.S.I.

ness proceeded leisurely. Leaving Agra on the 14th, he had only marched twenty miles by the 16th when he heard of Rose's arrival at Morar. The remainder of the journey, sixty miles or so, was accomplished on the 17th, and the Maharajah joined Sir Hugh that evening after the battle of Morar was over. On the 19th the battle of Gwalior was fought, the fortress was taken, and Tantia Topi was driven into Rajputana.[1]

Meade's Horse was left in Morar during the battle of Gwalior, but on the 20th was ordered to join a pursuing column, consisting of Lightfoot's battery of Bombay Horse Artillery, 60 men of the 14th Light Dragoons, 150 of the 3rd Bombay Cavalry, and 250 of the 3rd Cavalry Hyderabad Contingent, under General Robert Napier.[2] This force left Gwalior at 7 A.M. on the 20th, and at sunset, after marching twenty-five miles in heat to which many succumbed, reached the village of Samauli, and heard that Tantia's army, 10,000 strong, was only a few miles distant.

After a short rest in bivouac the march was continued, and on the morning of the 21st the enemy was found in position near Jaora Alipur, his guns— taken from Gwalior— in the centre, with infantry on either side and cavalry on the flanks.

Lightfoot's battery, escorted by the 14th Light Dragoons, galloped to the left, screened from view by some rising ground, and opened an enfilading fire on the enemy's guns. His infantry turned and

---

[1] During the battle of Gwalior the Rani of Jhansi, in male attire, was shot dead by a trooper of the 8th Hussars.
[2] Afterwards Lord Napier of Magdala.

fled. Our cavalry took up the pursuit: 300 of
the enemy were killed, the country for six miles
round was cleared of rebels, and twenty-six guns,
mostly English six-pounders, were dragged back in
triumph to Morar.

On the return of the pursuing column Sir Hugh
Rose handed over the command of his force to
General Napier, and left Central India to assume
command of the Bombay Army. The rains now set
in, and Napier cantoned his troops, some at Gwalior,
some at Jhansi, and some at Sipri. Meade's Horse
was posted at Gwalior.

Their rest was disturbed by the action of one of
Scindia's chieftains, Man Singh, Rajah of Narwar,
who had quarrelled with his liege lord. On the
2nd August he seized the fort of Paori.[1] He had
no quarrel with the English; but he had broken
the peace, and, since he refused to submit, it was
necessary to punish him. Smith's brigade from
Sipri moved out against him, but, being without siege
ordnance, was too weak to take the place. Smith
could only wait until Napier, with heavy guns and
mortars and a hundred horse and foot, Meade's
Horse included, came down from Gwalior. Operations were commenced on the 20th. A very short
bombardment was enough for Man Singh, who
evacuated the Fort on the night of the 23rd, and,
with his cousin Ajit Singh and all his followers,
fled through the jungles to the south. He was
followed by a column under Colonel Robertson of
the 25th Bombay Infantry, composed of detachments

---

[1] Paori lies about twenty miles to the west of Sipri. It is the place where we used, generally, to start our hot-weather shoots.

from two British and two Indian regiments, four guns, a squadron of the 8th Hussars, and Meade's Horse. On the evening of the 3rd September the enemy was located some twenty-three miles ahead at Bijapur on the Parbati, not far from Goonah. Marching through the night the column reached the bank of the Parbati at daybreak. The rebels, about 600 strong and all dressed in red—they were mostly men of the late Gwalior Contingent,—were observed on some rising ground on the other side of the river. They were by no means prepared for action. Some, in fact, were walking down to the river to bathe. Robertson sent his cavalry across to get behind them. They fought bravely. Lieutenants Stewart and Page of Meade's Horse were wounded. But the surprise was complete. At least 400 rebels were killed, and the rest under Ajit Singh, for Man Singh himself was not present, escaped towards Sironj. Robertson then returned to Goonah.[1]

Meanwhile, after his defeat at Jaora Alipur, Tantia Topi had made his way towards Jaipur. He was headed off by a force under General Roberts from Nasirabad. He fled to Tonk, where the Nawab's gates were closed against him; but he seduced the Nawab's soldiers and acquired four guns. Roberts was still at his heels, and drove him to Bundi. The Maharajah of Bundi was not only loyal but powerful. Tantia received no help here whatever. Turning westwards he made for the hills of Udaipur, and

---

[1] Scindia was so much gratified by the result of Sir Hugh Rose's operations that he proposed to give a medal to the Central India Field Force. The proposal was supported by Sir Hugh, and approved by the Duke of Cambridge. The medal was designed, but, as far as I know, was never issued.

Roberts overtook him at Bhilwara, half-way between
Nasirabad and Neemuch. Here he made a very
short stand, and went on to Kotrah.[1] He was again
overtaken by Roberts, who fought him at the village
of Kankraoli and deprived him of his guns. But
now he doubled on his track, eluded a force which
had been sent from Neemuch to intercept him,
crossed the Chambal, and entered Jhalra Patan.

He rested five days at Patan, and made the most
of his time. The Maharajah was unwilling to help
him, but, as so often happened, the State troops
mutinied and joined the rebels. Tantia demanded
a contribution from the Maharajah of twenty-five
lakhs of rupees, of which fifteen were promised and
five were paid. He then marched off with his booty
towards Indore, where he hoped to spread rebellion
in Holkar's territory and so gain further reinforcements. With his army augmented by the Patan
troops and the Maharajah's guns, thirty in all, he
found himself on the 12th September at Rajgarh;
and here he became aware of the approach of other
pursuers. General Michel, commanding in Malwa,
had, towards the end of August, despatched two
small columns from Indore and Mhow with orders
to cover Ujjain. The first of these, marching through
Ujjain and Agar, reached Susner on the 4th September, and halted to await the arrival of the other.
On the 8th the two columns joined hands at Nalk-
hera, and on the following day General Michel
himself took command of the combined force, which
now consisted of the 22nd, a wing of the 92nd Highlanders, the 4th Bombay Rifles, two guns of Le

---

[1] Forty miles south-west of Udaipur.

Marchand's battery of Bengal Horse Artillery, a squadron of the 17th Lancers, and two squadrons of the 3rd Bombay Cavalry. Mir Amjad Ali and his men, who had been acting as escort to the Agent to the Governor-General at Indore since December, were attached to this force and used as scouts. They were still dressed in the red achkans of the Gwalior Contingent, a fact which sometimes led to no little confusion. Indeed on one occasion a small party of our native cavalry, coming up with them during a reconnaissance, retired somewhat speedily and very nearly created a panic. On the 10th General Michel moved towards Rajgarh, but rain now fell heavily. The black cotton soil became almost impassable. With great difficulty he reached Chapaira, and there he was obliged to halt. Tantia was in the same predicament. Both sides lay for three days within striking distance of one another, unable to move.

On the morning of the 14th the march was resumed. The cavalry and guns, starting at 4 o'clock in the morning, reached Rajgarh twelve hours later. The enemy was in camp, but our infantry, completely exhausted, was still three miles behind, and the General decided to defer the attack till the following day. Tantia disappeared during the night, leaving, however, a strong rear-guard. Next morning Lieutenant H. E. Wood[1] of the 17th Lancers, attached to the 3rd Bombay Cavalry, with a subaltern and a few sowars were skirmishing through the jungle ahead of the column, when they came suddenly upon 500 infantry drawn up in line with

[1] Afterwards Field-Marshal Sir Evelyn Wood, V.C.

cavalry on their flanks. The infantry fired a volley and the cavalry came forward at a gallop, and the skirmishers had to seek safety in flight. Our guns and infantry were soon, however, on the scene, and after a few rounds from the former the enemy's rear-guard followed his main body towards Biaora. Our cavalry were sent in pursuit. Tantia escaped through Biaora with the major part of his army, and made for the big jungles round Maksudangarh; but many of his men were slain by our troopers, and all the guns he had taken from Jhalra Patan fell into our hands. That night General Michel's force encamped under the trees at Biaora.

Whilst this action was proceeding, Mayne's Horse, not yet up to strength but fit for service and ordered to join Michel as rapidly as possible, was pelting down the Grand Trunk Road from Goonah. It arrived at Biaora too late to cut off Tantia's retreat, but was a welcome addition to General Michel's column. Tantia, after crossing the Grand Trunk Road, went on without halting to Sironj, where, exasperated by the loss of his artillery, he blew his Artillery Commander from the muzzle of a gun. Michel halted a day at Biaora, then dived into the jungles to the east. At Narsingarh the rain came on again in those torrential downpours which herald the end of the monsoon. Tantia had reached Sironj, but Michel was brought to a standstill at Bersia. Here the news indicated that the enemy was likely to move down the Betwa to Chanderi or Lalitpur. Our infantry and guns were waterlogged. Only the native cavalry was capable of rapid movement. Mayne, therefore, in command of his own regiment and the 3rd Bombay Cavalry, was ordered to follow Tantia to the north; whilst Michel, who retained Amjad Ali's detachment and the squadron of the 17th Lancers, resolved to push on to Sironj as soon as the weather cleared. Mayne made for Isagarh. Approaching Dhakoni he received an order to join General Smith's brigade, which, freed for action by the dispersal of Man Singh's followers, was now moving southwards to close the circle upon Tantia. He was therefore obliged to change his direction to the north-west. Twenty miles farther on he joined General Smith, who then marched into Isagarh, only to find the place sacked, many of the inhabitants butchered, and the last of the rebels hurrying away. Mayne was very angry. He implored the General to allow him to pursue at once or to join his own column, which, with finer weather setting in, would be on the move in the direction of Tantia's line of retreat. It was not until he received a peremptory order from General Michel to come back to him that he was allowed to go. He proposed to march thirty miles that day, but was restricted to ten. And so he crawled down to Mangauli.

There he arrived on the 10th of October and, to add to his chagrin, was greeted by General Michel with the news that an action had been fought on the previous day. General Michel, who had hurried on through Sironj as soon as the rain had ended, was, on the morning of the 9th October, pitching his tents at Mangauli when a picket of Amjad Ali's men came galloping in with the customary shout of "Dushman hai."[1] The report was unmistakably

[1] "The enemy is there."

correct. There was Tantia, with his advanced guard and his main body all in column of route, quietly approaching the village from the northern side. No time was to be lost. General Michel deployed his infantry, and, with the guns in front, went forward to the attack. Tantia had the advantage of higher ground. He formed his masses along a slight eminence commanding the English approach, with five guns, which he had taken from Sironj and Isagarh, in the centre. His cavalry, acting with greater boldness than usual, and menacing the flanks, penetrated to the rear of the English line and got in amongst the dooli bearers. They were quickly put to flight by a few of the 17th Lancers under Sir William Gordon; and meanwhile the advance of the infantry continued unchecked in spite of heavy fire from the guns. The crest was gained and the guns were captured, and the enemy fled across the Betwa, leaving 300 dead on the field. Pursuit was impossible for want of cavalry, and Tantia disappeared into the Jaklaun jungles.

On the 11th Mayne's Horse was sent forward to reconnoitre. The jungles were infested by Bandelas and Serias, who not only gave no information but made progress extremely difficult. It was first thought that Tantia would make for Saugor, and Michel marched in a south-easterly direction to cut him off from that place. Then Mayne discovered that he had gone to Lalitpur. Direction was changed, and on the 18th, at Narhat, definite news came in that he was contemplating a raid on the territories of the Maharajah of Orcha and was actually in camp at Sindwaha, not twenty miles away. At

3 o'clock on the following morning Michel went forward. The rains were over, spirits were high, and every man in the force felt confident of rounding up Tantia before evening. A little before eight our cavalry came in sight of a few sowars under some trees near the village. These retired at once, and our men, galloping after them, soon descried the whole of Tantia's army in position. He had 10,000 men and four guns disposed along a low line of hills, in front of which, at a distance of about 600 yards, ran a marshy nullah, some 30 feet wide and 2 feet deep in water, bordered by fields of high jowari.[1] Our infantry was still some way behind, and the enemy, believing that he had only a few horsemen to deal with, began to push forward. Some of his infantry came down into the jowari fields, and his cavalry appeared on our right front. Meanwhile our guns, escorted by two squadrons of the 3rd Bombay Cavalry under Lieutenant Wood, had unlimbered near the bank of the nullah opposite the enemy's centre. The rest of the cavalry was sent to the right ready to cut Tantia off from Orcha. The action began with an artillery duel, during which the 3rd Cavalry suffered somewhat severely. Presently the hostile cavalry, emboldened by our apparent weakness, trotted down the hill to the nullah. They found a crossing on our right, beyond the jowari fields, and came over. Our squadrons were at this moment moving still farther to the right. Sir William Gordon, who was leading the rear squadron, turned his men about and charged. He was followed by the remainder of the cavalry, Mayne's Horse amongst

[1] Millet.

them, and the collision occurred on the bank of the stream. The mêlée lasted for some minutes. Men and horses were flung into the water, several of our troopers were killed, and many horses galloped riderless away. The enemy was completely overcome, and those who succeeded in recrossing the nullah fled onwards up the hill. Our men pursued them for some distance. On the edge of the jowari fields Mayne's Horse came upon a 'gol,' or irregular square, of infantry prepared to receive them. Mayne led straight at the square. Lieutenant Bradford,[1] who was riding with him, perceived that the point of the square nearest to them, where impact would occur, was very lightly manned. He turned his horse to the left and galloped in at the flank, where the men were eighteen to twenty deep. He was followed by twenty Sikhs. He himself came through it unwounded,[2] but there were many casualties. The square was overthrown. Those of the rebels who had escaped destruction darted back into the jowari fields, and Mayne's Horse went on after the pursuing cavalry. These two charges decided the day. They occurred in full view of the enemy on the ridge. The sight was too much for them. Moreover, the British infantry could now be observed coming up at the double. They left their guns and fled. There was now no further use for our artillery, and Wood brought his two squadrons round to the crossing. Galloping over ahead of his men, he was suddenly faced by a bunch of rebels who ran out

---

[1] Afterwards Colonel Sir Edward Bradford, K.C.S.I.
[2] When asked by his friend Wood whether he used the cut or thrust on this occasion, he replied, " I don't know. I shut my eyes and galloped."

of the jowari fields—probably the same men who had been scattered by Mayne's Horse. He charged them single-handed, and engaged a tall Wilaiti, whom he overthrew. He then engaged the next man; but the Wilaiti jumped up again and attacked him from behind. At this moment his orderly came to the rescue and cleft the Wilaiti's skull. Wood killed his man by a sword thrust through the chest, and the remainder were accounted for by the men of the 3rd Cavalry, who now came galloping up from the nullah.

A regular pursuit was now organised. The cavalry were rallied, formed into line, and moved forward solemnly at a walk. We have learnt since then that such methods are useless. They were as futile on this occasion as on any other. The enemy disappeared, though not without leaving 6 guns and 500 dead behind him. Our losses were 5 officers and 20 men killed and wounded.

Michel halted on the 20th, and on the 21st marched to Lalitpur. Tantia was now hard pressed. The circle round him was drawing uncomfortably close. His only chance was to break through to the southward and, if possible, cross the Nerbudda. He was in camp north of Lalitpur when he decided on this course. On the 21st he passed the whole of his army between Lalitpur and the Betwa within four miles of Michel's camp without either side being aware of the proximity of the other. As soon as Michel learnt of this movement he doubled back in pursuit. Multowa was reached on the 23rd, Khemlasa on the 24th. On the 25th, near the town of Kurai, Tantia's army was observed marching southward in two distinct wings. The rearward wing was composed of infantry, mostly tired men, many of them mounted on ponies. Our infantry advanced in line against them, and they prepared to defend themselves; but they had no heart for combat, and, at the sight of our stately movement, went about and fled in all directions. Our cavalry was soon upon them. Breaking up into three parties, under Mayne, Gordon, and Curtis, they continued the pursuit for many miles, and returned to camp at nightfall with a tale of 350 dead and the remainder of the wing completely dissipated. Mayne was highly pleased with the conduct of his regiment on this occasion, and expressed his pleasure in the following order :—

"The Commanding Officer is highly gratified with the conduct of the men of the Corps who were present in the fight of yesterday. All behaved well, and none left the ranks to plunder. Therefore great results were obtained. Upwards of 150 rebel sepoys were slain, forty miles of ground were traversed (fifteen being at the gallop), and the troops were for thirteen hours in the saddle. Naeb Risaldars Indar Singh and Mir Kasim Ali, Jemadars Najaf Ali, Garja Singh, and Muzaffar Ali led their men well, and Dafadars Koer Singh and Ziauldin have been reported to General Michel for conspicuous bravery."

Tantia escaped and made his way to Bagrode. He had saved one wing of his army by the sacrifice of the other; but he had gained twenty-four hours on his pursuers, and he pitched his tents at Bagrode, in full confidence that he had broken through the circle and could now cross the Nerbudda without further molestation. A surprise was in store for him. That night a couple of strange-looking peasants were observed in his camp. Their answers to questions were unsatisfactory. They were beheaded; and Tantia decided to move on. Next morning the impedimenta was despatched before daybreak due south to the Nerbudda. The army, mostly cavalry now, and about 4000 strong, halted in line a short distance out of camp to allow the baggage to get clear. And then the new danger was revealed. Some horsemen were seen on a hill to the south-west. They could not belong to the force which had defeated him yesterday. They had come from the opposite direction. Tantia was mystified. Who were these strange warriors, mounted on Arab stallions and dressed in green? He had little time for reflection. Three British officers came galloping down the hillside, followed by 300 yelling sowars. Tantia's line stood for a moment or two, then wavered, broke, and fled. The enemy were soon amongst them; and for five miles, through scrub jungle, high grass, and nullahs the pursuit went on. The losses were not heavy. With a majority of more than ten to one in his favour, Tantia had not very much to fear. The baggage was untouched; the army escaped towards Bhilsa, and a few days later crossed the Nerbudda some forty miles above Hoshangabad.

The cavalry which so distinguished itself in this action was the 1st Regiment of Beatson's Horse. They had arrived that morning from Jalna, 220 miles away, whence they had started on the 3rd September under orders from the Commander-in-Chief to join General Michel's column. Their gallant leader, Colonel Charles Becher, late of the 5th Bengal Light Cavalry, who in spite of his thirty years' service had still all the dash and intrepidity of youth, did not wait to estimate numbers. He charged Tantia's cavalry at sight, and his sowars, with less than nine months' service apiece, followed him to a man. The pursuit, like that of Kurai, broke up into three parties, led by the Colonel, the Adjutant,[1] and the Doctor,[2] armed with Bodraj hog spears. In the nature of things it could not last long. Some forty or fifty rebels were killed. The regiment was then rallied and returned to camp.

Meanwhile Michel's force, continuing the pursuit after the action at Kurai, reached Hoshangabad on the 9th November. On the 11th Mayne's Horse was detached, and returned to Goonah.

Becher crossed the Nerbudda on the 8th in advance of Michel, and was in time to save the Treasury at Baitul. He went on into the Tapti valley, and thence over the Satpuras to Khargaon. He was then called away northward, and henceforward, sometimes alone, sometimes as a unit in one of the many columns which were at this time chasing Tantia, his regiment marched incessantly, through Central India and Rajputana, until the spring of 1859, when it came to rest at Bersia. Becher's Regimental Orders are purely 'routine.' It is possible only to follow the movements of his regiment from day to day. There is no account of any fighting whatever. The only allusions to the action of Bagrode occur in Orders

[1] Lieutenant H. C. Clay.
[2] Dr John Sylvester, a very remarkable man. He was an eminent surgeon, but his heart was in soldiering. He wrote a book on the Central India campaign, which I have used freely.

of 7th November 1858 and 25th January 1859. The first strikes some horses off the strength as "having been lost in action on the 26th October," and the second strikes off two sowars, "Davy Singh, 1st Troop, and Ram Singh, 4th Troop," as "having been missing since the affair at Bagrode." These two men had volunteered to go in disguise and spy out the enemy's camp. They were, in fact, the two 'peasants' who were discovered and beheaded by Tantia on the night before the action. Their names must be recorded.

Tantia was not long on the left bank of the Nerbudda. Columns from the south, set in motion by Sir Hugh Rose, now Commander-in-Chief of the Bombay Army, blocked his way into Kandeish and the old Mahratta strongholds he was making for. He recrossed the river and tried to enter Baroda, but was driven farther northward into the hills of Udaipur. Towards the end of January 1859, sickened by constant disappointment and "tired of running away," he was persuaded by the emissaries of Rajah Man Singh to leave the remnants of his army on the borders of the Bikaner desert and to join that chieftain in his hiding-place in the Paron jungles. Thither we must follow him.

He reached Paron towards the end of February. At this time Meade's Horse, still under General Robert Napier, with its Headquarters at Sipri, was split up in detachments along the Grand Trunk Road and in the jungles on either side of it. Two squadrons were at Goonah. These had formed part of a column, under Captain Rice of the 25th Bombay Infantry, which on the 22nd December had intercepted Firozeshah[1] on his way from Oudh to join Tantia and had relieved him, at Barod in the Aron jungles, of much baggage and many horses. Another detachment, with a squadron of the 14th Light Dragoons, two guns, and a company of the 86th, under Colonel Scudamore, had scoured the jungles for three weeks without finding Tantia or any of his followers. Meade himself was commanding a mixed force of European and Bombay infantry, with fifty of his own men, at Bijraon.[2] On the 27th February, Napier ordered him to march to Sirsi, to clear the roads through the jungles between Paron and Sipri and attack Man Singh and Tantia whenever opportunity should occur. He reached Sirsi on the 3rd of March. On the 8th the Thakur of the place, a relative of Man Singh's, came into camp and opened negotiations for the surrender of the Rajah. The negotiations were protracted, and meanwhile Meade went on with his road-making. From Sirsi he moved to Museri. He cleared the road up the pass here from the Kunu River on to the main Central India plateau some twenty-five miles north of Goonah, and then marched through Garla to Mahudra[3]; and here on the 2nd of April Man Singh came in. The next few days were spent by Meade in endeavouring to discover the exact whereabouts of Tantia Topi, who was known to be still in hiding in the neighbourhood. Man Singh at length resolved

---

[1] The impostor who had been defeated at Mandesore in November 1857, and had fled thence into Rohilkhand.

[2] Bijraon is about seven miles to the west of Badarwas, the second halting-place on the Goonah-Gwalior road.

[3] About eight miles north-west of Badhaora.

to betray his friend; and on the night of the 7th, with a small party of the 9th Bombay Infantry under a Jemadar, he went to Tantia's lair in the jungle, roused him from his slumbers, and brought him back to Meade.

Tantia was tried at Sipri for waging war against the British Government, and was hanged there on the 18th April 1859.[1]

The drama of the Mutiny was over, and it was Meade who rang down the curtain. There remained but a few scattered bands, some 8000 or 9000 all told, led by some of Tantia's old lieutenants, wandering through the jungles round Sironj and Maksudangarh. These were dealt with by detachments of our regiment in the ordinary course of its activities, but several years went by before they were completely subdued.

[1] A cairn, commemorating the event, with inscriptions in English, Urdu, and Hindi, was erected on the spot where the execution took place by the 71st Highlanders, who were present on the occasion. It became an object of worship. I have seen it daubed with ochre and surrounded by cocoanut shells. It was demolished some years ago, but was standing as late as 1892.

CHAPTER III.

MEADE'S HORSE, BEATSON'S HORSE, AND MAYNE'S HORSE.

1. MEADE'S HORSE.

WHEN the Gwalior Contingent broke into mutiny at Morar in the middle of June 1857 a small party of officers, led by Major Macpherson, the Resident, made their way to the Maharajah's palace. Scindia, powerless to protect them, could only despatch them in his own carriages and with an escort of his own bodyguard to Agra. Their journey was eventful. In the ravines bordering the Chambal a body of 200 rebels lay in wait. As the procession approached the river there were signs of hesitation amongst the escort. Some of the sowars left the road and disappeared into the ravines. The carriages were halted; and at that critical moment a troop of horsemen was observed galloping up from the rear. The whole of the escort then vanished. The leader of the troop, Thakur Baldeo Singh of Jarreh, who had reason to be grateful to Macpherson for mediation with the Maharajah on his behalf, rode up to the carriage in which he was seated and offered to defend him and his party with his life. The carriages were then conducted by circuitous ways to the bank of the river; the rebels feared to leave their hiding-

CAPTAIN RICHARD JOHN MEADE.
(From a photograph by VANDYK.)

place, and the party, crossing in safety, was received on the other side by an escort sent by the Rana of Dholpur. It reached Agra without further molestation. Meade was one of this party, and a few months later, when he was called upon to raise his regiment—the date of the Governor-General's order is in fact the 31st October 1857,—his thoughts turned to his deliverers, and he invited Baldeo Singh to send him some of his men. Baldeo Singh at first hesitated, but Meade's persuasions and his own loyalty finally wrung consent from him ; and before the end of the year his eldest son, a handsome young leader of the name of Gopal Singh, rode into Agra at the head of some seventy followers. These men became the 5th Troop of Meade's Horse, and eventually the 2nd Troop of the 2nd Regiment Central India Horse. They were an interesting tribe. Brahmins by caste, they called themselves Dandotia Thakurs. Their home, the village of Jarreh, lies just off the Grand Trunk Road about half-way between Gwalior and the Chambal River. We used to know them as the ' Chambal Horse.' They were expert swimmers, and they distinguished themselves greatly at the crossing of the Kabul River near Jalalabad during the Afghan War some twenty years later. Gopal Singh himself rose to the rank of Risaldar Major, and eventually became Aide-de-Camp to the Viceroy. Physically and intellectually a giant, he was one of the most impressive men I have known. On horseback his appearance was magnificent. His long flowing beard, dyed by the time I knew him, and the ' pag,' which in uniform he wore invariably, might have led one to mistake him for a Sikh. He was, however, a Brahmin to the core. His men worshipped him, almost abjectly. He had complete command of his troop, and indeed of the whole regiment. His view was wide, his methods perhaps not always very scrupulous. He made immense sums of money for the regiment by purchasing grain direct from the producer. Whether the producer often got a good bargain is possibly open to question. Gopal Singh was a difficult man to argue with. He usually had his own way, with the result that the men lived cheaply. His operations earned for him a certain degree of unpopularity amongst the civil authorities, and in the regiment the affectionate nickname of 'Gulloo.'[1] His faith in the British Raj and the British officer was manifest to the last. From his death-bed he sent 10,000 rupees to Colonel Masters, the Commanding Officer of the time, with a request that he would keep the money for his young son and hand it to him when he came of age. The trust was, of course, fulfilled.

The Dandotia Thakurs were not actually the first to be enlisted in the new corps. In Agra, Meade found many men, faithful men from unfaithful regiments, with very little to do. There were some fifty or sixty Sikhs, for instance, and about the same number of Panjabi Mahomedans. These he quickly enrolled, and so made his 1st and 2nd Troops. A little later he was strengthened by the arrival of a body of Jats from Rohtak, who became the 3rd Troop. The 4th Troop were Christians, bandsmen and drummers whose regiments had mutinied or been disarmed. The 6th was composed

[1] 'Grainie.'

chiefly of Rajputs, both Hindu and Mahomedan, but was classed as 'Mixed.'

The British officers who assisted Meade in the organisation and training of his regiment were Captain H. A. Cockburn, Second-in-Command, who has already been mentioned, and Lieutenant W. M. Gibbon, the Adjutant. Captain Cockburn, originally in the 53rd Bengal Infantry, was in the 1st Cavalry, Gwalior Contingent, at the outbreak of the Mutiny, and happened to be at Agra with a detachment of his regiment when the troops at Aligarh broke out. Thither he was despatched to relieve the Europeans. Half his men deserted him and joined a crowd of angry villagers. With the other half he lay in ambush, sending meanwhile a bullock cart along the road with a purdah [1] round it and three or four sowars inside—a trick with which we became somewhat familiar on regimental manœuvres in the days of my youth,—and the ruse was so successful that nearly half the rebels were killed and the rest were not heard of again. The whole of the regiment mutinied soon afterwards, and Cockburn found refuge in Agra. He broke down in health before Meade's Horse was pronounced fit for service, and so missed the campaign in which the regiment figured so conspicuously.

Lieutenant W. M. Gibbon belonged to the 44th Bengal Infantry, and had been severely wounded by his own men at Muttra. He was appointed acting Second-in-Command in addition to his other duties when Cockburn was invalided, and was with the regiment throughout the campaign in Central India.

[1] Curtain.

Besides the above two officers there was another Englishman, Sergeant Hartigan, V.C., of the 9th Lancers, who seems to have been attached to the regiment as Riding-master. He had a difficult task, for the sowars of the Christian troop, who all belonged to infantry regiments, took a good deal of teaching. His name does not appear in any Army List. He left the regiment before it marched down to Gwalior, and was afterwards promoted to commissioned rank.

The Troop Leaders were Risaldar Sher Singh, Sirdar Bahadar; Risaldar Ghulam Mahomed Khan; Risaldar Hyland; Rissaidar Kurram Singh; Rissaidar Gopal Singh; and Rissaidar Rahim Dad Khan.

That a regiment so constituted should have been pronounced fit for service within five months of its birth is remarkable testimony to the ability and driving power of Meade and his officers. With five of the troops, composed as they were of well-to-do men of the fighting classes, the work, though strenuous, was straightforward. In the Christian troop, however, new problems arose. The men, two-thirds of whom were Eurasians, were penniless. It was impossible to entertain them in a corps of Irregular Horse without some modification of the Silladar system. Meade therefore prevailed upon the Government of India to advance them the price of their horses, which was to be recovered by monthly cuttings from their pay. He tried also to obtain special allowances for the Eurasian members of the troop who were accustomed to a somewhat higher standard of living than their purely Indian comrades; but here he was unsuccessful, and the result of all this was that these Christian sowars, like most paupers exceedingly improvident, were nearly always in debt. Nevertheless they were turned into good soldiers in time for the closing episodes of the Mutiny, which are described in the previous chapter. They endured, in Meade's own words, "some peril and much hard and harassing work," and they came through it all with credit.

Before the regiment left Gwalior in pursuit of Tantia three other British officers and a surgeon were appointed—Lieutenants Burlton, Case and Page, and Assistant Surgeon Dalzell. Case came from the 67th Bengal Infantry. Page seems to have been a civilian volunteer. He is ranked in the Army List of July 1858 as ' Local Lieutenant.' He was wounded at Bijapur, but must have returned to civil duty soon afterwards, as he is not shown in the Army List of January 1859. The other officer who was reported wounded at Bijapur, Lieutenant Stewart, is not shown in any Army List. Burlton rejoined his English regiment, the 5th Foot, after Bijapur, and went home. He returned to India a few years later, and was posted to the Central India Horse. Dalzell had been the doctor of the 6th Infantry of the Gwalior Contingent. He and Case were with Meade's Horse throughout its career.

Several honours were gained during the campaign. Gopal Singh was admitted to the Order of British India with the title of ' Bahadar,' and to the First Class of the Order of Merit. Two Dafadars, both of the name of Dewa Singh, received the Order of Merit for "conspicuous gallantry and exemplary conduct on various occasions during the past disturbances," and Nishanbardar (Colour - Sergeant) Michael Rigot was granted an increase of 50 per cent to his pay and allowances for "conspicuous gallantry in the action of Bijapur."

After the execution of Tantia Topi the regiment remained at Sipri, with several detachments still in the jungles. In September 1859 Meade left it to take up political duties, and handed over temporary command to Cockburn. In February 1860 Cockburn marched the regiment down to Agar. His orders for the march have a familiar ring. Particular emphasis is laid upon the well-known regulation that there shall be "no noise such as knocking tent-pegs, loading camels, etcetera," before 'Reveille.' The early rising habits of the Indian soldier rendered such an order just as expedient then as it is now. History does not relate whether it was just as frequently disobeyed.

At Agar life was varied by an occasional hunt for dacoits. A Dafadar of the name of Prem Singh was decorated with the Order of Merit for his "active exertions under Risaldar Bahadar Isri Parsad against the notorious Soondeah leader 'Umbajee,' who was killed. Isri Parsad, who was at this time in the Bhopawar Levy, afterwards became Risaldar Major of the 1st Regiment Central India Horse. We shall hear more of him later on.

At the end of May 1860 Meade was appointed permanently to the Political Department as Resident at Gwalior, and Travers, the hero of the Indore Residency, succeeded him.

No records are available to show how the regiment

was armed or dressed. That the uniform was khaki is more than probable, since Meade declared that he based his organisation "on the plan of the Corps of Guides." The chief weapon was certainly the curved sword, which was of a more slender pattern than that used in our regiment now. Probably, as was the custom of the time, a certain number of men had muzzle-loading carbines or pistols; but this is not more than a conjecture. The horses must have been country-breds of the old wiry type from Poshkar and Batesar, which has practically disappeared; and the saddle the old 'charjama,'[1] with a sharp bit and a standing martingale.

Undoubtedly Meade's Horse was a good regiment. Discipline was strict and punishments severe—so severe, in fact, as to produce a feeling of repugnance in the modern mind. Floggings are frequently recorded. Yet it was of such stern treatment that good soldiers were made, and Meade's men were no exception to the rule. Though scattered in detachments all over the jungles, the most trying ordeal that discipline can undergo, with but little excitement to relieve the monotony of their daily marches, they made their mark in history. Meade may well have been proud of them.

2. BEATSON'S HORSE.

Early in the year 1858—on the 12th of February to be precise—there came to Hyderabad a veteran of thirty-eight years' service and fifty-five years of age with orders from the Government of India to

---

[1] A saddle made of cloth and felt.

raise two regiments of Irregular Cavalry, which were to be fit to take the field in six months' time. This was Lieutenant-Colonel William Fergusson Beatson of the 65th Bengal Infantry, Meade's regiment. Though belonging originally to the dismounted branch and weighing fourteen stone, he was a horseman of some reputation,[1] and, in spite of his years and his weight, he still retained an amount of energy which sometimes surprised his officers. Handsome in appearance and dignified in bearing, he was a soldier of the austere and earnest type. He lived camp fashion, and very uncomfortably, too. He was on horseback every morning before daybreak, and, in order to be prepared for emergencies, he rode invariably with a supply of biscuits and sultana raisins in his wallets—an example which was followed by a Colonel of a later day, Gerard. His task was difficult. True, there was plenty of material. Delhi had fallen; Lucknow had been relieved. Sir Hugh Rose was pressing on his relentless way towards Jhansi. The fortunes of the British Raj were rising. Young men in plenty, and old men too for the matter of that, were ready to join the English standards and to draw English pay. Nor was there any dearth of horses. Hyderabad territory was a noted breeding ground, and Bombay, with its Arabs, was close at hand. But neither men nor horses were all of the right stamp, and there was little time for discrimination. The result was that the two regiments were up to strength in a very few weeks; but thereafter a process of elimination

[1] He had been in the Nizam's Cavalry and, in the Crimean War, had commanded a Corps of Bashi Bazouks.

COLONEL WILLIAM FERGUSSON BEATSON.
(From an engraving by D. J. POUND.)

became necessary. Many an undesirable was found in the ranks, and had to be discharged and replaced. All sorts of disqualifications came to light. Jailbirds, deserters, men who were not 'ashraf,' had been enlisted. There were even cases of men being discharged from the service "for having been a khitmatgar," or "for having been a barber." In the 1st Regiment alone, with a nominal roll of 500 sowars, 630 enlistments were made before the end of August.

The difficulty in regard to the remounts was one not of quality but of sex. It was the custom to ride entire horses. Gelding as a regular practice was not thought of; but there were not enough entire horses to go round. Beatson was therefore obliged to purchase animals of either sex or none, and he posted the stallions to the 1st Regiment, and the mares, with a very few geldings, to the 2nd. About 50 per cent of the horses of the 1st Regiment were bought in the Arab stables at Bombay, a practice which we continued in the Central India Horse until the Arab was superseded by the Queensland horse, or Bounder, about the beginning of the present century.

Each regiment was organised in six troops, and had four British officers—the Commandant, the Second-in-Command, the Adjutant, and the Doctor, —19 Indian officers, including the Wardi Major,[1] 48 dafadars, and 500 sowars. There was little attempt at 'classification.' Mahomedans and Hindus seem to have been posted to troops indiscriminately in the proportion of about five to three. All came from Hyderabad territory. A large percentage of

[1] Indian Adjutant.

the Hindus were Brahmins, but there was no Hindu officer appointed until the 30th of August. There were a few Sikhs.

The uniform was green, with red turban and kamarband. The main weapon was the curved sword. These were issued by Government in steel scabbards, which were promptly returned to store and replaced by wooden ones made locally. A few men were armed, to begin with, with old matchlock carbines or pistols. New carbines—282 per regiment, with slings—were sent up from the arsenal at Bombay in August. The men were taught to load and fire on horseback. No accidents are recorded, but it must have been risky work. In Beatson's Horse alone of our three regiments is there any record of lances. Five 'spears' were allowed in each troop. They were not a Government article, but were ordinary hog spears purchased by the British officers from the celebrated Bodraj of Aurangabad.

Beatson had as his first Brigade-Major a certain Major Hackett, who belonged to an English regiment, or a Queen's regiment as it was called in those days to distinguish it from a company's regiment, the 44th Foot. He resigned his appointment on the 5th of May, and was succeeded by Captain E. G. Wood of the 6th Madras Cavalry, Mayne's Regiment.

The two Commandants were Lieutenant-Colonel C. G. Becher of the 1st Regiment and Captain T. F. Wilson of the 2nd. Becher came from the 5th Bengal Light Cavalry, and had distinguished himself in the Sikh wars. Entering the service in 1828, he had been a subaltern for twenty-three years, but he received his Brevet-Majority on the same day that he was promoted Captain. His leadership of Beatson's Horse in the field has been recorded in Chapter II. Wilson belonged to the 13th Bengal Infantry.

The Seconds-in-Command were Lieutenant Henry Thurburn, who had been Interpreter of the 42nd Madras Infantry, and Lieutenant T. T. Turton of the 47th Madras Infantry, attached to the Hyderabad Contingent, to which, after a very few months, he returned. Lieutenant W. Thompson of the 7th Madras Cavalry filled the vacancy.

The Adjutants were Lieutenant H. H. Foord, 16th Madras Infantry, and Lieutenant C. E. Lennox of the 1st Madras European Fusiliers. Foord went back to his regiment on the 16th of April, and was succeeded, on paper, by Lieutenant J. B. Tudor of the 5th Bengal Infantry. The latter, however, did not join until the 26th of March 1859, just after the 1st Regiment had finished its long trek through Central India and Rajputana and had come to rest at Bersia. Meanwhile Lieutenant Clay of the 13th Bengal Infantry, a much younger officer than any of the others—he had only two years' service—was appointed to act for him. Lennox remained with the 2nd Regiment, becoming eventually Second-in-Command, until the end of May 1859.

The doctors were Assistant Surgeon John Sylvester and Assistant Surgeon T. Beaumont. Sylvester had been working in the Jamsetjee Jeejeebhoy Hospital at Bombay, and had a lucrative private practice as well; but he was of an adventurous nature, preferring soldiering to surgery, skilful surgeon as he was, and so he got attached to the first column that left Bombay for the relief of Central India. Tim Beaumont, a genial Irishman, served for many years afterwards in the Central India Horse, and finally became Residency Surgeon at Hyderabad. He had the Irishman's wit as well as his brogue, of which, however, he was supremely unconscious. It was related of him that he once described a new recruit to his service as "just a raw Irish lad and he calls Doblin 'Doblin.'"

The Indian officers were appointed gradually, mostly by transfer from the Hyderabad Contingent or the Nagpur Irregular Force. For this reason it was impossible even to commence the organisation by troops until the end of June. Up to this time the regiment paraded by Paigahs, a Paigah being a bunch of horses owned by one Silladar. The troop organisation was completed in the 1st Regiment in time for the march into Central India, but in the 2nd not till some weeks later. The names of the first Troop Leaders were:—

1st Regiment.

Risaldars Rustam Ali Khan, Imam Khan, and Bhawar Khan.
Rissaidars Mir Ghulam Ali, Kher Mahomed Khan, and Mirza Hatim Beg.

2nd Regiment.

Risaldars Safdar Khan, Mir Tajmal Hosein, and Sift Ali Khan.
Rissaidars Gokal Parsad, Babar Khan, and Sher Ali Khan.

The two Wardi Majors were Salar Masrud and Kadir Khan. The only one of these officers of whom I knew anything was Mirza Hatim Beg, a good Mahomedan, who, even after his retirement, kept a large sum of money in deposit with our regiment, and always declined to take interest on it.

During the first few months of its existence the Brigade of Beatson's Horse was encamped at Bolarum, Brigade Headquarters being established at the Residency. Beatson's orders, issued from here, are long and didactic, which is not surprising seeing that so many of his British officers came from infantry regiments and were obviously not well posted in the details of cavalry work. Such offences as off-saddling too soon after exercise and galloping in cantonments frequently evoke his condemnation. He notes that " in countries where saddles are never taken off, except to clean the horses, sore backs are unknown " ; and he quotes Sir Charles Napier's order that " we have all heard that if you put a beggar on horseback he will ride to the devil; but neither beggars nor any other persons have a right to send other people to the devil; galloping in cantonments is therefore prohibited." He had to rely to a great extent on his own exertions, for Becher alone of his subordinates had real experience in the training and handling of men. The other British officers had to learn as well as teach.

On the 25th of May both regiments left Bolarum for Jalna, where Headquarters were established on the 15th of June. A march of 240 miles, with several rivers to cross, was a severe ordeal for a half-fledged corps, but they accomplished it creditably, and

Beatson complimented them in Brigade Orders. By
the end of August all the clothing, arms, and accoutrements had been received, and then the two regiments
separated. The 1st, under Becher, with Thurburn,
Clay, and Sylvester, started on the expedition which
is narrated in Chapter II. The 2nd, still somewhat
behindhand in the matter of organisation and still
short of Indian officers, remained at Jalna till the
18th of November. On this day was formed the
Jalna Field Force, one of the several forces organised
by Sir Hugh Rose to block Tantia's way into the
Mahratta country. It consisted of the 18th Royal
Irish, a battery of Bombay artillery, a wing of a
native infantry regiment, a detachment of the 8th
Hussars, and the 2nd Regiment of Beatson's Horse,
all under the command of Colonel Beatson. The
force marched to Asirgarh. Tantia was not encountered, but his object was defeated, and he escaped
across the Nerbudda to the northward. At Asirgarh
the two regiments were for a few days in touch with
one another, the 1st having pursued Tantia from
Hoshungabad. The latter, however, was now ordered
to recross the river, the 2nd remaining with the
Jalna Field Force watching the fords between
Barwai and Akbarpur and the country between the
river and the Satpura hills.

The British officers with the 2nd Regiment at
this time were Captain E. G. Wood, officiating
Commandant; Lennox, Second-in-Command; Stanley Clarke, Adjutant; and Dr Beaumont. Thompson
had resigned in October. Lennox had been succeeded in the Adjutancy by Lieutenant R. Johnstone
of the 18th Bombay Infantry, but this officer had

also resigned and had returned to his regiment. Stanley Clarke belonged to the 15th Madras Infantry. In December two new officers came in. On the 3rd Lieutenant Tweedie, a young subaltern of the 4th Bengal European Regiment, was appointed 'to do duty'; and on the 15th Major De Renzie Brett, an elderly Captain and Brevet-Major of the 3rd Madras European Regiment—he had thirty-four years' service—was appointed to command. E. G. Wood then resumed his appointment of Brigade-Major of Beatson's Horse, to which the duties of Brigade-Major, Jalna Field Force, were added.

The force went forward from Asirgarh to the bank of the Nerbudda, but thenceforward had little work. There were marches and counter-marches, varied by halts of several days at a time. Some of Tantia's followers might still be in the hills and attempt to break down into the plain and cross the river. None, however, were seen. Life, in fact, was uneventful, and even became boring. The British officers, unaccustomed to the jungle and unaware perhaps of the opportunities for sport offered by the Satpura forests, found nothing to do. Beatson roused them with a Brigade Order reminding them that " When duty does not require officers in camp there are Tigers, Pigs, and other animals in the neighbourhood, all of which would afford manly sport to young officers; and going after which would be much more creditable to officers than lying in bed on halting days."

The expedition, however, did not last long. By the end of January the Jalna Field Force was back at Adjunta. By the end of February it was dissolved. The 2nd Regiment, Beatson's Horse, then moved to Aurangabad, and later on, in October, to Baitul, where it remained during the rest of the year 1859.

Meanwhile the 1st Regiment had lost its gallant Commander. Becher had brought his regiment through the long march and into permanent quarters at Bersia; but here he broke down, and was ordered by the doctors to take a long sea voyage. He died on his way to the sea at Indore. The regiment was thus left with but two British officers, Thurburn and Dr Sylvester; for Clay, who had had a quarrel with Thurburn, had reverted to the 13th Bombay Infantry. Tudor joined on the 26th of March, and took up the Adjutant's duties. Captain E. G. Wood was appointed to succeed Becher, but did not assume command until the 19th of May. Lieutenant H. E. Wood of the 17th Lancers, the dashing subaltern of Sindwaha and the future Field-Marshal, succeeded him as Brigade-Major of Beatson's Horse.

Life at Bersia provided much more excitement than fell to the lot of the 2nd Regiment at Aurangabad and Baitul. South of the Nerbudda, Tantia had left no trace whatever; but in the Sironj jungles Firozeshah and the Rao Sahib, though no longer themselves accounted fighting men, were still in hiding, and their followers occasionally gave trouble. Bradford, with Mayne's Horse, was in the neighbourhood at this time, the hot weather of 1859, and it is reasonable to assume, though no official records are available, that the two regiments were often in co-operation. During the month of May squadrons under Captains Wood and Thurburn were out 'rebel hunting'; and on the 16th of July a very successful attack was made by the 1st Squadron, 100 sabres strong, led by Risaldar Rustam Ali Khan, against 500 rebels at the village of Ganoni near Sindhora. Thirty-five of the enemy were killed and several prisoners were taken. For this Rustam Ali Khan received the Order of Merit. No forays are recorded in August and September, though the outposts were strengthened from time to time, and the rebels were kept on the run.

In Regimental Orders of 24th September occurs a well-known name, that of Lala Tikha Ram, who was appointed Persian Writer on that date. He was for many years Munshi of the 2nd Regiment, Central India Horse, and was a great favourite with all ranks. He kept the Regimental Accounts in the vernacular, and taught the subalterns, with varying success, how to keep them in English.

At the end of September Beatson relinquished his command.[1] Brigade Headquarters were then shifted to Bersia. They soon ceased to exist. In November the brigade was dissolved, the two regiments remaining as independent units. Captain E. G. Wood, who had been appointed to act for Beatson during this short period, returned to the Madras Cavalry, and H. E. Wood, the Brigade-Major, succeeded him in command of the 1st Regiment.

Wood found much to correct. Since Becher's death discipline had slackened; the horses were in bad condition; there were still a good many men in

---

[1] Before he retired he commanded first the Allahabad and then the Umballa Division.

the regiment hardly fit to be soldiers. Moreover, the British officers had not recently shown that united front which is expected in all good regiments. Tudor had resigned in May, and Lieutenant Sheppard, who succeeded him, had returned to his Regular corps. The Adjutant was now Stanley Clarke, who had been transferred from the 2nd Regiment. He was the only combatant officer on duty when Wood joined, Thurburn being absent on sick leave.

Reforms were put in hand, and meanwhile 'rebel hunting' continued. On the night of the 26th December, whilst the three officers were dining, a message came in from the outpost at Sindhora that a band was in the neighbourhood. Wood started at once, and rode in to the outpost on the evening of the 28th to find that the rebels had, on the previous day, carried off a loyal and influential landowner of the name of Chaman Singh. The detachment of Beatson's Horse had been in pursuit of them, unsuccessfully, all day, and had just returned to camp. Wood found a man in the village who was willing to guide him to the rebels' bivouac, but what could be done? Men and horses were tired; little could be expected of them even if he had called upon them for further exertions. Yet it was important to save Chaman Singh's life, to which end an immediate resumption of the pursuit was imperative. The rebels were said to number from twenty to twenty-five men. Wood decided to take a corporal and nine men of the Bareilly Police who formed part of the outpost, four sowars of Beatson's Horse, who had been on guard in camp during the day, and one

gallant fellow, Dafadar Barmadin, who had been
out with the detachment but insisted on coming ;
and at 9 o'clock he set forth. About midnight the
light of the bivouac fire was seen in the distance.
Wood dismounted, and, leaving the horses in charge
of three sowars, crept slowly forward through the
jungle, followed by the ten policemen, one sowar,
and Barmadin. An hour's crawl brought them to
the edge of a dried pond ; and there, asleep round
the fire, was a much larger body of men than Wood
had expected to find. There were, in fact, eighty-
three of them, and the only one awake was the
sentry, besides Chaman Singh, who was tied to a
tree. The sentry challenged. Wood gave the order
to fire and charge, and then, tripping over sleeping
forms they had not observed, he and Barmadin
and the sowar tumbled headlong into the middle
of them. Most of the rebels picked themselves up
and hurried away. Only five or six stood their
ground, and of these, in a struggle by the light of
the fire, the three Beatson's Horsemen each accounted
for one. The others made off. Wood pursued them
until he felt sure that all were too frightened to
come back, and then returned to the pond, where
the Bareilly Police had halted to reload. Four or
five rebels who had been wounded by the first volley
had crept into the jungle. Chaman Singh had been
released, and was already on his way to Sindhora.
Wood's party then went back to the horses, and
Wood himself, leaving Barmadin to take the men
back to the outpost, rode on without halting to
Bersia. He received the Victoria Cross for this
exploit. Barmadin was decorated with the Order

of Merit. A year later he was promoted to Jemadar, and eventually rose to the rank of Risaldar in the 2nd Central India Horse. He was a remarkable man. His bravery alone won him his honours. He was illiterate and a little eccentric; but as a faithful soldier he commanded considerable respect. A strict Brahmin, he lived pure, and touched neither meat nor alcohol, and he was the strongest man in the regiment. A favourite trick of his was to get two or three subalterns to hold on with all their strength to his ears, when he would shake them off as a horse shakes off a fly.

Early in the year 1860 it became known that both regiments of Beatson's Horse were to be incorporated in Mayne's. The order of the Government of India to this effect was issued on the 16th of April. On the 10th of May the 1st Regiment marched to Goonah. The 2nd followed from Baitul a few weeks later under Captain Dun, who had recently taken over command from Major Brett, with Lieutenant Fraser, also a recent appointment, as Adjutant. Both these officers then returned to their units in the Madras Army. In fact, the only British officers of Beatson's Horse who remained with the corps after it became part of Mayne's were H. E. Wood and Stanley Clarke, besides the two doctors, Sylvester and Beaumont.

3. Mayne's Horse.

In a long despatch to the Government of India, written during the autumn of 1857, reviewing the situation resulting from the failure of the Contingents, Durand had suggested, as part of a system to replace them, the formation of a Brigade of Irregular Horse, with its Headquarters at Goonah. His plan was approved, but the orders of Government, for the formation of a single regiment only to begin with, were not issued until the 5th of February 1858. Meanwhile, however, the situation was so critical, and the need of a loyal body of horsemen to keep open the communications with Agra so urgent, that Durand acted on his own responsibility, and, in the letter which is quoted at the end of the first chapter, he ordered Mayne to go ahead. The new regiments were to be modelled on the system of the Hyderabad Contingent Cavalry, of which Durand had formed a very high opinion during the Malwa campaign. "Nothing," he wrote in the above despatch, "could be more satisfactory than the conduct of the Hyderabad Cavalry in Western Malwa. Ready, quick, soldierly at all times, and in action bold, I have nowhere seen superior Irregular Horse; and as Captain Mayne was trained in that service and appears to be, in every respect, well qualified to organise a similar body of Cavalry, I have no hesitation in putting into his hands the initiative, and trust that Government will not be disappointed in the issue." "It would be well, too," he added later on, "if the Brigade of Irregular Cavalry adopted the Panjab Guide Corps colour." We have often compared ourselves in efficiency with these two corps, but it is perhaps not known to many of us that they were actually our official models. Whether the copy has equalled, or even excelled, the model is a question whose answer must depend upon the point of view.

Mayne, with his friend Cunliffe Martin, and Dr Brodrick, marched into Goonah on the 5th of February 1858 at the head of about a hundred men. The regiment was at this time organised in four skeleton troops, but the composition and the names of the Troop Leaders are known only in the case of two, the 1st and the 4th. The 1st Troop was composed of Hindustani Mahomedans of the late 2nd Cavalry, Gwalior Contingent, under Risaldar Amjad Ali, with Mir Kurshed Ali and Sheikh Najaf Ali as Jemadars; and the 4th of Sikhs of the Bhopal Contingent, under Naeb Risaldar Indar Singh and Jemadars Narayen and Garja Singh.

Recruiting proceeded daily, loyal men from disbanded regiments dribbling in; but the records in this respect are meagre. It is a pity so few documents concerning the early days of Mayne's Horse have been preserved. No Order Book even is extant.

Training was not impeded by the difficulties which hampered Meade, for many of the men had already some experience of soldiering; but it was interrupted in April by the approach towards Sipri of 6000 rebels from Kotah, with four guns, making their way to Jhansi. Mayne, with 80 sowars, hurried up to Kolaras, where he joined a force of 800 of Scindia's men under Captain Sheikh Daud, and succeeded in forcing back the rebels and preventing them from reaching their destination. He then returned to Goonah and set to work again. The regiment was to be raised to a strength of 800 sabres, so no time was to be lost. In June, as soon as Tantia Topi had been driven from Gwalior, Mir Amjad Ali was despatched thither from Indore on recruiting duty; and Cunliffe Martin was sent to Rajputana on a similar errand. Amjad Ali returned to Indore in time to join General Michel's Force in Malwa, and was present, as we have seen, at the battle of Rajgarh—where Mayne was not—as well as in several other engagements during the pursuit of Tantia. He and his detachment did not actually join Headquarters of Mayne's Horse until its return to Goonah, towards the end of 1858. Martin, on his return from Rajputana, was appointed Adjutant of the 1st European Light Cavalry at Cawnpore, and remained there for a couple of years.

Mayne, however, was not entirely bereft of British officers. Before Martin left him he was joined by Lieutenant E. R. C. Bradford, whose gallant behaviour at Sindwaha has already been described. Bradford had only five years' service, but had seen much fighting. Originally in the Madras Cavalry, he had been selected by General John Jacob for active service in Persia with the special object of assisting in the organisation of Irregular Horse. On the outbreak of the Mutiny he rejoined his regiment, and was continually engaged with rebels, first in the Jubbulpore district and then in the North-West Provinces, until he was appointed Second-in-Command to Mayne, when he came down to Goonah, with the smoke of battle on him, in time for the march to Biaora and the attempt to catch Tantia as he fled from Rajgarh.

Another officer was appointed about the same time

as Bradford. This was Lieutenant J. J. Blair of the 31st Bengal Infantry. He joined the regiment in August and was sent up to Gwalior, probably to command a small detachment there and to continue the recruiting begun by Amjad Ali. He does not appear to have accompanied the regiment to Biaora, but to have been left at Gwalior or Goonah, or perhaps at both places alternately, to carry on the training of recruits whilst Mayne and Bradford were engaged in more active enterprise.

Just before the regiment left Goonah on its march down the Grand Trunk Road it was augmented by the arrival of a troop of ninety sabres from Gwalior under Naeb Risaldar Mir Kasim Ali, Amjad Ali's son. This troop went down with Mayne, and Kasim Ali distinguished himself at the action of Kurai.

The regiment was not absent from Headquarters for long. It left on the 11th of September, and marched back into cantonments on the 3rd of December, elated by its exploits at Kurai and Sindwaha, and ready for as much more active service as Tantia and his friends might care to provide. It was at this time not more than 350 strong, including the new 5th Troop under Kasim Ali. During the next twelve months life may be said to have consisted of recruiting, training, tiger shooting, and rebel hunting. Recruits were brought in by Indian officers from Jaipur, from Gwalior and from Mehidpur, and other places, and were pretty severely tested before they were enrolled. Mayne wanted tough men. They were put over the jumps and made to engage in mounted combat; and the test was not so much one of skill as of courage. It is recorded of one 'umedwar'[1] that he begged his adversary not to hit him too hard. He was promptly rejected. Training in horsemanship and the use of the curved sword—we hear nothing of lances in these early days—went on regularly so long as it was not interrupted by rebel hunting. Such occasions, however, were frequent. Of the tiger shooting we have no precise accounts. No Game Book is extant. Possibly none was kept; but it was the only available form of recreation, and the name of a certain Captain Rice[2] of the 25th Bombay Infantry, then stationed at Goonah, is never mentioned without an allusion to his prowess in the sport. He it was who led an expedition to the Aron jungles against Firozeshah. Leaving Goonah on the 17th of December with fifty-five sabres of Mayne's Horse under Blair, as well as two squadrons of Meade's Horse and some of his own men, he found Firozeshah near Barod on the 22nd, and attacked him at night. The rebels fled to Rajgarh without resistance, and Rice rode back to Goonah with 100 of their horses and a good deal of their stuff.

In December and January rebels were again hunted through the jungles round Ragogarh on one side of Goonah and Nahargarh on the other, though there were few close engagements and no casualties. February was a quiet month. The whole of March was spent in a trek through the Sironj jungles in pursuit of Rao Sahib and his followers, who had

[1] A candidate for enlistment; literally 'hopeful.'
[2] He wrote a book on 'Tiger Shooting,' full of glorious illustrations, which was published by Smith, Elder & Co. in 1857. He shot all his tigers on foot with a D.B., M.L., 8-bore rifle by Westley-Richards. In three years he and a few friends killed 68 tigers, 3 panthers, and 25 bears.

separated from Tantia and were gradually dispersing. The pursuit was unsuccessful. Rao Sahib was not, in fact, captured until three years later, when he was found in the hills in the garb of a Sunyasi, brought down to Cawnpore, and hanged. Firozeshah was never caught. He escaped, in the disguise of a pilgrim, to Karbala, and there he died many years afterwards.

The regiment returned to Goonah on the 28th of March, and on the same day orders were received to send two troops to join Colonel Rich's column in pursuit of some of Firozeshah's men. Bradford and Blair, with the 4th and 5th Troops, started immediately, and an action occurred at Nainwar, near Lateri, where some men of the 71st Highlanders were killed. The expedition lasted ten days.

On the 9th of May Bradford was again on the war-path. Leaving Goonah before daybreak, with a wing of the regiment, he marched over sixty miles to Basoda on the Betwa, and attacked and dispersed a body of rebels before nightfall. Captain Roome of the 10th Bengal Infantry, who commanded the column operating in this region, wrote in his despatch that "These men had marched a distance of sixty-seven miles before coming on the enemy, and yet they could not have charged with greater spirit had their horses been fresh from the stables." It is a tribute not only to the spirit but to the mobility of the regiment, for Bradford started at short notice, and was prepared to be absent from Headquarters for a considerable time. He and his wing remained, in fact, in the neighbourhood of the Betwa throughout the hot weather and rains, forming part of the Basoda and Sironj columns alternately, and acting with whichever wanted him most. The jungles were infested with rebels, and skirmishes, of which little is known, occurred very frequently.

Meanwhile Headquarters at Goonah were still busy raising men. By the beginning of May three more troops had been formed, bringing the regiment up to its full strength in administrative units, though the units themselves were still undermanned. Mayne was particularly fond of the Sikh. The loyalty and courage displayed by the troops of this community during the early part of the rebellion, coupled with instances of individual bravery which had come under his own notice, had so impressed themselves on his mind that he determined to have a large Sikh element in his corps. Unable to find sufficient numbers in Central India, he had, in September 1858, sent a Risaldar to Umballa to recruit from the Panjab. This was discovered by the Government of India, who had prohibited any further enlistment of Sikhs, and Mayne was ordered to recall his Risaldar. He appears, however, to have obtained a few Cis-Sutlej men before the order reached him, and with these he had made a second Sikh Troop, under Risaldar Rai Singh and Jemadars Surmakh Singh and Kan Singh. Thus half the regiment consisted of Sikhs and Hindustani Mahomedans; the remainder were Jats, Rajputs, and Khaim Khanis from Rajputana, the Troop Leaders being Risaldars Mir Amjad Ali and Rai Singh and Naeb Risaldars Indar Singh, Mir Kasim Ali, Mahadeo Singh, Saledi Singh, Syud Mohiuddin, and Mir Bunyad Ali.

E

Only one other British officer was appointed to the regiment during this period. This was Lieutenant H. L. Hawkins of the 30th Bengal Infantry, who was gazetted Adjutant on the 25th October 1858. He does not appear to have taken up his duties until the 21st of April 1859; but he did a lot of recruiting work at Jaipur both before and after this date. He was not long with the regiment. On the 9th of October he was permitted to resign his appointment, and went to the Political Department.

By the end of September the regiment was complete in personnel, and Mayne, who was in bad health, found it necessary to take three months' leave. He handed over his command to Bradford on the 17th of October, and went to friends at Cawnpore. Here, however, he did not escape from his military responsibilities. Durand's proposal for the formation of three regiments was revived about this time. On the 9th of November the Government of India gave a provisional assent to the raising of two additional regiments; and on the 12th Mayne sat down and wrote a long letter to the Agent to the Governor-General at Indore—on many pages of blue foolscap—embodying his proposals for the composition and organisation of his brigade.

Bradford meanwhile, feeling the need of reinforcements in the Sironj jungles, called the Headquarters wing down to him. The whole regiment went into camp at Maksudangarh, and remained there during the greater part of the cold weather of 1859-60.

CHAPTER IV.

CENTRAL INDIA HORSE.

MAYNE rejoined from leave in February 1860. His regiment had returned to Goonah a little earlier than this, with the exception of one troop, which remained in the Sironj jungles under Bradford until May. He had now definite orders to proceed with the raising of two additional regiments, which, with his own, were to be formed " for service, ordinarily, in Central India, but available, on emergency, for general service anywhere in or out of India." They were to be placed under the orders and at the disposal not of the Commander-in-Chief or of any military authority but of the Agent to the Governor-General at Indore. Each regiment was to consist of 578 Indian ranks, a Second-in-Command (which remained the official title of each Commanding Officer until the office of 'Commandant, Central India Horse,' was abolished), an Adjutant, and two 'Doing Duty' officers, besides the Doctor. In addition to his military duties, the Commandant of the three regiments—who was not made a Brigadier-General—had certain political duties to perform; and since then it has always been a question whether our Commandant was mainly a soldier or mainly a

'Political.' We have had many distinguished soldiers as Commandants. Some leaned in one direction, some in the other. When rumour of war was in the air they were all very much soldiers; but in the less exciting times of peace, when a soldier has but his imagination to stir his enthusiasm, it was natural that they should turn with zeal to the more constructive if more prosaic work of politics. The majority worked hard at their political desks, and several of them became eventually 'Politicals' pure and simple. Mayne, in the long letter referred to in the previous chapter, estimated the time occupied by his political duties as six hours a day, and claimed a commensurate allowance, which surprised the civil authorities very much indeed. Sir Richmond Shakespeare, who was now Agent to the Governor-General, was indignant. He wrote that Major Mayne, in so far as his political work was concerned, "should do very little and appear to do less." The Government of India agreed with him. Mayne was informed that his force "was raised for military purposes and for these alone," and his estimate for an allowance was handled somewhat severely. This did not disturb him. He had at any rate plenty to do. He was determined to have three good regiments, and he had made his plans.

He still cherished the idea of enlisting Sikhs, and now it seemed that the opportunity of putting it into practice was presented to him. So indeed would have been the case had he been at liberty to pick and choose. But it happened that at this time there were, in Central and Northern India, many irregular regiments of Horse, raised for service in the Mutiny, some of which might no longer be required. If any of these were broken up, Government would be compelled to provide for the discharged soldiers by transferring them, where possible, to other regiments ; and what more natural than they should be drafted into Mayne's Horse ? Most of the regiments in Northern India were retained. Hodson's, Probyn's, Watson's, Murray's, Cureton's, Robarts', and Fane's Horse became the 9th and 10th, the 11th, the 13th, the 14th, the 15th, the 17th, and the 19th Bengal Cavalry, or Lancers, respectively ; but there were other bodies, like the Rohilkhand Levy and the Mainpuri Levy, which were doomed. In Central India there were Beatson's Horse, Meade's Horse, and the Mahratta Horse. The latter raised at Indore and Gwalior, was retained, and became the 18th Bengal Lancers. Meade's Horse also was left alone for the moment ; but Beatson's Horse, like the Levies above mentioned, could justify its existence no longer. The inevitable happened. Eckford's Mainpuri Levy and both regiments of Beatson's Horse were ordered to be transferred to Mayne's.

In April, Mayne called Bradford and H. E. Wood to Goonah for consultation. Wood gave him a poor account of the quality of his own regiment. Mayne's hopes revived. If all the inefficients were as inefficient as they were said to be, he would, by discharging them—as it would become his duty to do—reduce his new regiments below the authorised strength, and so find room for some Sikhs after all ; and it was not long before he entered into correspondence with Brigadier-General Neville

Chamberlain, commanding the Panjab Frontier Force, with this intent.

Meanwhile Beatson's Horse and the Mainpuri Levy received their orders to march to Goonah. The 1st Regiment of Beatson's Horse arrived on the 17th of May, with Wood, Stanley Clarke, and Sylvester. Mayne began discharging unwanted soldiers at once. He had estimated that, with the arrival of the three new corps, he would have 741 supernumeraries; so the Agent to the Governor-General, who had been getting a little anxious lest he could not fulfil his promise to hold Central India with three regiments, had suggested the formation of a fourth, to replace the recently disbanded Aden troop, then much stronger than it became on its revival in later years and differently constituted, which had been holding Mehidpur. This was not allowed, and the discharges went on until all, and more than all, the supernumeraries disappeared. The Mainpuri Levy, 477 strong, arrived on the 31st of May. None of its British officers remained at Goonah. The 2nd Regiment of Beatson's Horse did not march in until the 7th of July, having been detained on the road for more than three weeks by an outbreak of cholera.

The orders of the Government of India for the formation of the brigade, which were conveyed in a letter to the Agent to the Governor-General dated the 5th of April 1860, made the following appointment of officers :—

> Captain H. O. Mayne, 6th Madras Light Cavalry, to be Commandant.
> Lieutenant A. G. Mayne, 1st Bombay Lancers, to be Brigade-Major.

First Corps.

Lieutenant E. R. C. Bradford, 6th Madras Cavalry, to be Second-in-Command.
Lieutenant J. J. Blair, 31st N I., to be Adjutant.
Lieutenant D. T. H. Sampson, 20th N I., to do duty.
Assistant Surgeon H. C. Brodrick to be in medical charge.
Mir Umjad Ali, Sirdar Bahadur, to be Risaldar Major.

Second Corps.

Lieutenant H. E. Wood, H.M. 17th Lancers, to be Second-in-Command.
Lieutenant C. Beadon, 1st Madras Light Cavalry, to be Adjutant.
Lieutenant E. S. R. Carnac, 1st Bengal European Light Cavalry, to do duty.
Assistant Surgeon R. Bateson to be in medical charge.

Third Corps.

Lieutenant W. G. Morris, 1st Madras Light Cavalry, to be Adjutant.

Lieutenant A. G. Mayne (Ashton Mayne) was a cousin of H. O. Mayne and nephew of Brigadier-General William Mayne, who had commanded the Hyderabad Contingent. Dudley Sampson was a well-known horseman of his day. Beadon was a son of the Secretary to the Government of India in the Foreign Department. Dr Brodrick was at home on sick leave. His place in the First Corps was taken by Dr Bateson. Sylvester was then posted to the Second and Beaumont to the Third.

It will be noticed that in these first orders certain appointments were left vacant. Only two, instead

of six, 'Doing Duty' officers were appointed and
only one Risaldar Major; and no officer was named
as Second-in-Command of the Third Corps. Two
'Doing Duty' officers were shortly found in Lieutenant Stanley Clarke of Beatson's Horse, who was
posted to the Second Corps, and Lieutenant W. H.
Jennings of the 2nd Bengal Light Cavalry, who was
brought in to the Third. The Risaldar Majors Mayne
hoped to get from the Panjab. To command the
Third Corps the Viceroy, Lord Canning, selected a
very distinguished young officer, Lieutenant C. A. De
Kantzow, who was at the time acting in command
of Robarts' Horse. He was allowed to bring with
him to Goonah fifty of his own men. De Kantzow's
exploits were widely known. He was at Mainpuri
when the Mutiny broke out with a detachment of
his regiment, the 9th Bengal Infantry, whose Headquarters were at Aligarh. This regiment behaved
for some time extremely well, and, even when the
men could resist temptation no longer, they just
walked out of cantonments and went off quietly
to Delhi. The detachment at Mainpuri was ordered
to march out of the station. It started, but, on
reaching the boundary of the parade ground, the
soldiers refused to proceed farther. What followed
is thus described in Kaye and Malleson's History:
"Meanwhile De Kantzow, dismounted, had been
opposing to the mutinous Sipahis a firm and courageous will. He implored them, he upbraided them,
he threatened them. Muskets were levelled at him
in vain. The courageous attitude of the solitary
officer, endeavouring to recall to duty men whose
hearts told them they were doing wrong, overbore

for the moment physical force. Not indeed that he entirely mastered the Sipahis. But they did not kill him. They still rushed on madly towards the Treasury, bearing with them their earnestly gesticulating, madly imploring Lieutenant. Arriving at the iron gates of the Treasury, De Kantzow made one last appeal. Turning suddenly from his own Sipahis he threw himself on the loyalty of the Civil Guard of thirty men. They responded; they rallied round him; the officials of the gaol added their efforts; and for the first time since the actual outbreak on the parade ground the torrent was stemmed. Even more—it was stopped. Not indeed at the instant. De Kantzow, with a wisdom beyond his years, avoided precipitating a conflict. He forbade the Civil Guard to fire, but drew it up to oppose a resolute front to the halted Sipahis, whilst with all the energy of an excited nature he again implored these not to add plunder and murder to mutiny. For three hours his arguments, backed by the physical efforts of the Civil Guard, kept the rebels at bay." The soldiers eventually withdrew, plundered their lines, and left the station. Lord Canning, in an autograph letter to De Kantzow, wrote that " you have given to your brother soldiers a noble example of courage, patience, good judgment, and temper from which many might profit." After this incident De Kantzow was employed in raising, or helping to raise, both the Mainpuri and the Rohilkhand Levies. The special qualification which he displayed in dealing with raw troops marked him out for appointment to the command of a new corps.

The classification of all three regiments was the same—namely, one squadron of Mahomedans of the North-West Provinces, one squadron of Sikhs, one troop (half a squadron in those days) of Nagars and Khaim Khanis, and one troop of Jats and Rajputs. These, at least, were Mayne's proposals, and they seem to have received the approval of Government, as they certainly did of the Agent to the Governor-General. Mayne was constantly urged to admit a few Brahmins to the Hindu troops. This he resolutely declined to do, and so created another bone of contention between himself and the Agent to the Governor-General. There were many Brahmins in the Mainpuri Levy. He would not keep them. The only exception he seems to have made was in the case of Barmadin of Beatson's Horse. Moreover, Sir Richmond Shakespeare wished to appoint as Risaldar Major of one of the regiments a Brahmin of the name of Isri Parsad, who, as we have seen, had already done loyal and gallant service. Mayne objected to this, not only on the ground of caste, but because he was negotiating for the transfer of Sikhs for two of these important billets; and he had his way.

It is curious that both the Government of India and the Agent to the Governor-General should, in the first instance, have supported Mayne in his Sikh scheme, in spite of previous opposition ; but it is certainly a fact. It seems that he was expected to take Sikhs only if he could get them to buy the ' assamis ' of inefficients of Beatson's Horse as these were discharged ; but he was told at the same time not to hold up discharges if Sikhs were not immediately available. Thereupon he proceeded to dismiss every man whom he did not consider fit to be a soldier, with the result that in a very short time his brigade was 308 sabres below strength. This brought down upon him the undisguised wrath of the civil authorities, and some very strong letters passed between the Government of India, the Agent to the Governor-General, and himself. His negotiations with the Panjab came to light. He was reminded of the original prohibition of October 1858, and was severely reprimanded for disregarding it. He was ordered to break off his negotiations, and forbidden to enlist new men of any denomination until further orders, "as there may be other bodies of Irregular Horse to be provided for." Sir Richmond Shakespeare complained, too, that the discharges were causing much irritation. Disbanded soldiers, trekking along the Grand Trunk Road to their homes, were creating discontent in many places, at Gwalior, Biaora, and Hoshangabad especially; but he made an effort to support Mayne in procuring Sikhs, as he agreed with him that commanders of "other bodies of Irregular Horse" would send him their worst rather than their best men, and that in any case the Sikh had established his reputation as a soldier. He suggested, however, an alternative—namely, that "if there were any Irregular regiment about 308 strong it should be transferred bodily." The Government of India seized upon this suggestion, absolutely forbade the Sikh experiment, and stated that measures would shortly be taken to transfer a whole corps—namely, Meade's Horse.

In reading these old letters one is struck by the tone of irritation that runs through them. It is not to be wondered at, at any rate in Mayne's case. The hot weather at Goonah is not conducive to placidity, and Mayne had not recovered from the sickness which had forced him to take leave in October. He was indeed very ill. His officers, too, were frequently on the sick list. Wood and Bradford were often ill, De Kantzow constantly down with fever. Only their gallant spirits kept them going. And they had much to do both in the office and in the jungle; for whilst the work of organising the new regiments kept them busy in the Lines, rebel hunting went on just the same. All were out at one time or another. It was in June that Bradford, with sixty men, was ordered out after a band, larger than usual, in the jungles round Ragogarh. He took with him Lieutenant Jennings, at the latter's urgent request; for his father, the Chaplain of Delhi, had been butchered by the mutineers, and he was spoiling to avenge his death. The party marched through the night. Shortly after daybreak the rebels were observed on a rocky hill above them, completely unconscious of approaching danger. Bradford, who had twenty men with him, the rest having been sent round on a detour, gave the order to charge, and rode, as fast as the ground would let him, straight up the hill. Followed by a few Sikhs he got in among the rebels, and killed several before they could prepare to resist. Jennings was less fortunate. His horse fell twice, and before he reached the summit a few of the enemy were ready for him. One man, more courageous than his friends, withheld his fire until the last moment, and Jennings fell dead, shot through the body. Bradford, who had followed the rebels for some distance and taken a few prisoners, did not learn of his subaltern's fate till he returned from his pursuit. Jennings was buried where he fell; and many years afterwards a monument, sent by relatives from England, was set up over his grave by officers of a later generation.

One of Bradford's prisoners turned out to be a celebrated rebel leader of the name of Madhoo Singh, who had been often hunted by detachments both of Mayne's and Beatson's Horse. This man, when brought to Goonah, made a statement to Mayne implicating the Rajah of Narsingarh, who was alleged to be sheltering two Mahomedan Risaldars of Beatson's Horse, recently discharged for misconduct and turned rebel. They had been ringleaders of an incipient mutiny at Bersia just before the regiment marched to Goonah. The mutiny was nipped in the bud by the action of Dafadar Barmadin, who, unknown to Wood, had kept the Hindus of the regiment under arms all night, and so forestalled the intended attack upon the Commandant's house. The Risaldars were marched under arrest to Goonah to be dealt with by Mayne, who sent them about their business. It was these two men who had caused the trouble amongst other discharged soldiers at Biaora, which had aroused the fears of the Agent to the Governor-General. On receiving Madhoo Singh's statement, Mayne forthwith ordered Wood to proceed with a troop to Narsingarh and apprehend the Risaldars by means of the Rajah himself. Wood, starting at 3 o'clock in the morning, reached Narsingarh—forty miles from Goonah—twelve hours later. Leaving his troop near the entrance to the Fort, he rode, accompanied only by a Risaldar and a trumpeter, to the palace, where he demanded a private audience of the Rajah. The latter assured him that the rebel Risaldars were nowhere near Narsingarh. Wood, however, was persistent. He had actually seen one of them; and the Rajah had finally no choice but to conduct him to their quarters, where he arrested them. There was still one other rebel to be taken, a man of the name of Baba Dhatt, the Rao Sahib's Kamdar,[1] who was known to be living in a house in the town. Wood invited the Rajah to accompany him in search of this man. The Rajah, who denied all knowledge of Baba Dhatt, made the semblance of preparations for a start. He sent at intervals for his horse, for his sword, for his kamarband, for many other necessary or unnecessary things. His servants made no haste. He kept up the pretence for an hour or more till Wood lost patience and threatened him, quite politely, with arrest if he refused to move. Finally, he requested Wood to precede him out of the courtyard, promising to follow. And then he retired into the palace, whence, of course, he sent a messenger to say that he had a stomach-ache and could not come. Wood was obliged to find his own way to Baba Dhatt's hiding-place, but the bird had flown. He returned to Goonah next day.

Sir Richmond Shakespeare found this incident particularly disquieting. He believed that the Native

[1] Minister.

States in Central India had settled down, and that the behaviour of the discharged soldiers along the road, though troublesome, was only temporary. An indignity to an important chieftain might renew a conflict which he hoped had ended. It was perhaps just as well for his peace of mind that Wood had agreed to lead the way out of that courtyard. "If Lieutenant Wood had arrested the Rajah," he wrote, "he would probably have lost his life, and would have involved us in a petty and most inconvenient warfare." He could not, however, blame Wood, who only obeyed orders, and was, indeed, supported by the highest military authorities; but his anger fell unstintingly upon Mayne, who was thenceforward in very bad odour indeed.

Meanwhile the hot weather and the arduous duties imposed upon the British officers were telling on their nerves. Mayne and De Kantzow in particular, both remarkable men, were in their nature, in temperament, and in inclination so different that they found it impossible to work together. So long as Mayne was at Goonah and De Kantzow rebel hunting in the jungles, or *vice versa*, all went well; but when both were in the Lines their methods clashed, and difference of opinion developed into open hostility. De Kantzow discharged some men without gratuity. Mayne rebuked him in an angry letter. De Kantzow replied in terms for which, in a junior officer, there was no excuse; and all this was reported to the Agent to the Governor-General, who took De Kantzow's part. Shortly afterwards De Kantzow failed in the Higher Standard Examination in Hindustani; and Mayne in reporting it remarked

—as he had every right to do, seeing that all new appointments to the regiment had been made conditionally on the passing of this examination within a certain time—that there seemed to be no reason why he should not be removed. De Kantzow was, as a matter of fact, a brilliant linguist; but it was so obvious that these two good officers, if left together much longer, would mar rather than make the new regiment that the Agent to the Governor-General might himself have made De Kantzow's failure an excuse for obtaining some other, but equally honourable, appointment for him. Had he done so we should not, perhaps, have become 'Central India Horse.' As it was he took up the cudgels for him against Mayne. He wrote a long letter to Government setting forth the latter's iniquities. And not only did he criticise his attitude over the examination, but he referred also to the Narsingarh incident and to another incident, which he had reported previously, concerning a silver pencil-case. De Kantzow had been President of the Committee of Adjustment on the estate of Lieutenant Jennings, and had made up the 'lots' for the sale of the effects. Amongst these was one containing a looking-glass, a bundle of carpets, and a writing-case. Sylvester wanted the carpets, and bid seventeen rupees for the 'lot.' De Kantzow outbid him, and bought it for eighteen rupees. A damaged silver pencil-case of little value was afterwards found in the writing-case, and Sylvester, Stanley Clarke, and Wood accused De Kantzow of putting it there when he made up the lots, with the intention of buying it cheap at the sale. Mayne referred the matter to a Court of Enquiry composed of officers of the 89th Foot, then quartered at Goonah, who recorded their opinion that the charge was frivolous and De Kantzow entirely free from blame. Sir Richmond Shakespeare recommended that Mayne should be removed from his command, but that De Kantzow should be allowed a second trial for his examination, and that a censure would be adequate punishment for his insubordinate letter. The Government of India took the view that both should go; so both were relieved of their duties. Their services were placed at the disposal of the Military Department, and, as a final indignity to Mayne, his name was deleted from the title of the regiment. We were to be called in future 'The Central India Horse.'

De Kantzow served afterwards in many appointments, both military and civil, and is still (1923) alive. Mayne was posted to the Madras Army, whence he came; but he did very little more service. Broken in health and spirit, he left Goonah only to die. For some months he held out; but, the fever constantly recurring, he applied for leave to England, and he died, on his way to Calcutta, at Government House, Allahabad, at the age of forty-two. The 'Pioneer,' in reporting his death, wrote that " None can feel more regret than ourselves at the death of one of those who stood so firmly in the van in the hour of India's danger. The gallant old army of India has had its day, and is rapidly passing away. But it can point proudly to many a gallant record of the services of those who have gone, amongst whom the list of Major Mayne's services entitles him to no obscure place."

CHAPTER V.

TRAVERS.

THE date of the letter from the Secretary to Government which flung Mayne and De Kantzow out of Central India was the 8th of September 1860. It was followed immediately by another letter, making the following appointments :—

> Colonel J. Travers to be Commandant of the Central India Horse.
> Lieutenant Cunliffe Martin to be Second-in-Command of the 2nd Regiment.
> Lieutenant W. P. Conolly to be Second-in-Command of the 3rd Regiment.

It is a curious fact that in the first of these, the 'bombshell' letter, the new title given to the regiment is 'Central Indian Horse.' We are sometimes thus addressed, in error, even to this day. We have always disliked it, and we may perhaps be thankful to the writer of the second letter for relieving us officially of the burden of a meaningless and ugly name.

Travers handed over the command of Meade's Horse to Cockburn at Agar on the evening of the 25th September, and started next morning on the first of those many rides between regiment and regiment which were accomplished at one time or other by most officers of the force during the years when the regiments were united by the existence of a Commandant of the whole. The distance was 130 miles. For the first thirty miles there was only a bullock track. We sent horses on to Kanar and Barodia, and galloped, over the red laterite and the black cotton soil alternately, to Sarangpur on the Grand Trunk Road. Here was a small guard of the regiment; and thence onwards to Goonah there were detachments, consisting usually of a Naeb Dafadar and three sowars, at posts ten or twelve miles apart. At Biaora, the half-way house, in Rajgarh territory, with the town of Rajgarh on one side and Narsingarh on the other, the detachment was necessarily stronger. It was by this means that we discharged our duty of keeping the road open, and it was not often, though occasions were known as late as thirty years after the Mutiny, that a travelling bania was looted or the mail-carrier knocked on the head.

The remainder of the ride was done on the horses belonging to these detachments. Whether this was fair to the owners of those horses was a question which occasionally disturbed the mind of a conscientious Commanding Officer. It was generally answered in the affirmative. After all we were on duty—we were never considered to be on leave within the boundaries of Central India—and the only alternative to the horses were the camel-cart which travelled at six miles an hour, and the bullock train which travelled at two; and neither of these had springs. Nor did the men object to it as much as was fancied, if at all. Road guard duty, though occasionally exciting and presenting now and then opportunities for distinction, was on the whole a comfortable and inexpensive interlude. There were no parades. The horses were not highly fed. The local inhabitants undoubtedly did the men well; and when the day of reckoning came and a keen-eyed Adjutant inspected the horses on their return to cantonments there was always a plausible excuse for poor condition. " That horse is lame, Dewa Singh; how did it happen ? " The answer came invariably and without a moment's hesitation: " Ussi din jab Sahib ne sowari kiya." [1]

The ride usually took two days. Very rarely did an officer gallop through without halting. The duty of inspecting the detachments which was always discharged, more or less thoroughly, occupied an hour or so, even allowing but a short ten minutes for each inspection ; and by the time Biaora was reached the desire for food and rest suggested a night at the dak bungalow. Travers adopted this plan, and rode into Goonah on the evening of the 27th. Changes in the British appointments were in progress. Mayne and De Kantzow had left. Bradford was on the sick list. Wood, who had lost the favour of the political authorities since the Narsingarh incident, had sent in his resignation, and was on the point of departure for England. Sylvester had applied for a transfer, and had been appointed to Probyn's Horse, then in China. Three of the younger ' Doing Duty ' officers—Sampson,

[1] " On that day when the Sahib rode him."

Carnac, and Morris—had been posted elsewhere. New men were coming in. Cunliffe Martin returned to the regiment on the 3rd of October, and relieved Wood. Conolly assumed command of the 3rd Regiment, *vice* De Kantzow, a few days later. The three new 'Doing Duty' officers were Cornet J. Low from the 3rd European Light Cavalry, Lieutenant J. Jacob from the 22nd Bombay Infantry, and Lieutenant C. James from the 43rd Madras Infantry, who were posted to the 1st, 2nd, and 3rd Regiments respectively. On the 12th of October, Bradford, compelled to take fifteen months' leave to England on medical certificate, handed over his command of the 1st Regiment to Major H. Forbes, the Commandant of the Bhopal Levy. Thus only four officers who knew the men—the Brigade-Major, Ashton Mayne, and the three Adjutants, Blair, Beadon, and Stanley Clarke—remained to help Travers in his new duties. Training, however, had gone well forward. Mayne had expressly urged the Government of India to allow the Headquarters of all three regiments to remain at Goonah until they were pronounced fit for service. He had felt that if they were distributed in their raw state throughout Central India, training would certainly be intermittent and might become unmethodical. At Goonah, in spite of occasional rebel hunts, every man would be under his own eye. His request was granted. The result was that the regiments quickly took shape, and before the cold weather set in the 1st Regiment, complete and efficient in every respect, was ordered to Mehidpur. Three months later it moved to Agar to relieve Meade's Horse when the latter marched to Goonah to be incorporated with ourselves. It remained at Agar during the next six years.

Before the end of the year 1860 three more ' Doing Duty ' officers were appointed—namely, Lieutenant C. J. O. Fitzgerald from the 42nd Madras Infantry, F. Pike from H.M. 91st Foot, and K. Neave from the 24th Bombay Infantry. Fitzgerald (the father of Oswald Fitzgerald of the 18th Lancers, Lord Kitchener's Private Secretary [1]) was posted first to the 3rd Regiment and then to the 1st, and in May 1862 became Adjutant of the 2nd. He left shortly afterwards to join the Hyderabad Contingent, in which he had a distinguished career. Pike went to the 2nd, but was not long in the regiment. Neave, who was posted to the 1st, was killed by a tiger near Goonah on the 9th January 1861.

Mayne's departure had paved the way for the consummation of Sir Richmond Shakespeare's project of appointing a Brahmin Risaldar Major. Of the two Sikh sirdars whom Mayne had invited to join him one only had accepted the invitation. This was Risaldar Panjab Singh of the 2nd Panjab Cavalry, who became Risaldar Major of the 2nd Regiment. The other had declined, and Isri Parsad, already a well-known figure in Central India, was appointed Risaldar Major of the 3rd. Isri Parsad —' old I. P.' as he was familiarly known—was a Brahmin of a very different type from Gopal Singh, though undoubtedly just as able and just as powerful. He was a fiery soul. Short and lean, sharp of

---

[1] He was drowned, with Lord Kitchener, when the *Hampshire* was sunk in 1916.

feature, daring and exceedingly clever, a brilliant detective rather than a military leader, he was the terror of every miscreant in the Malwa jungles. Whenever a dacoity took place within the area of the Central India Agency, Isri Parsad was called upon to hunt down the perpetrators, and he very rarely failed. Sometimes with a few men of the regiment, sometimes by means of his own agents and spies, he would follow up a gang through one petty State into another, and even into British territory, until every member of it was brought to justice. Agar gaol was full of his victims. Umer Singh, Daoran Khan, Lachman Jharia, Chitoo, and Bhowan, all notorious outlaws of their time, were amongst them; and even after his retirement he spent three years in the pursuit of the celebrated Tantia Bhil, whom he captured a few months before his death. He died on the 26th of September 1890 at Indore, a member of the First Class of the Order of British India and a Companion of the Order of the Indian Empire.

He had little to do in earlier years with the organisation and training of his regiment. The 3rd Regiment, in fact, hardly knew him, for he was dacoit hunting during the greater part of the hot weather of 1861, and in July the Government of India found itself compelled, for financial reasons, to hold the jungles with two regiments instead of three. The 3rd was therefore disbanded, and Isri Parsad was posted to the 1st in the Grade of Risaldar, though retaining his title of Risaldar Major as a complimentary distinction.

Meanwhile Travers was occupied with the reception and distribution of the officers and men of Meade's Horse. These people had been aware for some months of their approaching dissolution. They had tried very hard to avert it. Meade himself, now Resident at Gwalior, had protested that his regiment was one of the earliest raised in the Mutiny, and deserved a better fate. " It was raised for General Service," he pointed out, " under the direct orders of His Excellency the Governor-General, and was embodied and on active service before any of the Corps composing the Central India Horse and long before many other regiments which are still kept on." But all in vain. On the 12th of November definite orders were issued for the regiment to march to Goonah, there to be incorporated in the Central India Horse. Certain favours, however, were allowed. The rates of pay, which were higher in Meade's than in Mayne's or Beatson's, were to remain intact; and as a mark of distinction to a regiment which had deserved well of the Government of India orders were expressly given that it should not be broken up, as others had been, but that, retaining its organisation, it should be transferred bodily. Cockburn marched his regiment up the road in February 1861, reaching Goonah on the 14th. The men hoped, undoubtedly, that they would simply become the 3rd Regiment Central India Horse. This was, however, impossible. There was already a 3rd Regiment. Nor was it even practicable to transfer whole squadrons, as had been suggested by the Agent to the Governor-General. This, however, did not matter very much. The administrative unit at that time was the troop, and each troop, not each squadron, was of a distinct class. Squadrons were known only on parade, and were composed of two troops, and there was no Squadron Leader officially appointed as such. The senior Troop Leader led the squadron, handing the command of his troop to his senior Jemadar. Meade's Horse was therefore transferred by troops to the 2nd and 3rd Regiments, Central India Horse. The 1st, 5th, and 6th Troops—Sikhs, Brahmins or Dandotia Thakurs, and Rajputs respectively—went to the 2nd Regiment; and the 2nd, 3rd, and 4th Troops—Panjabi Mahomedans, Jats, and Christians respectively—to the 3rd. These additions brought the two regiments up to full strength, but they produced a large number of supernumeraries in the commissioned and non-commissioned officer ranks. The men who had been in Beatson's Horse complained of this. They had simply been disbanded regimentally and enlisted in Mayne's Horse individually, some of them in ranks lower than those which they had previously held. The favouring of the men of Meade's barred their way to promotion. They were told that they had no grievance, as the conditions of their disbandment and re-enlistment had been made clear to them, whilst Meade's Horse had remained an entity. This did not satisfy them; but many of them, recognising their own inefficiency and the hopelessness of promotion, were willing to accept the gratuities offered to them of a month's pay for every year's service and to leave the Army. Others were compelled to do so by the indisputable pronouncement of Medical Boards.

The British officers of Meade's Horse, with the

exception of Dr Dalzell, left Goonah as soon as the incorporation was completed; but the men soon settled down. The only difficulty which confronted Travers in regard to them was the question of the maintenance of the Christian troop. Although a few of these Christian sowars, more thrifty than their comrades, had paid off the advances made to them for the purchase of their horses and were comparatively well off, the majority were still in debt, and, if discharged, could realise nothing on the sale of their assamis.[1] It was impossible to retain such men on the Silladar system strictly followed; and yet there were reasons for their retention which made it incumbent upon Travers and the Government of India to find a way out of the difficulty if they could. The Eurasian problem has been before Government ever since the English first went to India. These people are employed upon the railways and as clerks in Government and other offices, but there are many of them who still claim the right to perform military duty. The men of Meade's Horse in particular had already done good work in the field, and had no desire to cast their uniforms. What was the solution? Travers suggested that Government should give them their horses, refunding to them the amount of the advances which had been repaid. His advice was not followed. He was ordered to arrange with the Commandant of the Lahore Light Horse for the transfer of the whole troop to that regiment. This officer agreed to take all men of good character who were not married and could speak English. Unfortunately many of the

[1] Horse and equipment. See chapter vi.

THE THIRD REGIMENT DISBANDED

men were not only married but, *more indico*, had parents and aunts and uncles living with them as well; so negotiations hung fire. And then came, quite suddenly, the financial crisis involving the dissolution of the 3rd Regiment.

The records on this point are meagre. There is nothing to show how the disbandment was carried out. The Christian troop at any rate disappeared. Some of the men, no doubt, went to the Lahore Light Horse, and the rest were transferred to the 2nd Regiment, amongst them an amusing character of the name of John Turner, whose two sons, Charles and William, both excellent trumpeters, formed the last remnants of the Christian troop. Of the other troops the Indian officers and men were presumably discharged with gratuity in the usual way, though about seventy of the younger soldiers seem to have replaced casualties in the other two regiments. Of the British officers Conolly and Stanley Clarke went back to their Regular corps; and James replaced Ashton Mayne, not as Brigade-Major, for that title was now abolished, but as Staff Officer of the force, the latter becoming Adjutant of the 2nd Regiment in the place of Beadon, who left about this time.

Travers' tenure of command was a short one, and can have given him little pleasure. From the moment he had carried out the incorporation of Meade's Horse and so completed the formation of the brigade designed by Durand for the preservation of the Pax Brittanica in the Central India jungles, he was obliged to begin pulling it all to pieces. Not only was he ordered to disband the 3rd Regiment, but, as if that was not sufficient mortification, he was further commanded to reduce the other two from a strength of 578 sabres each to 420. The remainder of his time was therefore occupied in this unpleasant duty, and he went home on the 18th of December, leaving to his successor an attenuated force, no longer a brigade, barely sufficient in importance to lure an aspiring soldier from the command of some other regiment. Yet his successor was neither Cunliffe Martin nor Bradford. The latter was never Commandant of the Central India Horse ; the former had to wait fifteen years, and meanwhile the force was commanded by a succession of five distinguished warriors from the North.

CHAPTER VI.

THE SILLADAR SYSTEM.

ALLUSIONS have been made in previous chapters to the system of organisation known as the 'Silladar System,' on which our regiment—as well as many others—was raised and maintained until the Great War forced upon Government the adoption of the 'Regular System' throughout the Army. It has now ceased to exist, and, before many years have passed, may be completely forgotten; but it was an interesting system, and therefore, in case our young officers of the future may care to learn how varied was the work of their predecessors and how many questions of administration occupied their minds in addition to and sometimes, as its opponents always averred, to the detriment of their purely military duties, I propose to give here a short description of it, and to show how it worked in our own particular corps.

The idea underlying the Silladar System went beyond that of simple personal service. It involved a greater risk, with the probable consequence of a greater reward. It implied that an individual who was sufficiently loyal and sufficiently confident in the power of the State to win its battles and to pay its way, was prepared to place not only himself but a great part, or even the whole, of his resources at the disposal of the State for military duty. It was not feudalism. Service was not a condition of land tenure. No man was bound to serve or to provide the personnel or material of war. It was an ordinary bargain between the State and the individual, who gave his services and lent his property in return for a cash payment. It followed that the Silladar was, unlike the ordinary soldier, a man of substance. He might have much or little, the essential point being that he must have something to bring in to the service of the State beyond his own person and his own goodwill. If he were a large landowner, as Gopal Singh was, with men and horses at his command, he would bring in as many of these as he could muster. He then became a 'Silladar'—or Sillah bardar, an armour-bearer, an esquire. Each horse, with all the saddlery, arms, and equipment, was known as an 'assami';[1] and for the upkeep of each assami Government paid to the Silladar, in addition to his own salary, a sum which, until the closing years of the nineteenth century, was more than enough to cover his expenses. His men were called 'Bargirs' (horse takers), and were paid by Government at the same rate as infantry soldiers. A group of horses belonging to one Silladar was known as a 'Paigah.'

[1] 'Assami' is a very comprehensive word meaning, originally, a name on a muster roll, and hence the situation or appointment held by the owner of the name. Or it might mean his official equipment. It might be applied to the man himself, or to his belongings, or to both. In the military service it usually meant the belongings only. On the land an 'assami' is a tenant or cultivator.

BE-NOKAR SILLADARS

A case like Gopal Singh's, however, was, after the Mutiny, very rare indeed. In practically every instance the Silladar produced only the money; and the State, in the person of the Commanding Officer of the regiment, having purchased horses and equipment, sold the assamis to him, and enlisted the Bargirs where they could best be found. The purchase of a number of assamis was, in fact, regarded as a good investment; and it sometimes happened that such investments were made by civilians—rich merchants, for instance—who had no intention of performing military duty in their own persons, and were not compelled to do so. These men were known as 'Be-nokar silladars.' There were several of them in Beatson's Horse; but the arrangement was unsatisfactory, and when the crisis of the Mutiny was over, all 'Be-nokar silladars' were persuaded either to pass on their assamis to fighting men or to re-sell them to Government, who then held them as 'Government assamis' until soldiers of sufficient means or sufficient credit could be found to purchase them.

A regiment of cavalry organised on the Silladar System thus consisted, in earlier years, not of a number of well-to-do men, as soldiers of the latter half of the nineteenth century knew it, but of a few wealthy leaders, who commanded troops either of their own servants and followers or of indigent men, mostly agriculturists, enlisted by Government recruiting officers. The Silladar, however, as the owner of a large Paigah, gradually died out. More and more smaller men took to buying assamis; and so by degrees the composition of the regiment changed, and, even before the Mutiny, we find Silladars in all ranks and the proportion of Silladars to Bargirs gradually increasing. This increase continued. The Bargir, a man of lower social standing than the Silladar, himself died away; and in 1871 our Commandant, Colonel Dighton Probyn, who "can testify from personal experience what a beneficial change it made in his own late regiment, the 11th Bengal Lancers, when he abolished Bargirs in that corps," did away with him altogether. "Bargirs are to leave," he wrote. "Why should the Central India Horse any longer retain a system which causes the Force to run a risk of being inferior to other regiments of Native Cavalry in India?" Exceptions were made in the case of Troop Commanders and the Wardi Major, who were allowed to retain one Bargir each. The remainder, with the exception of those who had saved enough money to buy their own horses, were gradually discharged; and henceforward no man was enlisted who could not put down at least Rs. 200 in cash, the rest of the money—about Rs. 150—required for the purchase of his assami being advanced to him by the regiment. A man who thus owned his own horse and no other was known as a 'Khudaspa.' The last Bargir (he was Gopal Singh's) disappeared from the regiment in 1883; and since then there has been no Silladar in the original sense of the term.

On his enlistment as a Khudaspa the recruit took over, at a valuation made by a Committee of Indian officers, the assami of the man whom he replaced. The price of the horse was, however, always the same, whatever its age or its service; for all trans-

THE CHANDA FUND

actions in relation to horses were carried out by the Chanda Fund, to which every man paid a small monthly subscription. The recruit paid Rs. 200 into this fund for his horse, or he brought in his own, which, if considered fit for service, the fund took over; and thereafter, in virtue of his monthly subscription, he was entitled to be remounted by the Chanda whenever his mount became a casualty. It was hardly realised in the later days of Silladar cavalry how completely, in earlier times, a man's horse was his own. It was at his disposal not only for Government duty but for his own convenience. He was held responsible for keeping it fit for service, and if, through his own neglect, he failed to do so, he was put on 'dismounted' pay—the pay of a Bargir—for a period during which the Chanda took the difference between the 'mounted' and the 'dismounted' pay and fed the horse; but so long as the animal was well he might do what he liked with it, and no questions were asked. He might ride it on his own private business or for pleasure, and very often did; and he always took it with him on furlough. He rode to his home, in fact, and not too slowly either, and this was a privilege which was greatly prized. Not only did it make for economy, but it gave to the cavalry soldier, riding into his village, considerable prestige compared with the infantry man who walked. Moreover, he could take his horse away with him on his discharge. A good many men used to avail themselves of this right; but it was somewhat prejudicial, if exercised too freely, to the stability of the Chanda Fund as well as to the efficiency of the regiment. There was, however, another side to the bargain. He might wish to leave his horse behind him, but the Commanding Officer might decline to buy it; and if it was in bad condition owing to the man's neglect he did so—a severe punishment, with, however, a stimulating effect upon those whose discharge drew near.

The organisation of a Silladar regiment was, until 1888, by troops, six troops forming a regiment of three tactical squadrons; but the basic unit was the 'Juri' or Couple. In addition to their horses, arms, uniform, and saddlery, every pair of men owned between them a pony and a tent, and employed a syce or grass-cutter. Thus the complete 'Juri' was a small self-contained unit; and the obvious advantage of the system was that any portion of the regiment, from a couple of sowars to a squadron, or the whole, could march off at any moment to any place in India and remain there for an indefinite time. This was not a mere theory: it was a constant practice. A Naeb Dafadar and three men for a post on the Grand Trunk Road, a Dafadar's guard as escort to treasure, a troop for the pursuit of dacoits or the regiment ordered on active service or to a Camp of Exercise, all went out in the same way and could start immediately. For every two men, and for each officer, there was a pony loaded with the tent and baggage and a syce in charge of him. The duties of the syce and pony did not, however, end with the transportation of the baggage. Arrived on the camping ground the syce was obliged to go to some spot, pointed out by the Civil Authorities, and there either to cut sufficient grass for the three animals for the day, or

THE 'JURI'

collect it if already stored, load it up on the pony, and bring it back to camp. The syce, in fact, had a particularly hard time, for, having brought in the grass for the horses, he was expected by his masters to help to groom them. The ponies, before 1890, were tiny little fellows, not more than 13½ hands high; but they had wonderful endurance. They were nearly all stallions. They were supposed to carry a couple of maunds.[1] They often carried more, and the syce on top of it all; and they invariably travelled faster this way than when led by the syce, who was never a fast walker.

It is obvious from the foregoing that a Commanding Officer of a Silladar cavalry regiment had much to think of besides soldiering. He was, indeed, a trader with quite a large business. He had to buy and sell everything necessary for the life of the regiment. The horses he either bought himself or he entrusted the purchase to the best judges of horseflesh amongst his officers. Before the introduction of the Waler nearly half these horses were Arabs, purchased, of course, in the Arab stables in Bombay. An extra charge of Rs. 50, over and above the regular horse price, was always made for an Arab, who was an expensive animal; and there were always men ready to pay for it. The remainder of the horses were country-breds of the old type, which has practically ceased to exist. They were, in fact, real Indian horses, hard, wiry, excitable little fellows of all sorts of colours—the dun being very prominent—and for the most part of very high quality; and they were bought at the large fairs held annually

---

[1] A maund is eighty pounds.

at Batesar near Meerut, at Poshkar near Ajmere, and at Balotra in Rajputana. The ponies were bought locally, very often by the men themselves, though a few came down from the fairs, the Marwari pony from Balotra being especially prized. In the old days it was not easy to make a profit on the Chanda Fund. A horse's length of service was, on an average, ten years. The correct procedure, therefore, was so to adjust the sowar's monthly subscription to the fund that he should subscribe in ten years an amount not less than the average price of a horse. Any excess which he subscribed, plus the price obtained for casters, which, however, was negligible, went to the credit side. If he subscribed too little the Chanda fell into debt; if too much the regiment was liable to become unpopular, and recruiting consequently to fall off. In later days, however, when the height of polo ponies was raised to 14.1 and 14.2—that is to say, to the same height as our regimental troop horses—many horses were trained and sold as polo ponies, and large profits were made.

Clothing, leather for saddlery, iron for horse-shoes, &c., were purchased in large quantities at Cawnpore, Bombay, and other places. The saddlery and most of the clothing was made in the regimental workshops; and all completed articles were stored and sold to the men as they were required at a price slightly higher than the cost of production, the profit going to the 'Wardi' Fund. For the shoeing of their horses the men paid a regular subscription to the 'Forge' Fund. The only article not bought and sold by the regiment was the carbine, which

THE 'AFISERAN COMMITTEE' 101

was supplied by the Ordnance Department. Swords were made in England, mostly by Bourne of Birmingham; lance shafts of male bamboo were cut by parties sent out yearly into the jungles for the purpose. We used to supply Wilkinson of Pall Mall with a certain number of these. The heads and butts were made regimentally.

All these transactions, however, gave but little trouble, and occupied but little time in comparison with the perpetual question of food. The business of feeding 600 horses and 600 men, involving as it did somewhat extended operations, required a sort of regimental Army Service Corps. It was entrusted to a Committee of Indian officers, known as the 'Afiseran Committee,' of which the Risaldar Major was President, working always under the supervision of the Commanding Officer. The members of this Committee were usually able men, with a good knowledge of business as well as of agriculture, and they worked very hard indeed. The custom was, until the year 1885 or thereabouts, to deal, in the matter of grain, direct with the cultivators. A member of the Committee, very often the Risaldar Major himself, would at seed-time go out to the districts—to Shujawalpur in the case of the regiment at Agar, and to Shadora in the case of the Goonah regiment—and negotiate with the farmers for the purchase of the crops when harvested. Large advances were made to the farmers to cover their intermediate expenditure, and as a result of these, the price agreed upon was considerably below the wholesale market price. At harvest-time the crop, being reaped, was buried in the villages until the grain was required, when it was brought to the Lines and handed over at wholesale price to the regimental banias,[1] who were allowed to make a small profit on retailing it to the men. The regiment made considerable profits in this way; and Scindia's officials—for, of course, these operations took place in Gwalior territory—complained that the cultivators were being treated unfairly. We were accused of robbing the poor. There was no doubt some truth in this. Our 'Afiseran Committee' could drive a hard bargain, though on our side we wondered whether the Gwalior officials had not other interests to consider besides those of the poor zamindar.[2] We were, however, defeated. The fiat went forth from the Indore Residency that the system of advances must cease, and that we must in future buy ' Khush Kharid '—in the open market. Thenceforward much of our grain was imported from the Panjab.

Mention has been made of the regimental banias. There was a bania to each troop. They constituted the regimental bazaar, and they supplied the men with most of their requirements and kept their accounts. Each regiment, too, had its own banker—the ' Seth ' as he was usually called. These seths and banias had other dealings than those with the men. They came to the assistance of impoverished British officers. The names of some of them, of Harna Mal in particular, are remembered with affection by some of the old officers to this day. We could borrow money from them, plenty of it, at $7\frac{1}{2}$ per cent on a simple note of hand

[1] Corn-dealers and money-lenders.   [2] Farmer.

—it is enough to make the modern subaltern's mouth water,—and many of us were in debt to them for years; but to the best of my belief neither Harna nor any other bania was ever let down.

The provision of grass for the horses gave more trouble even than the grain. There was no question of purchase. The stuff was there for the taking. The Maharajah of Gwalior placed large grasslands —' Birs ' as they were called—at our disposal. All we had to do was to go and fetch it; but that is just where the trouble began. Immediately the rains had ceased the syces used to go daily to the bir to cut as much grass as the pony could carry, and bring it into the Lines. So far all was plain sailing; but this could not go on for many months. It was necessary to cut all the grass on the bir before it withered, and to stack it within view of the Quarter Guard for consumption during the ensuing hot weather and rains. An army of coolies, many of them women, and a great number of bullock carts were employed on this service during the cold weather; but before they could commence operations a protracted altercation took place between the Gwalior officials and the ' Afiseran Committee '— which demanded all one's sense of humour to endure without irritation—as to the hire of the carts and the weight to be carried by them, and the amount to be paid to the coolies for every thousand ' pulas ' cut. Now a ' pula ' has been aptly described as a bundle of grass as thick as a tree and as long as a piece of string. It was therefore necessary, before fixing the price of cutting, to agree upon some approximate size or weight. It is said that in olden times the thickness of the 'pula' was deemed sufficient if it was equal to the girth of a sowar; and tradition had it that we enlisted a specially corpulent recruit for this purpose and fed him up annually to be at his fattest in October. I have not, however, been able to trace this story beyond the region of legend. From time immemorial the amount of grass—it cannot be called 'hay'—has been reckoned in India by the 'pula,' and, in contracts for cutting or for purchase, the number of 'pulas' to the seer[1] has been usually stated. In our case it was decided that they should weigh either two pounds or half a pound. The 1st Regiment usually chose the larger 'pula'—I do not know why—and the 2nd chose the smaller, because any error in weight was likely to be in favour of the regiment. When the grass was stacked it was often found that there was more than the regiment required. The surplus was therefore sold to local farmers and dairymen for their cattle. This, too, was a profitable business, and the Gwalior officials either winked at it or were ignorant of it until the early years of the twentieth century, when they insisted that the grass was given as food for horses and not as merchandise, a contention which could not be rebutted; so the practice of selling ceased, and the surplus grass was taken by the Durbar.

The profits made on these agricultural dealings were placed to the credit of a fund known by various names—in the 2nd Regiment it was called latterly the 'Sowars' Reserve Fund,' to emphasise the fact

[1] Two pounds.

that it was theirs and no one else's—and were devoted to the interests of the men. Occasionally it was found possible to use the fund for a free issue to the whole regiment of certain articles of equipment, such as new saddlery or new greatcoats. Such occasions, however, were rare. They enhanced the prestige of the Commanding Officer who found them, but they caused a heavy drain upon the fund.

The accounts were kept in the vernacular by the regimental Munshi, and in English by the second senior officer. It was the official duty of the latter; but in practice every officer took a turn at the accounts at some time or other in order to acquire some experience of regimental economy. Subalterns usually found them difficult and very boring, and inspecting Generals who had not been brought up on the Silladar System gave them up as completely incomprehensible.

This is not the place for a discussion on the merits of Silladar as compared with non-Silladar cavalry. The taunt of " nanga ata nanga jata "[1] was often thrown by the men of the former service at their friends of the latter; but the theory that a man is a better fighter because he is better off, and perhaps of better social standing, is open to argument. On the other hand, a man who has staked his property as well as his person in the service of the State is less amenable to the persuasions of the agitator or the Bolshevik. Undoubtedly, too, the Silladar System took less out of the taxpayer. Cattle and goods are better tended by the owner than by the hireling. Nevertheless it is obvious that, how-

[1] "Naked come and naked go."

ever suitable to Asiatic campaigning of fifty years ago, the system cannot stand the strain of modern warfare for a day. Whether it could be maintained in peace time, for cheapness' sake, and a transition made to the Regular System on mobilisation, is a question which might still be revived. But cheapness is not always economy.

CHAPTER VII.

HENRY DALY.

THE close of Travers' tenure of command found the Central India Horse reduced to the formation by which it was characterised during the next five-and-thirty years—namely, a small force of two regiments, stationed always at Goonah and Agar under one Commandant, whose Headquarters were for the first few years at Goonah. The regiments were not linked in the same way as the battalions of an English territorial regiment, for there was no common local recruiting ground and no depot for the service of both. Recruiting, in fact, was never local. Promotions of British officers were made in the 'Central India Horse' and not in one particular regiment; and even temporary postings, to replace officers on leave or on the Staff without being seconded, were made by the Commandant and not by the Second-in-Command. Thus an officer was not always a 1st Regiment man or a 2nd Regiment man. He was liable to be, and often was, transferred from one to the other. At any moment he might receive his marching orders, when he would just send on his horses and baggage a week or so ahead of him and then gallop up or down the road as the case might be. But in all other respects the regiments were completely independent of one another. The Indian ranks were never interchangeable. The title of 'Second-in-Command,' which was held by each Commanding Officer, would seem to suggest some limitation of authority. This, however, was not the case. The Second-in-Command had all the responsibilities and all the powers of a full-fledged regimental commander, and he exercised them freely. The Commandant, though responsible to Government, took little part, of course, in the administration or training of the regiments, and brigade training was practically unknown. Never in war, and only on two occasions in peace, did he find an opportunity of parading his two regiments together. The very *raison d'être* of the force precluded this. The nature of the work required that it should be done for the most part by small detachments. The Central India Horse was never called upon to act as a brigade in Central India, nor could more than half of it be spared from Central India for any length of time. Consequently not more than one regiment could proceed on active service or even to manœuvres; and it was the custom, in order that each regiment might have its fair share of such opportunities, to send on these occasions a combined regiment consisting of a wing of each under one of the Seconds-in-Command, though the Commandant himself led his combined regiment through the Second Afghan War. Thus in Central India the Commandant, as a soldier, had very little to do. He was rarely in uniform. His pay, moreover, was but Rs. 100 a month higher than that of a Commandant of a single regiment. It is a fact, nevertheless, that the appointment was highly prized. If there was little military interest, there were attractions of another sort. The political duties, alluded to in an earlier chapter, provided in fact the charm which drew from Northern India some of the most distinguished heroes of the Mutiny.

At the time we are speaking of the designation of the Commandant, in addition to his military title, was 'Political Assistant at Goonah,' his immediate superior in this respect being the Resident at Gwalior. Before the Mutiny this office had been held by Captain Burlton of the Gwalior Contingent, who lived at Goonah, a solitary Englishman, for many years; and when Mayne began to raise his first regiment he assumed the duties which Burlton had performed. Later on, as we have seen, the Government of India expressed disapproval of so much political activity. Closer restrictions were placed upon Mayne than the Agent to the Governor-General himself was prepared to impose. He was forbidden to correspond with the chiefs, and his duties were limited to those of Magistrate in the town and cantonment of Goonah and to the protection of life and property on the Grand Trunk Road in cases only where British subjects were concerned. During the few years following the Mutiny there were British troops at Sironj and Lalitpur, as well as at Sipri and Goonah; and small detachments, sometimes without even a non-commissioned officer, were constantly moving up and down the road. These constituted, in nine cases out of ten, the British subjects whom it was necessary to protect. It soon became evident that, without wider powers,

Mayne could not discharge even this simple duty. The reason for this lay in the fact that in the jungles round Goonah, interspersed amongst Scindia's provinces, were the territories of certain petty chieftains—interesting but pathetic offshoots from the noble families of Rajputana, with revenues in some instances of less than £500 a year—and here, so long as Mayne had no authority, miscreants could find shelter without fear of molestation. The Agent to the Governor-General had foreseen this difficulty, and had authorised Mayne, " in the event of robbers and rebels again threatening to disturb the peace of the country," to act freely on his own discretion, to address any of the Thakurs and chiefs, and to take any steps he might deem essential. The hint was taken. Mayne resumed his former duties. He held his durbars. The Vakils from all the States, petty and otherwise, resumed their attendance at Goonah; and henceforward no band of dacoits was allowed to rest in any one territory for long. Succeeding Commanding Officers were invested with these fuller powers. The 'allowance' was negligible, not more than sufficient to pay for clerks and stationery; but the opportunity was there for studying the intensely interesting question of the feudatory States, and might lead, as it had already done in the case of Meade, to higher appointments in the Political Service. So the Mutiny men came down to us.

They were all of them Piffers.[1] They had won their spurs at Delhi and Lucknow. Their names

---

[1] The word is derived from the initials of the Panjab Irregular Frontier Force.

were known in England. Three were Victoria Cross men, and the other two were so in all but name. Henry Daly,[1] the first of these illustrious soldiers, had already raised two regiments and commanded two others; and he was the hero of a historic march. He had fought at Multan and Gujerat. At the close of the Sikh War he raised the 1st Panjab Cavalry, and six years later was sent to Oudh to form the 1st Oudh Irregular Cavalry, which he commanded until a few weeks before the Mutiny broke out, when he returned to the Panjab to take command of The Guides. He had hardly done so when John Lawrence ordered The Guides with all haste to proceed to Delhi, the first unit of that continuous flow of reinforcements from the Panjab which saved the situation in India. With 150 cavalry and 350 infantry Daly set off, at six hours' notice, on a march of 590 miles; and twenty-two days later, on the morning of the 9th of June 1857, on one of the hottest days of an Indian summer, he joined the Delhi Field Force on the Ridge. On the 19th occurred the action of Nawabgange. To save some guns of the Horse Artillery, which were in jeopardy from a large body of the enemy which had moved round our right rear, Daly, followed by a few men of The Guides Cavalry, charged the enemy's infantry, broke through them, and reached his artillery. He was very severely wounded and carried off the field; but his charge gave time for the arrival of reinforcements, the guns were saved, and the day was won. The deed cried out for the bestowal of the Victoria Cross, and had Daly be-

[1] Afterwards General Sir Henry Daly, G.C.B., C.I.E.

longed to the Queen's Service he would have been recommended for it without hesitation. It happened, however, that neither officers nor men of the Indian Army were eligible for the distinction at this time; and when, in 1859, it was thrown open to the Indian Service, though to British officers only, Daly was precluded on the ground that he had become by then a Brevet Lieutenant-Colonel and a Companion of the Bath. The Victoria Cross was not opened to Indian officers and men until 1914. It is strange that a decoration of this kind should ever have been closed to any soldier of the British Empire.

In November The Guides returned to Hoti Mardan, and Daly, whose wound had kept him out of action throughout the siege of Delhi, went with them. He was not allowed to remain long inactive in the Panjab. Early in 1858 he was called to Lucknow, and when Hodson was killed on the 11th of March, he succeeded to the command of Hodson's Horse, which he led during the remainder of the campaign.

He arrived at Goonah on the 31st December 1861. Few changes were made and few new British officers were appointed during the next two years. Bradford returned from leave in February 1862, relieving Forbes, who went back to the Bhopal Levy, in the command of the 1st Regiment at Agar. Martin commanded the 2nd at Goonah. The Adjutants were Blair and Ashton Mayne; the Doctors, Beaumont and Dalzell; and the Risaldar Majors, Amjad Ali and Partab Singh. Three new 'Doing Duty' officers came in. Lieutenant M. J. Mignon from the 15th Bombay Infantry was posted to the 2nd Regiment, and Lieutenants F. H. T. Cumming from the

22nd Bombay Infantry and G. R. Peart from the General List of the Bombay Army were posted to Headquarters for duty with either regiment as occasion might require. Cumming left before the year 1862 was out, and his place was taken by Lieutenant J. S. Irvine of the 2nd European Light Cavalry.

It was about this time, when the remnants of Tantia Topi's army were disappearing from the jungles and the despatch of rebel hunting detachments was becoming less and less frequent, that were originated those regular hot weather shooting parties which became an important feature in the life of the Central India Horse. The party, usually of five or six guns, half or more perhaps being guests from other regiments or from Europe, set out from Goonah about the 1st of April, and, starting from the neighbourhood of Paori, shot the jungles round Shahabad and down the Kunu River on the west side of the Grand Trunk Road. It was necessary to return to Goonah in time for Muster Parade on the 1st of May. This was a remarkable ceremony. It was abolished before the end of the nineteenth century, but up till then the Pay Department had resolutely declined to pass the pay of any officer or man or follower who had failed, without reasonable excuse, to answer to his name on the 1st day of the month. The regiment was paraded for this purpose, with everything belonging to it. Every officer and man, every horse and pony, all the syces and the bhishtis, the hospital dressers, and the dooli bearers, even the civilian clerks in the office; everyone was there. The names were called. The Adjutant reported to the Commanding Officer that everything was correct, and then all filed solemnly away. It will be remembered that the officers with the shooting party were not on leave. Both they and the shikaris and orderlies were reckoned to be 'on command' so long as they remained within the confines of Central India. It was a special privilege of service in the Central India Horse; but it was considered advisable not to say too much about it, especially to the babus[1] of the Pay Department, whose duty it was to draft the monthly 'Objection Statement'; so the shooting party returned to Goonah in time to answer to their names. A day or two later it went out again, usually to the jungles on the east side of the Grand Trunk Road, to Sironj and Isawas and Maksudangarh, and again returned to cantonments before the end of the month. The usual bag in early days was about five-and-twenty tigers, five or six lions, and a few panthers and bears. The lions gradually died out or were shot out. The last lion in Central India was killed in 1876. In 1861 there is a record of sixteen tigers and as many bears being killed in one month.

There is no record of the party in 1862. In this year a smart young Jat Dafadar of the 1st Regiment, of the name of Jiwan Singh, distinguished himself in a dacoit hunt. He was sent out in command of a detachment from Agar to the westward. He came upon his foe at Poonakheri near Jaora, and, acting boldly, succeeded in capturing the whole band. For this exploit he received the Order of Merit. He served for many years afterwards, rising to the rank

[1] Clerks.

of Risaldar before he retired. He was a very popular
fellow, and will always be remembered as the wittiest
Indian officer we ever had.

In 1863 Martin organised the usual shooting
party from Goonah. Bradford joined him from
Agar, and one of the guns was Captain Curtis of
the Inniskilling Dragoons, who had fought alongside of Mayne's Horse at Sindwaha. The first half
of the shoot was over and eighteen tigers had been
killed, when Curtis was obliged to leave the party
in order to join his regiment at Mhow before the
expiration of his leave. Bradford accompanied him,
and the pair marched southwards from the Kunu
valley into the jungles of Jhalra Patan. At Deglan-
pura, some fifty miles north of Agar, there was news
of a tiger, and a beat was organised. A large male,
attempting to break out at the side, was wounded
by one of the 'Stops.' He galloped back into the
beat towards Bradford, who was in a tree overhanging a pond. Bradford gave him both barrels,
wounding him again; and he came to the foot of
the tree and stood there. Quietly Bradford took up
his second gun, but, as he pressed the trigger, the
hammers were caught in a twig, and both barrels
missed fire. The tiger then sprang into the tree,
and Bradford, seeing no means of escape, jumped
down upon him, thrusting his left arm into the
tiger's mouth. He was dreadfully mauled; but
the tiger, sick from his wounds, soon left his victim,
and lay down on the edge of the pond. Curtis and
an orderly, impotent witnesses of the struggle, were
then able to finish him off. Bradford was placed
on a charpoy and carried towards Agar, a sowar

being sent on ahead with the news. The doctor, Tim Beaumont, galloped out with all speed, met the party some thirty-five miles from Agar, and there and then, under a mango-tree by the roadside, without any kind of anæsthetic, he amputated the arm. Bradford recovered; and the empty sleeve which he wore henceforward was never an effective handicap.

In the following year, 1864, the cadre of British officers was augmented, two being added to each regiment; and for the first time the term 'Squadron Officer' appears in the Army List. The three senior officers were thus designated, the Commanding Officer himself, from his new title of 'Second-in-Command and Squadron Officer,' being charged with the duty of commanding a squadron as well as a regiment. He delegated the former duty, of course, to the senior 'Doing Duty' officer. This system continued for many years. It was not, in fact, until the two regiments were separated that the duty of commanding a regiment was registered officially as a whole-time job. Two comparatively senior officers were brought in to command the second squadrons, Captains Peter Luard of the 104th Foot and John Durham Hall of the 4th Bombay Infantry being posted to the 1st and 2nd Regiments respectively. The third squadrons were commanded by Lieutenants Peart and A. J. Bannerman, the latter coming in from the 9th Bombay Infantry. The new 'Doing Duty' officers were Lieutenants E. E. Gibson from the 103rd Foot, and John Colledge and C. B. Horsburgh, both of the General List, Cavalry. Blair left the regiment early in this year, and went to the Political Department. Both doctors, Tim Beaumont and Dalzell, left also, the former to be Residency Surgeon at Indore. Dr Brodrick came back in relief of Beaumont, and Dalzell was replaced by Assistant Surgeon Odevaine.

In 1865 the Headquarters of the force were transferred from Goonah to Agar. The move was welcome to Daly, for it gave him larger political responsibilities, and brought him into closer touch with the Agent to the Governor-General at Indore. Hitherto the Second-in-Command of the 1st Regiment at Agar had not been overburdened by his civil duties. He was certainly 'Political Assistant at Agar,' just as the Commandant had been 'Political Assistant at Goonah,' but he had no dealings with any of the chiefs. He was Assistant to the Political Agent in Western Malwa, who lived at Mehidpur, and in practice he was only a Cantonment Magistrate; but in this year the Political Agent at Mehidpur relinquished his appointment, and the Government of India, instead of relieving him in the ordinary way by appointing a regular officer of the Political Department to succeed him, brought Daly down from Goonah to Agar and made him Political Agent in Western Malwa. His charge included the States of Jaora, Ratlam, Sitamao, and Sailana, besides certain outlying districts belonging to Gwalior, Indore, Dewas, and Tonk. "So you see," he wrote himself, "there are few Agencies with more varied interests." Succeeding Commandants of the Central India Horse were all invested with the same political authority; whilst the duties at Goonah, hitherto discharged by the Commandant, devolved, of course, upon the Second-in-Command of the regiment stationed there.

There were few changes amongst the British officers either in this year or the next. Mignon and Irvine left, and Lieutenant James Miller came in from the 27th Bengal Infantry. Lieutenant L. F. Jamieson of the 7th Hussars was attached to the 1st Regiment as 'Doing Duty' officer for a few months only. At the end of 1866 the two regiments, for the first time in their history, changed places. The 1st Regiment, after six years at Agar, marched out on the 4th of December, and reached Goonah on the 16th. On the following day the 2nd began its march to Agar. This was not the usual custom in later years. The exchange was henceforward, with very few exceptions, triennial; and both regiments, starting simultaneously, marched into Biaora on the same day. Here there was a day's halt, occupied by sports and games, and on the following morning both set off again.

Early in 1867 Daly gave up the command. He ceased to be a soldier. His wise and genial spirit was not, however, lost to Central India. During the next four years he was Resident at Gwalior, and then he succeeded Meade as Agent to the Governor-General. In February 1881 he left India for good; and twenty-five years later his son Hugh,[1] who had passed into the Political Department from the Central India Horse, sat in his father's old office at Indore.

---

[1] Afterwards Colonel Sir Hugh Daly, K.C.S.I., K.C.I.E.

CHAPTER VIII.

OTHER MUTINY HEROES.

DALY was succeeded by Colonel William Templer Hughes,[1] a man less widely known than his predecessor or than some of his successors. He had been less fortunate. In his youth he had been attracted, like so many good soldiers, by the opportunities for active service offered by the Panjab Irregular Frontier Force, and had entered that corps, from the 48th Bengal Infantry, as Second-in-Command, under Henry Daly, of the 1st Panjab Cavalry. He had succeeded Daly in command of that regiment, as he succeeded him later on in command of Hodson's Horse, and was following him now at Agar. When The Guides went down from Mardan to Delhi Hughes was with his regiment at Asni, a station since abandoned for Rajanpur. He received the news that a crisis had arisen at Multan, so, without waiting for orders from superior authority, he marched thither forthwith and placed his regiment at the disposal of Major Crawford Chamberlain, who had been ordered by Sir John Lawrence to disarm two native infantry regiments at that place. The disarmament was accomplished on the morning after

[1] Afterwards General Sir William Hughes, K.C.B.

his arrival without bloodshed. It was a difficult and dangerous task, but the rapidity and decision with which the situation had been handled unquestionably saved Multan.

Meanwhile it was becoming increasingly clear that the small force on the Ridge was insufficient for its purpose. Further reinforcements were demanded, and Hughes, with his 1st Panjab Cavalry, was ordered from Multan to Delhi. With joy he set his face in that direction. At Karnal, however, within sixty miles of his objective, his hopes were shattered. A telegram from the Adjutant-General informed him that, Hindustanis being considered unreliable and his regiment consisting mostly of men of that race, he was to remain at Karnal until further orders, sending on only John Watson's squadron of Sikhs and Afghans. He spent many hours of that day at the telegraph office. He implored the Adjutant-General to allow him to proceed, insisting upon the fidelity of all his men. But orders were imperative and immutable. With tears in his eyes he saw Watson off on the mission which was to bring him so much credit and rode back, a very sad soldier, into camp. His confidence in his men was not misplaced. Within a few days he led them against the insurgent town of Bulleh, which was stoutly defended. With the aid of a couple of Patiala guns and a few infantry he carried the town, killing 150 of the insurgents. Writing to Watson shortly afterwards, he said, "I congratulate you on joining the Army. Your men will win you promotion." His own men, faithful throughout, won him promotion too. He led them through the Meerut District and into Oudh towards the end of the year 1857, fought in all the battles of the Oudh campaign, and came out of the Mutiny a Brevet-Lieutenant-Colonel and a Companion of the Bath. A stern soldier, with a much softer heart than he professed to own, he cared little for the political duties imposed upon him in Central India. Within a couple of years of his arrival at Agar he was promoted Brigadier-General, and his services were replaced at the disposal of the Commander-in-Chief. He finished his career in command of the Umballa Division.

The period of his command at Agar was somewhat uneventful, though one well-known dacoit was brought to trial. This was a man of the name of Daoran Khan, a Mekrani of unenviable reputation. He was a ruffian with nothing romantic about him, a mere 'hired assassin,' ready to commit any deed of villainy for pay. In the year 1867 one of Holkar's Thakurs, who had quarrelled with the Durbar, employed him to make trouble in Indore territory. The Durbar appealed for help to the Agent to the Governor-General, who called upon Isri Parsad to deal with the case. This was enough for the Thakur, who promptly submitted. Daoran Khan, however, could not give himself up so readily. He knew what the consequences would be. He decided to fight for his life rather than surrender, and he found himself opposed to a small detachment of the 2nd Regiment Central India Horse under Dafadar Barmadin,[1] who, after a pursuit of some weeks, took him by surprise and brought him in to Agar. Barmadin was promoted from the 2nd to the 1st Class of the

[1] The same Barmadin who was with Wood when he won his V.C.

Order of Merit for this action, and was now well on his way to commissioned rank.

In this year the Army List shows another change of nomenclature. The exceedingly awkward title of 'Doing Duty' officer is abolished and that of 'Squadron Subaltern' takes its place. Ensign R. J. H. Wyllie from the 103rd Foot and Lieutenant A. F. Taylor from the 108th Foot were appointed 2nd Squadron Subalterns during the cold weather of 1866-67. In March 1867 Captain Ashton Mayne was appointed to officiate as Cantonment Magistrate at Morar, and Captain H. M. B. Burlton relieved him as 3rd Squadron officer of the 1st Regiment. Both these officers left the regiment a little later on, Mayne becoming a Political Agent and Burlton a Cantonment Magistrate. Lieutenants H. F. Showers of the 104th Foot and A. H. S. Neill of the 103rd were appointed Squadron officers on probation early in 1868. The latter was a son of General Neill of Cawnpore fame, who was killed at Lucknow.

Hughes' successor, Colonel Sam Browne[1]—"Shambrun Saheb" as he was always known by Indian soldiers—took up the reins at Agar on the 18th of March 1869. He had served in the Sikh War as a subaltern of the 46th Bengal Infantry. He then joined the Panjab Frontier Force, and for some years before the Mutiny had held the command of the 2nd Panjab Cavalry. Like Hughes, he was obliged to see a junior officer, Charles Nicholson, march off to Delhi with a squadron of his regiment; and, like him too, he followed himself later on. His regiment was sent down into Oudh, and, after Luck-

[1] Afterwards General Sir Sam Browne, V.C., G.C.B.

now had been finally relieved, he led it in a most gallant charge against the rebels at the village of Kursi. "Five times he rode clean through them, killing 200 and taking 14 guns." In the following year, during the operations which were known as 'The Pacification of Oudh,' he was at Philibhit when news came in that the important town of Nuriah, ten miles distant, was occupied by the enemy. With his own two squadrons and 350 infantry Browne was ordered to drive them out. During the attack, whilst the skirmishers were advancing, the enemy's guns began to play upon the cavalry soldiers, who had halted and dismounted on an open road. One gun in particular opened with grape at eighty yards. Sam Browne and his orderly were mounted. Followed by the latter he galloped into the battery and engaged the gunners in a hand-to-hand fight. They closed round him. He was quickly wounded by a sword cut on the knee; and immediately afterwards his left arm was severed at the shoulder,[1] whilst his horse, wounded at the same moment on the head, reared up and fell back on him. His Wardi Major and some sowars, who had mounted and galloped after him, were just in time to rescue him from his perilous position; and then the remainder of the force closed in upon the defenders, and the town was taken. The deed was recognised at the time as one of the bravest of the

[1] A friend had lent him a couple of curb chains to wear on his shoulders. This friend was killed and, shortly before this incident, another friend, who had bought two of the former's bridles, mentioned as a curious fact that neither had a curb chain. "I know where they are," said Sam Browne, and taking them off his shoulders handed them to him, and went into action without replacing them.

Mutiny, and the Victoria Cross was awarded to him without question. He recovered from his wound, and in later life was able to do as much with one arm as most men can do with two. Being a great sportsman as well as a great soldier, he had a practical turn of mind. He invented many contrivances to enable him to shoot, to play billiards, or to kill a salmon; but for all his prowess as a sportsman and a leader of men, he is now best known to fame as the inventor of the Sam Browne belt. He held the command of the Central India Horse during two short months, at the end of which he reverted, on his promotion, to the Military Department.

He was followed by Colonel Dighton Macnaughten Probyn[1] of Probyn's Horse, who in his turn was succeeded by Colonel John Watson[2] of Watson's Horse. It is impossible not to mention these two happy warriors together. They were devoted and lifelong friends. I have heard each say of the other that the Almighty could not find too good a place for him. Yet they differed much, in style as well as in appearance. Probyn, tall, dark, bearded, exceedingly handsome, was the living embodiment of the pomp and circumstance of war. Watson, fair haired, blue eyed, very powerful, and of medium stature, cared less for appearances than for practical efficiency. Both were superb horsemen; but Watson rose in his stirrups instead of bumping the saddle in the fashion of English cavalry, even on ceremonial parades. Probyn called this " jogging along like an

---

[1] Afterwards General The Right Honourable Sir Dighton Probyn, V.C., G.C.B., G.C.S.I., G.C.V.O.

[2] Afterwards General Sir John Watson, V.C., G.C.B.

old farmer." Both were great swordsmen; and here they were alike, for they both used a curved sword, and "Hit first and hit hardest" was their only rule. And they were alike in a simple faith, which they were not too bashful to express. To read family prayers, to go to Church at least once every Sunday, and to sing hymns in the drawing-room after tea was their constant habit. It sounds a little strange in the twentieth century, but in Victorian days there were many like them.

Watson was the older by a few years. As a subaltern in the old 'Bombay Toughs,' Henry Daly's regiment, now the Dublin Fusiliers, he had been present at the storming of Multan, at the battle of Gujerat, and at the final surrender of the Sikhs at Peshawar. He then found his way through the 28th Bombay Infantry and the 2nd Balooch Battalion to the 1st Panjab Cavalry, Hughes' regiment, of which he soon became Adjutant. Probyn joined the 6th Bengal Light Cavalry in 1849, was transferred to the Panjab Frontier Force in 1852, the same year as Watson, and became Adjutant of the 2nd Panjab Cavalry, Sam Browne's regiment. He was sent down from the Panjab to Delhi with a squadron of his regiment under Charles Nicholson, John Nicholson's younger brother; and when the latter was appointed to command the 1st Panjab Infantry in place of Coke, who had been severely wounded during the siege of Delhi, he came in to the command of this squadron. He and Watson and Younghusband, the latter with a squadron of the 5th Panjab Cavalry, arrived on the Ridge early in July, and henceforward, until the fall of Delhi and onwards until the final relief of Lucknow, they were in action almost every day. Life was full of adventure. During the assault on Delhi, when our column on the right had been repulsed, the cavalry was moved down from the Ridge to take up a position in front of the Mori Bastion, under the very walls of the Fort, to cover our successful columns on the left; and there they stood in line for two long hours, the 9th Lancers in white drill, with pennons fluttering, in the centre; Watson's steel blue swordsmen on the right; and Probyn's sowars in scarlet achkans on the left, a target—and what a target!—for the guns on the Burns Bastion. There were many casualties. At dusk they were withdrawn to Ludlow Castle; and as soon as Delhi had fallen they started, with Greathed's column, for Lucknow. There was fighting on the way—at Bulandshahr, at Aligarh, and at Agra. Agra was reached on the morning of the 10th of October after a night march. The people who had been shut up in the Fort flocked out to greet the column which went into camp on the brigade parade ground, some two miles distant. It was believed that no enemy troops were in the neighbourhood, so the camp was pitched at leisure; no pickets were posted, and many of the officers, Watson and Probyn and Roberts[1] included, rode into the Fort for breakfast. During the meal the sound of guns was heard. "With our mouths full," wrote Watson in his diary, "Roberts and I jumped on our horses and rode for camp. The scene was wonderful; the whole of the people, male and female, black and white, who had been pent up so

[1] Lord Roberts.

long in the Fort had poured out towards our camp, as they thought in perfect security; but on the sound of the guns they all fled back again, and we had to force our way against the stream at a gallop. I fear I must have knocked over a good many, but there was no time to beg pardon." As senior of the three Piffer officers Watson was ordered to take the three squadrons—which he delighted, of course, in calling his 'Brigade'—to the right, and to fall upon the enemy's left flank. This he did with conspicuous success, capturing two guns and several standards. It was in this mêlée and the pursuit which followed it that Probyn so greatly distinguished himself. The award of the Victoria Cross, which came to him at the end of the Mutiny, was not made for one particular act of valour, but for continual daring. Many gallant deeds were recorded of him. On this occasion there was a running fight along the road to the Kali Naddi, ten miles from Agra. At one time Probyn was separated from his squadron, and found himself surrounded by half a dozen sepoys, of whom he killed two before his men rejoined him. On another occasion he singled out a standard-bearer, and in face of a number of the enemy, killed him and took the standard; and these are only two of the incidents which stamped him as one of the bravest young soldiers of his time.

On the 9th of November, near Cawnpore, the column joined Sir Colin Campbell's force for the relief of Lucknow. During the operations which followed, Watson, on one of his many reconnaissances, found himself with his own and Probyn's squadrons on the bank of the river Gumti, when a considerable body of the enemy's cavalry was observed formed up under some trees half a mile off. It was impossible to attack them, as the only available open space, between the river and some high grass jungle, was too narrow for deployment, and, moreover, it was not known what guns or other troops were with them. Watson sent his squadrons back about a quarter of a mile to some open ground near the Martinière College, remaining himself under a tree to watch the enemy's movements. He saw some riflemen creeping through the jungle towards a village not far in rear of his observation post, and in order to prevent its occupation by these fellows he dismounted, and, with his trumpeter, began to fire it. Leaving the trumpeter to complete the work, he presently remounted and rode back to his tree. He had no sooner reached it than he saw a long column of cavalry galloping up six abreast between the jungle and the river, their leader not twenty yards from him. In the moment of thought allowed to him, he felt that to go back would be fatal. His men might misunderstand it. He rode straight into the enemy's column, engaging the leader, whom he killed, and was immediately surrounded by the troopers, who began hammering away at him, he guarding their blows as best he might. The unequal contest lasted for some minutes, when Probyn, who had seen the charge, brought up the two squadrons at full speed, and the enemy was soon in flight, leaving about a dozen on the ground. Watson was bruised all over, but he lost no blood, and was not off duty for a moment. Sir Colin rode up soon afterwards and rebuked him severely for firing the village; but he recommended him for the Victoria Cross, which was, of course, bestowed upon him.

Shortly after this Watson was ordered to raise a regiment of Sikh cavalry, and as soon as Lucknow had fallen he handed over his squadron to Captain Cosserat, who had recently joined him, and went up to Lahore to begin his new duties. The regiment which he raised, called at the time the 4th Sikh Cavalry, became the 13th Bengal Lancers, and is still known as Watson's Horse. Probyn was entrusted with a similar duty. He raised the 11th Bengal Lancers, Probyn's Horse, but he did not begin this work until some months later than Watson, being obliged first to take sick leave to England.

Probyn came to Agar on the 21st of May 1869. His aim during his two years' tenure of command was to emphasise the fact, enunciated in one of the earliest of the letters from the Government of India concerning Mayne's Horse, that the Central India Horse was raised "for military purposes and for those alone." He observed a disposition, especially amongst local civilian authorities, to regard the regiment as nothing more than a body of Military Police. Certainly it was our business to police the road and the jungles on either side of it; but this very obvious duty had a tendency to obscure others which were less obvious and for which a different kind of training was required. Probyn never lost sight of the fact that we might be called upon at any time to serve anywhere, in or out of India. He saw, too, that the need for so much constabulary work must diminish, and might even disappear, and that if, when this happened, we were not trained as an efficient military body, we might cease to exist. A threat of reduction was actually made before he had been many months at Agar. The Government of India suggested that one regiment was now sufficient for the work in Central India. The Agent to the Governor-General, Henry Daly, replied convincingly that, owing to the distances to be covered and the continued prevalence of dacoity, he could not be responsible for the maintenance of order with less than two, and there the matter ended; but it strengthened Probyn in his determination that the Central India Horse should be soldiers, and thereafter he lost no opportunity of inculcating soldierly ideals. He was keenly alive to the necessity of his regiment being brigaded sometimes with other troops. Accordingly he set to work to have them sent to a Camp of Exercise, and in this he succeeded.

There were several changes amongst the officers during the years 1869 and 1870. In 1869 two new doctors were appointed in the place of Brodrick and Odevaine—namely, Lionel Spencer and Denis Keegan, both of whom distinguished themselves in their profession. The former became in course of time Residency Surgeon and Chief Medical Officer in Rajputana. The latter, who acquired a European reputation, especially for operations for stone, finished his Indian service as Residency Surgeon at Indore.

In December of this year old Panjab Singh, Risaldar Major of the 2nd Regiment, died at his home in the Panjab. He was a gallant soldier, who, to use Henry Daly's words concerning him, had " so borne himself in the field and in quarters as to make his name a household word among Englishmen." In his honour his son, Dafadar Ala Singh, was immediately made a Jemadar. He was succeeded by Risaldar Gopal Singh, the leader of the ' Chambal Horse.'

Early in 1870 Bradford left the regiment to become Political Agent at Jaipur. After many years' service in the Political Department, culminating in the appointment of Agent to the Governor-General in Rajputana, he became, after his retirement from India, Chief Commissioner of Metropolitan Police. Of great courage and great ability, he was one of the most gentle of men. The command of the 1st Regiment, which now became vacant, was not permanently filled until eighteen months later, when Captain Henry Buller was brought in from the 11th Bengal Lancers.

An important event of this year was the Viceroy, Lord Mayo's, Durbar at Ajmere in October. The 1st Regiment marched up from Goonah to act as personal escort to His Excellency, who complimented them on their appearance and behaviour. Lieutenants H. A. Wilson and J. B. Watts of the Bengal Staff Corps, Ensign H. A. Vincent of the 96th Foot, and Lieutenant M. G. Gerard, R.A., were posted before the end of the year. Wilson and Watts remained for a few months only. Vincent and Gerard served for many years. The latter, in fact, became Commandant, and was the last Commandant of the two united regiments.

In the spring of 1871 there was some recrudescence of trouble along the Grand Trunk Road, and Probyn found it necessary to warn our patrols that " they must invariably carry loaded firearms, and, if necessary, they need not hesitate to use them." The firearm of the period was a smooth bore muzzle-loading carbine. A few weeks later this order was followed by another, directing officers commanding troops " to have the swords of the men under their command properly sharpened. They are responsible that the above weapons are always kept in a fit state for immediate use." Since then it has been a point of honour with Troop Leaders that every sword is always sharp. A special follower, who could do little else, was maintained for this purpose. He was known as a ' sigligar.' There was one in each troop. He sharpened the men's swords on weekdays, and on Sunday he spent the morning in the Squadron Leader's, or Squadron Subaltern's, verandah sharpening and polishing that officer's sword, his knives, his hog spears, and indeed every kind of steel instrument he possessed. These ' sigligars ' usually went on active service with their troops. They certainly did so in the Mutiny. After one of the fights near Lucknow a Sikh Risaldar of Probyn's squadron, because he had not completely cut an adversary in two, fined his ' sigligar ' a rupee, and was very indignant with Probyn for remarking that the poor fellow was not much to blame, seeing that the man was at any rate completely killed.

In September 1871 Probyn was promoted Major-General, and left India. During the remainder of his long life he was in the Household of Albert Edward, Prince of Wales, afterwards King Edward VII., and of Queen Alexandra. In his farewell order to the regiments he issued a final reminder of their military responsibilities. " The Central India Horse," he wrote, " is perhaps nominally a Local Corps, but notwithstanding this, General Probyn trusts that

A CAMP OF EXERCISE

all connected with the Force will ever remember that they are Soldiers and not Mounted Constabulary; that all will continue to strive to do their utmost as they have hitherto done to increase the efficiency and add to the good name of the regiments; and that when troops are required for active service there is no reason why the Central India Horse should not be the first called upon to join Her Majesty's Army in the field either in this or in any foreign Country."

Watson rode in from Indore through the mud, for there was no pakka road then, on the 14th of September 1871, the anniversary of the assault on Delhi. Though accustomed to the wild tracks of the Frontier, he found the hills of Malwa wilder still. Like so many officers after their first ride up to Agar, he felt not only that it was a very difficult place to reach but that there was nothing beyond it. "No! no! my dear fellow," he said as Probyn came out to greet him. "For God's sake let me ride a little farther. I am sure I shall come to the end of the world." His first military duty was to make preparations for the coming Camp of Exercise at Delhi, to which, owing to Probyn's exertions, the regiment had been summoned. He himself was appointed to command the Cavalry Brigade of the 3rd Division, of which the Central India Horse was to be one of the units. A composite regiment, consisting of one squadron of the 1st under Neill and two squadrons of the 2nd, the whole under Martin, marched from Goonah on the 8th of November, and was absent from Central India for nearly four months. It was the first occasion on which we were brigaded with other troops, and great was the anxiety to do well. We were not discredited. The Divisional Commander, Sir Harry Tombs, wrote a very complimentary report; and Watson, endorsing Probyn's views of the importance of a military training, published it in Brigade Orders with the following introduction: "In small stations such as Agar and Goonah there is but little to stimulate such endeavours, but where they are earnestly and unflaggingly made in a true soldierly spirit, the day will surely come when, not merely at a Camp of Exercise but on the Battle Field, they reap their true reward."

In July 1872 the Government of India, being at length persuaded that the Indian officers and men of the Central India Horse were quartered just as far from their homes as were those of the Panjab Frontier Force, sanctioned to the former the same privilege in the way of leave and furlough as were enjoyed by the latter. Under the new rules one-sixth of the men in each regiment—equivalent to one troop in the days of three squadron regiments—was allowed to be absent from Headquarters on furlough throughout the year. It was a great boon to the men. The length of the furlough depended upon the distance of a man's home from Central India. Pathans from across the border were allowed seven months; Sikhs whose homes were beyond the Sutlej had six; Jats and others from Delhi and Rohtak districts had five; and men who were unfortunate enough—in this respect—to live within 100 miles of the Lines were limited to three. In addition to these furloughs it was always within the power of a Commanding Officer to give a man two months' leave on urgent private affairs. British officers of the Panjab Frontier Force were allowed three months' privilege leave every year; but this indulgence was not extended to British officers of the Central India Horse.

In December of this year the Viceroy, Lord Northbrook, came down to Central India to open the new railway bridge over the Nerbudda at Barwai, and Watson seized the opportunity, denied to his predecessors, of bringing his two regiments together. After a few days of brigade training at Indore they marched thence to Barwai, where they were reviewed by His Excellency, and returned to their Headquarters before the end of the year.

Meanwhile there had been but few changes in the personnel of either regiment. In September 1871 Risaldar Major Amjad Ali of the 1st Regiment retired, and Isri Parsad became Risaldar Major in fact as well as in name. In October Dr Spencer left the regiment. He was succeeded by Dr Harvey, who, however, did not take over his duties until May 1872, Dr Roberts acting for him in the meanwhile. After three years' service with the Central India Horse, Dr Harvey became Civil Surgeon at Simla, where he was well known for many years. In October also Lieutenant J. de Burgh of the Bombay Staff Corps was posted as officiating 3rd Squadron officer of the 1st Regiment. He served for two years only.

Early in 1873 Watson was appointed to act for Henry Daly as Agent to the Governor-General at Indore. He was absent on this duty, and on the furlough which followed it, until the end of 1875; and meanwhile the command of the force devolved upon Martin. During this period occurred the great famine in Bengal. Sir Richard Temple, Lieutenant-

Governor of Bengal, had invited the assistance of volunteers from the Indian Army in the arrangement of relief measures and the distribution of food. A party of Indian officers and non-commissioned officers from both regiments under Captain Neill was sent into Tirhoot and Champaran, the scene of the greatest distress, and remained there throughout the hot weather and rains of 1874. Lieutenant G. E. Money, who was appointed to the 1st Regiment from the 16th Lancers in June of this year, went out later on to help Neill with the transport. It was a difficult and distressing duty; but the party came through it successfully, and the following individuals, in addition to Neill and Money—namely, Risaldar Mahtab Singh, Jemadar Murad Ali Khan, Jemadar Sheikh Wazir Ali, Jemadar Wazir Singh, Wardi Major Mir Al Rasul, Dafadars Ramadin, Partab Singh, Bishan Singh, Saheb Dad Khan, Khushab Singh, and Wazir Singh, received the thanks of Government.

In the jungles there was still dacoit hunting. At the same time as the famine relief party was at work a detachment of thirty sabres of the 1st Regiment was in Bandelkhand hunting a band led by a notorious outlaw of the name of Randhir Singh. Ashton Mayne happened to be Political Agent at Tehri at the time, and the detachment came under his orders. It took twelve months to capture Randhir Singh; but he was eventually brought to bay, and in the final combat, in which Naeb Dafadar Tara Singh and three men took a very prominent part, he was made prisoner and brought in to Indore. A sowar of the name of Mian Singh was promoted for his gallant conduct on this occasion.

Early in the year the 2nd Regiment had a small

party out at a place called Tappa after some Bhils led by a man of the name of Oonkar. Isri Parsad was also out during the hot weather with a party of the 1st Regiment after Lachman Jharia and his band, who were found in the Nimbahera district, and put up a stiffer fight than was expected. The whole band was captured. One of our men, Sowar Disa Singh, was severely wounded, and two horses were killed. Disa Singh, who behaved with great boldness, was promoted Naeb Dafadar and decorated with the Order of Merit.

In January 1874 Dr Edis was appointed to succeed Dr Harvey. He left the regiment about a year later, and was followed by Dr Barclay. In July Lieutenant Alexander Masters, from the 5th Lancers, was posted to the 2nd Regiment.

In 1875 Dr Keegan left the regiment to take two years' furlough before following Tim Beaumont at Indore. He was succeeded by a very remarkable man, Dr Randolph Caldecott, always known as ' Puffy,' a convivial soul with a heart of gold, who followed ' Stuffy ' Keegan, as the latter had followed Beaumont, to Indore, where he left behind him a very pleasant name as a surgeon, kindly and especially skilful in diseases of the eye.

Two other officers were appointed in this year, Lieutenant The Honourable J. P. Napier and Lieutenant E. D. H. Daly. Neither of them stayed very long. The former was the eldest son of Lord Napier of Magdala, and the latter the eldest son of Henry Daly. Napier returned to his English regiment, the 10th Hussars, and Daly, who had a great fondness for animals, went within a couple of years to the Remount Department.

Watson returned to Agar in November 1875, and again found his regiments preparing for a Camp of Exercise at Delhi. This camp was considered to be of greater importance than that of 1871 by reason of the fact that the Prince of Wales, afterwards King Edward VII., was to be present. Watson was appointed to the command of the Cavalry Division, which consisted of four brigades, thirteen regiments in all, a larger body of cavalry than had hitherto been brought together in India. The composite regiment of Central India Horse, which formed part of the Second Brigade, consisted of two squadrons of the 1st and one squadron of the 2nd, all under Buller. Probyn, who was now on the Prince of Wales' Staff, had given Watson a hint that His Royal Highness disliked slow movements. In consequence there was, when the Prince was an onlooker, a good deal more galloping than usual, or perhaps than necessary; but the casualties in horseflesh are not recorded. On return from the camp Watson issued his well-known Brigade Order about bumping the saddle at the trot. He considered that this method "may possibly be the best for British cavalry, but the Commandant being firmly of opinion that it is the worst for Asiatic cavalry, he hereby directs that it is never to be used in the Central India Horse, and that the sowars who have been taught to bump the saddle may be sent to school to learn to rise in their stirrups." It was many years before rising in the stirrups was allowed in the English service; but meanwhile Watson lost no opportunity of pressing his views on superior authority. At Delhi he had caused some astonishment amongst the Prince's Staff by rising in his stirrups

at the final Review, and Probyn had accused him of
" going by like a huntsman and not like a soldier " ;
and at Malta a few years later, when in command
of the Cavalry Brigade which went to Cyprus, he
incurred the wrath of the old Duke of Cambridge.
His Royal Highness had come out from England to
inspect the Indian troops. Rising in the stirrups was
a thing for which he was completely unprepared.
He was horrified. Nor would he listen to explanations concerning the comfort of the men as well as
of the horses. " Nonsense, nonsense," was his reply ;
" we must have discipline, sir, discipline. Give 'em
something they don't like." But Watson lived long
enough to see his views adopted.

After his visit to Delhi the Prince of Wales made
a tour of Rajputana and Central India. He spent
one day, in March 1876, at Indore. The 2nd Regiment, then at Agar, marched down to take part in
the reception of His Royal Highness.

On the 24th of March, Horsburgh, the Adjutant
of the 2nd Regiment, died at Agar. He was succeeded in the appointment by Masters. No new
British officer was, however, appointed until August,
when Lieutenant Neville Chamberlain came in from
the 11th Foot, now the Devonshire Regiment. On
the same day, the 21st of August, Lieutenant Algernon
Durand, from the 65th Foot, was appointed to the
1st Regiment. The latter was the third son of Sir
Henry Durand, the Agent to the Governor-General
at Indore at the outbreak of the Mutiny. He served
throughout the Afghan War. From 1889 to 1893
he was British Agent at Gilgit, and was severely
wounded when in command of the Hanza-Nagar
expedition in 1891. Later on he was Military

Secretary to the Governor-General, the Earl of Elgin, and on his retirement became a member of H.M.'s Corps of Gentlemen-at-Arms. Neville Chamberlain, now Sir Neville, who was on the personal Staff of Lord Roberts for many years, distinguished himself in the campaign of Afghanistan, where he was wounded, and of Burmah in 1886-87. He served again on Lord Roberts' Staff in South Africa in 1900; and then, for sixteen years, commanded the Royal Irish Constabulary as their Inspector-General. He was a nephew of Field-Marshal Sir Neville Chamberlain, the Adjutant-General in India at the outbreak of the Mutiny, and afterwards the Commander of the Panjab Frontier Force.

At the close of the year 1876 a detachment of fifty sabres of each regiment, under the command of Captain Neill, went to Delhi as escort to the Agent to the Governor-General in Central India during Lord Lytton's Imperial assemblage, when Queen Victoria was proclaimed Empress of India.

In 1877 another change appears in the Army List. The title of 'Squadron Commander' is introduced and that of 'Squadron Officer' is substituted for 'Squadron Subaltern.' The cadre of British officers remains the same—namely, three Squadron Commanders, of whom one is the Commanding Officer, and two Squadron Officers, of whom one is the Adjutant. Officers appointed to fill temporary vacancies, caused by furlough or Staff employ, are now for the first time shown as 'attached.'

In April of this year Watson was appointed Resident at Gwalior. Little did he think that he would again take up the sword. Within eighteen months, however, he was called from his civil duties to command the Cavalry Brigade in the force which Disraeli sent from India to Europe to shake in the face of Russia ; and this was followed by two years in command of divisions in Afghanistan. When peace returned he went back to the Political Department as Agent to the Governor-General at Baroda.

His successor was Cunliffe Martin. Little of importance occurred during the next two years. Before the end of 1877 Lieutenant H. E. Ravenshaw of the Bengal Staff Corps and Lieutenant Ivor MacIvor of the 3rd Hussars were posted to the 1st Regiment. The latter went very soon to the Political Department. In August 1878 Dr P. M. Grant of the Malwa Bhil Corps, known familiarly as Peter Grant, was appointed in succession to Dr Barclay ; and in October Lieutenant J. G. Morris of the 44th Foot came in for a while, but did not take up a permanent appointment. Lieutenant C. J. B. H. Dressner from the 9th Lancers was posted to the 2nd Regiment about the same time. In this year also old Jemadar Garja Singh, one of the heroes of the Indore Residency, retired on his double pension. He had served in the Central India Horse for twenty years, and for twenty years before that in the Bhopal Contingent. In the appointment of his successor a very interesting experiment was made. A sporting young Parsee from Mhow, of the name of Merwanjee Cooverjee, was made a Jemadar on probation. He was the only Parsee who ever entered the Army. He served through the Afghan War, and made a very efficient Quartermaster, but when the war was over he left the regiment to become a Superintendent of Police, and the experiment was not repeated.

CHAPTER IX.

THE SECOND AFGHAN WAR.
1878-80.

BY COLONEL SIR NEVILLE CHAMBERLAIN, K.C.B.

THE spring and summer of 1878 passed quietly, but in the month of September the Amir Sher Ali received a Russian mission in Kabul. Shortly afterwards, his unfriendly refusal to permit a British mission under General Sir Neville Chamberlain to proceed through the Khyber Pass to Kabul led to an open rupture with the British Government. Negotiations ensued, but when these proved to be unavailing, orders were issued to the British forces at Jumrood, Kohat, and Quetta to cross the Afghan frontier. They advanced on all three lines on 21st November 1878, and in due course occupied Jellalabad, Kandahar, and the Kuram Valley up to the Shutrgurdun Pass.

The Amir Sher Ali died in February 1879, and three months later the treaty of Gandamak was signed with Amir Yakub Khan.

In July our Envoy, Sir Louis Cavagnari, accompanied by Mr Jenkyns, his Secretary, Lieutenant Hamilton in command of the escort of twenty-five sowars and fifty sepoys of the Corps of Guides, and

Dr Kelly, arrived at Kabul, where he was received with every form of outward honour by the Amir. On the morning of 3rd September some Herati regiments mutinied and attacked the Residency in the Bala Hissar, their numbers swelled by the armed rabble of the city. From eight in the morning until four in the afternoon the garrison made a heroic defence against overwhelming odds, and then the end came as the Afghans surged into the blazing ruins of the Residency.

Cavagnari's head was borne in triumph through the bazaars by the excited crowd, and thus history repeated itself; for in December 1841 our Resident at Kabul, Sir Alexander Burnes, and the British Envoy, Sir William Macnaghten, were murdered by the Afghans within a rifle-shot of the Bala Hissar, and their bodies were dragged into the city of Kabul and exposed with every mark of indignity in the bazaar.

A month later Lieutenant-General Sir Frederick Roberts, with 4000 men and 18 guns, completely defeated at Charasiab a strong Afghan force, and the following day he entered Kabul. The abdication of Amir Yakub Khan followed, and our troops set to work to prepare the defences of the Sherpur cantonment, into which they had moved, and to collect provisions for the winter which was ahead of them. It was well that they did so.

Thirty-eight years previously our army had commenced its disastrous retreat from Kabul, and it was annihilated in the Khurd Kabul and Jagdalak passes. In 1879 every detail of that thrilling story was doubtless told and retold to the rising generation in every village in Afghanistan by the greybeards, many of whom had participated in the scenes they described. The result was that, when a call went forth to the nation to gird up their loins like their forefathers and destroy once more the infidel invaders, the response to it was immediate and universal.

On 11th December 1879 the storm broke. From all points of the compass armed contingents of Afghans concentrated on Kabul, when heavy fighting ensued, and by the evening of 14th December Sir Frederick Roberts states in his 'Forty-one Years in India,' "It was difficult to form an accurate estimate of the numbers opposed to us. . . . It was calculated by those best able to judge that the combined forces exceeded 100,000 men, and I myself do not think that an excessive computation."

That evening he decided to withdraw and concentrate the force in Sherpur. Though hard pressed by swarms of Afghans, who were flushed in the hopes of victory over the handful of men who were retreating before them, our soldiers retired with perfect coolness and precision, and soon after dark the troops and baggage were safely inside Sherpur.

Before the telegraph wires were cut that night Sir Frederick Roberts wired full details regarding the situation to the Viceroy and the Commander-in-Chief in India.

Throughout the period which has been described since the outbreak of war, the Central India Horse continued to perform its normal duties in Central India. A few of the officers of both regiments had the good fortune to serve in various appointments with our forces in Afghanistan, and details regarding their services will be found at the end of this chapter. In addition, a detachment of thirty sabres from the 1st Regiment was employed for nearly nine months with the transport train of the 2nd Division, Khyber Force, between Jumrood and Jellalabad, and performed excellent service. To the great regret of all ranks, Jemadar Ramadhin, who had commanded the detachment, died of cholera at Lundi Kotal in June, and a Regimental Order paid tribute to his memory.

A week after the stirring news had been received in India of the withdrawal of the British force inside Sherpur, the Central India Horse received orders to prepare for immediate service in Afghanistan. Three days later 250 sabres of each regiment left Augur and Goona, and by the 28th January 1880 both parties had reached Peshawar. On 2nd February the regiment marched to Basawal, and until the 2nd April the corps was employed on escort and patrol duties along the section of the Khyber line from Jumrood to Basawal, a distance of forty-two miles. On 4th April the regiment moved to Jellalabad, leaving some detachments in posts along the road from Barikab to Rozabad, a distance of thirty miles.

On arriving at Jellalabad one of the first points the Commandant had to consider was the method to be adopted in crossing the Kabul river should he be called upon to do so, for previous disasters in that neighbourhood [1] while carrying out such an

[1] In January 1879 five men of The Carabiniers were drowned when crossing the Kabul river, and in the following April forty-seven officers and men of the Xth Hussars, out of a squadron seventy-five strong, were drowned when endeavouring to cross a ford of the river late at night.

K

operation were fresh in the mind of every soldier in the regiment.

Measures were therefore carefully thought out, and when the time came were put into operation.

Early in May news was received of a hostile gathering in Besud, east of Jellalabad, where a certain Mulla Khalil was reported to be collecting a large force to make a raid on the Jellalabad district. Major Buller was ordered to reconnoitre the enemy's position, and on 15th May he, with 50 sabres of the Central India Horse, crossed the Kabul river, then in flood from the melting snows in the Hindu Kush mountains. He was able to ford a portion of the river, but the northern branch of it was a deep channel, 150 yards broad, with a current of between five and six miles an hour. The horses and baggage ponies swam across the river, and they, with all the baggage, &c., of the detachment, were in Besud in an hour's time. They joined a small force of infantry at the Dabela fort, and reconnoitred to a distance of twenty miles on the two following days. On the second afternoon they came under fire of the enemy, and Major Buller was able to send in a valuable report to the Headquarters of the Brigade.

On 18th May the force in Besud was increased, and, as reports were received that the Mulla was moving forward, at dawn the next morning the following troops took up a position facing the hills to the north :—

    2 guns—No. 1 Mountain Battery.
  200 rifles—1st Battalion 5th Fusiliers.
  200 ,, 1st Battalion 12th (The Suffolk) Regiment.
  100 ,, 1st Madras Native Infantry.
  105 Sabres—Central India Horse.

ACTION AT BESUD

The whole under command of Brigadier-General J. Doran, C.B.

The Mulla's force, which numbered some 4000 safis and men of the Kunar district, was seen when the light became stronger to be leaving the hills, and to be moving across the broken ground in the direction of the Jellalabad ford, which it was their intention to seize and thus, if possible, to cut off the line of retreat of the small British force.

The action only lasted half an hour, when the enemy streamed away to the hills, where they found safety.[1]

The despatch submitted by Brigadier-General Doran after the engagement contained a special reference to the Central India Horse. After describing the successful advance of the infantry under cover of the guns, he stated :—

" News of this being brought to me I ordered the cavalry to charge, and the Central India Horse at once swept along between the hills and the fort, led by Lt.-Colonel Martin, and killed here and in other parts of the field 25 of the enemy. Whilst this was going on the few sabres of the Central India Horse which were present, a weak troop in all,[2] had swept along the back of the fort down the enemy's line, but many of the latter had been given shelter in the

---

[1] An amusing story was current in the regiment after the fight. Shortly after it commenced the Brigadier, an experienced veteran of distinction, came up to one of our native officers, an old friend of his, who was in command of a small party of the regiment acting as escort to the guns, and asked him how he thought the fight was progressing. The native officer imagined that our Commander was becoming nervous as to what might happen. He at once endeavoured to reassure him by saying, " Dharrao mat, Sahib, hamara fauj zarur gitega !" (Fear not, sir, our force will certainly win the battle !)

[2] Presumably the escort with the guns.

village of Besud by the very people we were protecting them against. Some were pursued by the Cavalry to the banks of the Kumar river, and there slain or forced into its waters. In this dashing charge many deeds of valour were done by both officers and men. . . ."

The casualties in the regiment were fortunately insignificant. The gallant Jemadar Fahim Khan, and Sowars Nund Singh and Khadi Khan (1st Central India Horse), were severely wounded. One horse was killed, and five badly cut with knives. Lieutenant-Colonel Martin, after recording the names of the wounded in regimental orders, added : " The following officers and men, in addition, did good service against the enemy : Major J. Colledge, Duffadar Mugger Sing,[1] Lance Duffadar Zairulla Khan,[2] Sowar Hurnam Sing (1st Central India Horse), Duffadar Abdul Rahman, Lance Duffadars Mardan Khan and Mahtab Sing [3] (2nd Central India Horse)."

Subsequent to the action the troops were employed in disarming the people of the district, and the towers and forts of those who had assisted Khalil Khan were blown up.

[1] Duffadar Mugger Sing was a fine swordsman. On more than one occasion he won 1st prizes for swordsmanship at Camps of Exercise against all comers.

[2] Lance Duffadar Zairulla Khan. When he died in 1909, having attained the rank of Ressaldar, after a most brilliant career, a Regimental Order stated : " . . . At the action of Besud he saved the life of his brother, Jemadar Fahim Khan, who was severely wounded, and killed several of the enemy with his own hand."

[3] Lance Duffadar Mahtab was one of our leading shikaris, and a cheery staunch comrade. He was terribly mauled by a tiger in 1875, but his nerves were in no way affected by it. A braver man never lived, and to our great regret he was killed some years later by a runaway horse on parade.

On 22nd May the force began to recross the river. The water had been rising daily, but by the evening the guns and the detachment 12th Foot had moved across, and they took up a position to cover the passage next morning. Dawn on the 23rd showed that the river had cut in behind the abutment of a bridge which had been constructed, and soon after the whole structure was swept away.

The portion of the force still in Besud had now to cross the whole breadth of the Kabul river in full flood. Some rafts made of skins (massaks) were rapidly constructed, and by their means the equipment of the troops was got across the river.

"The whole of the horses and a large proportion of the men of 3 troops of the C.I. Horse, and the mules of a division of No. 1 Kohat Mountain Battery, with some of their drivers, swam the formidable river at a place 400 yards in width,[1] and having a velocity estimated at between six and seven miles an hour.

"This was achieved with the loss of one driver and one Cavalry horse. In very many cases the horses were swum across with their owners or drivers riding them, or swimming alongside. Some of the men of the C.I. Horse crossed as often as 10 times this day to swim horses and ponies over." (Brig.-General Doran's despatch.)

The Brigadier added that he "believed no record of such a feat can be found in our Military history."

Looking back after all these years on this fine achievement, we can picture to ourselves the scene. The burning May sun overhead, the icy cold of the water from the melting of the snows on the upper

[1] To form an idea of what a river in flood, 400 yards broad, looks like, it may be of interest to state that the Thames at Waterloo Bridge is about 400 yards across; for the actual breadth of the bridge itself is 1380 feet.

ranges, the courage and physical endurance of the officers and men who toiled throughout the long hours with such conspicuous success, and the assistance they received from their good horses.

It was a fitting wind-up to the operations that week, when the regiment had ' made good ' on the first occasion that it was tested in the field, and we can well appreciate the feelings of the Commandant when he referred in a Brigade Order on the 2nd June to the share the regiment had taken in the operations, and added, as regards the crossing of the river, " This was a feat which will add greatly to the reputation of the Central India Horse."

On 3rd June 200 sabres of the regiment accompanied a strong British force into the Kama district. Again the river had to be crossed by swimming. No opposition was met with, and the force recrossed the river on 6th June. The Regimental Records state as regards the return journey: " Crossing began at 4 A.M. and continued without intermission until 9 P.M. A long tiring day's work." We can well believe it. In the two crossings only one horse was lost, as it was carried down to a whirlpool and drowned.

During the remainder of June nothing of importance occurred. On 2nd July Lieutenant Durand, with thirty sowars, was reconnoitring about six miles south of Jellalabad, when he came across a hostile party of tribesmen who opened fire on our men. Two of the enemy were killed, eight were taken prisoners, and the remainder escaped to the hills. Our only casualty was one horse killed.

During the summer of 1880 the experiment was tried of sending some parties of sick troops from Jellalabad to Dakka on rafts, to spare them the fatigue of a journey by land of nearly forty miles. Up to the beginning of July the passage of the rafts had been unmolested, but on the morning of 13th July news was received at the Elachipur post that a raft was in danger, having grounded in the middle of the river, and that fire had been opened on it from the opposite bank. Captain Fenwick, 1st Madras Infantry, who commanded the post, accompanied by four sowars of the Central India Horse, succeeded with great difficulty in crossing the numerous deep channels of the river by means of an extempore raft made of three 'massaks' and two spears, and on reaching the raft under a heavy fire they found Lieutenant-Colonel R. Smith, 8th Native Infantry, 2 other British officers, a European orderly, and 2 sepoys, one of the latter having been wounded.

The raft had been deserted by its raftsmen, and it was exposed to fire from the bank, 250 yards distant. Lieutenant-Colonel Smith was too ill to move, so a small party of the 1st Madras Infantry and thirty sowars, under Ressaldar Major Gopal Singh, 2nd Central India Horse, crossed the river on a raft which was discovered higher up-stream. The infantry were extended along the bank to keep down the fire of the enemy. Captain Fenwick graphically described in his report what followed:—

"Lt. Price, and Ressaldar Major Gopal Singh and his men, went coolly forward with a couple of 'dhandies,' which the bearers were too frightened to bring up, to the raft. They lay down and extended on the river's bank, in the open and out of cover, until Colonel Smith was ready; and then Lt. Price and the Ressaldar Major, themselves assisting in bearing the weight of the dhoolie, brought the Colonel calmly and slowly away at a walk, and the two dhandies full of officers' property, out of fire; the Enemy, many armed with rifles, redoubling their fire."

Six years later the Viceroy appointed Ressaldar Major Gopal Singh to be native aide-de-camp on his personal staff, in recognition of his services during the Mutiny, and also his gallant conduct at Elachipur.

So far back as the month of May 1880 negotiations had been opened by the British with Sirdar Abdurrahman, who had fled to the Oxus on the accession of Shere Ali to the Amirship in 1869. After various pourparlers the Sirdar realised the friendly feelings of the British Government towards him, and moving south he crossed the Hindu Kush and arrived in Kohistan on 19th July. Three days later it was announced at a public Durbar in Kabul that we accepted him as the Amir of Afghanistan.

The following day Lieutenant-General Sir Frederick Roberts left Kabul and rode down to visit the line of communications. He reached Jellalabad on 26th July, where he was the guest of the Central India Horse in the Wuzir's garden; a lovely spot, shaded by splendid plane and yew trees, with running water flowing through the centre of it—a welcome haven to the distinguished visitor after his long hot ride from Kabul. That afternoon he visited the remains of the fortifications round Jellalabad, which the 'illustrious garrison,' under Sir Robert Sale, had constructed and held for four months in 1842, and he was shown the site of a bastion where a British sentry, on 13th January 1842, descried a European mounted on a pony slowly making his way to the Fortress. It proved to be Dr Brydon, the only individual who reached Jellalabad out of General Elphinstone's force, numbering about 4500 fighting men and 12,000 followers, which had left Kabul seven days previously, and had been annihilated in the passes by the Afghan tribesmen.

Next day he started on his return journey, and when he reached Butkhak the following afternoon he was met by Lieutenant-General Sir Donald Stewart, who had ridden out from Kabul to tell him the very grave news, that the previous day the force at Maiwand, under Brigadier-General Burrows, had been totally defeated by Ayub Khan, and that Lieutenant-General Primrose, with the remainder of his force, was besieged in Kandahar.

On the 3rd August the Government of India sanctioned the despatch of a force from Kabul for the relief of Kandahar, under the command of Sir Frederick Roberts, and from what he had seen of the Central India Horse at Jellalabad a few days previously, when he had walked through the lines of the regiment, talking freely with the British and native officers and men, as was his wont, and critically examining the condition of the horses, he specially asked Sir Donald Stewart that the regiment might accompany him to Kandahar. This was sanctioned, and orders were issued for the regiment to proceed at once, by forced marches, to Kabul.

On 4th August the wing of the 1st Central India Horse left Jellalabad, and it reached Beni Hissar, two miles from the Bala Hissar at Kabul, on 8th August. The wing of the 2nd Central India Horse arrived there the following day. The forced march to Kabul had been a very trying one, in the heat of summer. The altitude of Jellalabad is 1950 feet, and *en route* to Kabul (5800 feet) the regiment had to cross the Jagdalak Kotal (5200 feet) and the Latabund Kotal (7400 feet). The road was narrow and stony, and it was much worn by the passage of troops and convoys since the previous winter. The dust *en route* was extremely trying to both men and horses; scarcely any forage was procurable, and extreme vigilance had to be exercised when passing through the many defiles which had to be traversed. From Jellalabad to Beni Hissar the distance is ninety miles, and some detachments of the regiment had to join their headquarters from posts eighteen miles beyond Jellalabad. Yet the horses showed no signs of fatigue, and four days later Hensman,[1] describing the Cavalry Brigade as it passed Amir Kila, fifty-nine miles farther on, stated : " . . . the horses looked in grand condition, the Central India Horse seeming none the worse for their hurried march from Jellalabad."

At Beni Hissar the regiment was formed into three squadrons, under Majors Buller, Colledge,

[1] 'The Afghan War, 1879-80.'

and Gerard. Total strength 495 sabres, with 10 British officers—

    Lieutenant-Colonel Cunliffe Martin, Commanding.
    Major H. Buller.
        ,,   J. Colledge.
        ,,   M. Gerard.[1]
    Lieutenant A. Masters (Adjutant).
        ,,   A. Durand.
        ,,   N. Chamberlain.[1]
        ,,   H. Ravenshaw.
        ,,   G. Daly.[1]
    Surgeon-Major Keegan.

On the afternoon of our arrival at Beni Hissar several officers and men rode over and visited the Sherpur Cantonment, where the force under Sir Donald Stewart was encamped, prior to handing it over to the Amir Abdurrahman on 11th August, when the troops started on their return journey to India. Sherpur Cantonment will always possess a special interest to our fellow-countrymen. It was erected by Amir Sher Ali on the very ground which the British force occupied in the spring of 1840, until it was forced to move out in January 1842 to the tragedy of its disastrous retreat through the passes. In the early part of this chapter it has been described how Sir Frederick Roberts's force was besieged there in December 1879.

Forty-nine years later Lady Humphrys, with nineteen women and children, walked through the snow from the British Embassy during the night

[1] Major Gerard and Lieutenant Chamberlain rejoined the regiment from duties on the Staff at Kabul. Lieutenant G. Daly joined the regiment from The Guides Cavalry.

of 22nd December 1928 to Sherpur, which had been turned into an aerodrome by the Afghans, and the following morning they were carried away in safety to Peshawar by our Air Force.

The force which was proceeding to Kandahar numbered approximately 10,000 men, and consisted of four cavalry and twelve infantry regiments, with three batteries of mountain guns (18 guns).

There were also about 8000 followers and 8200 transport animals.

The Cavalry Brigade, under Brigadier-General Hugh Gough, V.C., C.B., was composed of:—

Regiments	Europeans		Natives	
	Officers	Men		
9th Lancers . . .	19	318		
3rd Bengal Cavalry .	7		394	
3rd Punjab Cavalry .	9		408	
Central India Horse .	10		495	Total
	45	318	1297	1660

The Regimental Record states: "9th August. Camp Beni Hissar. Marched at 3 P.M. to Zahidabad, 17 miles, not reaching Camp till 10 P.M. Joined the Cavalry Brigade, under command of Brigadier-General Hugh Gough, V.C., C.B."

We were glad to reach camp that night, but we could not have foreseen the welcome we received there. Pitched alongside of us was that splendid regiment, the 3rd Punjab Cavalry, and awaiting our arrival in the darkness were Major Vivian, its Commandant, and representatives of the officers and men. They had prepared a most excellent supper for all ranks of the Central India Horse, and had placed on our camping ground food for our horses. Never was hospitality more timely or more appreciated, and the history of our march would be incomplete without this record of our gratitude.

Space does not permit of a detailed description of the march to Kandahar. An excellent account of it was written by a very distinguished officer of the regiment, the late Lieutenant-General Sir Montagu Gerard, K.C.B., K.C.S.I., entitled ' Leaves from the Diary of a Soldier and a Sportsman,' published by John Murray in 1903. His book also describes most graphically various incidents in his life while in the Central India Horse. Mr Howard Hensman, Special Correspondent of ' The Pioneer,' who accompanied the force to Kandahar, wrote a picturesque and very accurate account of the march in his book ' The Afghan War, 1879-80,' published in 1881 by W. H. Allen & Co.

The force moved on from Zahidabad on 10th August 1880 and reached Ghazni,[1] without opposition, on 15th August. The following day the road led over a desolate and arid country to Zergatta, passing *en route* Ahmed Khel, where Lieutenant-General Sir Donald Stewart's force, as it marched

---

[1] Ghazni had a special interest for one of our officers, Lieutenant Durand, for it was his father, Lieutenant Durand, Royal Engineers, who fired the train which blew in the gate of the Citadel of Ghazni on 23rd July 1839, and thus opened the way for the storming column of the force commanded by General Sir John Keane.

from Kandahar to Kabul in the previous spring, had defeated in a very sharp and brilliant engagement a large force of hostile tribesmen on the 19th April 1880. This march of twenty miles was a very trying one. A heavy dust storm came on during the afternoon, and our Regimental Record states: "Started at 4 A.M. Reached Camp 3.30 P.M. The rear-guard did not get in until 9 P.M. Men and horses all very tired. Only a little Indian corn procurable." To which may be added that, for cooking purposes, it was necessary to collect such 'camel-thorn' scrub as could, with difficulty, be found, which was our only firewood at most of our halting-places.

Four days later Hensman wrote: "August 20th will always be remembered by those who survive the operations now being carried on, as a day full of privation, and calling for much endurance by officers and men.... Water was so scarce that followers fell exhausted by the wayside, and we had to send back *bheesties* with *mussuks* of water to save the Kahars and others from dying of thirst. The heat was greater than ever in the day, although in the early morning the air had been bitterly cold. One company of a native regiment lay down in an irrigation channel, the water of which was too muddy to drink. Not a tree gave shade in any direction, and the arid plain with its scrub-growth seemed to grow red-hot." He went on to describe our arrival in some villages where we encamped that evening, where "we had water and supplies more than enough for our force, but the struggle to reach this oasis broke down many a man and beast."

DUST AND HEAT

In his famous book, 'Forty-one Years in India,' Lord Roberts described some of the difficulties his troops had to contend with during the march, and added: "The variation of the temperature (at times as much as eighty degrees between day and night) was most trying to the troops. . . . Scarcity of water, too, was a great trouble to them, while constant sand storms and the suffocating dust raised by the column in its progress, added greatly to their discomfort."

And here we must pause to pay a warm tribute to our splendid infantry who, under a burning August sun, reeled off mile after mile of their journey as they pressed on to Kandahar, their only preoccupation being their fear that Ayub Khan and his army would not await our arrival. Often, for many miles, no water was obtainable, and as we neared Kandahar the drinking water was brackish. Day after day British and native infantrymen marched cheerily and steadily through the heat and the choking dust raised by the column. Only those who witnessed it can realise the strain it imposed on them. The officers and men were, however, veterans who had served for a long time in Afghanistan, and all weaklings had been eliminated by medical examination before we left Kabul.

The strain, too, on our followers was even greater. Of poorer physique than the soldiers, they also marched on resolutely with the force, and it was not until the greater portion of our journey had been covered that they commenced to drop out on the line of march. Our rear-guards were often hard put to it to retrieve and bring safely to camp many followers whose strength had failed them. Several of them strayed off the road to lie down and rest, and if they had not been discovered they would inevitably have been murdered after our troops had continued on their journey.

On 23rd August the force reached Khelat-i-Ghilzai,[1] where we got into communication by heliograph with Kandahar, and were assured of the safety of the garrison. The small force at Khelat-i-Ghilzai, under Colonel Oriel Tanner,[2] which had shown a bold front since its communications with Kandahar had been cut off, was withdrawn, and it accompanied our troops when we moved on two days later. On the morning of 31st August we marched into Kandahar, having covered a distance of just over 313 miles since the force left Kabul on 9th August, and 403 miles from Jellalabad.

That afternoon a reconnaissance was made of the right of the position held by the Afghans, and when our troops retired to camp swarms of the enemy's skirmishers followed them up in a determined manner, only withdrawing when they found a considerable force of infantry under arms in front of them. On the morning of 1st September the enemy's position was attacked.

The troops advanced about 9 A.M., and in a short

---

[1] Khelat-i-Ghilzai is memorable for the gallant defence made there, in the spring of 1842, by the garrison under Captain Craigie, numbering about 900 men. On 21st May a determined assault was made at night on the fort by about 6000 Ghilzai tribesmen. They were repulsed with heavy loss, and a fortnight later the garrison was safely withdrawn to Kandahar.

[2] The garrison consisted of 2 guns of C/2 Royal Artillery, 145 rifles of the 66th Foot, 100 of the 3rd Sind Horse, and the 2nd Baluch Regiment, 639 strong.

time the First and Second Brigades of our infantry, which had been detailed to turn Ayub Khan's right flank, were heavily engaged with the enemy, who held a strong defensive position in the villages of Gundigan and Gundi Mulla Sahibdad, which were connected by a network of orchards and gardens. Away to our right large numbers of the enemy moved down to our line, while, farther on, the Baba Wali Pass was crowded with Ghazis.

Our infantry were irresistible. Highlanders and Goorkhas, Sikhs and Punjabis, carried one position after another at the point of the bayonet, and within four hours the rout of Ayub Khan's Army was complete. His camp was captured, as it stood, as well as thirty-one guns and two of our Horse Artillery guns which had been lost at Maiwand, and he himself fled early in the day towards Herat, with an escort of a few horsemen and a small party of infantry.

The Cavalry Brigade left camp at 8 A.M. and followed the infantry closely, but until the latter had cleared the way through the orchards by the capture of Gundigan it could not advance. Indeed it was not until about 11 A.M. that we were able to move off along narrow lanes and over many deep and unbridged water-courses to Kokeran, seven miles distant, where we forded the Arghandab river and emerged on a broad stony plain several miles in length.

The long delay at Gundigan and our slow progress to Kokeran had given ample time for the main body of the enemy to retreat—some followed the line of the hills, while others disappeared into the villages, where, as Lord Roberts states,[1] " . . . They quickly divested themselves of their uniform and assumed the garb of harmless agriculturists "—the invariable custom when an Afghan army and its attendant masses of tribal levies have to disperse. Away to the north-west some miles ahead of us we saw clouds of dust, which may have been Ayub Khan and his attendants; but whoever it was they had got too great a start for us to attempt to overtake them.

The Brigade moved rapidly along a line parallel to the Arghandab river, and as regards its share in the day's work Lieutenant-General Sir F. Roberts stated in his despatch describing the action of the cavalry: "During this movement none of the regular troops were encountered, but some 350 of the fugitive Ghazis and irregulars were killed."

The day was very hot and no water was procurable away from the river. This told severely on the horses after the long march from Kabul and the strain on them as we had pressed on over the watercourses to the ford at Kokeran. The plain over which the Brigade moved was about four miles broad, so when it became apparent that we could not hope to meet large bodies of the enemy, each regiment extended till it covered a wide front. From time to time we came across bands of armed fugitives moving across the plain in the hope of gaining the hills in the direction of Khakrez, who fought bravely when we came up with them.

Late in the afternoon one squadron of the Central India Horse, under Major Gerard, reached the foot

[1] 'Forty-one Years in India.'

of the hills on our left, and after charging home with effect into a number of the enemy who had almost reached safety, it was recalled by the Brigadier, as the Brigade had been ordered to return to Kandahar. By sunset the leading troops of the cavalry had recrossed the Arghandab river, but it was dark by the time the Central India Horse reached Ayub's camp, and we slowly picked our way up over the rough stones of the Babawali Kotal, the scene of many a stern hand-to-hand combat when General Nott was at Kandahar in 1841-42, till we came in sight of the lights of Kandahar below us.

The casualties in the regiment were as follows: Lieutenant Neville Chamberlain and five men wounded. Two horses were killed.

On 3rd September the Cavalry Brigade moved to Kokeran. There we got good water, which we had not enjoyed for many days, plenty of forage for our horses, and an abundance of delicious grapes. Three days later a small force of cavalry, under Major H. Buller, Central India Horse, searched the villages along the road to Maiwand for any of our men who had been taken prisoners, and the four remaining guns of 'E' Battery R.H.A., which had been lost at Maiwand and in the retreat. The limbers were found, and a few days later the guns were recovered—buried in one of the villages.

On the 8th September the regiment left Kokeran and accompanied the Second Infantry Brigade, under Brigadier-General C. Macgregor, on the return journey to India. During the first day's march we met the advance troops of General Phayre's force, which had advanced through Sind and the Bolan Pass at the hottest time of the year—a very trying experience,—and had pressed on to the relief of Kandahar despite many grave difficulties as regards supplies and transport. As we moved on towards Quetta the horses suffered from a scarcity of food and water.

"Camp Dubrai. No water nearer than 3 miles, after a 12-mile march."

"17th September ... a march of 20 miles, passing Dina Karez, where the water was undrinkable. This was a very trying march for our horses, and we lost six in one day from debility caused by want of food."[1]

At Kila Abdulla a small column, under Colonel Rowcroft, was detached to march *via* Kach and Kawass, to punish some of the Murree tribe who, since our reverse at Kandahar, had raided a number of our small posts and had even attacked a larger one, Dargai. One squadron of the Central India Horse, under Major Gerard and Lieutenant Chamberlain, accompanied this column, strength 100 sabres. The main body of the regiment moved on, and passing through Quetta reached the railhead at Sibi, 243 miles from Kokeran, on 30th September. Three days later the regiment arrived by rail at Mian Mir, where Lieutenant H. Ravenshaw died of typhoid fever. He had been for two years on active service in Afghanistan, and in a Regimental Order announcing his death our Commandant struck a true note when he referred to him as "a good soldier and a cheery and amiable comrade."

[1] Extract from Regimental Record.

Colonel Rowcroft's column moved off into the high mountain valleys in the districts of Kach and Kawass, a picturesque country through which merely rough tracks existed. Food and forage were easily procurable, but the bitter cold at night after hot days, at an elevation of about 7000 feet, was trying to both men and horses. Equipment had been cut down to its lowest limit in the march to Kandahar, and with only one blanket at night sleep was often impossible. No resistance was met with, and after some hostages had been taken to ensure good behaviour in future the force moved on towards Sibi. The squadron of the Central India Horse was then ordered to push on rapidly to Harnai, forty miles distant, in the hope that it might be in time to save the valuable stores in the large advanced railway depot there. Leaving tents and kit to follow we started at 6 A.M. and reached Harnai late in the afternoon to find that everything had been pillaged and destroyed some time previously. Until the main body rejoined us we were kept on the alert, but beyond an occasional exchange of shots with the local tribesmen nothing of importance occurred.

The column moved on to Kach, where a number of the enemy had occupied a steep hill under which our road wound its way along a narrow rocky path with the deep water of the river below. Some baggage animals were killed and wounded, and there were some casualties, including two men of the Central India Horse wounded, before our infantry cleared the heights and enabled us to continue our march. Two days later, after having been fired on as we left each camping-ground, we emerged from the hills and came in sight of the railway line a short distance from Sibi. Our men cheered lustily when an engine passed us, for we realised that we had seen the last of Afghanistan. We railed to Mian Mir, and rejoined Headquarters after a month's absence from the regiment.

Shortly afterwards a very interesting event took place—a review by His Excellency the Viceroy, Lord Ripon, of the troops which had returned from Afghanistan. At the conclusion of the parade His Excellency made an announcement which gave great satisfaction to the army, that a medal with five clasps would be given for 'Afghanistan,' and also a bronze star to those who had marched from Kabul to Kandahar. The troops which had been concentrated at Mian Mir then moved off to their respective stations, and we railed to Agra, and from there marched down the well-known road through Gwalior to Goona.

The Regimental Record states: "24th December 1880. The 1st Regiment marched in to Goona exactly a year after the date of quitting it to proceed on active service."

The wing of the 2nd Central Horse moved on to Augur when it had recovered from the Christmas festivities which followed.

It may be of interest to those who served in the regiment in later years, and to those still serving in it, if a brief reference is made to the equipment of the Central India Horse during the Afghan Campaign.

In 1878 we had muzzle-loading carbines of an

antiquated pattern. Our course of musketry used to consist in each man firing seven rounds at seventy-five yards once a year. On such occasions a bottle was hung over the bull's-eye, and any man who succeeded in breaking it was rewarded by the trumpeter blowing the 'salami' (salute), and the British officer in charge of the practice presented the successful marksman with a rupee. Very few bottles were broken! To our great relief Snider carbines were issued to the regiment when it proceeded on service to Afghanistan.

Men in the front rank were armed with lances and swords—those in the rear rank with swords only,—all carried carbines. During the campaign the lances were found to be too unwieldy, so when we returned to cantonments they were reduced to a length of nine feet. Every day on active service, after stables, each man paraded in front of his horse with his sword and lance. These were critically examined, and woe betide the unhappy sowar the point of whose lance was not sharp, or whose sword could not shave some hair off his arm if required to do so.

The regiment was armed with the 'Paget blade' sword, a weapon invented by the late Major-General W. H. Paget, 5th Panjab Cavalry, which had been proved by the Indian cavalry to be a most efficient weapon. Certainly our men used them with effect in the Afghan Campaign, for they had had plenty of practice in 'sheep-cutting' at Augur and Goona. Among several instances in Afghanistan one comes vividly to mind in the case of a fugitive Afghan, wearing a skull-cap. As one of our sowars galloped past him he sliced the top off the man's head, just above the ears, as cleanly as it is possible to imagine, and with apparently no effort. Nowadays the 'Paget' blades have been replaced by a long, straight, thrusting sword, and those who served in the Great War can decide whether it is a more effective weapon than the old one.

In the heat of a combat hereditary instincts are sometimes stronger than the careful training instilled on the parade ground. An interesting example of this occurred at Kandahar. A fine young sowar, one of the few 'Jats' in the regiment, armed with a lance, was pursuing a fugitive. Just before he overtook him the spirits of his forefathers must have whispered to remind him that they, for generations past, had belaboured the skulls of their adversaries in village fights with 'lathies,' or long wooden staves. He forgot all he had been taught since he joined the service—he stood up in his stirrups, and seizing his lance at one end with both hands he brought the long bamboo shaft down with a crash on the Afghan's head, felling him to the ground. Yet that sowar was a good tent-pegger and 'man-at-arms' in cantonments.

As regards the transport of the regiment, Sir Montagu Gerard, in his book to which allusion has already been made, sums it up admirably by stating: "The sowars, of course, having their own baggage 'tattoos' (baggage ponies) were on their normal footing, which is far and away the most practical mode of equipment yet discovered."

A most important factor in our equipment has been left to the last—our horses.

From statistics given in the Regimental Records of both the 1st and 2nd Central India Horse about that period, regarding the number and class of remounts purchased annually, it appears that there were about three Arabs to every two countrybreds, and that the average cost of a remount in those days was about 276 rupees. So we set out on the campaign with about 300 Arabs and 200 countrybreds, and they never failed us despite unceasing difficulties as regards food and water. We started from Jellalabad for Kandahar after six months' harassing patrol and escort duty on the Khyber line, a prolonged strain on horseflesh which it is difficult to estimate. The day after we rode into Kandahar we had a long hot day's ride, which severely taxed the courage and endurance of the horses.

WAR SERVICES OF OFFICERS OF THE CENTRAL INDIA HORSE DURING THE SECOND AFGHAN WAR, 1878-1880.

The following officers served throughout the period the regiment was employed in the campaign, taking part in the expeditions to Besud and Kama, the march from Kabul to Kandahar, and the battle of Kandahar :—

Lieutenant-Colonel C. Martin, C.B.—Commanded the regiment. Twice mentioned in despatches. C.B.

Brevet Lieutenant-Colonel H. M. Buller.—Mentioned in despatches. Brevet Lieutenant-Colonel.
Major J. Colledge.
Lieutenant A. Masters.—(Adjutant.)

Major A. J. Bannerman.—Served in the Khyber Field Force with the regiment from 10th February to 13th August 1880.

Major A. H. S. Neill.—Served in the Kuram Valley, Zaimukht Expedition, capture of Zawa.

Brevet Lieutenant-Colonel Montagu G. Gerard.—Served throughout the war. Was present with the second expedition in the Bazar Valley (mentioned in despatches). Advance to Kabul under Brigadier-General C. Gough (mentioned in despatches). Rejoined the regiment at Kabul—marched to Kandahar—battle of Kandahar (mentioned in despatches). Brevet of Lieutenant-Colonel. Brigadier-General J. Tytler's despatch, 30th March 1879, which referred to the punishment of the villages of Deh Sarak, beyond Pesh Bolak, on 24th March, contained a report by Captain Thomson, who commanded the cavalry (90 lances, 11th Bengal Lancers; 60 lances, 13th Bengal Lancers), who, when describing how the cavalry charged some 300 of the enemy, added: "At this moment I saw Captain Gerard, Central India Horse (who accompanied the column as a spectator, but who afterwards rendered me the utmost assistance), cutting down a man on my right. . . . We had by this time continued the pursuit to the foot of a small range of hills, where Captain Gerard did good work, he and Lieutenant

OFFICERS' WAR SERVICES

Gwatkin cutting down several men, the former accounting for five or six himself."

Captain G. E. Money.—Served with the Kuram Field Force. Khost Expedition.

Lieutenant A. G. A. Durand.—Served with the Mhairwarra Battalion throughout the first part of the campaign, taking part in both Bazar Expeditions. He rejoined the regiment and served with it for the remainder of the war, taking part in the expeditions to Besud and Kama, the march from Kabul to Kandahar, and the battle of Kandahar.

Lieutenant N. F. F. Chamberlain.—Served on the personal staff of Lieutenant-General Sir F. Roberts during most of the war, and was present at the capture of the Peiwar Kotal, the actions in the Sapari Pass and Khost Valley, the battle of Charasiab, and the operations in and around Sherpur, Kabul. He rejoined the regiment when it reached Kabul in September 1880, and marched with it from Kabul to Kandahar. Battle of Kandahar (wounded). Three times mentioned in Lieutenant-General Sir F. Roberts' despatches.

Extract from despatch from Brigadier-General H. T. Macpherson, V.C., C.B., dated Kabul, 4th January 1880: "When the head of our column rounded the south end of the Khoosh Kak mountain, our approach was so utterly unknown to the enemy passing down from Arghandeh, that some of their leading horsemen galloped in our direction to hail us as allies. One of them approached incautiously near, and was cut down by Lieutenant Chamberlain."

Lieutenant H. E. Ravenshaw.—Served in the first part of the campaign as a transport officer. Marched from Kabul to Kandahar. Battle of Kandahar. Died at Lahore 13th October 1880.

Lieutenant G. K. Daly.—Joined the Central India Horse from The Guides Cavalry. Served in the operations in the Koh-i-Daman, the second action of Charasiab. Marched from Kabul to Kandahar. Battle of Kandahar (mentioned in despatches).

Lieutenant E. E. Robertson.—Served with the 72nd Highlanders in the earlier part of the war. Night attack on rear-guard at Zahidabad, action of Charasiab; operations in and around Kabul. March from Kabul to Kandahar. Battle of Kandahar.

Lieutenant J. Edwards.—Served in the 8th The King's Regiment during the war, and was present at the capture of the Peiwar Kotal.

Surgeon Major D. F. Keegan.—Served with the regiment throughout the second part of the campaign. Marched from Kabul to Kandahar. Battle of Kandahar.

CHAPTER X.

MARTIN.

AFTER the Afghan War the two regiments settled down at Agar and Goonah for a long period of peaceful training. It was not, in fact, until sixteen years had passed that they were again called upon to leave Central India on active service; and during this time the effect of Probyn's teaching, which had shown itself in the fighting efficiency of the composite regiment in Afghanistan, was gradually paving the way to the absorption of both regiments in the regular Army under the Commander-in-Chief. We became less and less political and more and more military. Officers began to regard an appointment to the Central India Horse less as a stepping-stone to the Political Department than as a promising and agreeable opening to a military career. Army Headquarters viewed more and more jealously the existence of a corps, obviously of some merit, over which they had no control. Commanders-in-Chief took a lively interest in its condition, and one after another, with the concurrence of the civil authorities who ruled over us, found it convenient to pay us a visit of inspection; and when next the Central India Horse went into action, it did so as one of the Commander-in-Chief's own regiments and not as a loan from the Government of India.

Field-Marshal Sir Donald Stewart, who had known something of the behaviour of the regiment in the war, made it one of his early duties, after assuming the command of the Army, to come down to Goonah and Agar. This was in the cold weather of 1882-83. It was a great occasion. Never had the regiments been inspected by a Commander-in-Chief. Preparations were set on foot long beforehand, not as a symptom of that 'inspection fever' which is supposed to, and often does, affect a regiment before the arrival of the great man—we never suffered from that,—but simply because we desired to give His Excellency a warm welcome to Central India. Moreover, he and his Staff had to be conveyed. We could not ask them to travel by camel cart. We therefore borrowed carriages from the chiefs; we trained twenty teams of horses; we practised the roughriders in the art of postilion driving, and we galloped the party down the road from Sipri to Goonah, from Goonah to Agar, and finally from Agar to the railway station at Ujjain. His Excellency spent three days at Goonah, where he made a very careful inspection and distributed the medals for the Afghan War. One day was, of course, devoted to a tiger hunt. His Excellency killed a tiger in the Takhtaya beat, and a member of his Staff killed another, which was very satisfactory. Then he went on to Agar, where he carried out the same programme, minus the tiger; and shortly after his return to Headquarters he supplemented his pleasant speeches to the regiment by the gift, as a memento of his visit, of a silver claret jug, which still adorns our mess table.

At this time the 1st Regiment was commanded by Henry Buller, who had been made a Brevet-Lieutenant-Colonel for his services in the war; the 2nd by Andrew Neill, acting for Arthur Bannerman, who was at home on sick leave and, indeed, never returned to India. Hall had left, at the end of 1880, to command the Bhopal Battalion. Martin was still Commandant. He had been made a Companion of the Bath, and now, after so many years of regimental duty, he seemed glad to throw aside his uniform and to devote himself whole-heartedly to his political labours. He already knew the work very well, and was on good terms with all the chiefs. Tall and lean, suave in manner, with a pink complexion and very white hair, he looked the part to perfection. Moreover, he had a temperament so calm and patience so inexhaustible that nothing ever seemed to irritate or disturb him. He could sign his name to a docket, marked in red ink " 54th Reminder," without more than a quiet expression of regret. He was a cool undaunted soldier, and as a sportsman he had killed more tigers than he had taken the trouble to count. He once told the author that he must have killed " about 300," and nearly every one of these with a muzzle-loading rifle.

The Adjutants were George Daly and Harry Hughes, who, as staunch comrades, had served in The Guides at Kabul during the Afghan War, and in April 1880 had charged the enemy with their troopers during a sharp fight at Charasiab. Daly was the third son of Sir Henry Daly; he joined the

Central India Horse at Kabul, and marched with it to Kandahar. Hughes joined the regiment after its return to India. Both were men of outstanding character, and both were short-lived. Daly was killed at polo in the Bombay tournament in the autumn of 1886. He was riding a little roan country-bred pony called 'Sipidar'—those were the days of the '13.2 and under'—that was not up to his weight, for he was a heavily built man, and he wore no protective head-dress. The risks of the game had not yet impressed themselves on superior authority, and one could wear anything or nothing as one pleased. It was the custom, in fact, until Lord Roberts forbade it, to play bareheaded, or with only a cap, and the consequence was that a fall on the hard grounds of India was often serious. George Daly's was only one of the many fatal accidents which prompted the Commander-in-Chief's order that the head should be protected either by a puggree or a sola topi. His death was deplored throughout both regiments, for he was very popular amongst all ranks.

Harry Hughes was the eldest son of Sir William Templer Hughes, Harry Daly's successor. Soon after he joined the regiment he inherited a small property in Devonshire and took the name of Hughes-Buller. A fine specimen of humanity, a brilliant polo player, a good shot with gun and rifle, and an eager thoughtful soldier, he would have risen very high indeed had death not called him away. Fate, however, was against him. After three short years of service in Central India, the admiration of his seniors and his juniors alike, he was killed in a steeplechase at Mhow on the 4th of December 1884.

Two other young officers were appointed in 1881, Lieutenant E. E. Robertson of the 72nd Highlanders, and Lieutenant J. B. Edwards of the 8th or King's Regiment. Robertson was a celebrated character. He had a fiery red head and a temperament corresponding to it, and he was known all over India as ' The Pink 'Un.' He had served with his Highland regiment throughout the Afghan War, including Lord Roberts' march from Kabul to Kandahar. He was always good company, for he was a brilliant raconteur, and he was never known to tell the same story twice. He died at Agar in December 1897. Edwards had served with the 8th in the Afghan War, and in 1895 he went with the Chitral Relief Force as a Transport officer, for which service he was rewarded with a Brevet majority and the Distinguished Service Order. He was unfortunate enough to be promoted Lieutenant-Colonel before he could succeed to the command of either regiment of Central India Horse, and so was obliged to take the command of the 27th Light Cavalry, to which he was appointed on the 22nd of February 1904.[1]

In 1882 Majors John Colledge and Arthur Bannerman retired from the Service, and Lieutenants Bedford Allen of the 2nd Panjab Infantry, W. A. Watson of the Worcestershire Regiment, F. C. Grant of the South Wales Borderers, and Lionel Herbert of the Suffolk Regiment were appointed as ' Attached ' officers. Allen was a mere visitor. He served for

---

[1] He served also on the staff of The Czarewich of Russia during His Imperial Highness' visit to India in 1890-91.

M

barely twelve months. Watson, John Watson's eldest son, became Adjutant of the 2nd on the death of Harry Hughes-Buller. He held several Staff and other extra regimental appointments during his career, including that of Commandant of the Imperial Cadet Corps, Lord Curzon's attempt to satisfy the military aspiration of the Indian aristocracy, and was, indeed, absent from Central India from the end of 1894 until he took over the command of the 2nd in April 1906. He fought in the Soudan campaign of 1885 as Adjutant of the Suakin Camel Corps, and was with the China Expeditionary Force in 1900-01. In the Great War he commanded a Brigade of Imperial Service Cavalry during the operations on the Suez Canal, and on his promotion to Major-General went to Cairo for six months in command of the Delta District, after which he commanded the troops on the western frontier of Egypt during the final operations against the Senussi. In 1918 he was made Honorary Colonel of the Central India Horse. Grant served with the regiment during the Tirah Campaign of 1897-98. He succeeded to the command of the 1st Regiment on the 24th February 1907. Herbert spent nearly all his service as a Staff Officer, and held appointments on the personal Staff of several distinguished men, including H.R.H. the Duke of Connaught. He was D.A.A.G. of General Gatacre's Division of the Chitral Relief Force in 1895.[1]

Neill, who on Bannerman's retirement had been appointed to the substantive command of the 2nd

---

[1] He was severely wounded whilst with the Buner Field Force in 1897. He rose to the rank of Major-General, and died in October 1929.

Regiment, began about this time to organise his regimental workshops. He was paying, and consequently charging the men, high prices for saddlery and accoutrements; and it was obvious to him not only that it would be cheaper to produce these things at home, but that, if he had soldiers at hand, in the field as well as in quarters, able to execute repairs, he could increase the marching efficiency of his regiment without reducing its fighting strength to any appreciable degree. Accordingly he had metal workers and leather workers trained at Cawnpore, and enlisted one of each in each squadron. These fellows, of course, were obliged to undergo their squadron training, including their musketry, which, in the days of the Snider carbine, was indeed an ordeal; but they were let down as easily as possible, for their presence was required in the shops, not only to pursue their proper calling, but to supervise the civilian labour which it was often necessary to entertain; and from the time that these shops were established no article of saddlery, not an arch nor a stirrup-iron, not a buckle nor a strap, was obtained by purchase. The advantage to the men was great. A few years later Neill extended his operations, and made a number of transport carts for pony draught. These, however, were not a success. They added little to economy and nothing to mobility, except along the Grand Trunk Road.

Meanwhile the peace-time occupations of the Central India Horse, outside the limits of the parade ground—dacoit and tiger hunting,—still continued, though the quarry in each case was becoming rarer.

Polo was played; but the game was really only in its infancy, and not half the time or care was devoted to it as was the case in later years. In 1881, Isri Parsad, who did not go to the Afghan War, was again commended for a successful capture in the Malwa Hills. He was by this time a little too old to endure the hardships of active service in a country like Afghanistan, and there is little doubt that the Agent to the Governor-General was glad to be able to make this excuse for retaining him in Central India. His very presence did something to discount the absence of 500 sabres. On the occasion just referred to some of his subordinates, Jemadar Saheb Dad Khan, Dafadars Mahoiuddin Khan and Ghulam Nur Khan, and Sowar Khairulla Khan were associated also with him in the letter of thanks from the Government of India. Early in 1883 he was called upon again. The Bhils and Mekranis in the little State of Ali Rajpur were becoming too much for the Rajah. The Agent to the Governor-General found it necessary to proceed thither himself to inquire into the cause of the rising. As his personal escort he took with him a troop of fifty sabres under Captain Money; and Isri Parsad went down with another troop of sixty-five sabres to deal with the rebels in case they declined to listen to reason. On the 3rd of February they showed fight. A short action took place, during which one man of Isri Parsad's troop, Sowar Natha Singh, was killed; and this was followed by the immediate submission of the Bhils and the return of the two troops to Agar. In the following year, with a detachment of the Malwa Bhil Corps and a few men of the Central India Horse, he caught a well-known freebooter of the name of Nana Rawat. This was his last exploit as a serving soldier. In September he was transferred to the Pension Establishment, and was succeeded, as Risaldar Major of the 1st Regiment, by a man equally remarkable but of very different type, a big, burly, jovial Afghan of the name of Bahauddin Khan, of the 11th Bengal Lancers. Bahauddin Khan, familiarly known as 'Boggledike,' was a man of thirty-three years' service and of great renown. He had fought in the Mutiny and in China, where he received a severe wound in the stomach. He had been present with his regiment throughout the Ambela campaign and in the Afghan War. He was at Kabul with Cavagnari's escort when the massacre took place, and, escaping from that atrocity, had been instrumental in the discovery of the murderers. He served on the Afghan Boundary Commission in 1884-85. A great-hearted optimist, he knew neither fear nor dejection, and in the most critical situation he saw nothing ahead but success.[1]

During the year 1884 travellers on the Grand Trunk Road between Biaora and Goonah were harassed by an audacious dacoit of the name of Bankaji, whose lair was in the jungles about Maksudangarh. This fellow had the effrontery to place letters in the petition box outside the Kothi at Goonah warning the authorities that he proposed to hold up the mail on such and such a night. On one such occasion he actually carried out his threat, in spite of the reinforcement of the mail escort;

[1] He fought in sixty-six engagements.

but this escapade sealed his doom. His band was located in the old ruined fort of Isawas, and Gerard, who was acting in command of the 2nd Regiment for Neill, at home on furlough, took out a troop under Saheb Dad Khan, rounded them up, and brought them all in to Goonah. He started from Awan at midnight, and returned thither twenty-three and a half hours later, having covered a distance of over a hundred miles.

The hot weather shoot of this year was marred by the death of the old shikari, Harsa Singh, the bearer of the note from Travers to Hungerford at the time of the attack upon the Residency at Indore. The bag was a large one—twenty-two tigers; but there could be no recompense for such an accident. It happened at Gorasdeh, on the hills above the Kunu. Four guns were out. Gerard was in No. 1 'mool,'[1] a little in advance of the others, and on higher ground. A big tiger came up to him. He hit him hard, but did not stop him. The beast turned sharp right-handed, and galloped down the line of 'mools' a little too far in front of them to be seen. The beat was continued, and shortly afterwards a bear came up to No. 4, a guest, who fired and killed him. The beaters then stopped, and Harsa Singh came forward on the elephant. Unluckily he came to No. 4, whose orderly told him that the Sahib had shot a bear. He then returned to bring on the beat again, but after going a hundred yards or so, unaware that there was a wounded tiger in the jungle, he dismounted from the elephant.

---

[1] The position occupied by the 'gun,' generally, but not always, in a tree.

Dafadar HARSA SINGH.

In a moment the tiger was on him, shook him like a rat, and walked away. Gerard alone of the guns could see what happened. With a very long shot he killed the tiger; but he could not save the unfortunate victim, who was so badly mauled that he died that night. Harsa Singh was a great hunter. It was computed that he must have been in at the death of 800 tigers. In appearance he was a little, hard-bitten, wiry old man, with a short, shaggy, white beard and a very keen eye. He delighted in teaching young British officers how to shoot, his method consisting mainly of fining them a certain number of goats for every miss, five in the case of a tiger, three for a panther, and two for anything else. He made this the custom of the jungle, and was indignant if anyone suggested that the shot was difficult and the fine too severe. With many an aphorism used he to remind his pupils of the essence of sport. One in particular, " Dushman ko marna, apne jan ko bachana,"[1] he obviously intended them to apply to a higher game even than tiger shooting; and he would say it with an earnest look in his eye as if to emphasise, for their special attention, that " dushman ko marna " always came first. Gerard was greatly distressed by his death. He had killed many tigers himself, and this was his first fatal accident, and he never quite forgave No. 4 for firing at a bear in a tiger beat. Being a man of some wealth, he erected a fine monument to the old fellow's memory in the shape of a bund across the valley on the north side of the lines at Goonah, with a cairn on the centre of it and an inscription

---

[1] " Kill the enemy. Make safe your own life."

describing his exploits. The water held up by this bund is known to this day, and no doubt will ever be known, as 'Harsa Singh's Tank.'

Of the officers who joined during the years 1883 and 1884, two—namely, Lieutenant W. E. Evans-Gordon of the Madras Staff Corps and Lieutenant H. L. Pennell of the King's Dragoon Guards—remained but a very few months. The former, a somewhat senior subaltern with longer service than several officers who had joined the regiment before him, after a short apprenticeship as a Political Assistant, became Political Agent in Jhalra Patan.[1] The latter, whose chance of promotion was undoubtedly not improved by his transfer to the Indian Army, went back to his English regiment before the expiration of his probationary period. Lieutenant Hugh Daly, Sir Henry's fourth son, came in from the Gloucestershire Regiment in 1883, left the regiment eighteen months later to become Third Assistant to the Agent to the Governor-General in Rajputana—Bradford,—and finally, after serving for some years as Agent to the Governor-General in Central India, became Resident in Mysore. Dr Sedgefield was gazetted in August 1883 to succeed Dr Grant, who died of cholera at Agar. He was four years with the 1st Regiment, and was then appointed to the medical charge of the Lawrence Schools at Kasauli, where, shortly afterwards, he died. Dr Lowdell took over medical charge of the 2nd Regiment in March 1884 from Dr Caldecott, and for the next five years was officiating either for him or for Dr Sedgefield, and then was posted to

[1] He wound up his career as Sir William Evans-Gordon, M.P.

the Malwa Bhil Corps. In May 1884, Lieutenant Colin Campbell, originally of the Staffordshire Regiment, came in from the Sindh Horse. He was appointed for one season Brigade-Major to the Inspector-General of Cavalry, a billet reserved for the smartest young cavalry officer of the year. In 1895 he was in command of the Chitral garrison, was severely wounded during the siege, and was thus obliged to hand over the conduct of the defence to Townshend, afterwards Townshend of Kut. He served with the regiment during the Tirah campaign of 1897. He finished his career as Military Secretary to Sir Bindon Blood, the commander of the Northern Army in 1904, when he married and left India, and he died in America in 1923. He was a beautiful horseman, an impetuous and very gallant soldier, and a most lovable man.

The year 1885 began with rumours of war. For many years Russia's gradual advance towards India had been a source of anxiety to the British Government. First Khiva, then Merv had fallen into her hands, and now a fresh move was apparent in the direction of Herat. A Boundary Commission, under the leadership of Sir Peter Lumsden, was at this time on the Russo-Afghan frontier. A settlement had actually been reached and ratified by both Governments, by which it was agreed that neither Russian nor Afghan troops should make any further forward movement. The word of the Russia of the Czars was not, however, more reliable than that of Soviet Russia of to-day. Within a fortnight of ratification, General Alikhanoff, the Turcoman leader with the Russianised name, who for weeks past had been endeavouring to irritate the Afghan soldiers into commencing hostilities, attacked their entrenchments at Panjdeh and drove them back, with a loss of some 900 killed and wounded, towards Herat. The torch of war burst into flame. There was intense excitement in England as well as in India. Mr Gladstone made a warlike speech in the House of Commons. A vote of credit of eleven millions was passed. Regiments were mobilised. Ships were chartered. The world prepared to watch the great struggle for mastery in Asia. And then it suddenly fizzled out. The contending Governments agreed to continue the negotiations, and the long-expected conflict did not take place. A wing of each regiment of the Central India Horse was amongst the troops held in readiness to take the field, and it seemed that Martin, who had ceased to contemplate any further use for his sword, might again be relieved of his civil duties to lead his regiment for a second time on active service. It was a transient prospect. The excitement was quickly over; and the two mobilised wings, instead of proceeding to Afghanistan, marched up later in the year, under Neill, to take part in Lord Roberts' first Camp of Exercise at Delhi.

Meanwhile the whole of the Indian cavalry, including both regiments of Central India Horse, had been augmented. The order of the Government of India, which was dated the 20th August, directed that a squadron, consisting of 1 squadron commander (British), 4 Indian officers, and 126 other ranks, was to be added to each regiment, which would thus in future consist of 8 British officers and 625 Indian officers, non-commissioned officers, and sowars. The composition of the two regiments of Central India Horse was to be much the same—namely, three troops of Sikhs, two of Rangars, one of Ghakkars and Pathans for the 1st Regiment or of Panjabi Mahomedans for the 2nd, one of Jats, and one of Rajputs. The administrative unit was still the 'troop.' Hitherto, beyond a few Pathans—some of them very remarkable men, too, in the 1st Troop of the 1st Regiment,—neither regiment had enlisted Mahomedans from districts further north than Delhi. The Ghakkar and the Tiwana from the Jhelum were novelties. The 1st Regiment secured the services of a leading tribesman of the name of Ali Haidar, a very charming personality, who afterwards became Risaldar Major; and the 2nd transferred Dafadar Ghulam Mahomed Khan, a prominent Tiwana Malik of the Shahpur District, from the 18th Bengal Lancers and made him a Jemadar. He, too, rose to the highest Indian rank. The process of augmentation did not take long. The commanding officers toured the Panjab in search of recruits. The above two Indian officers, as well as others already in the regiment—for half of each new squadron were Sikhs,—brought in their relations and friends; and within a very few months both regiments were up to the new strength.

The Camp of Exercise which was held at Delhi in the winter was the outcome of the mobilisation in the spring, which had brought to light certain weaknesses in the organisation of the Commissariat and Transport Departments. The arrangements for the camp were made under the direction of Sir Donald

Stewart; the conduct of the manœuvres fell to the hands of Sir Frederick Roberts—as he then was,—who succeeded to the command of the Army in India a few weeks before they commenced. The troops, 35,000 of all ranks, were in two Divisions, one at Umballa commanded by Sir George Greaves, and the other at Gurgaon under Sir Charles Gough. We formed part of the latter. After a fortnight's Brigade and Divisional training the opposing forces marched against one another and met on the historic field of Panipat, where we suffered defeat. The whole then marched back to Delhi, where, on the 18th of January 1886, they were reviewed by the Viceroy, Lord Dufferin. The occasion was made memorable by a great storm. The weather looked threatening as we took our places in the line, the infantry in front, the artillery and cavalry—in line of quarter columns—in rear. At 9 o'clock precisely the Viceroy, clad in frock-coat and black silk hat, rode on to the ground, followed by a large Staff, which included twelve military representatives of foreign Powers. At the same moment the salute opened, and before its last gun was fired the rain began to fall. For the next hour there was a deluge, severe even for the tropics, accompanied by thunder and lightning, which seemed continuous. Lord Dufferin, drenched to the skin but smiling, rode slowly down the lines, and then took up his position at the saluting point. Unfortunately the mounted troops marched past first, with the result that the ground in front of the saluting base was churned into a sea of mud. The infantry thus had a difficult task. It happened that one Indian battalion, now no more, was shod with Indian shoes instead of the usual ammunition boot—an excellent arrangement in fair weather, but when the rain fell there was no one with sufficient presence of mind to order the shoes to be taken off and carried in the hand,—so the mud pulled them off, and the men, to whom it was obviously more important to retain their shoes than their formation, were not, as they passed the Viceroy, in that correct alignment which the military eye delights to see. With the exception of this little contretemps the troops came through the ceremony with credit, and the foreign attachés expressed some surprise at the discipline and bearing of the Indian Army. We had with us on this occasion the young Maharaj Rana of Dholpur, who had been made an Honorary Major in the 2nd Regiment in August 1882. The Nawab of Jaora, the son of Ghaus Mahomed, to whom we were so much indebted in the Mutiny, had been appointed Honorary Major in the 1st Regiment a little earlier than this; but he never joined the regiment even for a ceremonial parade, though he built a house at Agar and sometimes wore our uniform. The march past at Delhi was the first occasion on which the Rana of Dholpur paraded with us—and it was the last. It was an unpleasant experience for him. He was mounted on a thoroughbred white Arab named 'Desert Born,' a superb creature. As we wheeled into line on the saluting base, 'Desert Born,' who had been showing signs of discomfort, elected to lie down and roll; and the Rana, covered with mud from head to foot, was obliged to fall out without having had the satisfaction of saluting the representative of Her Majesty. It was an expensive day for British officers. In fact, it cost us each the price of a new tunic, a considerable sum even without new gold lace, for what happened was that the maroon colour from our facings streamed down over the drab cloth. We were a sorry spectacle as we rode off parade.

Whilst the Camp of Exercise was in progress the squadrons left behind in Central India changed quarters, and the depot of the 2nd Regiment at Agar was called upon to send a detachment of thirty sabres to Manpur in pursuit of a gang of dacoits led by Tantia Bhil. Isri Parsad, now a pensioner and a servant of the Indore Durbar, conducted the operations against this clever freebooter; but three years elapsed before, with the aid of one detachment after another of the Central India Horse, one in particular under Risaldar Barmadin, who behaved with his usual gallantry, he captured him in the hills of Khandeish and brought him in to Indore. Tantia Bhil was the last of the great dacoits with whom we were concerned. He was hanged at Jubbulpore towards the end of 1889; and for the part which he played in the capture Risaldar Barmadin was admitted to the Order of British India.

In the spring of 1885 Lieutenants E. C. B. Cotgrave of the Devonshire Regiment and A. B. Mayne of the Leicester Regiment were appointed squadron officers on probation. Cotgrave became a few years later Inspecting Officer of Imperial Service troops at Gwalior, and for two seasons was, like Campbell, Brigade-Major to the Inspector-General of Cavalry.

He eventually succeeded to the command of the
1st Regiment. Mayne was a nephew of Henry
Otway Mayne, and was said to have been somewhat
like him in appearance. He was an able and extraordinarily kind-hearted fellow, but the routine
of ordinary regimental life was uncongenial to him,
so he became tutor and guardian to the young
Maharajah of Jodhpore, and, indeed, spent some
years in the States of Rajputana, where he had
considerable popularity and some influence. In the
Great War he served in the Remount Department,
but broke down in health, was invalided to England,
and died in London before the war was over.

Soon after the return of the composite regiment
from Delhi, Risaldar Major Gopal Sing was appointed
A.D.C. to the Viceroy. His successor as Risaldar
Major of the 2nd Regiment was Murad Ali Khan,
a Rangar of Kalanaur, a typical Mahomedan gentleman, quiet, dignified, and very sensible. He was
Risaldar Major for the next nine years.

Buller and Neill still commanded the two regiments. In the following year, 1887, Martin went
home on a year's furlough previous to retirement,
and Buller became Commandant; but before this
happened Neill fell a victim to one of those strange
aberrations of the mind to which the Indian soldier
seems peculiarly liable. During the cold weather of
1886-87 the 2nd Regiment had attended some
cavalry manœuvres at Mhow. These were followed
by an 'extended reconnaissance,' during which
Captain Masters, commanding one of the advanced
squadrons, one day sent a man of the name of Mazar
Ali back to the reserve squadron to be seen by the

doctor. The man appeared to be suffering no pain, but he was mute; by no inducement could he be persuaded to utter a word. The doctor, Lowdell, was puzzled, could not clearly diagnose the case, thought it might be hypochondria. Neill, with some experience of human as well as equine sickness—he was a really good veterinary surgeon,—asserted, quite confidently, that it was a case of sunstroke. The patient was brought in to Agar and admitted to hospital; and after a fortnight or so was discharged, to all appearances completely recovered. On the 14th March the regiment paraded for 'field firing.' At 1000 yards from the targets the men were dismounted and advanced to the attack. At 300 yards the squadrons were in line lying down and pouring in a heavy fire. Neill, Cotgrave, and Watson, the only British officers on parade, were mounted, the former behind the 3rd Squadron, Cotgrave behind the 2nd, and Watson behind the 1st on the right. Suddenly Cotgrave cried out, "My God! Neill's killed." He and Watson jumped off their horses and ran towards Neill, and as they ran a bullet hit the ground between them. It was at once obvious that a soldier was shooting to the rear. It was indeed Mazar Ali. He was seized and disarmed by Sowar Jhanda Singh of the 3rd Troop and several others; but the first bullet, which nobody saw fired, had done its fatal work, and when Neill's two subalterns reached him they found him unconscious and dying, with a wound in his right side. In a few minutes he was dead.

Mazar Ali was tried on the capital charge by the First Assistant to the Agent to the Governor-

General. There was no doubt that he had actually killed Neill. The question whether or no he was guilty of murder turned upon the state of his mind. At the trial he was not represented by counsel. He was reticent and sullen. It was with the greatest difficulty that any kind of answer was extracted from him. He said that he had shot at a green pigeon; that a 'Wali'[1] had ordered him to kill the Adjutant. The medical officer could not, however, swear to insanity. The prisoner was sentenced to be hanged; and hanged he was, in front of the regiment on parade; but reading over the evidence again, after an interval of forty years, and especially that part of it referring to the prisoner's actions on the early morning of the crime, it is impossible to resist the conclusion that his act was the result of a momentary impulse upon a diseased mind brought on by the excitement of the firing, and that a British jury would have found him "guilty but insane." A few years after the event an author of the name of Forbes Mitchell added to his history of the Indian Mutiny an appendix in which he affirmed that Neill had been murdered in revenge for the acts of his father, General Neill of Cawnpore fame. It will be remembered that General Neill had forced the perpetrators of the massacre to sweep up the blood of their victims with a 'sweeper's' broom before they were executed—not a wise action perhaps, but with evidence of atrocity before one it is not easy to be wise. Forbes Mitchell's story was that one of these men, as he went to death, had adjured the onlookers to carry to his little son in

[1] A spirit.

Rohtak his father's dying command to him to avenge his death on Neill or any of his descendants; that accordingly a fakir had visited Mazar Ali, the little son in question, in hospital at Agar and had conveyed to him his father's injunction; and that Mazar Ali had thereupon seized the God-sent opportunity of 'field firing' to play the part expected of him. The story has unfortunately been repeated by Sir Evelyn Wood in his 'Winnowed Memories.' There is no truth in it, though it is not without foundation. Neill was a dark Scotsman, lean and lithe, a beautiful horseman and horsemaster. In his dealings with his subordinates he had a quick hot temper, which subsided as quickly as it rose. His first thought was for the welfare of his men. The men knew this, and reciprocated his affection. That there were creatures outside the regiment who were prepared to murder him if a good opportunity presented itself there was always at least a suspicion, and Neill himself was aware of it; but that one of his own men, in the possession of his senses, should raise a hand against him, even at the bidding of a fakir, was very improbable. It was not, however, impossible, and the story could not be ruled completely out of court but for the fact that Mazar Ali was not born until four years after the events of Cawnpore, and therefore cannot come into it at all. His impulse obviously was not to kill Neill in particular but to shoot at any person who happened to be behind him, and it was the misfortune of the regiment that the nearest man to him was Neill.

CHAPTER XI.

BULLER.

NEILL's death and Buller's promotion to the office of Commandant, which occurred on the departure of Martin to England in the spring of 1887, left the command of both regiments vacant. The 1st then went to Vincent, and the 2nd to Gerard. The former, a man of wisdom and much humour, held his command for four years, and was then made President of the Council of Regency at Rampur. Here his firm handling of an outbreak in the jail secured for him a permanent place in the Political Department. He became Political Agent in Bikaner. Gerard, although he succeeded Buller as Commandant a few years later on, was, after the Afghan War, seldom on duty in Central India. As a subaltern he had applied for appointment to the regiment mainly for the sake of the big game shooting which it offered to him, and in later life his love of change and adventure led him to seek employment more varied and more exciting than regimental duty in cantonments could provide, even with the tiger hunting thrown in. He was indeed, as he described himself in his book, a soldier and a sportsman, in each capacity highly distinguished. The political duties were most distasteful to him. Sir

Richmond Shakespeare's recommendation to Mayne that in this respect "he should do very little and appear to do less," he followed to the letter. Like Beatson, he preferred to live uncomfortably. He rode blood Arabs, and his wallets always contained biscuits and raisins, which he would munch even on regimental parades. He had hardly held the command of the 2nd Regiment for a year when he was appointed Assistant Quartermaster-General of the Umballa Division. He returned to the regiment for a short time in the following year, but left again in the autumn of 1890 to become Chief of the Staff to the Czarewitch of Russia, afterwards the last of the Czars, during His Imperial Highness's tour in India; and in 1892 he went as Military Attaché to St Petersburg.

Towards the end of Buller's first year as Commandant, 1887, both regiments were ordered to take part in a Cavalry Camp of Exercise at Rupaheli in Rajputana, a score of miles or so to the south of Nasirabad. This was a new departure. Hitherto, as we have seen, not more than half of each regiment, or the whole of one, could enjoy an experience of this nature at the same time. The jungles, however, were now quieter. With the disappearance of Bankaji and Tantia Bhil, who, though still at large, was at this time on the left bank of the Nerbudda, the journey on the Grand Trunk Road could be undertaken without much risk, so both regiments could be spared for a few weeks. The 1st marched from Goonah, and the 2nd from Agar, to Neemuch. Here Buller had the satisfaction of exercising them in brigade. They then continued the march, still in brigade, to Rupaheli ; but here they were separated. Of the three brigades of the division to be exercised, the 1st Regiment went to the third and the 2nd to the second, whilst Buller himself commanded the first. The division was commanded by General Luck, the newly appointed, and the first, Inspector-General of Cavalry in India. This appointment had alarmed many of the older officers of Bengal cavalry. The cry went up that we should be 'dragooned,' that the traditional characteristics of Irregular Horse would be swept away, and that we should become a mere machine without individuality or intelligence. The alarm was short-lived. 'Die hards' themselves were soon obliged to confess that uniformity of training might possibly be an improvement upon the old individual system, and that there might even be some advantage in the practice of manœuvre in large bodies. Not that cavalry had not been assembled in large bodies before. John Watson at Delhi, twelve years ago, had manœuvred thirteen regiments with some success ; at Rupaheli there were only six ; but henceforward brigade and divisional manœuvres were to become more frequent, and regimental training was to be inspected periodically and regularly by an expert. In the light of recent events one may be permitted to wonder that doubt should have been so openly expressed ; but the fear of loss of prestige and consequently, perhaps, of moral was so real that the Commander-in-Chief, Lord Roberts, found it expedient to publish a reassuring Minute which allayed suspicions until time began to demonstrate the advantage of the new system.

General Luck had served in the 15th Hussars, of which regiment he was at this time Colonel. He was a marvellous 'drill.' He expected precision of movement, and was wont to criticise without sparing men's feelings. Irreverent subalterns might jest about 'The Camp of Roaring Luck,' but Regimental and Squadron Commanders, with less reason for being light-hearted, were apt to find the joke too grim. We came through the manœuvres creditably, though our small horses sometimes had to gallop very hard indeed, and suffered much from Rajputana camel thorn. Both regiments returned to quarters before the end of February 1888.

Several new officers had meanwhile been appointed. In May 1886 Lieutenant The Honourable H. D. Napier of the King's Own Scottish Borderers, a son of Lord Napier of Magdala, was posted on probation to the 1st Regiment. He became in after years Military Attaché, first at Teheran, then at St Petersburg, and finally at Sofia. In 1887 Lieutenants J. L. Kaye and F. de H. Smith were posted to the 1st Regiment, and Lieutenants C. V. C. Townshend and H. L. Goodenough to the 2nd. Kaye went to the Political Department. Smith, a very promising young officer and a particularly charming comrade, died in London in January 1891. Townshend, afterwards known to the world as Townshend of Kut, began life as a Royal Marine, and had seen service in Egypt before he joined the regiment. As a young man he was a very amusing character, his love of conviviality and singing, to the accompaniment of the banjo, bringing him into great request wherever soldiers were gathered together.

But there was another side to his character. He was an earnest student. He owed his success less to natural ability than to labour and determination. He worked very hard indeed. Certain hours of the day were always set aside for the study of military subjects. Even his jokes and his yarns were studied, and studied so well that they always appeared spontaneous. He was not long in the Central India Horse, for he never felt quite at home on horseback, and so sought service with the Imperial Service troops in Gilgit, where, in the defence of Chitral, referred to in the previous chapter, he found his first opportunity for distinction. Thereafter he obtained an exchange into the English Army. Goodenough remained for a couple of years, but did not take up a permanent appointment in either regiment.

In the hot weather of 1888 a party of five guns, of whom three were visitors, went out from Agar into the Rampura-Bhanpura jungles, in Jhalawar territory to the east of Neemuch. No tiger had been shot from Agar since the Afghan War, and few before it; and these great jungles, renowned for the grandeur of their scenery as well as for their capacity for holding game, were practically unknown to our shikaris. The expedition was thus an experiment. It was on the whole successful. During the first twelve days the bag was just one tiger; for the forests around Hinglazgarh, which were, however, worth beating for their magnificence alone, held nothing more; and it was not until we left them behind us for the more open country on the left bank of the Chambal, north of Rampura, that our fortune changed. From here Mahmud Khan and

Kadir Baksh had sent in word that the country was an open plain with the tigers walking about on it like black buck! In the next ten days we killed seven tigers and three bears. One of the former was a very old fellow who had been known for twenty years, and was said to have a price of Rs. 500 on his head, offered by Colonel Nuthall, a well-known sportsman of Neemuch. Colonel Nuthall had retired, and the reward had lapsed; but this did not damp the ardour of Mahtab Singh, then our head shikari, who was determined to find him and bring him to book. After much labour he harboured him in the gorge of the Chambal at Kilchipur and drove him up to Napier, who wounded him. We had with us an elephant belonging to the Maharajah of Jhalra Patan, a fine old tusker called 'Kala Nag,' who knew his work thoroughly. He was brought up to my 'mool,' and I mounted and went off in pursuit. Napier, who had climbed on to the cliffs overhanging the gorge, could see that the tiger was hiding in a small rocky nullah running down into the main stream, and could thus direct our movements. Kala Nag, however, found the ascent amongst trees and rocks very difficult. His progress was very slow. It was long before he reached the spot which Napier indicated. Then suddenly the tiger came out with a roar straight at the elephant's head. Kala Nag curled his trunk into his mouth and stood like a rock, and the *coup-de-grâce* was administered before the charge could be made good; which was, perhaps, fortunate, for Kala Nag could be very angry, and a fight between a tiger and an elephant, when you are mounted on the latter, can be a very unpleasant experience. As soon as the shot was fired he became very restive, knocking down trees, and half an hour or more elapsed before he was sufficiently calm to allow me to dismount. On another occasion he demonstrated the fact that an elephant has as good a nose as a foxhound. A wounded tiger had galloped away on to an open plain covered with tall grass. Kala Nag was brought into action, and we followed a track through the grass for about a quarter of a mile. The track then forked. It was with great difficulty that the mahout persuaded him to take the left-hand track. He trumpeted and tapped his trunk on the ground with that metallic noise which elephants make when anxious or excited, and told us quite plainly that in his opinion the tiger had gone to the right. We followed the left track for some distance without seeing anything; and then turned round and left the rest to Kala Nag, who came straight back to the fork, turned up the right-hand track, and took us straight to the tiger.

Mahtab Singh[1] was the acknowledged and not unworthy successor of Harsa Singh. He was a weird-looking creature, with a grizzled and very untidy beard, parted horizontally by a perpetual smile. He had only one eye and not much more than three-quarters of a head, the rest having been clawed off either by a tiger or a bear. No one saw the accident, for it happened at night, and Mahtab himself could give no rational account of it. The damaged side of his head was, of course, always covered by his puggree. He had not the natural

[1] See page 148, footnote.

dignity of Harsa Singh; there was in fact something of the 'gamin' in him; but in his knowledge of the jungle and of the ways of beasts he was not inferior. He was reputed to be able to drive a tiger in any direction and almost to any 'mool' he pleased. He was not a teetotaller; but, like most Sikhs, could retire to rest when too intoxicated for service, and he could consume a considerable amount of alcohol before that condition supervened. A bottle of brandy, at the end of a long day, he could swallow as a glass of milk. He suffered from time to time from rheumatism and similar complaints. During the cold weather before this shoot he was in hospital at Agar with lumbago. We visited him daily during the stable hour, and one morning we found him considerably worse than he had been on the previous day. He was, in fact, in agony; he seemed to be at the point of death. We inquired the cause of these alarming symptoms, and were informed that Mahtab Singh, becoming impatient and dissatisfied with the administrations of the regimental doctor, Caldecott, had called in a celebrated 'hakim'[1] who lived in Agar city. Now it is well known to certain people that lumbago is one of those diseases which are best treated by occult means. In England, for instance, a patient will be cured, it is said, if the seventh child of a seventh son will dance barefooted on the seat of pain. The treatment is not necessarily disagreeable: it might indeed be quite pleasant, if the child is young and light of foot. But the Agar 'hakim' had gone one better than this. He had ordered the hospital attendants to procure a man

[1] Indian doctor.

who had entered this world of sin feet foremost to kick the patient in the back. Diligent search had been made for an individual answering to this interesting definition, who had been found in the person of a soldier who happened to be the champion wrestler of the district. He had performed his part with the desired vigour, and perhaps a little bit over, and had nearly kicked poor Mahtab into his grave. The old shikari, however, recovered; but he did not live very much longer. In the following cold weather he was killed on an ordinary ceremonial parade.

Besides Mahtab Singh there were seven shikaris out on the Rampura-Bhanpura shoot. Five of them were Sikhs—namely, Bhagwan Singh, Kapur Singh, Gurmakh Singh, Dewa Singh, and Atma Singh. Bhagwan Singh was a clever old Kote Dafadar, whose work as senior N.C.O. of his troop did not permit him often to come out into the jungles. Kapur Singh was a very smart Malwai Sikh Dafadar. He was eventually killed by a panther. The other three were sowars, Gurmakh Singh being a typical Manja Sikh, sturdy and reliable. Dewa Singh and Atma Singh were beginners, the former becoming in later years a very dependable shikari. The remaining two men, Mahmud Khan and Kadir Baksh, already mentioned, were young Rangars, each with a very distinguished career as a shikari before him. Kadir Baksh began as a pupil under Mahtab in Hughes-Buller's shoot in Rewa in 1884. Many stories are told of him. On one occasion Hoare, who joined in 1903, was walking home through the jungles near Patleh Koh at dusk, with Kadir, unarmed, leading the way, when a bear appeared in front of them and charged. Kadir stood his ground and shouted, and the bear, turning suddenly off the track, went bundling down the hillside over a rock. Hoare got in a couple of shots; and they found the dead bear a few yards below the track. There was no wound on him whatever. He was Kadir's bear. They were all such brave fellows, these shikaris. They carried their lives in their hands, and they never wavered. Kadir Baksh, as bold as a lion, was perhaps the steadiest of them all. When he became head shikari he maintained very strict discipline, and the others invariably saluted him, even in the hunting camp — a tribute not often extended to other non-commissioned officers. When he retired on pension in 1910 he took service, as head shikari, with the Maharao of Kotah.

Mahmud Khan began his career as an orderly, and had particularly distinguished himself on an occasion in the cold weather of 1884-85. In preparation for a beat at Kariakal, Gerard had lined up the beaters and ordered them to wait a certain time whilst he placed the guns. This he then proceeded to do, the last to be placed—excluding himself—being a guest of his, a visitor from England of the name of Wallis, to whom Mahmud Khan was attached as orderly. Having placed him Gerard went on to his own 'mool,' and, as he went, the beat began prematurely. He climbed into the nearest tree, telling his own orderly, Subha Singh, to go to another some twenty yards distant. As Subha Singh ran to the place indicated a tiger, that had been drinking just outside the piece of jungle to be beaten and was returning to his lair, saw him, pounced upon him, and mauled him very

Dafadar Kadir Baksh.

severely. Gerard was at the moment arranging his 'mala.'[1] Mahmud was performing a like office for Wallis who was standing at the foot of his tree, fortunately with his loaded rifle—a .450 Express—in his hand. Leaving Subha Singh on the ground the tiger charged Wallis, when Mahmud, without a moment's hesitation, jumped down from the tree and stood beside him. The tiger came on, and Wallis bowled him over dead within thirty yards of him. And then a curious thing happened. On Mahmud's advice Wallis fired three more shots in order to make sure that the tiger was dead. Whether or no the nerves, braced for the critical moment, had given way on reaction it is difficult to say; but the fact remains that only one bullet hit that tiger. Poor Subha Singh died from shock in Goonah hospital two days afterwards.

In September of this year the 1st Regiment was armed with Martini-Henry carbines. The 2nd did not get theirs until five years later. The Martini is now a museum piece; but in 1888 it was, to the Indian Army, a God-sent novelty. With what alacrity did we pack up the old Sniders and send them off to the arsenal. They were dreadful weapons. The calibre was .577 inch, almost as large as a 12-bore gun. After firing a dozen rounds or so one's shoulder was pounded to a jelly. It was quite impossible to expect the recruit to 'press the trigger gently.' He just shut his eyes, turned his head away, and pulled; and the bullet very often hit the ground nearer to the man than to the target. They were used, however, in the Afghan War. It was

[1] A stout leather cushion, with a rope at each corner, tied in the tree for the 'gun' to sit upon. One sometimes has to wait for hours.

for this campaign indeed that they were first issued to us. Before that time the firearm was the Brown Bess, a muzzle-loading weapon which carried a very short distance and was rarely used. It was intended, as we have seen, for use on horseback, and one of the feats of a tentpegging afternoon, at which Probyn was particularly skilful, was to shoot a bottle on the ground at full gallop.

Of the officers who joined in 1888 Lieutenant A. P. Browne of the 6th Dragoon Guards and Lieutenant W. D. Daunt of the 7th Dragoon Guards succeeded in course of time to the command, the former of the 1st and the latter of the 2nd Regiment. Browne, in fact, commanded the 1st Regiment, by that time the 38th Central India Horse, during the Great War in France. He was Sam Browne's second son, and, like his father, a great sportsman. Daunt held several staff appointments during his career. Lieutenant A. d'Arcy Bannerman of the Highland Light Infantry also joined in this year, went to the Political Department, and is now, 1928, Colonel Sir Arthur Bannerman, K.C.V.O., C.S.I., C.I.E., Political Aide-de-Camp to the Secretary of State for India. Major Arthur Bannerman, who left the regiment in 1882, was his uncle. His father was some time Agent to the Governor-General at Indore. Surgeon Gimlette was appointed temporarily to the 1st Regiment early in 1888. At this time the permanent Medical Officers were Caldecott and Lowdell, but the former was officiating Residency Surgeon at Indore and the latter was with the Malwa Bhil Corps. Gimlette had the misfortune, whilst with the regiment, to lose an eye from an accident at polo. He left early in 1889, and during the next three years Surgeons C. C. Manifold and G. B. Irvine officiated for Caldecott and Lowdell respectively.

The year 1889 saw the introduction of the new system of cavalry drill. It was almost as great a relief as the change from the Snider to the Martini carbine. The essential novelty was not the formation of, and movement by, 'squadron columns,' which had indeed come into practice so long ago as 1883, but the division of the squadron into four handy little bodies known as 'Zugs' in the German Army and 'Divisions' in our own. It was impossible in the first instance to call them 'troops,' as they are called now, for the troop was still the administrative unit and was twice the size of a 'Zug.' It was not until 1896, when the various classes of soldiers were grouped in squadrons instead of in troops, and the 'squadron' and 'half-squadron'—clumsy title—became the administrative unit, that the term 'troop' could be, and was, applied to the small tactical unit, the fourth part of a squadron. Before 1883 the 'Cavalry Drill Book' was a prodigious octavo volume full of instructions for the accomplishment of intricate and unpractical movements which seemed designed only to trap the unwary. Not only the Squadron Leaders but the Troop Leaders also were involved in the succession of varying 'words of command' which followed that of the Commanding Officer; and the newly joined subaltern wasted his time endeavouring to learn, yet often contriving to forget, what to say to his troop when the Colonel shouted an order like "Change front, half right back on the 2nd Squadron." The new system simplified every manœuvre and was very easily learnt. Movements, instead of being made by the wheel or wheel about of 'fours,' thus leaving an inexperienced Squadron Leader in doubt whether or no he had his rear rank where his front rank ought to be, a dilemma from which we in the Central India Horse were relieved by the fact that, in those days, only the front rank carried lancés, were made by the wheel or wheel about of troops; and henceforward the subaltern could devote his time to more important studies.

In March 1889 the regiment was again honoured by a visit from a Commander-in-Chief, Sir Frederick Roberts as he then was, who desired to examine for himself the condition of all local corps in Central India and Rajputana, and to ascertain what progress had been made in the recently formed Imperial Service troops. The question whether localisation was any longer necessary or should be abolished, and whether the corps concerned, even if remaining localised, would not become more efficient fighting units if administered and trained under the Commanders-in-Chief's direct orders, was in the air; and, whilst we welcomed the approach of the latter scheme, we viewed with some dismay the signs of the times which pointed to the eventual adoption of the former, and consequently to our removal from the jungles to the stereotyped surroundings of a cantonment. His Excellency came to Agar but did not, like his predecessor, see Goonah too. A squadron of the 2nd Regiment, under Grant and Watson, marched down, however, from Goonah to Agar for the occasion. It was a week-end visit. The party arrived on a Saturday and left on Tuesday morning. Saturday afternoon and the whole of Monday were occupied by inspection, His Excellency being particularly pleased by an 'attack' of the 4th Squadron, under Colin Campbell, which involved the swimming of the horses across an arm of the Agar lake. A panther, that should have been 'in waiting' at Jamonia, was not harboured until the morning of His Excellency's departure. He was shot that afternoon by Colin Campbell, after giving a good deal of trouble and slightly mauling a shikari and a beater.

There was little variation from the daily routine of squadron and regimental training during the next two years, though the 1st Regiment distinguished itself by winning the Lloyd Lindsay Competition at meetings of the Bengal Rifle Association six times in succession; but at the end of 1891 a combined regiment, consisting of three troops of the 1st and five of the 2nd, marched up under Money to take part in General Luck's Cavalry Camp of Exercise at Aligarh, a repetition of the exercise held four years previously at Rupaheli. Cameron and John Pinney killed many pigs on the march.

Several new officers were, meanwhile, appointed on probation; for at this period a good many senior officers were seconded for extra regimental employment. Most of the permanent Squadron Commanders were, in fact, absent on Staff and miscellaneous duties. The situation became a public joke, and certain pungent verses appeared in the 'The Pioneer' referring sarcastically to the varied activities of officers of "The Scented Minstrel Horse." In 1890 Lieutenants T. M. Ward, J. C. D. Pinney, R. L. Kennion, and H. A. Lash were posted. Of these only Pinney remained long in the regiment; and he went some years later to be tutor to the heir of the Maharana of Udaipur. After his retirement he served in the Great War as a Provost-Marshal. Ward returned within a year to the dismounted branch. Kennion soon entered the Political Department. Lash, after struggling for a few years against constant bad health, was obliged to retire from the service. In 1891 Lieutenants G. de H. Smith—a younger brother of the late F. de H. Smith,—D. H. Cameron, S. A. Cooke, and G. T. Carwithen came in. The latter was invalided to England in 1892 and did not rejoin. Smith and Cameron served for some years. The latter went to Imperial Service troops in 1897, and was afterwards employed as tutor and guardian to the young Nawab of Jaora. Finally he became Adjutant and then Commandant of The Imperial Cadet Corps, and retired in 1912. Smith served on the Staff of Sir George Wolseley both in the Panjab and in Madras, but he was badly placed in regard to the command of either regiment and retired in 1913. Cooke served with the regiment in the Tirah campaign and in the Great War, during which he died in hospital in England. In 1892 Surgeon Captain Townsend Shaw was appointed to act for Lowdell in medical charge of the 1st Regiment. He became the permanent Medical Officer in January 1895, when Lowdell was transferred to civil employ, and retired in 1897 to become a barrister.

CHAPTER XII.

GERARD.

On the 3rd of October 1892 Henry Buller died suddenly whilst on leave at Simla. A fearless, sweet-tempered, and very companionable man, he left behind him a memory of friendship and goodwill which endured for many years. Gerard was recalled from St Petersburg to succeed him, but did not assume command until the 18th of May 1893. Masters had, meanwhile, been appointed to command the 2nd Regiment, Gerard's departure for Russia having created a permanent vacancy. Vincent relinquished command of the 1st Regiment about the same time, his place being taken by George Money.

Gerard's tenure of command was short and, regimentally speaking, uneventful. He was away a great deal. He has left very little in the 'Brigade Order Book,' and it is curious that he, who lived for active soldiering and sport alone, caring little for his personal appearance, should be distinguished in that record principally by some very definite orders on the subject of clothing. Certain irregularities had crept in, especially in the matter of boots; and no previous Commandant had troubled himself, or his officers, very much about them. The correct footwear for all mounted duties had been hitherto the 'Napoleon,' a handsome and very military boot reaching above the knee; but this had been rejected, without permission, by certain officers—including one of the Seconds-in-Command—who had found it heavy and old-fashioned. They had called it the 'concertina boot' and had provided themselves, one after another, with the ordinary cavalry 'knee-boot' which had, in this way, become recognised unofficially as the regimental pattern. Gerard ordered a return to the 'Napoleon,' though the usual proviso was made, verbally, that officers in possession of 'knee-boots' might wear them out. Gerard, however, left the regiment before this undesirable situation developed; and the 'Napoleon' was never revived.

Our uniform has undergone several changes during the short period of our existence, though the main features, of colour and lace, have remained. It will be remembered that, in this respect, Colonel Durand had written that "It would be well if the Brigade of Irregular Cavalry adopted the Panjab Guide Corps colour." The Guides wore drab with red facings. We made our facings maroon; and the first tunic was of Hussar pattern, made of drab cloth, with collar and cuffs of maroon velvet. There were, in the first instance, only four lines of somewhat attenuated gold cording on the front of this tunic, but by the year 1872 the number had increased to five, and the cording was bolder. The full-dress breeches were white and should have been of leather, but were usually made of cloth.

The full-dress helmet was of strange design, gorgeous to the point of vulgarity. It was covered with maroon velvet; there was a large and florid gilt regimental monogram in front; there was a gilt rim round the edge, and the whole was surmounted by a scarlet horsehair plume. This was noticed by the Prince of Wales during his visit to Delhi in 1875-76. His Royal Highness seems to have objected not so much to the plume as to the colour of the helmet, which he considered too dark for the rest of the uniform. He ordered John Watson to change it; and when he next saw Watson, at Sandringham some five years later, his first remark to him was, " I hope you have abolished that helmet." This, of course, had been done, though the transition from the old to the new had taken some years and was not actually promulgated in orders until 1879. The maroon helmet, plume and all, was worn at Lord Lytton's Imperial Assemblage, though the plume was discarded soon after this, its place being taken by a gilt spike. In undress a maroon cloth helmet was worn, without the monogram or the gilt rim, a cotton puggree of the same colour being wound upon it.

The new head-dress, adopted two years after the Imperial Assemblage, was a drab helmet upon which was worn a broad puggree made of the gold-woven end of a Ludhiana lungi.[1] It was worn both in full dress and in undress, the gilt spike which surmounted it in the former being replaced

[1] A puggree.

in the latter by a drab button. Gerard now abolished this, and substituted, for full dress, the cavalry pattern white helmet with white cotton puggree and a spike, and, for undress, the ordinary khaki helmet with khaki puggree and button.

The overalls were always, as they are now, of drab cloth with a double line of gold braid down the sides, divided by a narrow strip of maroon velvet. With these gilt box-spurs were worn, even in the daytime, and our friends in other mounted units were wont to suggest that we had spent a late night and had forgotten to change them.

The first undress jacket, for mounted as well as dismounted duties, was a loose fitting, comfortable, single-breasted garment of drab cloth, with maroon collar and cuffs and spherical gilt buttons. The maroon collar and cuffs seem to have been discarded about the year 1864. A plain leather cross belt was worn over this jacket, the sword being attached by slings to a belt underneath it. The 'service jacket' did not come into use until the 'Sam Browne' belt was invented, shortly before the second Afghan War; and, about this time, the undress jacket was replaced, for dismounted duties, by a patrol jacket of drab cloth with four broad loops of drab mohair braid across the front. There was another jacket, too, which, however, was very rarely seen. This was the 'doggie coat,' as it was commonly called. It was a beautiful garment, though not particularly suitable to a warm climate. It was a patrol jacket similar to that just described, but with brown Astrakhan collar and cuffs and a broad strip of the same material down the front. Its origin is wrapped in mystery. There was one in existence when the author joined the regiment. It was never worn on any parade or duty whatever, but was just passed from one officer to another, mainly for purposes of photography.

The head-dress worn with the patrol jacket, when the sun was low, was the useless and singularly uncomfortable 'forage cap,' a thing like an enlarged pill-box made of maroon cloth and decorated with gold lace. It was worn on the side of the head, resting very often on the right ear, a conspicuously unserviceable head-dress though undoubtedly smart. This was followed by a maroon cloth 'fatigue cap,' which was rather like a 'Glengarry' without the tail; and this by the peaked cap now in use.

The 'service jacket,' mentioned above, was of Hungarian pattern, gathered at the waist, its chief feature being that the sleeves were buttoned at the wrist and that at the arm-pit was a large gusset to ensure freedom of movement. For winter use this was made of khaki serge with a thin line of gold piping round the top and bottom of a stand-up collar, and along the edges of the breast pocket flaps. The sword was carried in a 'Sam Browne' belt, and white buckskin gloves were worn, with large stiff gauntlets. For summer use this 'service jacket' was made, before Messrs Spinners invented a permanent khaki dye for cotton material in the 'eighties, of cotton grown at Agar, the colour being natural and rather red, the colour, in fact, of the laterite. The leg wear was drab Bedford cord breeches and black knee-boots with gilt spurs. Gerard abolished both the gauntlets and the black boots. In future the boots were to be brown, though no particular pattern was specified. The ' Elcho ' boot was introduced about this time, and most officers equipped themselves either with this or with the ' Field ' boot, which required less lacing. There was much discussion as to which was most serviceable. Gerard himself wore the ' Clarence ' boot, which was by way of being an Oxford shoe with a boot leg attached to it, and a few officers imitated him ; but this boot was not so comfortable or so serviceable as it pretended to be, and was very soon discarded.

There has been little change in the uniform of the Indian ranks. The full dress was always, as it is now, a khaki kurta, with scarlet kamarband, white pyjamas, black puttees, and ankle-boots with brass spurs ; and for head-dress a blue Ludhiana lungi, plain for the sowars but with gold-woven ends for the officers and non-commissioned officers, the rank being denoted by the amount of gold. It was not until July 1879 that Indian ranks were permitted to wind these lungis in accordance with the custom of their race. Before this date all had been wound alike. Indian officers used to wear ' Napoleon ' boots ; but these were dropped in favour of the puttee after the Second Afghan War. In undress, until the year 1900 when ' all khaki ' was instituted, the men wore exactly the same clothing as in full dress, with the exception that the pyjamas were of saffron colour instead of white.

Since Gerard's order there have been, in respect to the uniform of British officers, many petty alterations which have gradually brought the regimental attire to its present state; but these are hardly worth recording.

In 1895 both regiments lost their Risaldar Majors, Bahauddin Khan being appointed aide-de-camp to the Viceroy and Murad Ali retiring on pension. The former was succeeded by Risaldar Sanwal Singh, who held his position with great dignity and retired in March 1901. The new Risaldar Major of the 2nd Regiment was Risaldar Lehna Singh, the eldest son of old Garbha Singh, a Bhopali Sikh. He had previously been Wardi Major, and an exceedingly smart one too. He was a superb man-at-arms, a great polo player, a drill instructor without equal, and he knew the history of every man and horse in the regiment. He was one of the few Indian officers selected to attend Queen Victoria's Jubilee celebration in 1887, the first occasion on which Indian officers appeared in London on public duty. After his retirement in 1902 he built a house at Goonah and lived there for many years.

The British officers appointed during this period (1893, 1894, and 1895) were Lieutenants T. S. Tancred, R. C. Bell, A. S. Capper, A. H. O. Spence, G. H. Lawrence, and J. D. Cadell. Lawrence remained for a few months only, and Cadell died of typhoid fever on the 12th January 1897 at Jodhpore, where he had joined a party for pig-sticking during the Christmas week. Tancred went to the Burmah Military Police for a short time in 1899, and, succeeding to a baronetcy in 1910, retired in the following year; but he returned to the Army, temporarily, in 1914, and served with the regiment in the Great War. Spence fought in the Tirah campaign, and shortly afterwards went to Imperial Service troops, with which he served during the Boxer Rebellion in China. His health broke down soon after this, and he spent the remainder of his service in the Army Secretariat at Simla. Bell served with the regiment in France during the Great War. Capper eventually succeeded to the command of the 2nd Regiment.

Amongst the Medical Officers there were several changes. In March 1894 Dr Caldecott was confirmed in his appointment as Residency Surgeon at Indore. His place in the regiment was taken by Surgeon Captain Malcolm Moore, who was the doctor of the 2nd Regiment for the next five years, when he was transferred to the Political Department as Residency Surgeon at Bhopal. Both he and Shaw were on leave in England during the year 1895, and three Medical Officers were appointed, one after another, to act for them. Of these, Surgeon Major Baker and Surgeon Captain J. B. Jamieson remained for short periods only. The third, Surgeon Captain J. R. Roberts, well known in Central India and afterwards at Simla as 'Micky Roberts,' remained for five years in the regiment, was then posted to Gwalior as Residency Surgeon, succeeded Caldecott at Indore, was finally made Surgeon to the Viceroy, and was knighted for his distinguished services.

Two senior combatant officers were in this year, too, brought in from other regiments. These were Captain C. E. Baynes of the 2nd Bombay Lancers, who was appointed to command a squadron of the

2nd Regiment on the 27th March, and Major F. H. F. Drummond, who was transferred from the 11th Bengal Lancers (Probyn's Horse) to be a Squadron Commander in the 1st Regiment on the 30th July. Baynes returned to the 2nd Bombay Lancers at the end of 1897. Drummond was made Commandant of the 1st Regiment on the 8th February 1900. A few years later he became Inspector-General of Imperial Service Troops, was made a Knight Commander of the Indian Empire on his retirement, and died in England shortly afterwards.

Gerard, the last Commandant of the two regiments combined, left Central India on the 14th June 1895 to join the Pamir Delimitation Commission, of which he had been made a member, taking with him a Trans-Frontier Pathan Risaldar of the name of Zairulla Khan.[1] This officer and his brother, Fahim Khan,[1] were very prominent characters in the 1st Troop of the 1st Regiment. Fahim Khan, a very handsome soldier, was the model for the mounted figure in the silver statuette which was presented to Sir Henry Daly. He was very severely wounded in the Second Afghan War, in the action of Besud, and died in 1883. Zairulla Khan had seen much service. In his early days he had taken a conspicuous part in several 'affairs' with dacoits. He had distinguished himself in the Second Afghan War. He had travelled with Gerard in Persia, and had saved the latter from drowning in a river near Kermanshah. After the death of his brother he retired from the Army, though he did not cease to serve ; for, being a man of resource

[1] See page 148, footnote.

and exceptional courage who could be relied on in a difficult or dangerous enterprise, he was often called upon in circumstances where such qualities were required. In 1885 he again accompanied Gerard to Persia. From 1888 to 1890 he was in Chitral and Sikkim. In 1891 he was at Vincent's back during the outbreak in the jail at Rampur. Two years later he accompanied Sir Mortimer Durand on the Kabul Mission, from which he returned a 'Khan Bahadur.' All these services were rewarded by the grant of a commission; so he returned to the Army as a Jemadar in the 1st Regiment, Central India Horse. He served with the regiment in Tirah, was admitted to the Order of the British India in the New Year Honours of 1910, and died on the 19th April of that year.

Another soldier of the same race went also with Gerard on this expedition. This was Dafadar Ghazan Khan, who, with Zairulla, had been on Vincent's escort at Rampur and had behaved very well. The party was not long on the Pamirs, but Gerard himself never returned to the regiment. On the 10th April 1896 he was appointed to command the Hyderabad Contingent, and subsequently he commanded the Lucknow Division. On the 13th May 1904, having meanwhile been created a Knight of the Bath, as well as of the Star of India, he was, at the request of the regiment, gazetted Honorary Colonel of the 38th Central India Horse. He died in the summer of 1905 at Irkutsk on his way home from Manchuria, where he had been attached to the Russian Army during the Russo-Japanese War.

Money was appointed officiating Commandant on Gerard's departure for the Pamirs. He took leave to England in February 1896, and was relieved by Masters, who in his turn was relieved by Drummond; but no permanent appointment was gazetted, for the time was drawing near when news of the coming event, foreshadowed by the visits of two Commanders-in-Chief, was to be broken gently to us during that of a third, and the two regiments were to lose that very close tie which had bound them together since their formation and to become two units of the Bengal Army.

Meanwhile the 1st Regiment was called upon to send a wing to Jhalra Patan. The Maharajah of that place had chosen, in defiance of the expressed wishes of Government, to supply many of the Wilaitis, and other similar rascals who infest his kingdom, with firearms; and these people had become a menace to the peace of the State. They had even surrounded the camp of the Agent to the Governor-General in Rajputana, who was on tour, threatening grave disturbance. The wing, consisting of A and C Squadrons, covered the distance between Agar and Jhalra Patan, sixty-four miles, in two days, and arrived on the scene of anticipated disorder on the afternoon of the 8th January 1896, only to find that news of their approach had preceded them and the Wilaitis had discreetly vanished. They enjoyed, however, a very pleasant halt of four days at Patan, for it happened that the Political Agent there was Captain Evans-Gordon, who had served in the regiment and was noted for a generous hospitality.

The third Commander-in-Chief to visit the regiment was Sir George White, who came to Goonah on the 21st December 1896, inspected the 2nd Regiment, and informed them of the coming change. The news, however, had actually been communicated to the 1st Regiment a few days earlier than this by the Viceroy, Lord Elgin, whilst on tour at Indore. The 1st Regiment, with a squadron of the 20th Hussars, formed his mounted escort there, and His Excellency made a special point of reviewing it and, in a speech at the close of the review, of proclaiming his continued interest in its welfare and assuring officers and men that none of the traditions or privileges of the Central India Horse would be interfered with.

The office of Commandant of the two regiments of Central India Horse was thus abolished, and the two regiments became two distinct corps, each with a Commandant of its own, included in the Bandelkhand District of the Bengal Command. Moreover, the political duties ceased. Henceforward each Commandant was vested only with the powers of a second-class magistrate within a radius of five miles from cantonments. The Western Malwa Agency was placed, as it had been before 1865, under the charge of a regular officer of the Political Department, living, however, at Neemuch instead of at Mehidpur; whilst the Goonah Agency was handed over to the Resident at Gwalior. The Agent to the Governor-General at Indore, being responsible for the peace of Central India, retained a certain amount of military control. He was charged with the distribution of all troops localised in his area, and was empowered, when immediate movement became necessary, to order such movement on his own responsibility without first referring to the General Officer Commanding the District.

Money and Masters were the two first Commandants under the new dispensation, the former of the 1st and the latter of the 2nd Regiment. The new order came into force on the 15th February 1897. It delivered us from our fears of delocalisation, which, indeed, were expressly ruled out; nor were they revived until ten years later, when rumours of Lord Kitchener's reforming projects again spread a cloud of apprehension over us.

CHAPTER XIII.

AGAR AND GOONAH.

OF the two small cantonments occupied by the Central India Horse during the sixty years when it was privileged to keep the peace in the highlands of Central India, Agar—or Augur, or Aggar, or even Auggur, as it has been spelt at different times—lay forty-two miles to the north of Ujjain, in Western Malwa; whilst Goonah, or Guna, was on the Grand Trunk Road from Bombay to Agra, about half-way between the latter place and Indore. Both, until the advent of the motor-car, far removed from other haunts of Englishmen in India, for until 1894 there was no railway at either, and there is none within forty miles of Agar to this day; both, in fact, completely 'jungly'; they were nevertheless, in their aspect, in the kind of sport they afforded and in the facilities they offered for the movement of cavalry, two widely different places. Goonah was the more remote. From Agar, when the road permitted, an officer in need of a change could ride into the Indore Residency, where there was always a warm welcome for him, or he could go to the races at Mhow; but at Goonah the nearest railway station was at Gwalior, 130 miles off; and although leave dated from the moment of departure from Gwalior, he thought twice before taking a 'week-end' or even an 'extended ten days.' In spite of such apparent drawbacks, Goonah was always the more popular of the two; and it was a noticeable fact, regarded with some sense of superstition in the regiment, that, with the exception of Neave, who was killed by a tiger in 1861, no British officer of the Central India Horse ever died there. Agar cemetery told a different tale.

Agar was first used as a cantonment for troops in 1845. Up to this time Scindia's south-western districts had been protected only by detachments from units of the Gwalior Contingent at Gwalior, Mahona, and Goonah. For the better protection of Malwa a small mixed force, consisting of a battalion of infantry, a wing of cavalry, and a company of artillery, was in this year quartered at Agar, special stress being laid upon the necessity for mounted troops, since these districts were always infested by bands of mounted plunderers who did much mischief, and stood in no fear of infantry when not accompanied by cavalry. After the Mutiny there were, of course, no guns at Agar; but the infantry remained, in the shape of a wing of the Bombay Regiment, whose Headquarters were at Mehidpur, until the year 1881, when that regiment, the 18th, was disbanded on the reduction of the Bombay Army. It was a little earlier than this that the railway was opened from Indore, *via* Fatehabad, to Ujjain, and that the Gwalior Durbar consented to make a road thence to Agar. Hitherto there had been no metalled road from Agar to any place on earth, and one often felt that there was nothing beyond it. It was at all seasons a difficult place to reach, and in the rains almost impossible, for the major part of the journey was over black cotton soil. The railway and the road, which was completed in 1882, brought civilisation nearer to us.

There were no great jungles round Agar. It was open undulating country, with here and there an isolated hill, not unlike the kopjes of South Africa, rising abruptly from the plain, on which were patches of scrub jungle, usually dak [1] or karonda.[2] Hyena Hill on one side of cantonments and Jamonia and Kankar-ki-Baori on the other often held a panther or a sounder of pig; and on the former, as its name implies, hyenas were frequently found and ridden, though they are not a sporting quarry. Occasionally, though rarely, a tiger was killed. The death of what must have been the last is recorded by John Watson in his diary on the 29th March 1876: " General Montgomery came out on Inspection duty. We took him out and killed a tiger in the afternoon." It was always the tradition that inspecting Generals should be shown a sample of our sporting life. They were not always prepared for this form of hospitality, but, for the most part, they accepted it willingly and enjoyed it. There was, however, one important General Officer who found himself, without much enthusiasm, compelled to join in a hunt whilst actually inspecting the regiment on outpost duty. Colin Campbell, having posted a line of

---

[1] The 'bastard teak,' covered with brilliant scarlet blossom in early spring.
[2] A giant whortleberry.

THE HAPPY VALLEY

Vedettes, galloped back to the General, saluted, and reported, quite gravely, as follows: "I beg your pardon, sir, but the enemy is in one of those bushes on the side of the hill," and solemnly handed him a spear. The General, completely taken aback, was overheard to remark to his Staff Officer: "I say, what sort of a regiment is this?" But he took the spear and joined in the pursuit of the 'enemy'—a panther, which was finally killed by Campbell himself.

The cantonment was situated east and west along a ridge of red laterite sloping gently to the north, the southern edge ending in a steep cliff some 80 to 100 feet high, beyond which was the Happy Valley, a terrain of black cotton soil, of mango groves and maize and sugar-cane; and here during the monsoon the pig, coming down from distant hills, would feast the night long upon the sugar, destroying invariably much more than they consumed, and then lie up for the day. On such occasions some villagers would run up to the Lines at dawn; a shikari would hasten to the spot, and presently would break in upon us at breakfast with news that such a pig as he had never seen in his life was awaiting our attack. We all turned out on our ponies, British officers, Indian officers, non-commissioned officers, sowars—it was an enormous field,—and for the next hour or so were flopping through the mud in pursuit. The pig could travel faster through the black cotton soil than we could, and if he reached the laterite on the higher ground with too long a start he escaped; but we often killed a boar this way, and the Sikhs carried him home in triumph and ate him.

Pig-sticking as known in Guzerat, or at Muttra and in the Kadir country, was impossible at Agar; but the Sikhs, gourmands in the matter of pork, were always devising some new way of circumventing what to the Mahomedan is 'the unclean beast.' In later years the method known to us as 'pig mobbing,' which is circumvention literally, was adopted on the suggestion of Risaldar Teja Singh, a great shikari; and many a good day's sport and many a good dinner did he and his friends derive from it. It was practised by daylight or by moonlight, and always on foot; and it never failed, if pig were found, to provide excitement. The daylight method was feasible only in the rains. A solitary boar was tracked, in dead silence, through the mud, sometimes for several miles, to his lair, with dogs in leash ready to be loosed upon him when discovered. He was usually found in a clump of karonda bush, when the dogs, terriers of sorts and even 'pie' dogs, anything, in fact, except a bulldog or bull-terrier, overmuch courage being a disadvantage, went in and set him to bay. The hunters, armed with spears to which 'stops' were lashed, surrounded the bushes, and presently the boar would charge out. Generally was someone knocked over, but never was anyone seriously hurt; for Teja Singh always maintained that the boar on these occasions shut his eyes and blundered through, so that it was possible to dodge him. Breeches and coats, nevertheless, were sometimes cut by his tushes. The moonlight method could be practised at any time of year, but, since success depended upon finding a sounder of pig on the way to or from water, the hot weather was the best season. No tracking was necessary. A long line, formed on the edge of Agar lake, with intervals of five or six yards between each hunter, moved silently forward through the karonda bushes. The presence of pig was signalled by a whistle, and the dogs were let loose. Now it is no use tracking a sounder by the daylight method, for the sounder quickly scents danger and moves on, and the boar moves with it. But at night his behaviour changes. He acts as rear-guard to the sounder and stands to bay at once, whilst his family escapes. The dogs drive him into a bush; and he dies his gallant death in the moonlight as he did by day.

At the eastern end of the Agar ridge were the officers' bungalows, not very attractive residences, for, since no plant except the karonda seemed to thrive on laterite, there were no surrounding gardens; though there was a public garden, always known as the 'Company Bagh,'[1] on lower ground to the north, between the officers' quarters and the Lines. Near the mess was a racquet court, where Gabriel, the marker, one of the best professional players in India, would take on almost any officer at almost any handicap, and, provided that there was a rupee on the game, would always win. The 'slap' of his bare soles on the floor of the court must surely haunt it to this day. There was also a church, which was neither elegant nor imposing; but we were much attached to it. It was erected by subscription at the instigation of Colonel Martin, whom gossip alleged to have vowed to build a church

[1] The East India Company's garden.

and a temple on his safe return from the Afghan
War. He certainly interested himself in both; and
the temple of Bamganga, in a small wooded valley
about a mile to the north of Agar, was a thing of
beauty. It is strange that both gossip, and Martin
too, seem to have omitted the Masjid.[1] The church
was a square building of red stone with a domed
roof, a little porch at the west end, and a curious
oblong tower, which looked like an afterthought,
between the porch and the main building. Creepers,
bougainvillea, and bignonia soon covered its walls,
but could not hide its squat proportions. Service
was taken periodically by the chaplain of Indore,
and in his absence the Colonel, if of sufficiently
pious inclination, read prayers on Sunday evenings.

Towards the western end of the ridge was the
town of Agar, a walled city of some importance,
and below it the lake, on which we kept a sailing
boat or two.

The polo ground was in front of and a little lower
than the Lines, on the level where the laterite ended
and the black cotton soil began, so that it was
neither too hard, like the rock between the officers'
houses and the Lines at Goonah where we used to
play in the rains, nor too soft, like the Goonah
parade ground. It was, in fact, reckoned quite a
respectable ground; and it was very much played
on. In early days, before we took the game very
seriously and began to compete in first-class tournaments up-country, great numbers of men turned out
to play, and it was quite impossible to arrange
regular 'chakkars' of four a side. I have seen as

---

[1] Mahomedan church.

many as eight or ten a side, when no player, with the possible exception of the Colonel, was allowed more than two consecutive strokes. The men used sticks of male bamboo with no handle whatever and with heads of siras or babul wood, in shape more or less like a cigar, made and fixed at any angle by the local mistri [1]; but they drove the ball, as they do now, with that natural elegance and accuracy of timing which English players never cease to envy. It was from Agar that we first went out to tournaments. The earliest record is of a team consisting of Neill, Caldecott, Bannerman, and Ravenshaw winning a tournament down at Bombay in 1878. After the Afghan War this event was revived on a somewhat more ambitious scale; and we went down again and won again. We won, in fact, three years in succession, and the Challenge Cup became our property. Nothing like the preparation necessary nowadays was required for these old tournaments. Two or three fellows rode down from Goonah, a few games were played on the Agar ground, a team from both regiments was selected, and off we went. Nor did we use so many ponies. Ten or a dozen for the team was an outside figure. They were supposed to measure not more than 13.2, but no certificates were required. The ponies were all paraded on the day before the first match, and any team could object to any pony of any other team on the score of height. No objections were, in fact, ever made, each team being too conscious of a big 'un in its own ranks to venture on a challenge. This Bombay Tournament was

[1] Carpenter.

held at the end of September, so that, on the ride to the railway at Ujjain, we were sometimes obliged to cross the Kali Sind river in flood. This took time. There was neither bridge nor boat, though there were watermen—'bhois'—in plenty to help us over. The ponies and baggage, having been sent on beforehand, had been able to wait, if necessary, until a flood subsided, for these rivers on the Central India plateau subside in the rains as quickly as they rise; but if we arrived on the bank on the top of another flood we could not wait. It was imperative to cross at once. Each player, therefore, sat upon a small charpoy,[1] large garhas[2] being lashed mouth downwards to the corners, and with his saddle between his knees and his chest was pushed across by swimming 'bhois.' It was an exciting but moistening process, and the remainder of the ride, some thirty miles or so, was exceedingly uncomfortable.

It was in 1884 that we first entered for the Bengal Cavalry and the Inter-Regimental Tournaments; but this was an isolated and unsuccessful effort, which was not repeated until the railway came to Goonah. Meanwhile we had to be contented with down-country tournaments which could be reached from Agar without undue expense.

If Agar, in those early days, was the best station from the polo point of view, Goonah was incomparably the best for sport. There was scatter-gun shooting at both, and this can be said of almost any station in India; but Goonah was the country

[1] A small bedstead. [2] Globular earthenware water vessels.

THE RIDE TO GOONAH

of the rifle, of the 'Barra Ban,'[1] the great jungles, and the 'Barra Shikar.'[2] On the ride up the Grand Trunk Road the landscape presented little change of appearance until Biaora was reached, and then it altered completely. Villages and cultivation disappeared, and one rode into a land of hills and forest. Few travellers were met. A bania going down to Indore, silken curtains hiding the ladies in his bullock carts, and a sepoy or two beside them with drawn swords which were of little use when needed; a crowd of Brinjaras, their cattle loaded with grain; some Serias, perhaps, with a string of donkeys laden with antlers for the English market; or the Dak[3] runner jogging along with Her Majesty's mail slung to a lathi over his shoulder, his bells tinkling as he ran: these were the only signs of life. Occasionally some old castle came into view, the abode of some Rajput chieftain, or of 'bandit earls and caitiff knights,' reminding one of Cheetoo and the Pindaris or even of mediæval England. On the left the red walls of Chachora looked down from teak-clad hills about a mile away. On the right the grey towers of Ragogarh, just visible among the trees. And here the road became more tortuous, and one left behind those long straight stretches which, in the absence of good company, made the ride so dull. Rounding the hills at Rotiai, where the river Suket breaks through, and debouching from the defile at Garder Choki, one saw on the left an open plain, with patches of cultivation amongst

[1] Great Forest.   [2] Big game hunting.
[3] The Post.

the bushes, from which rose abruptly in the distance an isolated hill divided near the summit into three, like the Eildon Hills above the Tweed ; and a few miles farther on one reached the first house in Goonah, appropriately named ' Melrose Abbey.'

No other houses were visible. Goonah was all trees, bakain and siras and tamarind, with a few of the larger figs and an occasional mango. The officers' bungalows were dotted about amongst these without plan. They were, with one exception, wretched buildings, arising generally from four mud walls built round a tent. The exception was the 'Kothi,' the Colonel's house, which stood on a slight eminence in the centre of the officers' quarters. Here had stood before the Mutiny the residence of Captain F. M. H. Burlton of the Gwalior Contingent, who had been Political Assistant at Goonah for many years. He had been transferred to Kotah, where he met his death at the hands of the insurgents, and had left behind him at Goonah his little daughter, buried under a tombstone of Hindu design in order to prevent desecration. Few officers of the regiment were aware that the elegant little 'Chattri' in front of the Kothi stables covered the grave of an English girl. Of his house, after the Mutiny, there remained but four bare walls. There was no outbreak of insurrection at Goonah, for no troops were there at the time ; but the mutineers from Indore and Mhow burnt everything English as they passed through on their way to Agra. Whilst plans were being prepared for the reconstruction of the house, Mayne, during one of his rebel hunting expeditions, had found in the heart of the jungles a temple which, in his own words, he "bought ridiculously cheap," and transported stone by stone to Goonah. And so from the four bare walls there grew a quaint but exceedingly attractive residence with a long semi-circular verandah supported by slender sandstone pillars and arches on which were carved many deities of Hindu mythology, with here and there a floral decoration where the acanthus was prominent, a gentle reminder of the lasting influence on India of Alexander the Great. In front of the verandah stood two small sandstone elephants looking out on to an unusually pleasant garden.

In later years another good house was built by the Maharajah of Gwalior for his railway engineer, Mr Taylor. It stood within fifty yards of the Kothi, and when the railway was completed and the Maharajah had no further use for it, it became the Officers' Mess.

Goonah was an older cantonment than Agar. It was first mentioned as such in 1820, when, by reason of its being in the most disturbed part of the Maharajah's dominions, it was selected as the General Headquarters of Daolat Rao Scindia's Contingent. The village itself was of no importance. There were very few shops, and supplies were not easily obtainable; but it was within a couple of miles of the town of Bajrangarh, the Headquarters of the Subha of the district, and it became a halting-place on the Grand Trunk Road. The troops of the Contingent were encamped at the foot of Hanuman Tekri—the Eildon hills—on the south, the farther side of the village from the officers' quarters, the locality being still known as the 'Mahratta Chaoni.'[1] The Lines of the Central India Horse were built on the north side, on the road to Shadora and the Betwa river.

The country all round was, for the most part, dense jungle, and it was very difficult to find ground where a larger body of cavalry than a squadron could manœuvre for long. Goonah was not, therefore, a good station for training in shock tactics. This defect, however, was more than counterbalanced by facilities for a special form of training which Goonah and no other station in India could provide. In the pursuit of big game both officers and men learned to use their eyes and ears, and acquired a knowledge of woodcraft which was just as useful to them in the daily and nightly occurrences of warfare as all the drill in the world. Nor were the occasions rare for this pursuit. There were the annual 'shoots,' of course, when friends from other parts of India, or from England, were invited to join the party; but these were not the only opportunities. It was the custom, except during the monsoon, to beat the neighbouring jungles every Thursday and Sunday throughout the year. Thursday, before the Great War, was always a whole holiday for the Army in India, a concession granted by Lord Napier of Magdala when he was Commander-in-Chief. His Excellency had complained, so the story goes, of officers shooting on Sunday; and, on excuse being made to him that it was the only day available for such recreation, had replied, "Well, let them have Thursdays." It is a regrettable fact that the Army proceeded to take both; and, what-

[1] The Mahratta camp.

ever may have been the true reason for the concession, Lord Napier's name was always remembered with gratitude so long as the Thursday holiday remained a standing order.

It was never necessary to go far for game. Tigers have been shot within a mile of Goonah; and Amkoh, Takhtaya, Phatti Dant, Atasumba—we knew all the beats by name—were all within a radius of eight miles or so. In the absence of 'Khabbar,'[1] the particular jungle to be beaten was selected the day before. Early in the morning all the shikaris, all the recruits, and as many other men as cared for the sport, galloped out on their ponies to the meet, the British officers arriving an hour or so later, by which time the beaters had been assembled. Fifty or sixty coolies, supplemented by recruits and other soldiers, were enough for these 'ittafaq hankas,'[2] as they were called. For the big tiger beats a couple of hundred were usually required. They had a hard day's work, not unaccompanied by risk, though the mauling of a coolie was an extremely rare occurrence; and their wages for the day was two annas, which, however, in the nineteenth century was more than sufficient for the day's food. On the arrival of the 'guns' information concerning the whereabouts of game was weighed, prospects were discussed, the beat was arranged, and we went quietly to our 'mools.' Unless a tiger was known to be in the beat it was lawful to shoot at anything. The shikaris always pretended to know, even in the absence of news from villagers, what might be expected; but they were careful not to part with

[1] News.   [2] Chance beats.

this information until afterwards. Old Harsa Singh, in particular, had a set formula for his reply to questions on this point: "Hazur, Jangal hai. Nigah ke samne jo guzar awe so sach hai."[1] So we waited to see what we should see. Four or five stretches of jungle were beaten; then we assembled under a tree, reviewed the events of the day, fined somebody for a miss perhaps, paid the coolies, had a drink, and galloped home to dinner. It was an exception to see a tiger on these occasions. Three or four possibly were bagged during the year in addition to those shot by the big shooting party; but panthers, bears, lynx, sambar, and four-horned deer were often killed, and almost invariably there was a pig for the Sikhs. The Mahomedans were not so fortunate. A sambar, or any other kind of deer, was theirs if they could 'halal'[2] him before he actually expired; but deer were not so numerous as pig in the Goonah jungles.

One of Scindia's elephants, 'Randullah' by name, and a fine old fellow he was, stood at Goonah for many years. He was at our disposal for shikar purposes, and came out to most of our beats. Of all the elephants we ever borrowed, he was the only one to suffer the indignity of a mauling. It happened in 1886. Gerard and Edwards, with two guests of the former's, the Duke of Braganza, afterwards the last King of Portugal, and the Austrian Count Trautmansdorf, went out after a tiger and a tigress that had been harboured at Ganeshkhera. In the river beat, which has produced so many

---

[1] "Your Majesty, there is the jungle. We shall see what we shall see."
[2] Cut his throat.

AN ELEPHANT MAULED

tigers, the tigress came down along the right bank of the stream, swam across in front of the guns, and went on up the hill on the left bank, being fired at several times. The last shot, from Edwards, wounded her, and she rolled down the hill into the river bed, where she was wounded again. Then she lay up in the Jaman bushes between the guns and the beaters. Immediately afterwards the tiger came up to the Duke, who killed him. 'Randullah' was then brought to the 'mools,' together with another elephant borrowed from Badaora for the occasion; and the Duke on the former and Edwards on the latter moved slowly towards the place where the tigress had last been seen. She came out with a roar to meet them. The Badaora elephant turned tail and bolted; and the tigress, swinging away from him, charged 'Randullah' and got home on his head. He shook her off and pounded her for some minutes with his fore-legs. She crept away into the Jaman. Meanwhile the Badaora mahout, having regained control of his elephant, had brought him back to the scene of action. After a short interval both elephants were sent forward again, and the tigress was found dead, a mass of crumpled flesh and broken bones. 'Randullah's' wounds were serious. He took a year to recover from them; but his nerve was not affected, and for the remainder of his sporting life he was as staunch as ever.

After the advent of the railway polo was played at Goonah more regularly and with much greater attention to individual and collective improvement than it had ever been before. A new ground was made; and Colin Campbell, a very keen enthusiast, set to work to train a team for the Bengal Cavalry Tournament. He was immediately successful. In February 1897 he went up to Umballa with Capper, Ibrahim Khan, and Cotgrave, playing in the order named, he himself playing back; and the Challenge Cup, for the first time, was brought to Goonah.

The opportunity for competing in these big tournaments at Umballa and Meerut, which the railway now afforded, provided a new interest for the British officers of the regiment, which perhaps was somewhat needed; for the jungles were getting more and more empty, game was being shot out, and ' ittafaq hankas ' were becoming less frequent and less productive. Moreover, many of the great tiger jungles in Scindia's territory, which had been ours without question for shooting purposes during the minority of the late Maharajah, were closed to us when His Highness came of age. Thus Goonah became a polo centre, as much so as Agar ever had been; and we trained many ponies, we practised very hard, we entered for many tournaments, and, on the whole, we were very successful.

CHAPTER XIV.

THE TIRAH CAMPAIGN.

THE year 1897 was memorable for the surprising wave of hostility to the British Government which swept the North-West Frontier from the Tochi to the Malakand and forced us to keep an army of 40,000 men in the field for six months before our rebellious neighbours were finally subdued. The rising was sudden and completely unexpected. There was nothing on the surface to indicate the existence of a general discontent or even to suggest a possible cause for it. Beyond such trival excuses as the enhancement of the salt tax and the failure of the British Government to restore their runaway women, which were obviously insincere, the tribesmen gave no reason for breaking out. It is not, however, necessary to look further for the origin of trouble, in this or any other frontier dispute, than the religious fanaticism of the tribes and the cunning with which the mullahs seize the opportunities of the moment to set it aflame. It was unfortunate for the peace of the border that, in the spring of this year, Turkey had inflicted a severe defeat upon Greece. To the tribesman there is no difference between Greek and English. Both are Faringhi ;

and he believed, on the assurance of his mullahs, not only that Greece had been conquered and annexed, but that Aden and the Suez Canal were in the hands of the Sultan of Turkey and that England was tottering to her fall. Thus he was easily persuaded that the time had come to assert the superiority of Islam in the East by force of arms. He had one or two old scores to wipe out, too, though these he did not mention. He distrusted, in particular, the motives of the British Government in delimiting the frontier between Afghanistan and independent territory by the Durand Line. This work had been in progress during the last three years, and the tribes had taken every opportunity to hinder it. At Wano in November 1894 the Mahsud Wazirs had attacked the camp of the Boundary Commission and its escort, inflicting severe losses. Farther to the north-east, in the Mohmand country, the demarcation came to a standstill altogether. The tribesmen here would have no more of the Durand Line. The Amir of Kabul[1] was on their side, too, and would become an active supporter, so at least they had been told. His Highness—he had not yet become His Majesty at this time—had recently written a book on 'Jehad,' and had been proclaimed " Light of Union and of the Faith "; but his religious fervour did not carry him so far as to cross swords with the British Government. His attitude was, in fact, throughout the whole disturbance perfectly correct. The tribesmen, nevertheless, were confident that their hour of triumph was at hand. The summer months were

[1] Abdurrahman Khan.

marked by a series of outrages. On the 10th of June the escort to the Political Officer in the Tochi Valley was treacherously attacked. The Commander and one other British officer were killed, and the escort was forced to retire to Datta Khel. On the 26th of July the Malakand and Chakdara forts were attacked with equal suddenness. Here, however, the tribesmen were driven off. On the 7th of August the Haddah Mullah, with a force of 5000 Mohmands, made a raid upon the post at Shabkadr. He, too, was defeated, though he fought for three long days. There was severe fighting also during this month in the Kurram and on the Samana range. The posts of Gulistan and Saragheri were attacked. It was here that the Sikhs upheld their name so proudly. The little garrison of Saragheri held the fort until numbers overpowered them, and died at their posts to a man. These events led to a concentration of troops at Rawal Pindi as a precaution against further raiding. A movable column was at the same time formed at Peshawar. In the Khyber, however, there was no sign of disturbance until the third week in August. For sixteen years the tribal levies, which had developed during this period from a corps of ragged jezailchis[1] into 'The Khyber Rifles' under a British officer, had kept the pass open without disorder and almost without incident; but on the 21st of August it became known that an Afridi lashkar[2] of 10,000 men had set out from Bagh, the Headquarters of the clan in Tirah, to attack the Khyber posts. The serious nature of the trouble

---

[1] Men armed with 'jezails,' long-barrelled matchlocks.
[2] Army.

was thus disclosed. The whole border was up. The concentration of a few troops here and there along the frontier was no longer a practical solution of the difficulty. Swift and severe punishment of the offending clans was the only safeguard against further aggression; and so, in order that the whole Afridi tribe might be made to feel the weight of the British Government, it was decided that a force should march into their mountains, deemed by themselves so completely inaccessible, and exact reparation for their folly.

During September, therefore, a main column, consisting of two divisions, each of two brigades of infantry with divisional troops, was formed at Kohat for the invasion of Tirah. At the same time two subsidiary columns were formed, one at Kohat and one at Peshawar, to support the advance of the main column in such manner as circumstances might dictate. The whole was under the command of Sir William Lockhart. On 16th October the main column was in position along the line Hangu-Shinawari, ready for the advance. After severe fighting at Dargai on the 18th and 20th, made memorable by the attack of the Gordon Highlanders across the open spur below the enemy's sangars, the heights were cleared, and the troops moved down into the Khanki valley. On the 28th, after a week's halt devoted to road-making and the strengthening of posts on the line of communications, the column marched to Ghandaki at the foot of the Sampagha pass, which was captured on the following day. The bivouac that night was in the Mastura valley, between the Sampagha and Arhanga passes, and here a day's halt was called to allow the baggage to come up. On the 31st the Arhanga was attacked. It was the enemy's last position covering his stronghold at Bagh. He held it with his usual courage; but, reduced in numbers and short of ammunition, he was compelled early in the day to disperse, conquered but not yet subdued, to his homes in the Maidan valley. At 3 o'clock on that afternoon the advanced guard of the British column marched into Maidan, and next morning a small force of two battalions and a mountain battery was detached from the main body to occupy Bagh. A week later Sir William Lockhart decided, for political as well as strategical reasons, to encamp his whole force here. By the 21st November the move was accomplished.

Meanwhile the jirgahs were gradually coming in. The terms of the British Government were explained to them, and, for the most part, were accepted. There were, however, certain sections of the Orakzai clan who, with the Chamkannis, still remained defiant. These folk dwell in the rugged country between the Kurram and the head of the Maidan valley, which is drained by the Khurmana river. The fact that their territory lay on the western side of the intervening hills gave them a false sense of security. They reckoned that the main British column was too fully occupied in the Afridi country, on the eastern side, to risk an invasion of their own. In their reply to Lockhart's proclamation they even ventured to dictate terms to the British Government; but they reckoned without that subsidiary column which had been formed at Kohat and, now known as the Kurram Movable Column, under Colonel Hill of the 2nd Gurkhas, had moved up the valley to Sadda, where the Khurmana runs into the Kurram river. Lockhart now called upon Hill to co-operate with the main column in the punishment of these recalcitrant tribes.

The Central India Horse formed part of Hill's column. It was a strange country for cavalry. Yet there are occasions—the charge of the 13th Lancers at Shabkadr was one of them—when a tribal lashkar can be driven off a hillside into comparatively open country; and if cavalry is at hand on these occasions to charge down upon them they rarely fight again. Moreover, being now armed with a long-range firearm, cavalry is not wasted even if the opportunity for the use of the *arme blanche* does not occur. There were two regiments of cavalry with Hill's column, and they fought as infantry all the time.

It is remarkable that on this, the first, occasion on which four squadrons of Central India Horse were ordered on active service after the separation of the two regiments, when there was no longer a material link between them, when they had nothing in common but spirit, not only that they should have still desired, but should have been permitted by military authorities, to send not one regiment intact as might have been expected, but two squadrons from each after the usual custom. Such, however, was the case. Two squadrons of the 2nd Regiment left Goonah on the 11th September, and reached Kohat on the 19th. On the following day the two squadrons of the 1st Regiment arrived from Agar; and the combined regiment was formed, with Colonel George Money, the Commandant of the 1st, in command, Captain Bell as Adjutant and Captain Malcolm Moore in medical charge. The two squadrons of the 1st, commanded by Captain F. C. Grant and Lieutenant A. P. Browne respectively, were called 'A' and 'B.' The 2nd Regiment squadrons, commanded by Major Colin Campbell and Lieutenant A. Cooke respectively, were called 'C' and 'D.' 'A' and 'C' Squadrons were composed of Mahomedans, 'B' and 'D' of Sikhs. Browne's squadron of Sikhs, incidentally, was found on arrival at Kohat to be four sabres over strength, four furlough men having stowed themselves in the train at Amritsar. The Squadron Subalterns were Lieutenants Barr, Birdwood, Spence, and Hewlett. During the rest of September and the first half of October the regiment remained at Kohat, employed for the most part on escort duty, with detachments at Hangu, Thal, Doaba, and Sadda; and on the 15th of October regimental Headquarters were established at the latter place. On the following day Colonel Hill arrived at Sadda and assumed command of his column, which consisted of the 3rd Field Battery, Royal Artillery, the 6th Bengal Cavalry, the Central India Horse, the 12th Khelat-i-Ghilzai Regiment, the 5th Gurkhas, the Kapurthala Infantry, the Kurram Militia, and a Maxim-gun detachment of the Royal Scots Fusiliers.

During the next three weeks the column maintained a watchful attitude, with posts at all important points along the Kurram river between Thal and Parachinar, no forward movement being required

of it until the main column had dealt with the
Afridis on the other side of the hills. Meanwhile,
however, the Masuzai and Alisherzai sections of the
Orakzai tribe were becoming restive. On the 26th
October they built a barrier across the Khurmana
Darra, and a week later a lashkar of some 3000
men assembled in this neighbourhood with the
apparent intention of attacking some of our posts
in the main valley. To disperse these fellows, and
so to clear his flank of the menace to which it was
now exposed, Hill decided to make a reconnaissance
in force of the whole of the Khurmana Darra. On
the morning of the 7th November he led a small
force up the defile. 'A' and 'D' Squadrons of
the Central India Horse, the former mounted under
Captain Grant and the latter dismounted under
Lieutenant Cooke, with Birdwood and Hewlett as
their subalterns, formed part of it; the other units
being 100 rifles of the Khelat-i-Ghilzai Regiment,
260 rifles of the 5th Gurkhas, 100 rifles of the
Kapurthala Infantry, and 400 rifles of the Kurram
Militia, with the Maxims of the Royal Scots Fusiliers.
The defile was seven miles long, the steep hills on
either side being covered with a low scrub jungle.
No opposition was encountered until Hissar, at
the head of the valley, was reached at 11 A.M.
Here a few shots were fired; but the tribesmen,
unprepared for Hill's movement, could make no
serious effort to resist him. By the time, however,
that the retirement began—a couple of hours later—
the Masus had collected a large number of fighting
men and, in the manner of frontier tribes, began
from the outset to hamper the return to camp,

always for this reason a difficult operation, by following up the column along the spurs on either side of the route. The 5th Gurkhas, skilled in this form of warfare, formed the rear-guard; and detachments from other units, including 'D' Squadron Central India Horse and a non-commissioned officer and thirty-five men of the Kapurthala Infantry, were used to help them in crowning the heights on either side. The Kapurthala men were exceedingly unfortunate. They were posted, before the retirement began, on a hill overlooking the defile; and when the column moved off they were recalled by signal, which was duly acknowledged. They started to rejoin the rear-guard, but, descending by the re-entrant instead of by the spur, were quickly lost to view amongst the ravines at the bottom of the valley. The rear-guard waited for them, and, whilst so doing, were subjected to a fierce attack by the oncoming tribesmen, who, however, were driven back with heavy loss to Hissar. When the firing had ceased a report was made to the Commander that the Kapurthala picket had rejoined the column, and the retirement was continued; but it was not until after dark that the 5th Gurkhas and the dismounted squadron of the Central India Horse reached the camp at Sadda. Hill then discovered that the Kapurthala picket was missing. It was afterwards learnt that it had descended into a ravine where a jungle fire, ignited by the enemy, was burning fiercely. The enemy, from the hills above, then hurled rocks upon the hapless soldiers, who were hampered by the fire as much as by the difficulties of the ground, and finally closing down upon them destroyed them. Not, however, without feeling the fighting power of the Sikh; for the Masus themselves admitted that fourteen of their number had been killed. The 5th Gurkhas had one man killed and three wounded during the action. The Central India Horse had no casualties.

As a result of this reconnaissance the Orakzai tribe, with the single exception of the Masus, agreed to terms. The Chamkannis, untouched as yet, showed no signs of submission. Hill, therefore, received Lockhart's order to move again to Hissar and to co-operate with a column under General Gaselee, which was to advance in that direction from Bagh. 'B' and 'C' Squadrons of the Central India Horse, dismounted, under Browne and Campbell respectively, with Barr and Spence as their Squadron Subalterns, and half of 'A' Squadron, mounted, under Grant, formed part of Hill's column for this operation. It reached Hissar early on the 29th November. The village was taken at the point of the bayonet by the Kurram Militia, who fired it; and the column then moved on to Lwara Mela, where it bivouacked for the night. Meanwhile Gaselee's column, after some fighting on the Lozaka pass, had reached Dargai, at the head of the Khurmana valley, whence heliographic communication was established with Hill. On this day the Masuzai jirgah came into camp and expressed their willingness to submit. The only casualty during the day was Captain Grant, who broke his leg. On the following morning the two columns concentrated unopposed at Lwara Mela.

The subjection of the Chamkannis still remained to be accomplished. Accordingly Hill was called upon to march against their principal village, Thabai, seven miles from the camp at Lwara Mela. On the 1st December he advanced in two columns: the right under Colonel George Money, consisting of half a company of Bombay Sappers and Miners, the Kohat Mountain Battery, three dismounted squadrons of the Central India Horse, the 2nd Battalion 4th Gurkhas, and some Gurkha Scouts; and the left, under Colonel Gordon of the 6th Bengal Cavalry, consisting of 300 rifles of the Khelat-i-Ghilzai Regiment, 100 rifles of the 1st Battalion 5th Gurkhas, three dismounted squadrons of the 6th Bengal Cavalry, 100 rifles of the Kapurthala Infantry, and the Maxim-gun detachment of the Royal Scots Fusiliers. The right column, advancing through the Masuzai country past the villages of Mobin and Tsappar, and dropping a squadron of the Central India Horse at the former lest the Masus should be tempted into mischief, reached the Kotal commanding the Thabai valley at 10 A.M. without opposition. The left column was less fortunate. The track was very difficult and the tribesmen most pertinacious. A very sharp fight occurred, in which Battye of the 6th Bengal Cavalry was killed, and two British officers, one Indian officer and twenty men were wounded, the enemy too losing heavily, before the column reached the head of the valley; and it was not until noon that Gordon and Money joined hands. Meanwhile the Kohat Mountain Battery had shelled the village of Thabai and the Sappers and the Central India Horse had descended into the valley, whilst the 4th Gurkhas had occupied a hill on the farther side to protect the troops during the necessary work of destruction. It was impossible, however, during the time available to dislodge the enemy from all the surrounding crags. This operation was left until the following day, and at 4 P.M. the order was given to retire to Lwara Mela. The enemy as usual attempted to seize the heights commanding the line of retirement, but were forestalled by the Gurkha Scouts, and camp was reached at 6.30, one man of the Central India Horse being wounded during the march.

On the morning of the 2nd Hill took out a column, which did not include the Central India Horse, though Browne, Spence, and Moore accompanied him as orderly officers, to deal with the tribesmen hitherto unpunished. Advancing by the route taken by Money's column on the previous day, he found the hills round Thabai strongly occupied. The 5th Gurkhas, covered by the fire of the Kohat Mountain Battery, moved rapidly across the valley, attacked the sangars with spirit, and drove the enemy down the other side of the hill with the loss of only five of their own men. The Chamkannis left thirty dead bodies on the hill-top, and carried off many more, both killed and wounded. It was enough for them. They fought no more.

On the following day Hill and Gaselee parted, the latter moving to Khanki Bazar, whilst Hill, with the Kurram movable column, returned unopposed to Sadda.

The remaining days of December were passed on the upper waters of the Kurram river, regimental

Headquarters being first at Parachinar, then at Sadda. Before the end of the month they were shifted to Alizai, where the British officers spent a lively Christmas; and in January the regiment moved by easy stages down-stream to Thal, which was reached on the 8th. On the 26th all four squadrons left Thal for railhead at Kushalgarh on the homeward journey, and arrived at Goonah on the 6th of February.

During the operations described above, the depot wings, under Captains Baynes and Robertson (Masters, the permanent Commandant of the 2nd, being at this time on the staff of the Malakhand Field Force), changed places; and when the combined regiment returned to Goonah the two squadrons of the 1st remained there, whilst those of the 2nd continued the journey to Agar by road.

Of the four Squadron Subalterns who served in Tirah, Spence had succeeded Cameron as Adjutant of the 2nd in February 1897, but was sent with the Service wing because at the moment there was no other subaltern available. Barr, who came from the East Surrey Regiment, joined the 1st Regiment on 20th January 1896, and in 1900 was appointed personal assistant to the Resident at Hyderabad, his father. He died in England towards the end of the Great War. Birdwood joined the 1st Regiment on the 23rd February 1896 from the Worcestershire Regiment. He served with the Central India Horse in Persia in 1912, was given the command of the 27th Light Cavalry shortly afterwards, and during the Great War rose to the rank of Brigadier-General. Hewlett joined the 2nd Regiment just before the Tirah campaign. He succeeded eventually to the command of the 1st Regiment, which he led during the Great War in Palestine.

Two other subalterns joined in 1897, Lieutenants W. St C. Muscroft and A. N. Hood. The former, who was appointed in May, went to the Commissariat Department two years later. Hood joined at the same time as Hewlett. He was a very popular young officer of brilliant promise, but his career was a short one, for, after a period of duty as Adjutant of the Viceroy's Bodyguard, he went to the South African War and was killed at Yser Spruit on the 25th February 1902.

During Surgeon Captain Moore's absence with the regiment on field service the duties of Medical Officer in charge of the depot wing of the 2nd Regiment were discharged by Surgeon Major D. B. Spencer. Surgeon Lieutenant M'Ardle was, during this period, Medical Officer with the depot wing of the 1st Regiment. He had been appointed temporarily in June on Shaw's retirement; but when the service wings returned to Central India he relinquished this appointment, the permanent vacancy being filled by Captain Bruce Seton.

The two regiments now settled down again in Central India, under Money and Masters, to prepare themselves for their next encounter with an enemy, to beat the jungles, to play polo, and, since they were now under the direct control of Army Headquarters, to be inspected regularly by every kind of expert from a master-armourer to the Inspector-General of Cavalry, and to attend more manœuvres, assaults-at-arms, and Staff rides than it is possible or necessary to record. Money and Masters were not, however, much longer at the head of affairs. The former became Assistant Adjutant-General of the Presidency District in February 1899, and, on his retirement to England in September 1900, was followed in the same appointment by the latter. Both these officers had passed nearly all their service hitherto on regimental duty, Masters alone having had, in addition to his Malakhand service, a short break in an extra-regimental appointment in 1890 and 1891, as Inspector of Imperial Service Cavalry at Gwalior. Money died in Switzerland not long after his retirement. He was the best turned out man in the Army and, having a remarkable eye, was an adept at every game that was played. Masters, in his youth, was a skilful man-at-arms, with peculiar dodges of his own, and won some of the principal events at the Military Tournament in London in 1882. He was a gentle and very powerful horseman, and there was little that he did not know concerning the ways of the Indian soldier.

The next two commandants were strangers to the regiment, one comparative and one complete. Drummond succeeded Money on the 6th February 1899; and when Masters went to Calcutta Colonel Dawson of the 9th Bengal Lancers, familiarly known throughout the Bengal Cavalry as 'Uncle,' was brought in to take his place.

CHAPTER XV.

BETWEEN TIRAH AND PERSIA.

THE interval of fourteen years between the last and the next expedition, more peaceful and less romantic than any period which the regiment had yet known, was marked, officially, by certain important administrative changes and, in the realm of sport, by considerable activity on the polo field. Within a year of the return of the two wings from Tirah what was known as the 'Squadron System' was introduced throughout the Indian cavalry, and the 'Troop,' as an administrative unit, ceased to exist. The date of the Gazette of India notifying the change was the 18th February 1899. Regiments were in future to be classed by squadrons instead of by troops, and the Risaldar, or Rissaidar, was to hold administrative command of a 'half squadron,' though in the field he could only command a tactical troop, the Squadron Leader both for tactical and administrative purposes being a British officer. The classification of each regiment of Central India Horse was to be two squadrons of Sikhs and two of Mahomedans, the latter being, in the 1st Regiment, Pathans and Ghakkars, and, in the 2nd, Tiwanas and Rangars; and this classification lasted until the reconstitution of the whole of the Indian cavalry after the Great War.

Four years later another, and more startling, change was made. Until the year 1895 there had been three armies in India: that of Bengal, that of Madras, and that of Bombay. The Bengal Army was commanded by the Commander-in-Chief in India, who was responsible to the Viceroy; but the Madras and Bombay Armies each had a Commander-in-Chief of its own, who was responsible to the Governor of the Presidency. When these Presidential Armies were abolished, and the whole of the Army in India was brought under one chief, the Presidential numbers and designations of regiments remained unaltered, and thus, in 1903, there were still three distinct bodies of cavalry, with not a little jealousy between them. Officers of Bengal cavalry, and of the cavalry of the Panjab Frontier Force, considered their regiments vastly superior to those of Bombay or Madras. Cadets did not as a rule apply to be posted to either of the latter, though they accepted appointment gladly if they wished for mounted service and could get no other; but to become a Bengal Lancer or a Piffer was the ambition of every young soldier who was fond of a horse and could not afford to satisfy his sporting instincts in England. Not that there was much, if anything, to choose between the three bodies in the matter either of efficiency or of fighting value. There were magnificent regiments in the Madras and Bombay Armies, with stories of very honourable fighting on their records; but there was reason for the young men's choice. There was glamour in the name of 'Bengal Lancer.' The *beaux sabreurs* of the Mutiny had raised regiments of their own; to these had been given the name of 'Bengal Lancers,' and at the end of the nineteenth century the echoes of the Mutiny had not died away. The Central India Horse had belonged to no Presidency. It was a local corps, belonging to no Commander-in-Chief, and the names of officers of all three Presidencies were entered on its rolls; but we shuddered if any suggestion was made that we were not in essence Bengal cavalry, and we found some satisfaction in our unofficial recognition as such when we were allowed to compete in the Bengal Cavalry Polo Tournament.

On the 2nd October 1903 all Indian regiments were brought on to one list, with their numbers running consecutively throughout. The thing was very cleverly done. Changes are always unpopular in an army which, irrespective of politics, is invariably conservative to a man; and twenty-two years previously the introduction of the Territorial system in the English infantry, with the abolition of the old regimental numbers, had caused a great deal of dissatisfaction. So bitter, indeed, was the feeling that one gallant regiment went so far as to incur the displeasure of the War Office by burying, with full military honours, an effigy of itself under the old numerical title, which certain soldiers of the battalion exhumed during the night and deposited near the quarter-guard labelled "Ninety twa, not deid yet." The Indian authorities, possibly mindful of this incident, were careful to reduce irritation to a minimum. They tempered the wind. The Bengal cavalry regiments, which together formed about half of the cavalry force in India, were allowed to retain their old numbers from one to nineteen. The other numbers had to be altered, but the Piffer regiments, from being 1st to 5th Panjab Cavalry, merely became 21st to 25th, which was not a severe break. Similarly the Bombay regiments became 31st and 32nd Lancers and 33rd Light Cavalry instead of 1st, 2nd, and 3rd Bombay. The Poona Horse, Sindh Horse, Jacob's Horse, and the Baluch Horse, which were really the 4th to 7th Regiments of Bombay Cavalry, became the 34th to 37th, and retained their personal and local titles. The Hyderabad Contingent and Madras regiments were obliged, however, to suffer a complete change. The former became the 20th, 29th, and 30th, and the latter the 26th, 27th, and 28th. Likewise the two regiments of Central India Horse became the 38th and 39th, whilst retaining the old local denomination. We disliked the new numbers very much. There was a tendency, too, especially amongst Departmental babus, to address us as " 38th and 39th Horse " ; but of this we made complaints, which were successful. The feeling did not last long. In the nature of things it could not do so, and the older generation soon became uncomfortably aware that young men were growing up who were positively proud of the objectionable new numbers. The only regiment which retained its old title without the infliction of a number was The Guides, and we were as jealous of them as we could be.

Meanwhile life at Agar and Goonah was becoming more and more civilised. The Grand Trunk Road had become much safer and, to British officers, less well known; for the dacoit had practically disappeared, and, since transfers of officers from one regiment to another now very rarely took place and could be carried out by railway when they did, the long rides through the jungles were no longer necessary. Big game, too, had become less abundant, though the 'ittafaq hankas' continued, albeit less frequently, a hot weather 'shoot' was organised whenever possible, and a certain number of tigers, panthers, and bears were bagged every year. Polo consequently became the principal amusement. It became a study, almost a profession. Before 1896 there was but little collective practice. The old tournaments at Bombay were marked by brilliant individual performance rather than by team work. There were no 'numbers.' There were just three forwards and a back, though the youngest member of the team was expected to do the 'riding off' for the other three. Moreover, the ponies were so small, the limit being 13.2, that very little preliminary training was required. The new purchase was taken straight into a game instead of being broken gradually for a period of six to twelve months, or even more, according to his temperament and aptitude. As the height limit was raised the necessity for gradual training became more urgent, and before the end of the nineteenth century this had become the chief occupation both of officers and men when off duty. For the men were in this, as in all things, our stand-by. Our peculiar situation, alone in the jungles, made this inevitable; and it was very pleasant. It is fair, without boasting, to express a doubt whether officers of any other corps formed so close a touch with their soldiers. The men were with us in all our doings. They told us much about themselves, and, on the polo ground or in the shikar camp, were wont to discuss all sorts of matters, even politics, with a frankness which would have astonished officers of most other regiments. Many of them played polo, on their baggage ponies in early days, and were engaged, as the game developed, in training troop horses for the purpose. Colin Campbell was the first to organise a semblance of a Polo School, and to this he owed his success in the Bengal Cavalry Tournament of 1897. A couple of years later A. B. Mayne, who had been tutor to the young Maharajah of Jodhpore, returned to the regiment with a string of twenty-eight ponies. He had learnt the value of systematic training, for about this time several of the princes of India had taken up the game very seriously, and Jodhpore was one of them. The Maharajah of Patiala had indeed started the fashion in the 'eighties, assisted by the celebrated Hira Singh, who had left the 12th Bengal Cavalry to join him; but by now other chiefs, including Hyderabad, Bhopal, and Alwar, as well as Jodhpore, had followed his example, and, with the aid of better ponies and of players who did little else, had introduced a very high standard of play. Mayne began at once to improve the schooling. He had good material to work on. Spence and Cameron and Hewlett, who were then in the 2nd, were all good players, and Cotgrave, then in the 1st, was on his day second to none in India. Amongst the men, too, there were several fine performers. Maksud Ali of the 1st was worthy of a place in a tournament team, and often had one; whilst in the 2nd, Ibrahim Khan was already well known outside the regiment. He was indeed a great player. Dhokal Singh of Jodhpore and Shah Mirza Beg of Hyderabad were scarcely his superiors. He could play a wonderful game even on a half-trained pony. He could hit very hard and straight, and could 'bump' severely; he was in fact a difficult opponent. A Rangar of the village of Kalanaur, he rose to the rank of Rissaidar. He served with the regiment in Tirah and in Persia, and was killed on the polo ground at Agar just after his return from that country.

To put his schooling into practice Mayne organised a tournament at Goonah, the only one that was ever held there. It was intended that this should become an annual event, to be held alternately at Goonah and Saugor, but it did not survive. It was won by the 1st Central India Horse, who entered two teams, Cotgrave being the mainstay of the winners. Against us in the Bhopal team was playing a well-known man of the name of Abdul Wahad. He and his brother 'Godoo,' whose real name nobody ever seemed to know—it was Fakkaruddin Khan,—had, some years before this, been distinguished players in the 1st Regiment. They were sons of an old Risaldar, Sheikh Shubrati, a remarkable man who had been bandmaster as well as Wardi Major. Abdul Wahad continued to play for several years after this tournament. He led many a good team against the regiment, but never defeated it.

Mayne's next effort was in the Championship

THE IMPORTATION OF 'BOUNDERS'

Tournament at Lucknow in January 1900. A strong team, individually speaking, from both regiments, calling itself the 'Goonah Freebooters,' went up with thirty-five ponies in the hope of meeting the smart players from Patiala, who, however, withdrew at the last moment. Our players were Hewlett, Ibrahim, Mayne, and Cotgrave. Mayne, however, broke his collar-bone in a practice game, and Watson, who was on the Staff and came down as fifth man, was called upon to play for him. Very weak teams were opposed to us, and we won very easily. It was in fact an inglorious walk-over.

It was fortunate that in this year the height limit was raised from 13.3 to 14.1, for the price of ponies was rising rapidly, and it would have been impossible any longer for Indian regiments to compete in first-class tournaments with the limited resources at the disposal of their British officers. The new rule made it possible to play regimental horses. About this time, too, the small well-bred Waler from Queensland, commonly known as the 'Bounder,' was being imported in large quantities, and at a price which the Chanda Fund could afford to pay. These, therefore, were purchased. The Arab was discarded, though Watson during his tenure of command of the 2nd continued to buy a few of them; the Indian country-bred was by now dying out, and was practically unprocurable even if wanted, and the Waler thus became the stock remount of the Central India Horse. He is not so easily trained as the Arab, who has the polo temperament by nature, but, once made, he is, by reason of his scope and power, a better mount on the polo field, and he commands a higher quotation on the market.

After another attempt at the Championship and one at the Inter-Regimental, neither of them successful, Mayne left the regiment, and the polo schooling devolved upon Hewlett, who prepared a very good team for the tournament at King Edward's Coronation Durbar. This, however, was won by the Poona Horse, who beat us by a very narrow margin in the semi-finals.

Early in 1905, after winning a tournament at Bareilly, a team consisting of Eckford, Ibrahim, Hewlett, and Pitcher went on to Umballa for the Indian Cavalry Tournament. Here the 18th Tiwana Lancers beat us after a very exciting game. Near the call of time the score was Central India Horse, 3 goals and 3 subsidiaries; 18th, 3 goals and 1 subsidiary. In the last moments the 18th hit a goal, and so won. The subsidiary is now a thing of the past. It was invented to discount the number of ties which had become so frequent about the beginning of the twentieth century, and, since no number of subsidiaries was considered equal to one goal, should have solved the difficulty without injuring the play. This, however, did not happen. Players seemed just as content to hit a subsidiary as a goal, with the consequence that the art of straight hitting, which, young players will do well to remember, is an essential feature of the game, received much less attention on the practice ground than it deserved. The subsidiary was therefore abolished after a very few years' trial.

This match against the 18th was neither our first

nor our last against that gallant corps, who have ever been our particular friends and rivals. They were raised at the same time and in the same locality as ourselves, being known at the commencement of their career as the Mahratta Horse. We owed to them our fine squadron of Tiwanas. We admired them very much and very sincerely, but we were deadly enemies on the polo field, and we were always very evenly matched.

In the autumn of this year there was a small tournament at Indore which brought to light an exceedingly clever young player in the person of Jemadar Mahomed Bahadur Khan, a Tiwana Malik and nephew of Risaldar Major Ghulam Mahomed Khan, who forthwith became a regular member of the team. He played with his head, as the saying is, and, being a particularly straight hitter, was a useful man near the opponent's goal; but he lacked the fire of players like Ibrahim Khan and Dhokal Singh, and could not always 'get going' in the early part of the game.

In the spring of 1906 Colonel W. A. Watson, who had done no regimental duty for some years, took command of the 2nd. Being a keen player himself, and determined, moreover, to win the Indian Cavalry Tournament again, he allowed a good deal of latitude to other players in the way of leave for minor tournaments, and made the polo school more strenuous than ever. He was a very light weight and could consequently ride Arabs, invariably stallions, without suffering for want of pace. It was impossible, however, to enter at Umballa during the following winter; but there was a very good tournament at Agra during the visit of the Amir of Afghanistan, and Mahomed Bahadur, Watson, Hewlett, and Pitcher, playing in the order named, very nearly won it. After defeating several good teams, including the Royals led by De Lisle, they were just beaten in the finals by the 15th Hussars.

The ensuing cold weather began with the Indore Tournament, which was now becoming quite an important event. We entered two teams and expected to win it easily, but Watson, who was playing in the first, was in very bad form and both teams suffered defeat. The first team was then reorganised, Todd taking Watson's place, the other players being Mahomed Bahadur, Hewlett, and Pitcher. After winning the Cup at Cawnpore this team went up to Umballa in 1908 and reached the finals, when, however, it was beaten by the 4th Cavalry. In the semi-finals of this tournament there was the usual desperate encounter with the 18th, which was marred unfortunately by a bad accident. Clive Wigram[1] was knocked over by one of our players and carried off the field. The Umpire gave it a 'dangerous foul.' Now there was an excellent rule, in the case of a player being disabled by a dangerous foul, giving the fouled side the option of withdrawing a player from the other side and continuing the game with six players only. The Captain of the 18th, Captain Frank Maxwell, V.C., one of the most gallant of men killed in the Great War, quite rightly set this rule in motion;

[1] Afterwards Colonel Sir Clive Wigram, Private Secretary to H.M. King George V.

but unfortunately for his side he selected Pitcher, who, steady 'back' as he was known to be, was not the best player in our team. Todd, on the other hand, was brilliant in any place in the game, and, unknown to the 18th, was just as good a 'back' as Pitcher; and the result was that the match ended in our favour. In the finals against the 4th, however, neither Todd nor Pitcher was at his best, and, to our great disappointment, we thus missed a good double event; for whilst the 2nd Regiment was playing in the polo matches the 1st was competing in the Tentpegging Tournament, which it won. To have carried off both the Tentpegging and the Polo Cup would indeed have been a triumph; but it was not to be.[1]

After this, however, the team being in very good practice, successes came more frequently. We won the Indian Cavalry Tournament three years in succession, in 1909, 1910, and 1911. Mahomed Bahadur played on all three occasions; Watson, Hewlett, Todd, and Eckford each played twice, Walter Daunt replacing Eckford, incapacitated, during one of the games; and in the third year D. De M. Fraser was brought into the team as No. 1. In 1913 we entered again, but were unsuccessful.

At a later period—towards the end of the Great War in fact—Hewlett took command of the 1st Regiment in Syria, and, the war being over, devoted himself with his usual ardour to the preparation of

[1] We were not allowed to enter a combined team of both regiments for the Indian Cavalry Polo Tournament, though this was permitted in the case of the Inter-Regimental. We entered a combined team three or four times for the latter, but, before the Great War, did not succeed in winning it.

a new team. He found two unusually good players in Captain Williams and Lieutenant George, both of whom distinguished themselves on the polo field in years later than those covered by this book; and in the spring of 1920 he took these two, with Major Hutchison as 'back' and himself as No. 3, to Cairo, where he won the Inter-Regimental Tournament against teams from the English, the Indian, and the Egyptian Armies.

In other sporting contests during the period between Tirah and Persia the most conspicuous individual successes were those of Cameron and Hewlett with the hog-spear. Cameron, who had carried off the Jodhpore Cup in 1897, won the Kadir Cup in 1903, on a very bright little thoroughbred called 'Mousquetaire'; and Hewlett won the Guzerat Cup early in 1899, as well as the Pony Hog-hunters' Point-to-Point. He followed this up by spending the hot weather on leave at Cawnpore, where he won the Silver Spear for the highest number of 'first spears' taken during the season.

Of strictly military events during this period there were but few. Neither regiment, of course, took part in the 'White Man's War' in South Africa, though both sent out horses for the Mounted Infantry. In the year 1900 there was a famine in Western Malwa, with the consequence that very little grass could be obtained within reach of Agar, and it became necessary to send 240 horses of the 2nd Regiment from Agar to Patai, near Goonah, where they were kept until the cold weather, when the regiments changed stations. Soon after its arrival at Agar the 1st Regiment was obliged, for the same reason, to send some horses to Mehidpur.

The Order Book of the 1st Regiment for this year records, on the 25th September, the death of the office babu, Gopal Swamy, a genial friend to officers and men alike. He had been Adjutant's Clerk in Mayne's Horse, and had forty years of faithful service to his credit. The two regimental babus were, in fact, nothing less than regimental institutions. They knew every detail of administration, and were never flurried or unwilling to work. The clerk of the 2nd, Babu Maniruddin, though not such an amusing character as Gopal Swamy, was just as reliable and served just as long. Towards the end of his service he was granted, to his intense delight, a chair in Durbar,[1] and, on his retirement, was made an Honorary Magistrate. He had a peculiarly ornate but somewhat illegible handwriting, which, when we came under the orders of the Commander-in-Chief, brought us into occasional difficulties with the more sophisticated specimen in the office of Divisional Headquarters.

The next year saw a change in the armament of the regiment. Hitherto the official mistrust of Indian troops, born of the Mutiny, had condemned them to the use of a firearm inferior to that carried by their English comrades. When the latter were armed with the Martini-Henry rifle, the sepoy and the sowar were entrusted only with the Snider, and it was not until a superior weapon was issued to English troops that the Indian were promoted from

[1] This gave him the status of an officer.

the Snider to the Martini. But with the dawn of the twentieth century the idea, initiated by Disraeli, that Indian troops might be called upon not only to serve outside India but to fight alongside English against a European foe, began to shape itself as a coming reality; and it was obvious that for such a duty they must be equally well armed. The Martini was therefore relegated, like the Snider thirteen years before, to the arsenal, and in September 1901 was replaced, with equal jubilation, by the .303 Lee-Metford magazine carbine. Two years later this again was replaced by the long rifle, which enabled cavalry henceforward to conduct a fire fight on level terms with infantry.

Meanwhile there had been a revival of the old controversy as to which was the best *arme blanche*, the lance or the sword. There will always be advocates of both; but the lance has usually predominated, though the tulwar[1] is the natural weapon of the Indian fighting man; and indeed, when the 9th Bengal Cavalry was sent to Suakin in 1885, it was specially armed with lances for the campaign, becoming from that moment 9th Bengal Lancers. At the time we are speaking of the Central India Horse was armed with lances in the front rank only, whilst all carried swords. There is no record to show exactly when this system of armament was introduced, but in the year 1902 lances were issued to the rear rank also, and swords were abolished, only to be restored a twelvemonth later.

In the cold weather of 1901-2 the 2nd Regiment varied the usual custom of marching along main

[1] A curved sword.

roads to and from manœuvres by returning from Jhansi, where the manœuvres were held, direct through the jungles, and killed four tigers and a panther on the way. The regiment distinguished itself at these manœuvres by winning five first and eleven second prizes at the assault-at-arms with which they were concluded. Both regiments were equally good at this kind of work, and the 1st have undoubtedly more wins to their credit than are entered in their records or can be mentioned here; but the two rarely met in mounted or dismounted contests except at Biaora during the triennial changes. On the last of these occasions, in November 1900, the 1st swept the board in all the mounted events, whilst the 2nd won everything on foot.

In May 1902 Colonel Dawson went to England in command of the Indian Contingent on duty in London at the Coronation of His Majesty King Edward VII. Risaldar Major Ghulam Mahomed Khan went also, as Orderly Officer to the Commander of the infantry of that Contingent. Later in the year preparations were set on foot for the Coronation Durbar at Delhi. Again the two regiments were allowed to combine two squadrons from each to form a composite regiment for the occasion. The 1st Regiment squadrons marched up from Agar at the end of December and halted at Goonah for eighteen days. Drummond then took command of the composite regiment and marched it up to Safdar Jang, where it was brigaded with the Gwalior, Bhopal, Mysore, and Alwar Imperial Service Lancers to form the Fifth Brigade of the 2nd Cavalry Division of the Southern Army in the grand manœuvres round Delhi, which took place before the actual Durbar. During the Durbar itself the regiment formed the Divisional Cavalry of the 2nd Division under Sir Alfred Gaselee, and was mainly occupied in lining the routes of processions. On the 14th February 1903 it was back at Goonah, the two squadrons of the 1st Regiment continuing the march thence to Agar, which was reached on the 1st March. The British officers of the regiment seized the occasion of the Durbar week, when many past and present officers of the Central India Horse were amongst the large concourse of Englishmen assembled at Delhi, to organise the first 'regimental dinner' ever held, the precursor of the annual dinner now held in London, and gathered together a cheerful company of twenty-seven comrades, old and new, to discuss, in the way of regimental diners, the glories of the past and the dullness of the present, to congratulate the old on their youthful appearance and the young on their good fortune in belonging to such a corps, and finally to part with the expression of the usual hope that all would meet again next year.

Many new British officers had meanwhile been appointed to the regiment. Just before the return from the Tirah campaign Lieutenant J. G. Lyons was posted to the 2nd. He left before the end of 1898. During this year Lieutenant M. R. Pocock and J. T. Ferris also joined the 2nd. Neither remained for long. Ferris, in fact, was taken ill soon after joining, and died in the train on the 22nd August whilst being taken down to Bombay. Pocock was attached to the 1st for a short period and, after a couple of years, went to the Supply and Transport Corps. In 1900 Lieutenants R. C. Goodfellow, N. D. Horsford, and R. C. Burton were appointed to the 1st and Lieutenant A. Kettlewell to the 2nd. Goodfellow served with the regiment during the Great War. Horsford died at Agar on the 3rd February 1901 during the inspection of the regiment by Sir George Luck, who at that time was commanding the forces in Bengal. Burton retired from the service on the 24th June 1908. Kettlewell served in Persia with the regiment. In 1901 Lieutenant R. E. T. Hogg joined the 1st Regiment, and Lieutenants A. B. Eckford and D. Le G. Pitcher the 2nd. Hogg, after being tutor to the Rajah of Panna and Assistant Military Secretary to His Majesty the King Emperor, George V., during the Durbar of 1911, was appointed Personal Assistant to the Resident in Mysore. He returned to the fighting service at the commencement of the Great War, and had a distinguished career in the Royal Flying Corps. Pitcher became also a very distinguished flying officer. Eckford was killed in Persia. In 1902 Lieutenant R. B. M. Wood joined the 1st Regiment. He had already seen active service in the South African War, but after two years' duty in Central India he was transferred to the Burmah Command. The officers appointed to the 2nd Regiment during this year were Lieutenants F. A. C. Wrench, H. D. S. Keighley, and G. P. Hood. All three had very short regimental careers. Keighley went to the Burmah Police in 1904, and retired from the service not long afterwards. He joined the regiment, however, for the Great War. Wrench

S

was forced to take sick leave within a month of his appointment, and died in Ireland of blackwater fever. G. P. Hood, a brother of A. N. Hood and equally popular, was drowned in Agar lake on the 12th April 1904. Pitcher and Keighley received the Royal Humane Society's medal for their gallant attempt to rescue him.

Amongst the doctors there had been many changes. Seton and Moore, it will be remembered, were the two medical officers when the regiment returned from Tirah. In July 1900 Seton took six months' leave and thereafter, until May 1908 when he became Secretary to the Director-General of the Indian Medical Service, he was often absent from the regiment either on furlough or on officiating administrative appointments. The officers who acted for him on these occasions were Captain Ainsworth, Lieutenant Holdich-Leicester, Lieutenant N. S. Wells, Lieutenant G. O. Thurston, Lieutenant F. P. Mackie, Lieutenant S. W. Jones, Captain E. E. Charles, Captain Emslie Smith, Lieutenant G. E. Malcolmson, and Captain M'Cowen, all of the Indian Medical Service. Moore left the 2nd Regiment in March 1899 to become Agency Surgeon at Bhopal. Lieutenants A. F. F. MacArdle, T. Hunter, and Delaney acted for him for short periods; but he was succeeded in the permanent appointment by Captain J. Fisher, D.S.O., who went to Gwalior in May 1902 as Officiating Residency Surgeon. Captain T. B. Kelly acted for Fisher for a short time in 1900, and when the latter was appointed permanently to the Political Department in 1904 he was followed in the regiment by Lieutenant-Colonel W. G. Alpin, Lieutenants

H. B. Steen, W. D. Ritchie, and C. S. Parker having acted for him in the meanwhile.

Amongst the Indian ranks the 1st Regiment suffered, during this period, a very severe loss in the death, at Delhi on the 2nd January 1903, of Risaldar Major Magar Singh who had succeeded old Sanwal Singh in March 1901. Magar Singh was perhaps the best loved man in either regiment. He was of the finest type of Manja Sikh, cheerful, courageous in every sense of the term, with great charm of manner, and a sense of duty to which his own interests were always subordinated. In his younger days he had been an expert and successful shikari. During the Durbar at Delhi he caught a chill, and would not be persuaded to cease work. Pneumonia then supervened, and in a very few days he was dead. He was succeeded as Risaldar Major by Risaldar Umar Ali Khan, who held the appointment for the next three years. In the 2nd Regiment there was also a change of Risaldar Majors. Lehna Singh retired on his pension on the 30th April 1902, to be followed by Risaldar Major Malik Ghulam Mahomed Khan.

The change of stations which, in ordinary circumstances, should have taken place very early in November 1903, the 1st Regiment being then at Agar and the 2nd at Goonah, was delayed by an outbreak of plague at the former place, and the usual meet at Biaora did not occur. The 1st actually marched on the 5th as far as Kanar, where, however, it was obliged to halt during a quarantine period of eight days, Goonah not being reached until the 25th. The 2nd had meanwhile vacated the Lines at Goonah and were on manœuvres at Jhansi; but on their return, instead of proceeding straight to Agar, were compelled to go into standing camp at Singwasa until the plague abated. It did not leave Goonah until the 6th February 1904, when it was played out of cantonments by the 1st Regiment band. Each regiment, in fact, possessed a band. It was an unusual concomitant of Indian cavalry, Probyn's Horse being the only other Bengal regiment thus distinguished; and, although we could not boast of Royal Artillery form, we were always glad, not having super-sensitive ears, to listen to it on guest nights and to ride within sound of it on the march. It was maintained by the British officers and consisted only of sixteen musicians, half of them trumpeters and the remainder mostly line boys. The music was supplied by Boosey periodically for a subscription, though occasionally we selected something ourselves, usually the best valse of the day or the latest Comic Opera. Boosey sometimes sent out pieces with 'words' to them, and to hear the 2nd Regiment band singing 'My Valentine' or 'Little Wee Dog' never failed to cause much merriment. The bands, of course, went the way of the Silladar System.

In April 1904 we were again honoured by a short visit from the Commander-in-Chief. Lord Kitchener came to Goonah on the 16th in the early morning, inspected the 1st Regiment before breakfast, and left immediately after. Any opinion which His Excellency may have formed as to the suitability of Goonah as a cavalry station was not disclosed to the regiment; but other inspections were yet to come, and, since there was no warning before the outbreak of the Great War that our removal from Central India might be imminent, it may be assumed that on the whole it was favourable. Our fears, at any rate, were not intensified.

The winter of 1905-6 was marked by the visit to India of Their Royal Highnesses the Prince and Princess of Wales. The 2nd Regiment marched from Agar on the 25th October 1905 for escort duty during Their Royal Highnesses' stay at Indore, returning to cantonments before the end of November. On the 1st of January 1906 we were honoured by the appointment of His Royal Highness as our Colonel-in-Chief. To the pleasure which we very naturally derived from the honour thus bestowed upon us by so great a Prince was added the intense satisfaction, felt sincerely by all ranks, in being associated regimentally with so great a sportsman; and indeed, when a small party of British and Indian officers went to Gwalior to wait on His Royal Highness during a tiger shooting expedition, they found that the stories of his prowess which had reached them were no mere flattering tales; for His Royal Highness quickly demonstrated, to the delight of all, the fact that, besides being the best shot in England, he was a shikari of the first water.

In January 1906 Dawson left Agar to take command of the Madras Brigade. He handed over the 2nd Regiment to Grant, who hoped, not unreasonably, to succeed him in the permanent post, since Watson, who was at the time commanding the Imperial Cadet Corps, was expected to retain that billet for the rest of his service. Watson, however, was offered, and accepted, the more military appointment, and came down to Agar on the 1st April. To Grant this was a misfortune. He had, to a day, the same length of service as Watson, but having joined the regiment at a later date, was graded below him. Moreover, he had devoted all his time and energy to the service of the Central India Horse, whilst Watson had been, regimentally speaking, a truant; and now it seemed that the happiest period of a soldier's life—when he commands his regiment—was to be denied to him. He was, however, given the command of the 32nd Lancers at Neemuch, whence he returned in February of the following year, when Drummond was made Inspector-General of Imperial Service Troops, to command the 1st Regiment.

The next few years were somewhat uneventful. Lord Kitchener, however, paid another visit to Central India, and on the 15th November 1907, whilst staying at the Residency at Indore, found time to drive up to Agar to inspect the 2nd Regiment and to view the surrounding country. It was an interesting inspection. His Excellency was in a happy, almost boyish, mood. The frown of severity with which his name was associated was conspicuously absent. His attitude towards the Indian Army seemed to have become very friendly, and this was an unexpected pleasure to the Indian ranks. The men had, in fact, learnt to regard Lord Kitchener as a sort of ogre from whom nothing but the sternest discipline was to be looked for. They had never seen him; but they knew something of other English Generals, heroes of the South African War and new to India, of whom he was to them the archtype and whose demeanour was not agreeable to them, and they had therefore looked forward to His Excellency's visit with some degree of trepidation. Their surprise was immediate, their pleasure obvious. There was a broad smile on the chief's face as he rode down the line. He spoke with a cheerful voice. The Risaldar Major whispered, "Lat Saheb ka misaj bilkul badal hogiya."[1] Having finished his inspection His Excellency galloped to the front and made a very pleasant speech. He complimented the men on their appearance, he praised the horses, he chatted with the officers for a few moments, and finally he rode off parade singing 'D'ye ken John Peel.'

After such an inspection we felt that we had taken a new lease of life in Central India, more especially as Pitcher had driven His Excellency across country to show him that cavalry could manœuvre there. Lord Kitchener again made a short inspection of the 2nd Regiment at Goonah, on his way through to Kotah, in the cold weather of 1909-10.

On the 10th March 1910 Colonel Cotgrave took over command of the 1st Regiment from Grant, who retired from the service; he in his turn being succeeded four years later, on the eve of the Great War, by Colonel A. P. Browne. Watson, on his completion of his five years' tenure, was succeeded, in command of the 2nd Regiment, by Colonel J. A. Douglas of the 2nd Lancers, who took the regiment

[1] "His Lordship's disposition has entirely changed."

to Persia in the following year, and at the commencement of the Great War was appointed to the Embarkation Staff at Bombay.

Since 1902 the following young British officers had been posted. In 1903 Lieutenants R. J. Macnabb and G. Lewis joined the 1st Regiment. Macnabb went to the Political Department four years later, but returned for the Great War. Lewis also fought in the war. In the same year Lieutenants I. MacIvor, G. Pearse, and C. G. Hoare joined the 2nd. MacIvor was appointed Station Staff Officer at Bombay in 1911, and did not return to the regiment. Pearse went to the Supply and Transport Corps in 1905. Hoare distinguished himself as a flying officer in the Great War, rising to the rank of Brigadier-General. The officers appointed in 1904 were Lieutenants J. Gourlie, L. G. Henderson, and J. R. Hutchison to the 1st Regiment, and N. H. C. Russell and J. F. Todd to the 2nd. Gourlie eventually commanded the single regiment of Central India Horse when the two were amalgamated after the Great War. Russell exchanged six years later with Captain W. B. White of the 4th Hussars, who succeeded Gourlie as Commandant. Todd was killed in Flanders whilst serving with the 2nd Life Guards. The year 1905 saw no new appointments. Lieutenants E. J. D. Colvin, A. C. Bird, and W. A. K. Fraser were gazetted in 1906, the former to the 1st and the two latter to the 2nd. Colvin soon entered the Political Department. He served in Persia during the Great War. Bird was obliged to take sick leave soon after joining. The regiment did not see him again. Fraser saw a great deal of fighting in the Great War, in Persia as well as in France. The 1st Regiment had no new appointments in 1907 or 1908. Two officers, however, were appointed to the 2nd in 1907, Lieutenants D. B. Edwards and K. A. G. Evans-Gordon. The latter was another instance of an officer of the Political Department, which he entered in 1911, returning to military duty for the Great War. He served in Egypt. Edwards served in Mesopotamia and Persia. In 1909 four officers were appointed to the 1st, none to the 2nd. The names of the four were R. S. Abbott, C. O'B. Daunt, C. O. Harvey, and Sir Norman Leslie, Bart. In 1910 Lieutenant A. H. Williams was posted to the 1st and Lieutenants D. de M. Fraser and E. T. R. Wickham to the 2nd; and from this time until the 1st Regiment went to France the only officers appointed were Lieutenants G. B. Lucas and R. H. M. Martin— a son of Colonel Cunliffe Martin, so well known in Central India in former years,—who joined the 1st in the hot weather of 1912, and M. H. S. Jones, who joined the 2nd towards the end of 1913. All these officers served in the war with the exception of the last, whose health broke down and forced him to leave the regiment. Lucas was killed in France whilst flying.

Two interesting appointments were made in October 1910 when the two sporting young chiefs of western Malwa, the Rajah of Ratlam and the Nawab of Jaora, neighbours and intimate friends though of different religions, were made ' honorary officers ' of the 2nd Regiment. Ratlam was attached to the 1st Regiment in France. Jaora, however, the grandson of our staunch friend of 1857, was, for reasons of health, unable to proceed to Europe. Both had served in the Imperial Cadet Corps, and both were superb polo players.

On the medical side Captain W. H. Odlum succeeded Seton as permanent Medical Officer of the 1st Regiment in May 1908. He was followed a year later by Captain E. B. Shettle, who retained the appointment until the opening of the Great War. Lieutenants D. G. Cooper, C. J. Stocker, R. H. Candy, and Major Hodgson acted for him at various periods. Major Hodgson was in medical charge in August 1914, and accompanied the regiment to France. In the 2nd Regiment Colonel Alpin had a very short stay. He went on leave in April 1905, Lieutenant W. E. J. Tuohy officiating for him; and in November of this year Major Jay Gould was brought in to the permanent appointment. He, however, was less than three months in Central India when he was appointed Medical Store-keeper at Lahore, a title which was very soon changed to that of Staff Officer, Medical 'Mobilisation Stores.' Though he never rejoined the regiment his name was kept on the rolls until 20th July 1913, when he was succeeded by Captain F. M. Stevenson. In the meantime Lieutenants F. M. Reaney and S. T. Crump, Captain R. G. G. Croly, Lieutenant F. S. Smith, and Captain W. T. M'Cowen held medical charge successively. The latter accompanied the regiment to Persia.

Risaldar Ali Haidar Khan, of the 1st Regiment,

was appointed Risaldar Major on the 15th January 1906 in succession to Umar Ali Khan. He held the appointment for eight years, and it was during his tenure, and to him most certainly the happiest moment of it, that the Proclamation was read announcing the increase of the pay of N.C.O's. and sowars by Rs. 3 a month—and of Indian officers in proportion—in commemoration of the fiftieth anniversary of the assumption of the government of India by the British Crown. To celebrate the occasion the Indian officers invited the British to a Special Durbar whereat Ali Haidar delivered an address of his own composition, expressing in very graceful terms the gratitude of his regiment and the assurance of its continued loyalty and goodwill. He was succeeded, on the 11th July 1914, by Risaldar Amar Singh, a magnificent figure of a man, whose behaviour during the Great War won the admiration and the gratitude of all ranks.

The Risaldar Major of the 2nd Regiment, Malik Ghulam Mahomed Khan, relinquished his appointment on the 1st March 1913 on becoming aide-de-camp to the General Officer Commanding the Southern Army. Later on he was promoted to the honorary rank of Captain. His place as Risaldar Major was taken by Risaldar Bakshi Jaswant Singh.

On the death of King Edward VII. on the 6th May 1911 we became ' King George's Own Central India Horse.' Risaldar Major Ali Haidar Khan and Risaldar Rajendra Singh of the 1st Regiment attended the Coronation of King George V. in

London. Colonel Walter Daunt commanded the Indian Contingent on this occasion. The 1st Regiment also sent a representative detachment consisting of Risaldar Lal Khan, Jemadar Harnam Singh, and eighteen Indian other ranks, under the command of Colonel Cotgrave, to the Coronation Durbar at Delhi in December; after which Her Imperial Majesty, the Queen Empress, on her way to Rajputana, was graciously pleased to spend a few hours at Goonah and to review the 1st Regiment, to whom the visit will ever remain a proud and especially happy memory. The 2nd Regiment took no part in the Durbar. It had been detailed earlier in the year to attend the ceremony and to form part of the 5th Cavalry Brigade in the manœuvres preceding it; but owing to the lateness of the monsoon and the consequent scarceness of fodder the order was cancelled, and before the Durbar took place the regiment was ordered overseas.

CHAPTER XVI.

THE REGIMENT IN PERSIA.

At the time when Douglas assumed command of the 2nd Regiment the main anxiety of the Government of India, in its relations with neighbouring States, was centred in Persia. Victims of a corrupt administration and an extravagant Court, the people of that country were, at the beginning of the twentieth century, in danger of losing their independence owing to the pressure of two powerful and jealous neighbours, Russia on the north and Great Britain on the south, and were only saved by the action of these two Powers themselves, who, from very fear of one another, were obliged, in the year 1907, to guarantee the integrity of Persia, and to set a limit to their mutual progress towards collision by demarcating their spheres of interest, on the north and south respectively, with a neutral zone between them. Meanwhile the Persian people, growing more and more discontented with their governors and more and more disgusted with a Customs Tariff which demanded 100 per cent *ad valorem* duty on Indian tea, had forced the Shah to grant a Constitution. This Shah died in 1906, within a year of this act; and his successor, Mahomed Ali Shah, less enlightened or less timorous but certainly less wise, attempted to carry on a reactionary form of government during the next three years, when he was deposed by the National Assembly.

The excitement and uncertainty attending this national movement served only to produce an increase of that form of disorder from which Persia has never been free. Travelling became more hazardous than ever. There are but eight miles of railway in the country. Beyond this the only method of transport is by caravans; and these, in the absence of a strong Government, are at the mercy of predatory tribes inhabiting the hills along the routes. For the security of British traders in Southern Persia the Government of India could only place small guards of Indian troops at the Legation and at the Consulates, whilst the ports were guarded by British men-of-war. The guardianship of the roads was necessarily left to the Persians themselves. Suggestions had indeed been put forward that Indian troops should be employed on this duty; but it was so obvious that no independent country in the world could submit passively to the use of armed foreigners in the maintenance of order that they were not strongly pressed. The road from Bushire to Shiraz in particular, the main trade route from the Gulf to the interior, was of all the roads in Persia the most difficult to protect. It is 165 miles long, and runs for the greater part of that distance over rugged mountains, rising to 8000 feet above the sea by rocky zigzag paths whereon the mountain battery mule himself would find it difficult to keep his foothold and retain his load. No caravan could traverse it without risk of disaster, for the Persian guards were useless even when present. The situation became so alarming and the position of traders in the towns so unsafe that it was even contemplated at one time to proffer advice, which would not have been taken, to merchants and other British subjects in Persia to desert the interior and seek refuge in the ports, or to leave the country altogether. Meanwhile these same merchants, and their representative bodies in England, were clamouring for protection. None was available, and the robberies continued. In 1909 there were serious disorders throughout Southern Persia. The British community at Shiraz was menaced, and in July a party of Royal Marines from H.M.S. *Fox* was sent up from Bushire to reinforce the Consulate Guard. In August Mr James of the Indo-European Telegraph Department and Mr Wright of the Imperial Bank had to flee for their lives. In November the Russian Consul-General was attacked on his way down to the coast. Early in 1910 two sowars of Indian cavalry were killed whilst on escort duty between Shiraz and Ispahan. In the summer of the following year Persian soldiers actually entered the Consulate at Shiraz and wounded a man of the guard. Our reply to this was to send up the ordinary relief of the Consulate guard a little earlier than was necessary in normal times, in order to double its strength for a period during which it was hoped that disorders might subside; and half a company of the 7th Rajputs left India for this purpose in August, the relief not being due until October. Hopes were not fulfilled; disorders increased rather than subsided, for about this time the deposed Shah suddenly appeared upon the scene, and it became clearly impossible to maintain our position any longer without some show of force. Before the end of September the Government of India was authorised by the Secretary of State to send a regiment of Indian cavalry to Persia for the protection of the lives and property of British subjects in Bushire, Shiraz, and Ispahan, though not, emphatically, for the security of the roads. The regiment selected, partly because its commander had already served in Persia and knew something of that country and its inhabitants, was the 39th Central India Horse.

It was not too soon. English men and women continued to be subjected to indignity and even worse. On the day after mobilisation orders were received by the regiment at Goonah a certain Miss Ross, a missionary lady on her way south from Ispahan, was very roughly handled by Kashguli robbers at Abadeh, was again attacked and robbed when attempting to continue her journey, and was consequently held up at Abadeh until the 25th November, when she was released from her uncomfortable position by a squadron of the regiment.

We went to Persia in two wings. The right wing, consisting of 'A' and 'B' Squadrons under Eckford and Kettlewell respectively, with Wickham and W. A. K. Fraser as their squadron officers, left Bombay on the 20th and 21st October in the *Islanda* and *Ujina*, British India boats of some 5000 tons burden. 'A' Squadron sailed in the *Islanda*, together with Regimental Headquarters, which consisted of Colonel Douglas, Edwards the Quartermaster, M'Cowen the Doctor, and Hart of the Supply and Transport Corps who was attached to the regiment for transport duty. Hoare, the Adjutant, was at home on leave when the regiment was ordered to mobilise, but returned to India in time to sail with the left wing, W. A. K. Fraser meanwhile acting for him as Adjutant. Both ships arrived at Bushire on the same day, the 26th October. Evidence of Persian antipathy at once became apparent. The demands of the Consul-General for boats were answered by half-hearted endeavours on the part of the Persian officials; these again were weakened by the active opposition of the mullahs of the town, and in the end only five dhows, of different sizes, were procurable for the landing. The horses, mules, camels, and baggage were slung into these at the inner anchorage. Then came an hour's tow to a sandy beach a couple of miles beyond the town. Here was no landing stage whatever. An improvisation was made and the dhows brought alongside; but then another difficulty cropped up. The sides of some of these boats were so high, and the bottoms so uneven, that it was impossible to get the horses out without help. Accordingly a ramp, made of sacks full of hay, was constructed inside the boat and, as each horse was led up to it, the boat itself was tilted over by means of a rope fixed to the mast; then, with a slap on the rump, he had to fling himself out as best he could. The landing of the two squadrons occupied four days, although a few more dhows were obtained as the process went on. By the afternoon of the

30th it was completed, and on the following morning the *Islanda* and *Ujina* sailed for Karachi to embark the left wing.

On the 2nd November the right wing began its march to Shiraz. The ascent of the first range of mountains was a difficult and tedious operation. Fortunately it was not opposed, for the spectacle of his sowars leading their horses in single file up a precipitous goat track, dignified by the name of road, the reins in one hand and the lance in the other, was enough to satisfy the Commander that, if attacked, they were helpless for all the military precautions that could be taken. For the transport the physical difficulties were still greater, and many loads, coming in contact with projecting rocks, were upset and had to be replaced. Kazerun, however, ninety miles from Bushire, was reached on the 7th November; and Shiraz itself on the 13th. Here news was received of the attack upon Miss Ross and her detention at Abadeh, and Douglas was ordered to move out in strength to bring her in; for the road to the northward, though physically less difficult than that between Shiraz and Bushire, was known to be infested by robbers who took toll of almost every caravan that passed along. He set out accordingly on the 18th November with Eckford's squadron, the Maxim Gun Detachment and ninety-six men of Kettlewell's squadron, leaving the remainder of the latter on guard at Shiraz.

Abadeh, 168 miles from Shiraz, and exactly half-way between that place and Ispahan, was reached on the 25th. The weather, though without the rain which had hampered the movement of the wing on its way up from Bushire, was intensely cold, especially at night; for between Shiraz and Abadeh is another range of mountains, rising at Mount Dena to a height of 17,000 feet, and no part of the road is lower than 5000 feet; yet the men and horses suffered but little, the Sikhs of 'B' Squadron even scorning tents, content to bivouac under the shelter of their waterproof sheeting. From Abadeh 'A' Squadron went on to Ispahan, whilst Headquarters and 'B' Squadron returned to Shiraz, taking Miss Ross with them. Near Yazd-i-Khast Eckford, who was riding with the advanced guard, became aware that a caravan was at that moment held up by robbers a short distance ahead of him. With a couple of troops of his squadron he galloped to the rescue. The robbers fled on his approach and sought shelter in one of those towers presumably intended for the protection of travellers but more often used to their discomfort. Eckford, unable to cut them off, was obliged to content himself with preventing their egress, thus allowing the caravan to pass in safety; but they opened a heavy fire on him and the Commander of the right half of 'A' Squadron, Risaldar Major Malik Ghulam Mahomed Khan, was severely wounded in the thigh.

Meanwhile the left wing, under Capper, had landed at Bushire. 'D' Squadron, Hewlett and D. de M. Fraser, was detailed to guard the port. Capper, with 'C' Squadron, Birdwood and Pitcher, was ordered to proceed to Shiraz; but since it had been reported that the Khans of Daliki and Borasjun were prepared to oppose any further advance of foreign troops through their country, it was considered advisable that Hewlett's squadron should go with it as far as Kazerun. This was accordingly done. It was too much for the Khans, who remained quiescent; and the two squadrons reached Kazerun without incident. Here a detachment of the 79th Carnatics, who were relieved as Consulate guard at Shiraz by the 7th Rajputs, had halted until the arrival of the Cavalry. 'D' Squadron, with the Carnatics, then returned to Bushire; and 'C' Squadron continued its march to Shiraz, where it arrived on the 27th November, Capper proceeding thence to Ispahan where he took over command of 'A' Squadron.

During the next few weeks the attention of the Commandant was directed mainly towards the questions of accommodation and supplies. Both presented the sort of difficulties which are always encountered in a country which is neither friendly nor actively hostile. Money even seemed to have lost its attraction, and it became necessary to send an armed party into the bazaar to seize such supplies as were needed, in case the shopkeepers should refuse to sell them, and to give receipts to be settled later on. The construction of huts and shelters for men and horses was hindered also by a difficulty of another kind, for there was but little roofing material at Shiraz, and the lawless state of the country made it almost impossible to transport it, even if it could be obtained, from elsewhere. The greater portion of the men had consequently no shelter from rain or snow throughout the winter beyond their regimental tents, and the majority of the horses had none whatever. By the spring these difficulties were surmounted. Before the end of April men and horses were all provided for, and the British officers, who had spent the winter in very close quarters in a very small house, found a much larger residence placed at their disposal by the Persian authorities and were henceforward very comfortable.

In December 1911 Douglas was apprised of the fact that a quantity of specie was held at Bushire in readiness for transportation to Shiraz for the Imperial Bank of Persia. An escort was required. It was decided, against the wishes of Colonel Douglas, who had recommended the use of larger parties, that half of 'D' Squadron, under D. de M. Fraser, should proceed with the treasure as far as Kazerun, where it would be met by a detachment of similar strength from 'C' Squadron, under Birdwood, who would escort it thence to Shiraz, Fraser's party then returning to Bushire. At the same time opportunity was taken to add to this convoy a convoy of stores, the whole caravan thus consisting of 150 mules. The newly-appointed Vice-Consul at Shiraz, Mr Smart, also took advantage of the occasion and marched with Fraser's escort, which crossed the mountains in safety and reached the Rahdar caravanserai, eleven miles short of Kazerun, where the road drops down into the Kazerun plain, on the morning of the 26th.

Birdwood, accompanied, most fortunately as it turned out, by Captain M'Cowen, who went with him to attend Rissaidar Ibrahim Khan, lying sick at Kazerun, left Shiraz on the 19th and marched into Dasht-i-Arjin on the 21st. Here he was detained by a blizzard during the whole of the 22nd. On the following morning he was able to proceed, though the weather was still severe. He crossed the Pir-i-Zan pass, 7800 feet above sea-level, and descending by a very steep path on the further side reached Mian Kutal, about half-way down, where there is a caravanserai; and here he halted for the night. The next march took him to Kazerun, which, however, was not reached until 10 P.M.; for the Kashguli tribesmen, watching every movement from commanding positions on the hill-tops and observing that there were but fifty soldiers, encumbered by fifty horses and a baggage train, determined to offer resistance. It was indeed a strange land for the operations of a mounted force. Gurkha Scouts might have found themselves at home in it; not light cavalry. Between Bushire and the Rahdar caravanserai, and from the Kazerun plain to the top of the Pir-i-Zan, there is a succession of ridges, precipitous on the seaward side, each rising considerably higher than its predecessor, the few miles of ground between them being level but much broken. This was the sort of country which the regiment was required to negotiate. Had its opponents been Afridis, with the zest for fighting and the skill in musketry which distinguish that martial race, Birdwood's little force would assuredly have been annihilated.

From Mian Kutal there is a further drop of 1500 feet to the level ground between the Pir-i-Zan and the Kutal-i-Dukhtar. The road through the latter pass takes a curve, and as the advanced party of three men reached this spot they disappeared from the view of the main body. A few moments later Birdwood heard a shot ring out. He galloped forward to find about twenty Kashgulis trying to drag two sowars, whom they had treacherously disarmed, into a tower; whilst the third man, who had been wounded in the face, was keeping them off with his rifle. On the appearance of the main body the tribesmen retreated into their stronghold. Birdwood dismounted his men, letting the horses gallop away, for there was no one to spare to hold them, nor any shelter. Sending a few men on to an adjacent hill to cover his movements he rushed the tower, followed by M'Cowen, Jemadars Abdul Rahman and Amar Ali, and two or three sowars, only to find the door so strongly barricaded that entry was impossible. The little party was now in a position of some danger. Flattened up against a low wall at the foot of the tower, to avoid the fire from the roof and from loop-holes in the walls, Birdwood soon became aware that his transport, which he had left about three-quarters of a mile behind him, was being fired on from the hills leading up to the pass. He and his party could only make a second rush, leaving the wounded man, Sowar Nazar Mahomed Khan, who had been hit a second time, under the wall; but our men on the hill had driven the defenders of the tower into a lower storey, and he reached the transport without further loss. The loose horses, with the exception of Birdwood's own charger, were then collected; the baggage was retired to a safer position and a spirited attack was directed upon the hills. The Kashgulis soon fled in confusion, leaving several casualties behind them. Meanwhile the men in the tower had bolted down the further side of the pass to a small sangar commanding the road. Out of this, however, they were driven very speedily, and Birdwood was at last able to call up his transport and continue his journey. Sowar Nazar Mahomed Khan, who had behaved very bravely, continuing to fire on the enemy until he received his second wound, died just after the tower was evacuated. Two other men were wounded and two horses were killed. There were still nine miles to travel; but the Kashgulis withdrew and the weary squadron plodded through the dark into Kazerun without meeting any further opposition.

After spending Christmas Day at Kazerun Birdwood, on receipt of instructions from Douglas at Shiraz, for the tribesmen had not cut the telephone wires, moved out on the morning of the 26th to meet Fraser, taking with him Rissaidar Ibrahim Khan—who was found fit enough to return to duty,—Jemadar Abdul Rahman, and thirty men. The two parties joined hands at the Rahdar caravanserai where they halted to feed and water. During this interval Mr Smart, who had taken the opportunity to converse with some of the Kashguli road guards in the caravanserai, observed that their attitude was, to say the least of it, a little unfriendly. Birdwood, therefore, took the precaution of sending the convoy ahead of him with an escort under Jemadars Abdul Rahman and Bhaggat Singh. It was a wise precaution, for before he and Fraser, with the rear-guard, had proceeded more than a couple of hundred yards fire was opened on him from the caravanserai and from the hills on his flank. For the next two miles an orderly retirement was carried out without loss, the Kashgulis continuing the fire but not pressing their attack home. But from here onwards, until within two miles of Kazerun, the fight became much more severe. More tribesmen appeared, not only upon the hills but upon the road itself, and from every village and every tower armed men turned out to swell the crowd of enemies. The hospital assistant was soon killed; three or four men were down; many horses were hit. M'Cowen dressed the wounded and mounted them behind unwounded sowars. Fraser, whose horse was killed under him, handled the rearguard with great coolness; and so the action went on, the men behaving splendidly. Four miles from the Rahdar caravanserai Birdwood looked round for Mr Smart, but could not see him. No one had seen him. A mile farther on his horse came trotting by with a bullet wound in his neck. Mr Smart had obviously been wounded too, but no one knew where he had fallen. It was impossible to go back and search for him. Every rifle was too fully occupied. As a matter of fact he had wandered away from the convoy, had been wounded in the thigh, had then been picked up by Kashgulis and taken to a village a few miles away, whence he was brought in to Kazerun three days later.

The fight continued, Lance Dafadars Pal Singh and Lachman Singh using the Maxim gun persistently and most efficiently. At one point a body of tribesmen blocked the road in front. Birdwood mounted all his men and, with many horses carrying two riders apiece, cut his way through them; but there was further opposition beyond; and it was not until the town of Kazerun was in sight that the enemy began to slacken his fire and gradually disappeared.

Meanwhile Abdul Rahman and Bhaggat Singh had sent the convoy along the road whilst they themselves, with their men, took up a series of positions on either flank and held the enemy off; and consequently no determined effort was made to seize what would have been a very rich prize. Fifteen mules, however, were killed, though only six loads of ammunition, none of treasure, were left upon the ground. After five hours of fighting, the last three in drenching rain, Birdwood brought his convoy into Kazerun with the loss of two men killed, in addition to the hospital assistant, and seven wounded; eight horses being killed and many hit. He was made a Brevet Lieutenant-Colonel for his conduct of these two actions but, since the regiment was not pronounced officially to be 'on active service,' medals were not awarded, though Douglas was afterwards made a C.M.G.

When the news of the first fight, on the 24th, reached Shiraz, Pitcher was sent out to Dasht-i-Arjin, with the remainder of 'C' Squadron, with orders to hold the Pir-i-Zan pass and help Birdwood through on his return journey with the convoy. The more serious attack on the 26th threw a lurid light upon the attitude of the tribesmen and called for still stronger measures; for if, as seemed likely, the infection were to spread it would become impossible for Birdwood's small force, with its large convoy, even with the assistance of Pitcher, to overcome the opposition which might be expected. Douglas therefore decided to move out himself with all available men, 100 all told, to reinforce Pitcher.

It was not until 2nd January that the wounded men at Kazerun were fit to travel. They were carried in 'Kajawahs'[1]; and Birdwood set out again, Fraser and his men marching with him, for it was as unsafe as it was unnecessary for them to return to Bushire; and, for the better protection of the column, Mahomed Ali Khan, the Chief of the Kashgulis, was persuaded by Mr Smart to accompany it for a certain distance.

Meanwhile Douglas had marched over the Pir-i-Zan. Leaving all the horses with a guard of thirty men at Mian Kutal on the morning of the 2nd he marched, with the remainder of his men on foot, to the head of the Kutal-i-Dukhtar; and there he met Birdwood and brought him back to Mian Kutal, arriving late that night. The next few marches were accomplished under great difficulties; for the rain, turning to snow on the Pir-i-Zan, was continuous, the roads were fetlock deep in mud and the men were drenched to the skin; but the tribes made no attempt to reopen hostilities and the column reached Shiraz on the morning of the 6th.

These events, from the political standpoint, were exceedingly unfortunate. It had been easy to send a regiment into Persia. Should it now be extricated? And if so, how? Or should it be

[1] Panniers.

reinforced and the country occupied for a time? Moreover, what punitive measures, if any, could be taken to exact reparation from the tribes and to restore order in our sphere of interest? The alternatives of evacuation or occupation were much discussed. The natural difficulties of the country, more than the strength and character of the enemy, required, in the latter case, the despatch of a very large force; but the susceptibilities of our Russian neighbours on the one hand and of the Moslem community in India on the other had to be considered, and this alternative was therefore discarded, our Government contenting itself with remonstrances to the Persian Government, leaving it to the latter to punish the tribesmen and to organise a new system of road security. This was a great disappointment to the officers and men of the regiment who had looked forward to taking vengeance on their tormentors. They could still hope, however, for relief under the first alternative, for it was known that the despatch of a mixed brigade, with mountain artillery, was contemplated for this purpose; and they went into winter quarters at Shiraz in expectation of returning to India in the spring. They were again disappointed. Before the end of January it was announced that the Persian Government would raise a force of gendarmerie, 1400 strong, under Swedish officers, who would be responsible for the safety of the caravans. It was obvious that many months must elapse before such gendarmerie could be sufficiently trained to perform the simple duties required of them; but meanwhile no relieving force was sent, no satisfaction was obtained from the Kashgulis, who continued to be as troublesome as ever, and the regiment remained throughout the year 1912 in prison at Shiraz.

The position was humiliating and most difficult. It is not always realised how detrimental it can be to the 'moral' and discipline of troops to be confined for week after week and month after month in uncomfortable quarters whence there is no egress without escort, and no communication with the outside world except by means of the post or the wire, both very precarious as it happened, and there is not even the consolation of being 'on active service.' But the men stood it well. There was no despondency, no grumbling, and very little crime. Both officers and men were frequently subjected to insult and even to open attack. On one occasion W. A. K. Fraser and his orderly were fired on near the Consulate itself, the latter being hit. Desire for retaliation ran high; but Douglas kept his men in leash, and the civil authorities had reason to be grateful to him and his subordinates for the patience and restraint with which they endured their ordeal. Training was carried on under difficulties too, the country in the vicinity of Shiraz being unsuitable for cavalry manœuvre. There are many gardens close to the town; and on the plain beyond are large stretches of cultivated ground intersected by irrigation cuts, large and small. Consequently there could be no regimental exercises, though troops and squadrons were trained day by day and a certain amount of reconnaissance work was possible in the lower hills. For the recreation of the men certain games were organised; but these were robbed of half their pleasure by the dust, which, during the hot weather, was very unpleasant indeed. Even polo was played but intermittently during the summer months. The British officers enjoyed some shooting near at hand during the winter—duck, snipe, and chikor[1] being fairly plentiful; and Hoare and Edwards managed to import a couple of fox-hounds which, under the name of 'The Shiraz Vale Hunt,' and in pursuit of the herring, afforded a considerable amount of amusement. During the hot weather a few hog, the European not the Indian species, were speared as they returned from the crops to the marshes in the early morning.

In the autumn hopes of relief were revived, for it became known to the regiment that the Government of India was again on the point of sending a Brigade to bring it out. The scheme, if ever sanctioned, was not translated into action, and Douglas was obliged to make preparations for another winter. Capper's squadron was called in from Ispahan, where it was doing little good; and thus the whole regiment, with the exception of Hewlett's half-squadron at Bushire, which was now the only detachment, settled down in quarters which had been made much more comfortable, both for horses and for men, than they had been in the previous year. A new Governor-General of Fars arrived at Shiraz about this time; and, being a man of some strength of character, very soon made his presence felt in the town and its neighbourhood. Disturbances

[1] Red-legged partridge.

became fewer. Officers and men could move about more freely. Moreover, a section of the newly-raised Swedish gendarmerie were sent down from Teheran to take charge of the road between Shiraz and the Pir-i-Zan. A sense of security began to grow, prematurely indeed and, for the regiment, most unfortunately, for it cost the life of a very gallant officer. Eckford and Kettlewell applied for leave to go to Dasht-i-Arjin on a shooting expedition. With the consent of the Consul and the Governor-General himself the leave was sanctioned and, with an escort of an Indian officer and twenty-six men, they marched on the 10th December as far as Khan-i-Zinian. On the following morning, as they approached Dasht-i-Arjin, both officers riding with the advanced party, with a scout on some low hills to the left and the baggage, accompanied by the greater part of the escort, some 200 yards behind them, they were fired on from the hills. With the few men at hand they dismounted in some dead ground and moved up to attack their assailants, who retired in haste after firing a few more bullets at random. But one of these bullets hit Eckford, who fell dead, shot through the heart. At the same time about 150 tribesmen rushed out of a ravine at the mules; and although Dafadar Mahomed Zaman, who was in charge of the baggage guard, did his duty well and drove them back to their shelter, from which they did not again emerge, many of the syces fled in panic and several mules were lost.

Eckford's body was carried back to Shiraz and was buried in a corner of the Consulate garden.

He was of that rare type of earnest young soldier, taking life very seriously, that with opportunity rises invariably to fame. Ascetic and rather solitary, intent on exploration and adventure, a traveller and a hunter, he was never quite happy in the conventional life of a cantonment; but he commanded the respect and admiration of his brother officers, and the Indian ranks gave him their complete confidence. A stern note was addressed to the Persian Government demanding reparations and the punishment of the offending tribesmen; but the Persian Government, however willing, was powerless; so there the matter ended and Eckford's death remained unavenged.

Early in 1913 the question of withdrawal was again revived; but Douglas, who by this time had had enough of paper and ink to warn him that, unless he took action himself, his imprisonment, which had become closer since the attack on the shooting party, might be indefinitely prolonged, proposed that his regiment should find its way to Bushire without assistance. His proposal was accepted, and on the 6th April he led his men out of Shiraz on the homeward journey. No untoward incident occurred on the march to the coast; and before the end of May, in two voyages of the R.I.M.S. *Dufferin*, the regiment was brought back to India after nineteen months' absence on a service from which much had been hoped for but little won, a creditable but exceedingly disagreeable episode.

CHAPTER XVII.

THE GREAT WAR—FRANCE.

The thunderbolt fell on India during the quietest period of the military year. Nothing had occurred before the end of July 1914 to relieve the discomfort of the hot weather or to break the monotony of life in the rains. Many officers, as usual, were on leave; and many men too. The daily routine of squadron drill and musketry went on. The weeks passed by just as much without incident as ever. Even the Sarajevo murders were but an item of news. And then, with a start, men woke to a call which summoned them to a duty far transcending the ordinary notion of 'Active Service' and to an ordeal which none could foresee.

Undoubtedly all thoughtful soldiers were aware that a war with Germany must come sooner or later. Few, however, contemplated the possibility of India playing an important part in it. Least of all did the Government of India. The Indian Army was not intended or equipped for such a war. The military policy of the Indian Government had, for some years past, been one of retrenchment; and the scope of the Army was restricted to the prevention of internal disorder, the despatch of a small expedition overseas, such as to China, or a possible campaign in Afghanistan. And so, when the trumpet sounded, British officers wondered what chance they had of seeing service. Those on leave in England flocked to the War Office, eager for jobs. Headquarters at Simla were besieged by applicants for any posts, however menial, which could be obtained. It was little realised how unnecessary this was. Indian soldiers wondered too. They had forgotten the expedition to Cyprus; but had they not been rigidly excluded from that 'White Man's War' in South Africa? This, too, was a 'White Man's War.' It seemed more than doubtful that their services would be required. And yet there were many of them, Sikhs and Gurkhas especially, who felt that they were capable and should not be denied this time. In China they had seen Japanese soldiers to whom they felt no whit inferior. If these could contend successfully against a European Army why not they? They were loyal enough. The Imperial idea had not forsaken them, as it seemed to forsake the 'intelligentsia' of Bengal after the Japanese victories. They would not have been content to look on. Policy itself, apart from the greatness of the issue, dictated the despatch of Indian troops to the theatre of war; for if they had not been employed prestige and 'moral' would have vanished, and there would have been discontent such as had hardly been known since the Mutiny.

But whatever may have been the views of the Government of India, before 1914, concerning the use to which its Army should be put, there was no

question of inaction when England declared war.
From the Viceroy downwards every man in India
rose to the occasion. The elephant behaved all
wrong.[1] Princes and chiefs hastened to place their
armies and a great part of their treasure at the
disposal of Government. Expressions of loyalty
and promises of support were received even from
the least expected quarters. Little did the people
care for the incidents which actually provoked the
declaration of war; to Indian folk they were but
incidents; but they knew that England was
threatened by a great Power; her enemies were
their enemies; they were prepared for great sacrifices to sustain her honour, and the rest was in
the lap of the gods. It was welcome news to the
Imperial Government, who at once ordered the
mobilisation of an Army Corps and a Cavalry
Division. Before the end of August mobilisation
was completed and Indian troops, for the first time
in history, sailed out into the unknown with the
certain prospect of meeting a European foe.

The history of the doings of this Indian Corps
in France is written elsewhere. The men embarked
with the enthusiasm which always affects good
soldiers on the way to war; they accustomed themselves very quickly to the strange conditions in
which they were placed; they endured the agony
of the water-logged trenches of Flanders with such
faith and fortitude as even their own British officers
had hardly dared to predict, and when the Indian
Corps was withdrawn from France it was not only
because the men were deemed to have suffered

---

[1] See 'Punch,' August 1914.

enough, not only because the gap which they had filled so successfully could now be filled by freshly-trained troops from England, nor solely because their services were required elsewhere, but because there were no reserves to make good the awful wastage which men knew must continue.

The excitement at Goonah and Agar, as at every other station in India, was intense. The 38th, at Goonah, had the greater hope, since they were on the mobilisation list, though not in any formed brigade. The 39th at Agar were destined, as they knew, for 'Internal Security' and could only wait upon events. Neither regiment was called upon to form part of the cavalry division or of the divisional or corps troops, and British officers, it seemed, could now only hope for service in such extra-regimental and individual appointments as, with luck, might come their way. All officers on leave in India were recalled, those in England being retained by the War Office and attached to English units. The regiments stood ready. Two months later hopes were revived. The results of the early battles of the war soon demonstrated the need of further reinforcement from India. A second cavalry division was ordered to mobilise; and on the 24th October the 38th received orders to prepare for action. Lieutenant Charles Daunt, the Quartermaster, was immediately sent to Jhansi for the mobilisation equipment. But now was seen the effect of India's military policy. An expedition had gone overseas, and every article of equipment at Jhansi had gone with it. Daunt returned empty-handed. Henceforward daily telegrams were despatched to Headquarters reporting deficiencies, and by degrees, from all parts of India, the necessary stores dribbled in. Mobilisation, which at ordinary times should have been accomplished within a week, was, however, far from complete on the afternoon of the 9th November when the Goonah stationmaster presented himself at the Adjutant's office and reported that three troop trains would be ready for the regiment on the following day. Colonel Browne, who had received no notice of movement, thereupon informed the General Officer Commanding at Mhow that, in the absence of orders to the contrary, he would entrain on the following afternoon; and entrain he did; and thus, on the 10th November 1914, the Central India Horse started from Goonah for the Great War on the word of an Indian stationmaster.

The following British officers started with the regiment :—

Lieutenant-Colonel A. P. Browne, commanding.
Lieutenant Sir Norman Leslie, Bart., Adjutant.
'A' Squadron (Pathans) Lieutenant-Colonel R. C. Bell.
       Captain J. R. Hutchison.
'B' Squadron (Sikhs) Major R. C. Goodfellow.
       Lieutenant R. H. M. Martin.
'C' Squadron (Ghakkars) Captain R. S. Abbott.
       Lieutenant C. O'B. Daunt.
'D' Squadron (Sikhs) Captain G. Henderson.
Major Hodgson, I.M.S., Medical Officer.

Captain G. Lewis and Lieutenant G. B. Lucas were left at the depot.

On leave in England were Majors S. A. Cooke and R. E. T. Hogg, Captain J. Gourlie and Lieutenants A. H. Williams and R. H. M. Durand.

Major H. K. Barr was seconded as guardian to Mian Saheb Hari Singh of Kashmir; and Captain C. O. Harvey, who was at the time aide-de-camp to the Lieutenant-Governor of the Panjab, was posted to a brigade of Imperial Service cavalry which went to Egypt.

The trains were stopped at Jubbulpore on the 11th. Here the regiment went into camp with the other units—the Inniskilling Dragoons, the 2nd Lancers (Gardner's Horse), and 'Y' Battery Royal Horse Artillery—of the Mhow Brigade, of which it now formed part. Four days later it was entrained for Bombay, and on the 19th set sail in the *Euryalus* and the *City of Poona* which, shortly after leavng harbour, joined a convoy of sixty ships from Australia, under escort of a French cruiser named *Dupleix*. It is a strange reversal of history which chronicles the departure of British-Indian troops from India, under an escort named after British India's great enemy of 160 years ago, to fight in Europe on the side of France.

Marseilles was reached on the 13th December, and the troops were very warmly received by the French population. The men were delighted as they marched through the town, amid cries of "Vivent les Hindous," to the camping ground of La Barasse, some six miles beyond it. There was another kind of greeting, too, which at once gave them confidence in the higher authorities under whom they were about to serve. Warm clothing was showered on them in abundance. It was so different to India, where little could be obtained without difficulty and much was not obtainable at all. Serge uniform had certainly been provided by regimental funds, but the sowars had no underclothing. Here there was as much as the heart could desire; strange garments, too, some of them, which they had never worn before; but they put them all on, as proud as children with new frocks, and swaggered down the streets of Marseilles, until observed by the shocked eye of the British officer, with 'drawers, long woollen,' worn over their breeches. New rifles also were issued to them, together with a weapon which they had seen but never handled, strikingly indicative of the work which lay before them, the bayonet.

Six days were spent at La Barasse, six very wet though not very cold days. During this period four interpreters were attached to the regiment. Drawn from very different walks in life—one was a landed proprietor, another had been a buyer for Worth's, the third was a hotel manager, and the fourth a courier—they were useful in all sorts of ways. One in particular, Louis Nouguier, who very quickly acquired the affectionate nickname of 'Nuggett,' became as devoted to the regiment as the regiment did to him. A French gentleman of the old school, a scholar and a Royalist, a fine horseman, always immaculately turned out, always smiling, alert, and resourceful, he was everybody's friend; and, greatest of all accomplishments in the view of the war-worn soldier, he seemed to possess the faculty of conjuring food from the sky.

The next move was to Orleans, a two days' journey by rail. The discomfort here was great. To the rain, with which men and horses had become more or less familiar at Marseilles, was added a piercing wind. Moreover, the ground was badly drained. The horse lines were a quagmire, and officers and men, living in bivouac, were never really dry or, for all the warm clothing, ever really warm. They were being broken in quickly to worse conditions still. They endured nine days of this and were then entrained for another two days' journey, which brought them to the little wayside station of Blendecques. Guides met the regiment here and conducted it to the neighbourhood of Therouanne where, for the first time in its experience, it was distributed in billets.

The Mhow Brigade was now within thirty miles of that part of the long trench line between the sea and Switzerland which, from the end of October until the end of December, had been held by the Indian corps. The corps, with the First Cavalry Division, had arrived in France after the battles of the Marne and the Aisne had been fought and the race to the sea had ended in a draw, to be followed by four years of trench warfare with such discomfort and such constant fighting as had not been dreamed of. It had fought in the first battle of Ypres, in the first attacks at Neuve Chapelle and Festubert, and in the battle of Givenchy. It had suffered 9500 casualties, including 144 British officers killed and missing. Many regiments had lost all, or nearly all, their sahibs—their 'mothers and fathers,'—but they had set an example which their

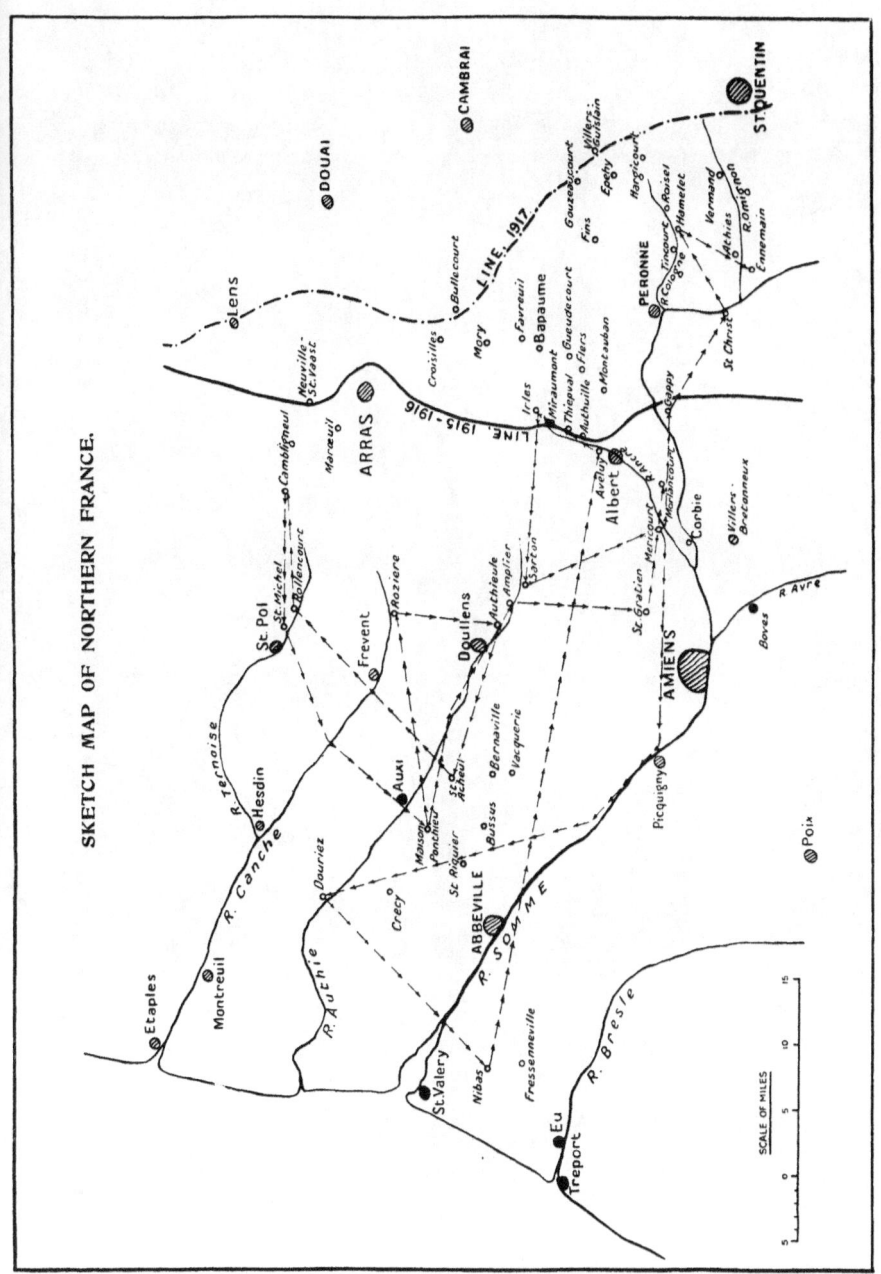

Movements of Central India Horse, 1916-1917. (From War Diary.)

successors may well follow but can never excel; and now, at the end of December, after two months' hard fighting from which there was no respite night or day, they had been withdrawn to billets behind the line.

The billets allotted to the Central India Horse were in the four villages of Upen d'Amont, Upen d'Aval, Westerham, and Dilettes, the latter being close to Therouanne itself. Regimental Headquarters were housed in a chateau at Upen d'Amont. Snow was falling as the process of billeting began. The men were at first somewhat bewildered by the novel experience. They were shown into barns and outhouses from which, during the first few days, they were too shy to emerge except when called out on duty; but by degrees they poked their noses out a little farther and a little farther until, before long, they were seen to be on very friendly terms with the villagers, who welcomed them heartily. Indeed not the least remarkable manifestation of the war was the easy way in which our Indian soldiers associated with the French people. They picked up a smattering, and in some cases more than a smattering, of the language very quickly, and used it too, mixed into an extraordinary jargon with a little English and a little Hindustani, in conversation with their English comrades of the brigade, with whom they developed, as the war went on, a camaraderie such as had never been known in India.

The distribution of squadrons in separate billets, sometimes a mile or more apart, and the certainty that they would often be called upon to act independently, involved a new departure in the way of British officers' messes. Squadron messes had to be formed, but this was no easy matter. There were not enough servants. Gussa Khan, the mess khitmatgar, staunch fellow as he was—he followed the regiment throughout the war,—could not be everywhere; nor could men for this duty be found from the ranks as in the English service. Many solutions of the difficulty were suggested, one being that British officers should learn to cook for themselves; but common-sense eventually prevailed and English soldiers, drawn mostly from the English regiment of the brigade, were attached in the proportion of one per officer. These men were invaluable. They entered into the life of the regiment as if they had been born in it. They took their share in the fighting and in games with equal zeal, and made many close friendships with soldiers in the Indian ranks.

Nor were these the only 'British other ranks' who were entered on the rolls of the regiment. During the first few weeks the transport and signalling services presented difficulties which the sowars could hardly be expected to overcome unaided. They had not been taught to drive. Consequently it was found expedient to attach English drivers for the Army Transport carts, which were replaced later on by General Service wagons. This difficulty, however, was speedily surmounted, for the sowar is not deficient in horsemanship, and he very soon demonstrated the fact that he could manage little affairs like this for himself. The telephone difficulty lasted a little longer; but before many weeks had passed the transport and signallers of Indian cavalry had become as efficient as those of any other branch of the service.

Captain James Gourlie and Lieutenants Williams and Durand joined the regiment early in January, and were followed shortly afterwards by Captain Rawdon Nacnabb, who was permanently in the Political Department but was allowed to rejoin the regiment for the war. He brought out the first batch of reinforcements from India.

During the first ten days of January the men were taught the use of the bayonet, and on the 11th were sent forward to the trenches to use it, perhaps, in earnest. At 10.15 A.M. on this day a party of thirteen British officers and 300 Indian officers, non-commissioned officers, and men was entrained in London omnibuses for Bethune, a journey of twenty miles. Parties of similar strength from the Inniskilling Dragoons and the 2nd Lancers were entrained, or 'embussed' as the term was, at the same time and for the same place. Bethune was reached at 12.50 P.M., and from here the brigade marched a distance of seven miles to the trenches in front of the village of Les Plantins, between Festubert and Givenchy. The Central India Horse here took over the section of the line which had been held by Jacob's Horse, whilst the 2nd Lancers, on our left, took over from the 29th Lancers, the Inniskillings being farther to the left still and Brigade Headquarters at the village of Rue de Bethune, a mile to the rear. It was pitch dark, reliefs being, of course, impossible by daylight. The men had to feel their way; and thus the introduction of

Indian cavalry sowars to the grim business of trench warfare in Europe was made under difficult conditions, only relieved for the good soldier by the din of battle which had grown louder and louder as the regiment marched up from Bethune. Moreover, the trenches at Les Plantins were typical of the Flanders trench of the winter of 1914-15. Originally the ordinary shelter trench, such as one digs on an ordinary field day, or a drainage ditch hollowed out along a roadside—for the deep-cut, drained and revetted subways with traverses and 'dug-outs' were not made until siege warfare had more firmly set in—they had been deepened and widened by former occupants; but this had only served to make them almost untenable since they were not yet drained. In most places they were waist-deep in water; men had sometimes actually to swim to get from one part of a trench to another, and in the battles of November and December wounded men had actually been drowned in the communication trenches whilst attempting to crawl to the rear. At Les Plantins the original fire trenches at the foot of the slope in front of the village had become too full of water for occupation, and the defenders were withdrawn some 500 yards to the support trenches on the outskirts. The mitigation of discomfort was, however, slight; for even on the higher ground many men had to stand in two and a half feet of water during their tour of duty in the firing line.

It was in these early days of the alternate occupation of trenches and of billets that the fine character of the Indian officer became so conspicuous. As a leader in time of peace it is one of his duties to see that his men are contented and give the least possible trouble to British officers, and he has ways of his own for accomplishing this end; but in the warfare in which he now found himself engaged his task was infinitely more difficult. Old customs and old prejudices had to go by the board. Endurance hitherto unthought of was required of his men. His peace time methods, his 'meharbani'[1] and 'tasalli' had to be forgotten. He could only call upon their loyalty and enforce a sterner discipline. He did it splendidly. In the fighting as in billets he set them a fine example. The men never grumbled, though there was no short leave to break the strain for the Indian soldier as there was for his English comrades. They fought and endured, no doubt, for the British Empire, though more really perhaps for their sahibs; but it was the Troop and Company Leaders who held them together.

This first turn of duty in the trenches only lasted two days, and was marked by a very plucky reconnaissance on the part of Dafadars Nadir Khan and Bostan Khan of 'C' Squadron. There was desultory shooting from the German trenches with an outburst of shell fire on the morning and evening of the 12th and 13th which, however, did but little damage. No. 20090 Dafadar Dayal Singh was wounded in the leg, our first casualty. At 7 P.M. on the 13th the Mhow Brigade was relieved, the trenches of the Central India Horse being taken over by the 18th Lancers, and returned by the way it came to its quarters round Therouanne.

[1] Kindness and consolation.

The night was intensely cold and the men, all soaked to the skin, were so benumbed by the ride on the busses, the outside passengers especially, that at the end of the journey they could hardly crawl to their billets. Therouanne was reached at 7.30 on the morning of the 14th, but it was some hours before the whole party was reported safely housed. That afternoon Risaldar Major Amar Singh went round to every billet with something more than a hint that no man should, on any account, report sick, with the result that the Central India Horse had fewer admissions to hospital after its first visit to the trenches than any other unit of the 2nd Cavalry Division, not excluding the English regiments. Lieutenant Martin was, however, invalided a few days later and, being transferred on recovery to the Royal Flying Corps, did not return to the regiment.

A period of training ensued, broken by an occasional inspection. On one such occasion the 2nd Cavalry Division was concentrated on a plain near the village of Enguingatte, the field of the 'Battle of the Spurs,' to be reviewed by the Commander-in-Chief, Sir John French. *En route* to the rendezvous the Mhow Brigade was put through a training exercise based on the general idea that "the Germans have landed at Etaples." At this early stage the men had hardly learnt to distinguish friend from foe, and, on nearing the appointed place, an advanced patrol from 'A' Squadron, which was acting as advanced-guard, observed in the distance certain horsemen whom they at once assumed to be Germans. They were, in fact, the Commander-in-Chief and his Staff. A man was sent galloping back with the news and the advanced party prepared for action. The commander of the advanced-guard, however, went forward in time to point out the mistake before fire was opened, and the contretemps was avoided; but the regiment had to suffer the gibes of other units in the division. Such contretemps are not infrequent in war. Indeed this very squadron had already distinguished itself at Les Plantins by wounding and bringing in a private of the Black Watch, whose utterances were completely unintelligible. He, however, was so well satisfied with his treatment, consisting mainly of his national beverage administered by his compatriot James Gourlie, that being alongside the regiment again, in Palestine a few years later, he called on the officers' mess to express his gratitude with a skirl of the pipes, and to receive, no doubt, further compensation for his wound.

The Mhow Brigade remained for two months in its quarters round Therouanne. It was here that Her Majesty's Christmas present was distributed. Each man was given a box of chocolates and a cholera belt. The chocolates were highly appreciated and very speedily devoured, and many of the precious boxes which contained them form now an old soldier's most cherished possession; but what to do with the cholera belts was as great a puzzle to the men as were those novelties in underwear which were issued at Marseilles. To wear them round the stomach was to subject Her Majesty's present to an indignity. It could not be done. In the end they wore them on their heads.

Captain Keighley, a retired officer of the Central India Horse, rejoined the regiment here; so also did Major Cooke, who on return from England had been posted to the depot at Marseilles. Major Goodfellow relieved him at the depot. Lieutenant T. R. Wickham of the 39th came out too as a reinforcement officer. About the same time Lieutenant T. Westmacott reported his arrival. He was a Calcutta solicitor, the first of the civilians who joined the regiment for the war and played their part so well. Wickham developed measles soon after his arrival, was sent to hospital in England, and did not return to the regiment.

On the 11th March the brigade was on the move again. Starting before dawn it reached Estrée Blanche soon after daylight. Here the Meerut Brigade joined the column, and at 9.30 A.M. the two brigades were halted in a wood round the Chateau Mont Eventé, behind the village of Lozinghem, with orders to be ready to move at an hour's notice. In front of them the battle of Neuve Chapelle was at its height. On the previous day the village itself, and the trenches on either side of it on a front of 3000 yards, had been carried by the 4th and Indian corps; but on the 11th the attack on the Aubers ridge, beyond the village, failed, and the enemy's counter-attacks were repulsed with difficulty. On the 12th the battle was renewed, and at 10 o'clock at night it ended. The salient in our line had been straightened out but no gap had been made in the German line to give occasion for the use of the Cavalry Brigades which had been waiting for it in the wood. No such occasion did, in fact, ever occur during the war in France, though sabres and lances were held in readiness over and over again.

On the evening of the 14th the cavalry retired to billets along the head-waters of the Lys, those of the Central India Horse being now at Estrée Blanche ; and during the next six weeks the regiments were shifted constantly from village to village, an irritating process for which, in his usual way, the regimental officer showered blame upon the Staff, forgetting that it might have been made necessary by the exigencies of war. The Central India Horse, for instance, was moved on the 18th to Clarques, and on the 7th April to Fontes. On the 12th it returned to Clarques for one night and then went back to Fontes until the 23rd. It was during this period that, in addition to the intensive training which went on daily, a novel but henceforward a recurring duty was thrown upon the soldiers of Indian cavalry, that of digging trenches for their infantry comrades, who were too deeply engaged in the more honourable though hardly more important business of fighting. The idea of sowars digging seemed almost ludicrous at first. In olden days they would have called it " Coolie work " ; but there was much coolie work to be done in this war, and they did it nobly. The need was now so urgent, and the opportunity for rendering some immediate service so attractive, that the men seized it with alacrity, and went off on the busses with a cheer. It cannot be said that they began like experienced sappers, and the sight of the sowar with a loaded wheel-barrow usually provoked laughter; to him it was a monstrous contrivance; but he worked with a will, and in process of time developed the required muscle and became quite a skilful navvy. These digging parties usually consisted of sixty to seventy men per squadron, with the usual complement of British and Indian officers, and stayed out for periods varying from a few days to a month. It was an arduous and monotonous duty, the work being carried out mostly by night, the men resting by day, very often two or three miles in rear of their work, in any old trenches or 'dug-outs' which they could find.

Meanwhile the cavalry still clung tenaciously to the hope that the day was not far distant when they would gallop through "the G in Gap"—as the local joke called it—and onwards to a glorious finale of the war; and no man hoped for this more ardently than the Commander of the Indian Cavalry Corps, General Mike Rimington—"The Iron Ration,"—who at this time was more than usually active in the inspection of regimental transport lest it should be too bulky or too slow for the mobility required. And so it happened that, as he stood on the side of the road whilst the regiment was moving between Clarques and Fontes, he observed amongst the General Service Wagons an innocent-looking cart which had got there, apparently by accident. But at that unfortunate moment a wheel came off this shandridan and out fell an assortment of impedimenta, obviously the property of a British officer, together with an excitable and voluble

French woman. The General had fallen upon the transport of one of the new squadron messes, somewhat amplified, with a lady 'chef,' whom Major Hutchison, with a fine sense for the historic precedent of the 'Vivandière,' had engaged for that service. The exact words used by the Corps Commander on this occasion are not recorded.

The second battle of Ypres, which opened on the 22nd April, was marked by the introduction by our opponents, for the first time in war, of the abominable weapon of poison gas. Our armies were taken completely by surprise. Whole divisions were overwhelmed. All available reinforcements were hurried up to the line. Even the cavalry was called upon, not to stand in readiness for a charge or for pursuit, but simply to be at hand, should the necessity arise, to resist on foot the determined effort which the Germans, aided by the new device, were now making to reach the Channel ports. The orders came to the Mhow Brigade at 4 o'clock on the afternoon of the 24th. At 5.15 the Brigade set out and, marching through Aire-sur-Lys and Wardrecques, reached a point three miles west of Cassel shortly before midnight. It was a distressing march. The regiments had not yet acquired sufficient experience in 'march discipline,' so often preached in the textbooks but so little heeded in practice, with the consequence that there was much ruffling of tempers and considerable damage to horseflesh. Moreover, there was heavy rain to add to the trouble. The Central India Horse, being the last regiment of the brigade, suffered most. It was a night of alternate galloping and halting; now bumping into the unit in front, now wondering whether there was any unit in front at all. As the war progressed regiments learnt, by bitter experience, the 'tips' which the text-books should have given them; but during the first few months the confusion of a night march was great. When the brigade came at last to the end of its journey, which was no longer than sixteen miles, the men were ordered into close billets, the Central India Horse being quartered in the village of Bavanchove, which, however, was not found and occupied until 4 o'clock in the morning. Here for the next three days it remained under orders to be prepared to move at twenty minutes' notice. Neither officers nor men dared to stray more than a few yards from their horses, and meanwhile the roar of the guns round Ypres was unceasing. Every man was on tenter-hooks, expecting orders every minute. The time seemed interminable. At last the brigade was moved forward a little nearer to the battle. It was now billeted around Haringhe, the Central India Horse at Houtkerke, and for five more days stood ready, eagerly waiting. No call to action followed. By the 4th May the battle was over. The long struggle for Hill 60 had ended in the enemy's favour, but his advance had again been stemmed, and the cavalry turned back towards the neighbourhood whence it had come. The ensuing night march was as unpleasant as ever, the 2nd Lancers being the rear regiment on this occasion and so the greatest sufferers; and on the morning of the 5th the Central India Horse found itself in comfortable billets at Amettes, three miles west of Lillers.

From now until the end of July its rest was unbroken, save by a move for a couple of days, the 17th and 18th of May, to Lozinghem during the battle of Festubert. It was a period almost of cantonment life. Sports and horse shows were held; polo was played. There was an attempt at pig-sticking in the woods near Nedenchelles; but the local gamekeeper, unaccustomed to this form of sport, drove the boar back into cover and no run was obtained. The Sikhs, who formed the line of beaters, were greatly disappointed. They described the boar as enormous and very hairy, and more like a bear than a pig. The King and Queen of the Belgians paid a visit to the corps. British officers were able to take a few days' leave. Weather improved. The men were more comfortable and happier. They were becoming more familiar with their surroundings and could now find their way about with remarkable ease. In July a digging party of 200 men was sent to Vermelles, some fifteen miles away, and the Adjutant, Leslie, afterwards recorded with pride that he experienced no difficulty in sending a message to it by a Pathan orderly who borrowed a bicycle, delivered the message, and returned almost as quickly as he could have done in India. One man of the digging party was wounded.

During these summer months of 1915 several additional British officers were posted to the regiment. Three came from British yeomanry regiments. These were Captain Prichard, Captain Pryce Jones, and Lieutenant Leslie Wilson. Prichard served with the regiment until he was killed in the Jordan Valley in 1918. Pryce Jones stayed until the winter of

1916-17. Wilson served for a few months with the regiment and then returned to his own unit.

In May Colonel Bell left for England to command a battalion of the new army.

In July another civilian was appointed. This was Lieutenant W. W. K. Page. He had a most distinguished career in the regiment, which he did not leave until the war was over.

On the 8th July Lord Kitchener inspected all the regiments of the Indian Cavalry Corps. On the 15th General Barrow relinquished the command of the Mhow Brigade to become Brigadier-General on the General Staff of the Tenth Corps, and was succeeded by Brigadier-General Neil Haig, a cousin of the Field-Marshal. His appointment was very popular, for he was well known and much respected. He was the heaviest player on the polo field and one of the best; a bold rider to hounds, an enormous hearty sportsman, with a fine command of military language and the delightful faculty of seeing the good in a man before the bad. The men in his brigade, English and Indian alike, were devoted to him.

At the beginning of August the Mhow Brigade moved down to the Somme and went into billets round Picquigny, the scene of the 'Field of the Cloth of Gold.' From here, on the 14th, the regiment was sent forward to take over the support trenches at Authuille from the 8th Seaforth Highlanders. It held them for eight days, during which there were eight casualties, including Captain Abbott, who was wounded by a shell which hit Regimental Headquarters. On the 25th it was relieved by

Jacob's Horse. The next week was spent in billets at Picquigny, a small party being sent meanwhile to dig reserve trenches in the neighbourhood of Senlis.

Whilst the regiment was at Picquigny it was strengthened by the arrival of one of its old British officers, Major Sir Thomas Lawson-Tancred, Bart., who had retired from the service before the war. Captain C. L. Leslie of the 35th Sindh Horse, and Lieutenant G. B. Walter of the Indian Army Reserve of Officers also came up, as reinforcement officers, from the base.

On the 1st September the Mhow Brigade was again sent forward to the trenches. Proceeding by way of Engelbelmer, where it bivouacked for the night, it passed through Martinsart to Authuille and here took over from the Umballa Brigade, at midnight on the 2nd-3rd, the front line trenches immediately opposite to Thiepval. Here the German trenches were within a few yards of ours. It was nevertheless a comparatively quiet sector. The supply of shell being limited, our guns were silent throughout the greater part of the day. The enemy's artillery was not more active. Our trenches were shelled for an hour every evening, and fourteen Indian soldiers were wounded. It was here that our men first used bombs. These were made up on the spot from empty jam tins and did but little damage, but they gave the men some employment and not a little excitement. On the 14th the regiment was relieved by the 30th Lancers and went back to Picquigny. On the following day the Mhow Brigade was transferred from the 2nd to the 1st

Indian Cavalry Division and moved to a new billeting area lower down the Somme, the Central India Horse being quartered at Bussus-Bussue and Yaucourt-Bussue. Before the end of the month another move became necessary, for the battle of Loos was in progress and the Indian Cavalry Corps was required to be in readiness for emergencies. During the first fortnight of October it was concentrated in rear of the Amiens-Calais railway, the Mhow Brigade in close billets at Villers L'Hopital; and here it stood listening but did no more.

Captain Lewis arrived from India about this time and took over command of 'D' Squadron from Captain Henderson, who left to join the Royal Flying Corps. He brought with him Lieutenant Roxburgh of the Indian Army Reserve of Officers.

The battle of Loos was the last battle in France in which the Indian Army Corps was engaged. It had lost 21,000 officers and men—killed, wounded, and missing—in Indian units alone, and, for want of reinforcements, it could stand the strain no longer. The Indian Army Reserve, never intended to provide reinforcements for a war on a large scale, had proved, of course, inadequate. The few reservists called to the Colours were found to be, for the most part, old or feeble and utterly useless, and their numbers were quickly exhausted; and so it became imperative to call upon regiments in India to fill the gaps. They were able to comply with demands for a certain time because recruiting, stimulated by the enthusiasm of the moment and furthered by the magnificent efforts of civil and military officers, Indian as well as English, had exceeded all expectations. But this business of cutting up a new stocking to mend an old one could not go on indefinitely. Moreover, the all-important question of British officers remained to be solved. The supply had run out. The old sahibs had been killed, and for the present could only be replaced by those who did not understand and were not understood. And so, in November, the Indian regiments of the Indian Corps, covered with glory, were withdrawn from France to rest and to fight again, after recuperation, in other fields.

The same difficulties did not affect the cavalry, which had not yet been seriously engaged and had suffered very few casualties. Regiments in India, augmented as they were, could easily fill vacancies without reducing themselves below normal strength. The cavalry therefore could be, and was, retained in the hope, still cherished by the Higher Command and by every mounted soldier in France, that those long waves of pursuit might some day surge upon a beaten enemy.

CHAPTER XVIII.

THE GREAT WAR—FRANCE—*continued*.

AFTER the battle of Loos the cavalry was withdrawn to a billeting area west of Doullens. During the next two months regiments were kept continually on the move from one village to another, mainly for the purpose of trench digging which now occupied most of their time, and finally, on the setting in of winter, they found themselves in comfortable quarters within a very few miles of the coast. The Central India Horse, during October and November, was billeted in turn at Bernaville, Wavans, Vacquerie, and Villers-Campsart, and on the 16th December went to Fressenville, where it remained until the 25th March 1916.

The following British officers were now present with the regiment : Lieutenant-Colonel A. P. Browne, commanding ; Majors Sir Thomas Lawson-Tancred, Barr, and Lewis ; Captains Hutchison, Keighley, Macnabb, Daunt, Pryce Jones, C. L. Leslie, and Prichard ; and Lieutenants Sir Norman Leslie, the Adjutant, Durand, Page, Wilson, and Roxburgh. Gourlie had been invalided with a broken collar-bone. He was appointed, on recovery, to the Staff of the Royal Flying Corps, and came back to the regiment in June 1916. Abbott also had a Staff appointment. Cooke was commanding an army school in the St Pol area.

The winter months were spent in turning the men into complete infantry soldiers. The close individual fighting, which was continuous all along the line, the fire trenches being in some places within a few yards of one another, had involved the introduction of devices of an earlier day, improved, of course, by modern science; and the bomb and the hand-grenade became as important as the rifle and the bayonet. Bomb throwing, therefore, was now the chief item of the daily programme. A few of the men had used bombs at Authuille, but these were clumsy missiles made of old jam tins with pieces of metal and a charge of explosive inside them. About this time the Mills grenade was invented, and supplied in large quantities, and every officer and man in the regiment received instruction in its use. The risk of a premature explosion added something to the excitement of the practice, and accidents, more or less serious, sometimes occurred. Major Lewis, in fact, nearly lost his life on one occasion, when he held one too long after lighting it, was severely wounded in the abdomen and was invalided to England. Defence against gas was also practised. The soldiers had to be trained to fight encumbered by a mask. These were first issued at Amettes, where the whole population was employed in making them. They consisted in the first instance of flannel hoods soaked in chemicals and were exceedingly uncomfortable. It was necessary to inhale through the nose, the chemicals in the flannel purifying the air before it entered the lung, exhalation being only possible through an india-rubber mouthpiece. The later gas-mask was a much more elaborate affair, with a tube from the nose to a box respirator. It was hideous, though of so little inconvenience to a man that he could even sleep in it.

When off duty both officers and men played football. The most sporting event of the winter was, in fact, a football tournament open to all Indian regiments of the Indian Cavalry Corps. It was won by the Central India Horse. Other contests, such as tugs-of-war and wrestling on horseback, took place, too, between the Central India Horse and their friends and neighbours, the 2nd Lancers, with no preponderance of victory on either side ; and an Indian officer of the 29th Lancers, who had challenged any Indian soldier of the division to wrestle with him, was defeated by Jemadar Ram Singh of the Central India Horse. Meanwhile there was no respite from trench digging. Parties were sent out constantly, one relieving the other, to be attached to the 37th Division, then at Souastre. Every regiment in the brigade was so employed.

On the 5th March 1916 the Indian Cavalry Corps ceased to exist, the 1st Division going to the 3rd Army and becoming the 4th Cavalry Division, and the 2nd Division to the 4th Army becoming the 5th Cavalry Division. On the 24th, winter training was concluded though weather was still severe. The Mhow Brigade was under orders to march to new billets on this day, but a heavy fall of snow prevented movement until the 25th, when it returned to its old area round Doullens. From this date until the end of July the regiment was in billets consecutively at Maison Ponthieu, Poziere, Authieulle, St Acheul, and Roellecourt. At Maison Ponthieu Norman Leslie left the regiment on appointment to the Royal Flying Corps; so did Lieutenant Lucas, who had recently come out from the depot at Goonah. Lucas was killed when 'observing' some three weeks later. Lieutenant T. Westmacott had left a little earlier than this to become, much to his disappointment, an Assistant Provost-Marshal, and Lieutenant W. F. Skene of the 16th Queen's Own Lancers had joined. The latter was an expert conjuror, with a repertoire of tricks which surprised the Indian officers very much. Obviously, if not witchcraft, this was at least an accomplishment which might be made useful as well as amusing; so a certain Jemadar invited Skene one day to smell out the thief who had stolen forty francs from one of his men's bedding. Skene blushingly declined. This was beyond him; but the Jemadar, not to be put off, paraded his troop and told them that Skene Saheb had promised, if the money was not refunded within three days, to divulge the name of the offender. The whole of the stolen property was returned during the second night. Skene went back to the reserve regiment of the 16th Lancers just before the Central India Horse went to Palestine, and died of pneumonia a few years after the war.

During this period the training was mostly in mounted duties, though the regiment could seldom muster its full strength on parade owing to the demands for digging parties which still continued, and indeed grew more and more pressing day by day. The men had, however, wintered well. They had been well clothed and particularly well fed for a year or more. They had put on weight and become extraordinarily self-reliant, and whether digging or drilling, whether mounted or dismounted, or merely polishing their accoutrements, were working very well indeed. They had lost some of their British officers from invaliding or transfer to other units or other appointments; but the vacancies thus caused had been filled, as we have seen, either by officers from cavalry regiments in India well up in the customs of the service, by men from the Indian Army Reserve of Officers who at least knew the language, or by subalterns from English yeomanry regiments who, although complete strangers to the mentality as well as to the language of the sowar, were for the most part of excellent type and quickly inspired the necessary confidence. The men were growing accustomed to these new officers. The regiment was eager for active work.

Before the Mhow Brigade left the neighbourhood of Maison Ponthieu all the machine-guns of the brigade were brought together into one machine-gun squadron, under the command of Captain Humphrey of the Inniskilling Dragoons. Williams and Durand joined this squadron. Barr and Goodfellow were both invalided about this time, and Lieutenants Wynyard-Wright, C. L. Reid, G. B. Walter, P. C. Mangin, and C. E. Milner of the Indian Army Reserve of Officers, and Lieutenant T. D. Wilson of the 10th Royal Hussars (Special Reserve), were posted to the regiment. Barr died in England shortly afterwards. Wilson served with the regiment throughout the remainder of the war, and died of malaria at Damascus just after the Armistice was signed.

From Roellecourt a large digging party, under command of Captain Macnabb, was moved up to Marœuil, near Arras, to relieve a party of Jacob's Horse. The strength and disposition of this party, which were similar to those of all others, are given here as an example, the extract from the War Diary being as follows :—

"*Digging Party:* 6 B.Os. 6 I.Os. 10 B.O.Rs. 266 I.O.Rs.
6 *Followers.*

Moved up to Marœuil and relieved digging party of 36th Jacob's Horse.

Disposition as follows :—

H.Q. at Marœuil. Capt. R. Macnabb (Comdr.)
Lt. W. K. K. Page (Adjt.)
' A ' Sqdn., Captain C. L. Leslie. Abri Sablier.
' B ' Sqdn., 2nd Lt. Wynyard-Wright. Marœuil.
' C ' Sqdn., Major R. G. M. Prichard. Abri Centrale.
' D ' Sqdn., Lt. C. L. Reid. Marœuil."

On the eve of its departure steel helmets were issued to the regiment. The Sikhs, owing to their religious scruples, were allowed to retain the lungi. The Pathans applied, through their Risaldars— Kamaluddin and Lihaz Gul,—for the same concession, which, however, was not granted since, unlike the Sikhs, they had no real scruple of any sort. They simply considered the new helmets to be ugly. After being made to wear them as long as they were in the trenches they seem to have changed their minds concerning their æsthetic value. Before long they took to wearing them on all occasions, and nearly every man in the squadron had his photograph taken in his smart new head-dress.

The month of August was spent in further preparations, in billets behind the Amiens-Calais railway, the regiment moving before the end of the month to Cambligneul. Early in September every available cavalry unit was moved down to the Somme to be ready to take advantage of the success which was hoped for in the great Allied offensive which had been in progress since the 1st July. By the 13th the 4th Cavalry Division was concentrated on the right bank of the Somme, about Querrieux. On the 15th it moved forward to a preparatory position near Morlancourt. On this day an attack of eleven British divisions was launched against the German positions between Combles and Courcelettes. The first two stages of the battle were accomplished successfully, according to plan. The British line fought its way 3000 yards forward, overrunning its first two objectives, but was held up by the defences in front of the villages of Morval, Les Bœufs, and Gueudecourt. The capture of these three villages was to have provided the opportunity for the cavalry to break through to the country beyond, and there to form a defensive flank eastwards, covering the advance of the 4th Army through the gap and northwards towards Bapaume. It was now seen, however, that, without further deliberate preparation, our success could not be completely established. Another attack was therefore prepared for the 21st; but at this critical juncture, when time was the essence of victory, rain fell in torrents, preventing the aerial observation of new defences which the enemy had constructed. In this way four valuable days were lost, and when, after the capture of Gueudecourt, cavalry patrols were pushed out beyond that village, it was found that the Germans had had time to prepare new lines of trenches farther to the northward; and the opportunity was gone.

Meanwhile the cavalry was waiting at Morlancourt. At 3 o'clock on the morning of the 25th the Mhow Brigade moved forward to Montauban. Here Brigade Headquarters and the Central India Horse halted, whilst the Inniskillings and 2nd Lancers went on to a forward position between Bernafay and Trônes Wood. The plan for operations after the fall of Gueudecourt was known; but instructions had been received that, if the village was not taken by 4 o'clock in the afternoon, the cavalry would not be required. The morning wore on, the men standing to their horses, inactive but greatly excited, the thunder of the guns more intensive than anything yet known. The shells passed overhead; masses of German prisoners were marched through to the rear; the battle seemed to be going very well for us. But after noon the fire slackened. At 4 o'clock no further news or orders had been received. Officers looked at one another; their faces fell; and then, at 6.15, they heard that Gueudecourt was still untaken and the advanced squadrons were coming back to Montauban. A little later Colonel His Highness The Maharajah of Ratlam, who had recently joined the regiment and had been appointed regimental galloper to the brigade, galloped back over the shell holes with an order that the whole division was to return to Morlancourt. It got back somehow or other that night; but the road was so full of vehicles, going either way, that no regular formation was possible, and, troop by troop, the regiments shuffled into bivouac as best they could.

The 26th was a day of rest, and on the following morning the cavalry was sent back to billets on the Authie, the Central India Horse at Dourriez, close to the battlefield of Crécy; and here it remained throughout the month of October. On the 1st November it was withdrawn to winter quarters near the coast, about St Valerie, in the same district as the winter billets of the previous year, the Central India Horse having its Headquarters at Nibas, where it resumed its infantry training. The digging parties were now organised on a more permanent basis. Each brigade was called upon to form a Pioneer Battalion of three companies, one from each regiment, the strength of each Indian company being 6 British officers, 8 British other ranks, 5 Indian officers, and 255 Indian other ranks. The Mhow Battalion, as it was officially designated, was attached to the Third Corps, and was in the line at Mondicourt and Fricourt throughout the winter. Intended originally for entrenching duties, and employed on these alone during the winter of 1916-17, it became engaged later on in more serious work, and came in for some severe fighting during the following summer and autumn.

The winter of 1916-17 was unusually severe, and the Mhow Battalion, although accommodated in Nissen huts, suffered much discomfort. By this time, however, Indian soldiers had become so well acclimatised that admissions to hospital were remarkably few. One British officer of the Central India Horse, Major Cooke, was invalided, and, to the sorrow of the regiment, died in hospital in England soon after his admission.

The Mhow Battalion returned to billets early in March, and regiments had just commenced mounted training when, at 3 o'clock in the morning of the 19th, the 4th Cavalry Division was suddenly ordered to move forward. The order was unexpected and its cause unknown. Bustle and excitement pervaded the ranks, and on the march through Petit Laviers and St Ouen to Aveluy, which was reached on the 21st, every kind of report except the right one was passed along the column. At Aveluy the intention of the move was revealed. The effect upon the enemy of the battle of the Somme had at last disclosed itself, and the Germans were in retreat to the Hindenburg Line. The 5th Army was preparing to attack the enemy's positions round the village of Bullecourt. The cavalry was to take part. On the 3rd April the division marched up to Irles and bivouacked in the snow. On the night of the 9th-10th it was moved to a position of readiness in the Mory Valley, where it remained for a few hours, and then returned to Irles in a snowstorm. At 2.45 on the morning of the 11th it again went forward, and from the Mory Valley commenced an advance towards Bullecourt, the Sialkote Brigade leading, the Mhow Brigade in support. The ground was so difficult, owing to snow and slush and shell holes, that the men were obliged to dismount and lead their horses. It soon became apparent that the advance was premature and that all was not going well with the Sialkote Brigade, which had topped the ridge and disappeared from view. Loose horses came floundering back; and presently the order was given to retire to the position of readiness. It transpired that the 17th Lancers had fallen upon uncut wire behind which was a nest of machine-guns. Visibility was bad, for snow was still falling, or the losses would have been very heavy indeed. The division remained in the Mory Valley during the rest of the day. At nightfall it was withdrawn to Irles, where it halted until the 13th, when it marched back to billets on the Authie, the Central India Horse being now located at Sarton.

A period of rest followed. It was sorely needed, for men and horses had suffered much from exposure since leaving Nibas. The horses, when not in movement, had stood hock-deep in muddy snow. They had had no repose. The men were equally fatigued and very dirty. At one or two halting-places they had found bell-tents to sleep in, but for the most part had lain in the open. At Sarton baths were provided, new clothing was issued, and all lost or damaged equipment was made good. The weather improved too, black clouds and snow giving place to the warm sunshine of early spring. It was a quiet pleasant time disturbed only by occasional administrative difficulties, attributable in some measure to the change of season itself; for the young herbage was coming up and the sowar, whose first thought in war if not in peace is for his mount, took full advantage of it, with the very natural consequence that complaints were made to 'higher authority.' "Les Hindous" in fact became a little unpopular. 'Higher authority' soon made itself felt. Severely worded orders were promulgated, followed by visitations of Staff Officers—

> ". . . . threatening hideous fall
> One day upon our heads,"

and the indiscriminate grazing ceased abruptly. There was one Squadron Leader,[1] however, who scored a pleasing triumph over his tormentors of the Staff. A young officer of the Administrative Branch, riding round on a tour of informal inspection, chanced to come upon a twenty-acre field where to his horrified gaze was exposed the spectacle of fifty or sixty happy horses, unsaddled, grazing and rolling in the sun, whilst two completely nonchalant British officers were smoking their pipes under a tree. Back to Headquarters did he gallop, without making inquiries or even verifying his position on the map, with a picturesque report of the outrage. Authority was greatly agitated. Our friendship with France was in jeopardy. The culprit was eventually traced. All leave was stopped in the sinning brigade to which he belonged, and the Brigadier himself was called upon to report what disciplinary action he had taken. The

[1] Major Gourlie.

Squadron Leader smiled. He had rented that field from a farmer for 500 francs, paid out of his own pocket; and the Brigadier's report merely forwarded the receipt for this money, duly stamped and signed by the Maire. The Staff capitulated, leave was reopened, and the Squadron Leader smoked his pipe with greater scorn for officialdom than ever.

On the 15th May this restful period came to an end. The 4th Cavalry Division was on this day moved down to the devastated area in the bend of the Somme between Peronne and St Quentin. The Central India Horse went into camp near St Christ on the 17th and at once resumed infantry training. Five days later it moved to Ennemain, and from here the Mhow Battalion was sent up into the line east of Hargicourt to take over a sub-sector of the trenches from the South Staffords. The Mhow Battalion was commanded alternately by the Colonel of each regiment of the brigade, with an officer from one of the other regiments as Second-in-Command. On this occasion Colonel Paterson of the Inniskillings led the battalion, with Major Gourlie of the Central India Horse as his Second-in-Command. The Central India Horse Company was over 300 strong, with ten British officers.

Meanwhile the battle of Arras had been fought, and a great British offensive had just opened in Flanders. On the Somme the situation was thus comparatively quiet. It was expedient, however, to detain as many German units as possible in this part of the line, as well as to identify them; and with the arrival of fresh troops eager for distinction this quietness became a little less noticeable. During the next few months constant patrolling took place, and many a raid into the enemy's trenches was carried out, by day as well as by night, by small parties under a British officer or two, and much information was collected. The hostile trenches were, in this sector, a considerable distance apart, ' No Man's Land ' being in some cases half a mile broad or even more. It was nowhere possible to lob a grenade, without moving, into a German shelter, as our men had done at Authuille, where the trenches were almost contiguous. A raid consequently involved a dash across the open, or a crawl from tuft to tuft or from shell hole to shell hole, and was never unmarked by casualties. The first carried out by a party from the regiment was planned by Lieutenants Cameron and Durand to take place by daylight on the morning of the 29th of May. Cameron belonged to The Guides, and had recently come out from India with reinforcements for us. He and Durand had already formed a close friendship, and, from the moment when the Central India Horse Company took over the fire trenches in front of Hargicourt, had occupied themselves in the preparation of schemes for inflicting as much loss upon the enemy and obtaining as much information from him as possible. The German fire trenches were about 200 yards from our own, the particular trench in front of the Central India Horse being known as ' New Trench.' Our own fire trenches were not continuous. On the left Macnabb's trench—for it was he who commanded the Central India Horse Company on this occasion—

curved forward to a sunken lane, running parallel to the trenches, where for occupation purposes it ended. Beyond the lane, however, it continued

Trenches in Front of Hargicourt.

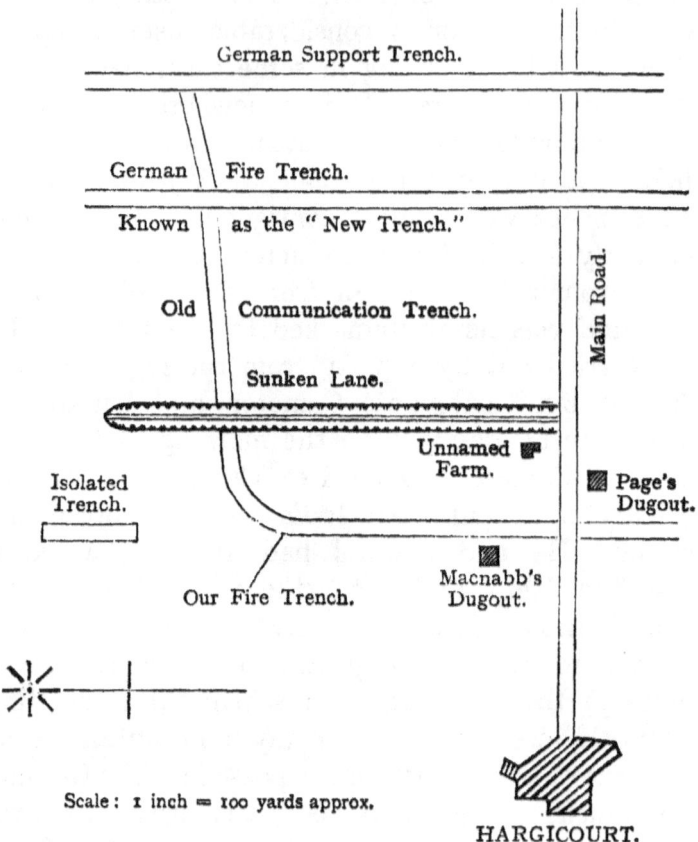

across 'No Man's Land' into the German system. It was, in fact, an old communication trench, with traverses, formerly occupied by the enemy. The subalterns' plan was to start from the sunken lane shortly before daylight, and, pushing along the old communication trench, lie up in some large shell holes about half-way across 'No Man's Land' until noon. Then, when the Germans were, as it was supposed, indulging in their mid-day potations, the party was to crawl back to the communication trench and work along it to the last traverse, from which point a couple of bombs were to be lobbed into 'New Trench.' At this moment a trench-mortar battery was to put down a barrage right and left of the trench junction and on the continuation of the communication trench between the two German lines, whilst the raiding party rushed in to take prisoners. The retirement was to be made by the same way, the occupants of our own trench covering the withdrawal by intensive fire from rifles and machine-guns. The plan was upset before it could be set in motion, for early in the afternoon of the 28th Macnabb was informed by two excited and indignant subalterns that they had been forestalled by a couple of privates of the Machine-Gun Corps, who, having overheard conversations, had borrowed a brace of revolvers and had themselves carried out the design that morning, killing, as they averred, at least one German but without bringing back any information whatever. Since it was important to learn what enemy unit was holding 'New Trench,' Macnabb decided to carry out Cameron's raid immediately, instead of waiting until the morning and thus giving the Germans an opportunity for the construction of fresh obstacles during the night. The members of the raiding party had been told off and were at hand at the end of the trench, the trench-mortars were in place and had done their registering, there need be not a moment's delay. Cameron, followed by Lance Dafadar Fateh Khan and Sowars Kutabuddin Khan, Habib Gul Khan, Dost Mahomed Khan, and Mahomed Sharif Khan, went over the parapet and dropped into the sunken lane. Macnabb and Durand watched them from the bank of the lane, which afforded a commanding view of the country and the trenches in front, whilst Lieutenant Woodhouse, with a few men as local reserve, stood ready at the bottom of the trench just behind them. The raiding party crept along the disused communication trench, but before reaching the end traverse, Cameron, suspecting that there were Germans in the trench, lobbed a bomb over an intervening traverse, and, having disclosed his position, was obliged to bomb his way methodically up to the junction. Seeing this, Macnabb sent a man forward with a fresh supply of bombs, and at this moment there was a burst of machine-gun fire from a position which could not be detected, the bullets striking the ground all round the raiding party. Woodhouse thereupon went over the top, closely followed by his orderly, Ghulam Mahomed Khan, climbed our wire, and ran forward to investigate. He observed that the firing came from an isolated trench on our left rear held by one of our own units, and climbing back on to the parapet he waved the 'wash-out' signal, which was eventually respected. Meanwhile the raiding party was approaching the objective—namely, the trench junction, and the trench-mortar barrage opened according to plan. Cameron, however, went farther than he was intended to go. He turned to the right and went bombing along the German fire trench and presently showed himself on the farther side of the barrage; but running short of bombs and not knowing that a fresh supply was on its way to him, he returned to the trench junction, though not without entering two or three deep dug-outs and collecting much valuable information in the shape of papers and articles of uniform. The German occupants of ' New Trench ' had sought the shelter of their support trenches and their dug-outs during this operation, but as the raiding party withdrew they emerged, and a sharp exchange of fire ensued. Durand, who had been greatly disappointed by Macnabb's refusal to allow him to accompany Cameron, was now showing himself well above the parapet using two rifles, his orderly loading for him in the trench below. He was ordered down, but, before descending, was wounded in the leg by a bullet which came through a loophole where Lance Dafadar Ahmad Yar Khan was using a Hotchkiss-gun with good effect. He, too, was wounded in the wrist. The raiding party, whipped in by Cameron, finally reached the sunken lane without casualty, and dropped safely into the trench.

On the following evening Cameron went out again, accompanied only by his orderly, Lance Dafadar Abdul Hakim Khan, to ascertain whether the German fire trench south of the main road was occupied at night. Starting from Macnabb's dug-out after dinner he went along the main road as far as ' Unnamed Farm,' an advanced post about fifty yards in front of our fire trench ; then, leaving the road, he crept forward slowly until he found himself held up by wire. He made his way through this without difficulty, and crawling on again, with his orderly at his heels, he was suddenly surprised by a challenge from a trench below him on his right. He was actually lying on a German traverse, with the German trench on three sides of him. Hoping that the sentry might think after all that he had been mistaken, Cameron lay still. The sentry, however, was not so easily satisfied. He hurled a bomb, which exploded between the two adventurers without hitting either of them. Still they did not move. The sentry then prepared another bomb, but before he could fire it Cameron himself flung one down into the trench, and, jumping up, the pair of them ran for home. They were pursued along the road for some distance, but with a good start in their favour, reached our fire trench unharmed. Cameron received the Military Cross for these two exploits.

Whilst these events were taking place on the left some Sikhs, under Lieutenant Page, were holding the right portion of our fire trench on the south side of the main road. A detachment from Page's squadron held the advanced post at 'Unnamed Farm,' which was subjected all day long on the 2nd June to a very severe shelling. Sowar Indar Singh was killed and Wardi Major Hazara Singh and eight men were wounded before Macnabb and Page arrived upon the scene, but by a rare combination of nerve and skill Page held the post during the remainder of the day without a further casualty. The episode is best described in Major Macnabb's own words: " We had all dispersed after breakfast, following on a night when I don't suppose any of us had more than three hours' sleep. Page, I know, had gone off to bed, and, if I remember rightly, I had managed to keep awake long enough to finish writing the usual reports, and was just going to turn in, when the Boshe began shelling Unnamed Farm. From the trench, at the door of the dug-out, Unnamed Farm was about seventy yards off on the sky-line rather to the right front, and it was easy to see the German shooting was pretty good. A moment later I was called up from the farm on the telephone. The report said that a shell had landed in the trench and that there had been a lot of casualties. I said I would be coming along, and went off to wake up the unfortunate Page. He had dug himself a shelter in a bank of the main road (where it was sunken enough to afford a covered approach to the Unnamed Farm), and was sleeping like a log when I got there. The shelling had not stopped, and it looked as if he was going to have an unpleasant morning of it. When we got up to the farm we found things in a pretty good mess. Evacuating the wounded was not easy, as, apart from the shelling, there was one place where a sniper could have a bang at you unless you crouched very low, just at the exit from the post before you got into the shelter of the sunken road. There was only a short bit of trench in the post, perhaps fifteen yards, and Page thought that even if the bombardment was to be followed by an attempt to rush the post it was no use trying to keep more than six or eight men up there. Accordingly we turned out some younger sowars; one, I remember, was very indignant about it, and another hid behind a traverse, and having escaped immediate removal stayed on right through the ordeal and was quite unshaken at the end.

"I then went back to my dug-out and Page carried on. The shelling was most methodical. The first shell would be a bit short, the second somewhere in or near the trench, and the third a little over it. Then the first of the next bracket would be a little to the right or left of the last three, and from that Page had to guess where the second and third were likely to go, and would shift his men accordingly from one end of the trench to the other. When a shell pitched in the trench there would be some frenzied digging till the trench was cleared again. This would have been a considerable strain on most people, but Page, of course, was entirely unmoved. Every now and again he would tell me on the 'phone how they were getting on, and his conversation would be interrupted by the scream of a shell followed by a placid 'Damn, here comes another one,' followed by the burst of the shell as heard on the 'phone, followed by the burst heard direct, followed by the tinkle tinkle of stone, earth, &c., falling on Page's tin hat, and then Page would go on with his conversation where he left off. For three hours the shelling never stopped, but after that it became more patchy. I offered at intervals to send somebody up to relieve Page, but he would not hear of it—much to my relief, as a new fellow going up there might have had half a dozen casualties in five minutes. Page never had a man touched after he got there, and I remember going up to meet his little party when they were relieved at dusk, and hearing Page having something to say about one of the men being out of step."

On the next day the Mhow Battalion was relieved, but returned to the same section of trenches on the 15th. On this occasion the battalion was commanded by Colonel Browne, with Major Terrot of the Inniskillings as his Second-in-Command. Macnabb again commanded the Central India Horse Company, the British officers with him being Captains Williams, Keighley, and Daunt, and Lieutenants Wilson, Filose, Durand, Pinney, and Reid. Pinney had recently left Sandhurst, had been gazetted to the Royal Fusiliers, had been for a short time an observer in the Royal Flying Corps, and was now posted to the regiment for permanent appointment. He was the eldest son of Major John Pinney, who had been for many years in the regiment and was now serving in Egypt. During the ensuing fortnight there was no close fighting, one man only being killed and three wounded by shell-fire; but on the 28th another raid was made upon the German 'New Trench.' This was carried out by two parties of 'B' Squadron, one of ten men under Durand and one of fourteen under Wilson. The first party was to move along the disused communication trench as far as the last traverse and there to await the signal of a Verey light, whilst the second crept by way of the shell holes to the German wire about fifty yards to the right of the trench junction. On the signal being given Durand was to seize the junction and to halt there until the arrival of Wilson and his men, who would jump into 'New Trench' and fight their way down to him. All went well to begin with. Both parties reached their starting points and the signal went up. Durand immediately climbed on to the parapet and threw a bomb into the trench junction. His orderly, from the trench below, handed up another to him, and as he was withdrawing the pin a German bomb exploded in front of him, wounding him in the body. In spite of this he led his party into the trench junction, posted men to block all three approaches, and waited for Wilson. The latter had jumped into 'New Trench,' followed by his men, had killed two or three Germans with his revolver, and had driven the rest of them in front of him down the trench towards Durand. These fellows, however, managed to escape by climbing out of the trench, which was shallow on the rearward side, and running across the open to their support trench; so Wilson joined Durand without prisoners. The latter ordered him to collect the sowars who were blocking the approaches and to prepare to withdraw; but he asked permission first to go down the German communication trench and round up a few of the enemy so as not to return empty-handed. Durand, however, insisted on immediate obedience, and Wilson went off to collect the men. When he returned he found that Durand had fainted. No one was aware, until this moment, that he had been hit. He was carried back to our fire trench and sent to No. 5 Casualty Clearing Station, where he died on the following afternoon. Eight Germans were killed during this raid, and, in addition to Durand, Wilson and twelve men were wounded, most of them on the return journey to our trenches.

Reggie Durand was thus the first British officer serving with the regiment to meet his death at the hands of the enemy. He was a gallant spirit. Like so many of those brave youths who left their bones in France, he seemed to enjoy danger for its own sake, and was never so happy as when, with his friends Dickie Cameron and Johnnie Pinney, both of whom were laid to rest near him in Tincourt cemetery a few months later, he was designing or carrying out some hazardous enterprise. Many were the deeds of selfless heroism performed by these young soldiers. It should not, however, be forgotten that whilst our British subalterns, those 'boy officers' to whom our former foes, the Sikhs, attributed our victories of 1848, were so conspicuous in their leadership, there were others, Indian officers and soldiers too, who in daring were no whit behind them. Of these, Risaldar Dilawar Khan was one of the brightest examples. He smelt the battle afar off, and where the greatest danger was, there was he. On the march neither fatigue nor cold could quell his ardour, so long as the music of the guns drew nearer; and in the trenches he was ever foremost to repel a German raid. Jemadar Ram Singh, too, steady like all good Sikhs, would gird up his loins for a dangerous patrol and carry it through with grim determination. Imperturbable Lihaz Gul, whom no crisis could shake, would rouse himself to fury in personal combat. Risaldar Kamaluddin Khan, an optimist like his father old Bahauddin Khan, was always eager for fighting. He happened to be in England when the regiment was finally ordered to Marseilles; 'wangled' through Norman Leslie, who was then at the Air Office, a passage in an aeroplane to Boulogne, and found his way across France with ease. They were all splendid. Sikhs, Ghakkars, and Pathans vied with one another in facing perils and difficulties, and no history should be written that has no record of their gallant behaviour.

The Mhow Battalion returned to Ennemain on the 9th July, the regiment having lost, since the raid of the 28th June, three men killed and two officers—Lieutenant Pinney and Risaldar Dilawar Khan—and eleven men wounded. It was during this short period that Lance Dafadar Achar Singh distinguished himself. He took out a patrol to attack a German working party and covering party which he himself had located on the previous night. He had, in fact, crept round the covering party, and had brought home one of the working party's rifles. The patrol, however, could do nothing more than take note of the work in progress, as the Germans did not wait for them.

Ennemain was the extreme right of the British line, which was separated from the French by the Omignon stream. Here the regiment had made itself pretty comfortable. Shelters for men and horses, with brick floors too, had been constructed from the ruins of the village; and the Squadron Messes and the Club were almost luxurious. British officers amused themselves, when off duty, with fishing in the Omignon, and polo was played regularly on a ground near Brigade Headquarters. Here, too, our friend Nouguier became engaged to be married to a lady who owned property in the neighbouring village of Athies, where she paid occasional visits to her ruined home. His betrothal was celebrated by a dinner in his honour. He remained, however, on duty with the regiment until the eve of its departure from France. The other interpreters had already been withdrawn.

The month of August passed quietly and pleasantly at Ennemain, a small digging party in the trenches being the only detachment. In September the trench business began again. The Mhow Battalion, in fact, had two turns of duty in the firing line during this month, with a week's interval between them, in the sector south of Hargicourt, a little to the right of the scene of the operations just described. On the 29th of this month Wilson distinguished himself in an endeavour, which unfortunately failed, to reconnoitre the enemy's wire. ' No Man's Land ' was here more than three-quarters of a mile broad, and the night was not sufficiently dark to give the patrol more than a sporting chance of reaching the wire unseen. Nor were there sufficient shell holes or undulations in the ground, or even tufts of grass, to give cover from view and fire. Wilson nevertheless crawled out with his men, Sikhs of ' B ' Squadron mostly, and reached a spot about half-way across, where he dropped the major portion of his party and crept on with two or three men towards the enemy's trench. At 200 yards from his objective he was observed by a German sentry, and a heavy fire of rifles and machine-guns was opened on him. He could now only lie flat for a few seconds and then crawl back, with his party, to the patrol, which he rejoined without mishap. It was at this moment, however, that casualties began to occur, for, a larger target being now exposed to view, the fire became more intense and the crawl onwards to our own trench was accomplished under very great difficulty. Sowars Kesar Singh and Bachan Singh were killed, and Sowar Harnam Singh was wounded in the head. Two privates of a patrol of the 8th Buffs, which accompanied Wilson's, were also wounded. At 3.30 in the morning the patrol reached our lines, bringing the dead and wounded with them. It was a gallant piece of work. The Sikhs kept their heads and behaved beautifully, Sowar Dhalip Singh being especially prominent. He was decorated with the Indian Order of Merit for his conduct on this night, and Wilson received an immediate award of the Military Cross.

Early in October the battalion was relieved, and the regiment again found itself concentrated at Ennemain. Lieutenant Hirst of the Indian Army Reserve of Officers and Captain R. Westmacott of the Calcutta Light Horse joined about this time; and a large batch of young officers, affectionately known as 'War Babies,' came out from England for appointment to the Indian Army. Of these Lieutenants Cox, George, Dalrymple-Hay, and Alington were permanently appointed to the Central India Horse. In November large reinforcements were sent up from the base. There seemed now to be a stir, as of preparation for important events. Staff Officers appeared to be more active than usual. Moreover, cavalry regiments were set to work at mounted training, somewhat intensively too, at this unusual season. The Mhow Battalion ceased to function as such. There were no digging parties. One large detachment, however, went out from the brigade, dismounted, under Lieutenant-Colonel R. C. Bell, on a mysterious mission. Obviously there was something in the air. Yet no one at Brigade Headquarters, or even in much higher quarters still, knew anything of projected operations. The preparation for the battle of Cambrai, which was now imminent, was, in fact, the best-kept secret of the war.

CHAPTER XIX.

THE GREAT WAR—FRANCE (*continued*).

It is unfortunately true that the battle of Cambrai was designed with the deliberate intention of giving Haig's fine body of cavalry, hitherto so useless as such, the opportunity which officers and men had been trained to look for, and that the plan just failed. Haig was a cavalry soldier. He was a follower of Bernhardi. He had preached the importance of the rôle of cavalry all his life. He had five Cavalry Divisions behind his line, and he believed that, given a good opening and a convenient terrain, his mounted warriors could still demonstrate the truth of the theories he had inculcated and crown a victory with a paralysing raid. It seemed that the moment had come. The enemy had weakened his line in many places in order to meet our attacks in Flanders and the French offensive on the Aisne, and it was necessary to show him that he could not do this with impunity. Many months must elapse before such another opportunity could arise, for no offensive on a large scale, to attract his strength, could be attempted in the winter, and meanwhile the tired German troops could rest, they could be redistributed, and reinforcements could be brought across from the Russian front. Haig therefore prepared the blow. Whether, before the end of October, he had actually decided to deliver it must remain doubtful. Against it were weighty arguments which he had considered very earnestly, for none felt more seriously than he the grave responsibility of a General in war, and it was no trifling matter to make a heavy call upon troops who had been fighting incessantly for many months. But whilst his arrangements were in progress there occurred the Italian disaster of Caporetto. There could be no question now that a blow in France was imperative in order to discount this Austrian victory, which, as the German High Command knew well, could have no importance whatever compared with an Allied success on the Western Front. Preparations were consequently hurried on. They were timed to be complete by the third week in November.

Though marked by some of the fiercest fighting and by some of the most gallant behaviour on both sides which the war had yet evoked, the battle of Cambrai was, in its inception, a local and, comparatively speaking, a minor operation. Nothing was projected beyond a sudden onslaught of infantry and tanks on a front of less than six miles between the two canals, the Canal de l'Escault and the Canal du Nord, followed by a burst through of cavalry, who would raid the communications and delay the arrival of German reinforcements, whilst fresh Infantry Divisions would follow them through the gap and exploit the country to the north-west towards the river Scarpe between Arras and Douai. The ground was especially suitable to the movement of the mounted arm. It was open down-like country, covered with short grass, not unlike the Southdowns near Brighton, with prominent beech woods here and there. There were as yet but few shell-holes. The enemy's defences, though lightly held, were, however, of a most formidable character. Lines of massed wire, in some cases a hundred yards broad, protected his trenches. For all the advantages provided by nature it would be impossible for cavalry to move with such barriers in the way. These, therefore, had to be destroyed. Yet guns could not be used for this purpose. Surprise being essential, there could be no artillery preparation, nor could tanks, though they might clear narrow paths for infantry soldiers, make roadways broad enough for cavalry formations to pass along without hindrance. The difficulty was solved—whether it was the Commander-in-Chief's own suggestion or the brain-wave of some Staff Officer who shall say?—by the formation of a special body of 500 dismounted men from the 4th Cavalry Division under Colonel Bell of the Central India Horse,[1] who would follow the infantry attack, tear away the wire, bridge or level the trenches, fill up the shell-holes, and thus carve a broad track through the German lines to the country where the Mounted Branch was to come into its own. Every detail had been thought out. Everything was ready by the appointed time; yet, with the exception of one or two officers in very high authority, and of the French Commander-in-Chief who had agreed to place a strong force in a position of readiness to help if help were required, nobody

[1] See Appendix I.

knew what was going on; not even the Germans. The enemy was, in fact, totally unprepared. Usually well informed, he remained, on this occasion, completely ignorant until the attack was actually launched. His spies had told him nothing, because they knew nothing. The few aeroplanes he sent over could see nothing. He had practically disregarded this section of the line. The single raid he attempted during the month of November brought him back nothing; and so our successes in the early stages of the battle were rapid and almost complete.

Six British divisions, with 324 tanks of the latest pattern, called Mark IV., formed the attacking force. Opposite to them were three German defence systems, the Hindenburg Line running from Banteux on the Canal de l'Escault to Havrincourt on the Canal du Nord and thence northwards along the Canal to Mæuvres, the Hindenburg Reserve Line a mile or so behind it, and behind this a line running from Marquion in a south-easterly direction through Masnières to Beaurevoir. It was calculated that no German reinforcements could arrive within forty-eight hours, and the Commander of the 3rd Army was informed that, unless results justified the continuance of the battle, the advance would be stopped at the end of that period. The principal objective, after the piercing of the first two lines, was not the town of Cambrai, but the village and wood of Bourlon and the ridge, running east and west, on which they stand. From this ridge the ground slopes down to the Sensée river, crossed by the Cambrai-Douai railway some five miles distant, and around here was the field of action for the cavalry. Bourlon was never completely taken. Whether, with the enemy in possession of the ridge, the cavalry could still have passed through farther to the right is a question which has been discussed, and will no doubt continue to be discussed, elsewhere. The fact remains that, with one small brilliant exception, no mounted troops went forward.

On Sunday morning, the 18th of November, the cavalry was warned to be in readiness. The Headquarters of the 4th Cavalry Division and of the Mhow Brigade were at Athies. The Central India Horse was still at Ennemain. Its orders now were to be prepared to move at any moment after 9 o'clock on Monday morning. The regiment was living very comfortably at this time. It was no quick matter to clear for action, for large quantities of spare clothing and other stores had been accumulated, and these had to be collected and formed into 'dumps.' This business occupied the whole of Sunday, and next morning the squadrons stood ready to go. Monday, however, was a quiet day. It was not until Tuesday morning that the regiment was on the move.

Meanwhile in the trenches the same quietness prevailed. There was no outward indication of the coming storm. No raids were made, no patrols sent forward. Save for a short and unaccountable outburst of firing in the small hours from a trench away on the left, no sound disturbed the stillness of the night. But before dawn the troops were alert. Officers had their eyes on their wrists, counting the minutes, the seconds, to zero hour. Then suddenly, at twenty minutes past six on the morning of the 20th November, the silence was broken by the roar of twelve hundred guns. On then went the tanks, rolling like great beetles over the downs, followed by the infantry and that detachment of Colonel Bell's, which set to work forthwith on its levelling mission, a mighty difficult task accomplished successfully but in vain. The Hindenburg Line was overrun almost without opposition. Tanks tore great lanes through the wire. Infantry, hidden by screens of smoke, went forward over the trenches. Occasionally a tank would dive into a trench and hurtle along it, crushing down every obstacle and slaying every living thing. But there was no stopping. On they went to the next line. Here, however, our troops encountered more stubborn resistance. Very severe fighting resulted in the capture of Ribécourt and Havrincourt; but at Flesquières the stout brick wall round the park of the chateau, and the gallantry of a German artillery officer, who worked his gun single-handed until he was killed, kept the 51st Division at bay. This village was not taken until the following morning. Forward, nevertheless, went the rest of the line towards the third objective. Marcoing, Graincourt, and Anneux were taken during the afternoon. At Masnières, however, there was another misadventure. The enemy had partially destroyed the bridge over the Canal de l'Escault, and the leading tank, attempting to cross it, completed the destruction. The infantry of the 29th Division were thus obliged to go on without tanks, and although they entered the village, they were unable to clear the northern portion, which remained in the hands of the enemy until late in the evening.

During this conflict the cavalry had come to their position of readiness. The Mhow Brigade had marched from Athies through lines of cheering French soldiers, and was now in Fins Wood. The weather was damp and dismal, and the mud as deep as ever. Little heed, however, was paid to such discomforts. The only thought was for news of the battle, and every news-bringer was questioned eagerly. All was going well: the 'day' seemed to be at hand. Certain units of the 1st and 5th Cavalry Divisions had actually taken part, dismounted, in the fighting on this day; and one squadron of the latter—it was 'B' Squadron of the Fort Garry Horse of the Canadian Brigade,—which had apparently escaped from its division, had galloped as far as Masnières, where it halted for an hour or so during the construction of a makeshift bridge. Orders sent to the commander not to cross the canal were either not received or not heeded. As soon as the bridge was ready over he went. He passed through the Marquion-Beaurevoir Line, charged a German battery in position to the east of Rumilly, and took the guns; then, continuing his advance, he dispersed a column of 300 German infantry, but finally, having lost more than half his horses and finding himself without support, he had to abandon the guns and seek the shelter of a sunken road, which he held till nightfall. After dark he made his way with difficulty back to our trenches, bringing with him several German prisoners as a token of his amazing ride.

On the 21st the battle was renewed, the cavalry still waiting. Flesquières was taken early in the morning. Masnières was held throughout the day against heavy counter-attacks from the direction of Rumilly by a fresh German division, which, most opportunely for our opponents, had just arrived from Russia. Farther to the left Noyelles was held by the 29th Division and some dismounted units of the 1st and 5th Cavalry Divisions. There was fierce fighting here. In the centre the infantry and tanks pressed farther forward, and seized before evening the villages of Cantaing and Fontaine-Nôtre Dame, but were held up by machine-guns on the edge of Bourlon Wood. On the left our troops entered the outskirts of Mœuvres. Thus at the close of two days' fighting all objectives had been seized with the one important exception of the Bourlon Ridge. The main body of the cavalry was not, therefore, brought into action; and on the following morning the regiments in Fins Wood returned disgusted to their quarters at Athies and Ennemain.

The battle, however, was not broken off. The forward positions already held could not be maintained without the possession of the commanding feature of Bourlon. Moreover, the situation on the Italian front made a pronounced success in France almost essential. During the next six days, therefore, the struggle for the ridge continued. The village was taken and lost, and taken again, but never firmly held. There was stubborn fighting on the left about Mœuvres. Ten thousand prisoners had fallen into our hands since the opening of the battle, together with 142 guns and 350 machine-guns; but still, in the end, we were not firmly established on the ground we had tried so hard to win. On the nights of the 27th and 28th the tired soldiers were relieved, and preparations were made to return with fresh troops to a second battle.

Meanwhile the Germans were preparing a counter-offensive. Indications were not wanting that reinforcements were in movement. There was much 'registration' carried out by the enemy's artillery. It was clear that he intended to regain full possession of Bourlon. What was not quite so evident was that he had contrived a scheme of some magnitude, and, not content with an endeavour to retrieve all his losses between Masnières and Mœuvres, had designed a second attack, on a much wider front, against the positions on our right between Masnières and Vendhuile, which were lightly held. This attack began at 8 o'clock on the morning of the 30th. Though not unexpected by Army Headquarters, it came as a complete surprise to the troops in the front line, who were overwhelmed before they had realised the gravity of the situation. After a short but intense bombardment the German infantry appeared in front of our trenches with a suddenness only possible on a chalk formation, and, without waiting to secure the stronger points of the line, pushed rapidly on through the weaker and up the ravines on either side of the Villers Guislain Ridge as far as Gouzeaucourt, which was captured at 9 o'clock. The villages of Bonavis, Gonnelieu, and Villers Guislain were thus taken in reverse, and the position of the 3rd Army had become critical. At noon the enemy was driven out of Gouzeaucourt

by a very gallant attack of the Guards Division;
but there was now a gap between here and Vendhuile, and the cavalry was sent for to fill it.

Little did the cavalry expect this sudden reversal
of the anticipations of ten days ago. The regiments
had, in fact, settled down again to the normal life
of training, plus digging parties. Bell's detachment
had returned to Headquarters, and on this particular morning the Mhow Battalion, under command of Colonel Paterson of the Inniskillings, had
actually started for a tour of duty in the trenches
at Hargicourt. The order to proceed without delay
to the Cambrai battlefield was received at Ennemain
a little before noon. Less than half of the men and
horses were present, for the trench party had gone
out mounted; but in a very short time the lances,
swords, and neck bandoliers of the absentees were
loaded on G.S. wagons, orders were sent to the
party to join Headquarters on the line of march,
and the skeleton of a regiment marched to the rendezvous at Estrées en Chaussée, where the Inniskillings
and 2nd Lancers were found in a similarly depleted
condition. The 4th Cavalry Division then marched
to Villers Faucon, where it remained until dark,
continuing thence to St Emilie, and halting there in
bivouac to await orders for operations on the following day. The trench party joined the column during the evening.

Whilst this march was in progress the 55th
Division was preparing a line of defence from
L'Empire through Malassise Farm to Vaucelette
Farm, which the enemy was expected to attack
early on the 1st December. Fragments of the 166th

Infantry Brigade, woefully shattered by the German onslaught in the morning, held the centre of this line in front of Epéhy and Peizière, contiguous villages; and the first indication of coming events received by the Mhow Brigade was that it would be required to act as reinforcement here. The attack, however, was not developed. It was anticipated by the action of the cavalry. Before daylight an order was received that the 5th Cavalry Division, with the Lucknow Brigade of the 4th Cavalry Division attached, and fourteen tanks co-operating, was at 6.30 A.M. to attack Gauche Wood and the village of Villers Guislain from the west, whilst the remainder of the 4th Cavalry Division was to assist the attack by seizing Villers Guislain Ridge. In compliance with these orders the Mhow Brigade moved forward at 5.30 A.M. on the 1st to a position of readiness at the northern end of Peizière, behind a railway cutting. Here it assembled in 'mass,' and here it stood for the next two hours exposed to a heavy shell-fire at a range of about 4000 yards. Fortunately the enemy's fuze-setting was bad, and the casualties remarkably few. Shortly after 8 o'clock it became known that the tanks had not come to the rendezvous, and that consequently the Lucknow Brigade, unable to attack, was supporting the infantry in Vaucelette Farm. This disappointing piece of news at once raised doubts in the Mhow Brigade as to the expediency of carrying out the attack upon the ridge, for it had been clearly understood that this movement was only intended to be subsidiary to the main attack upon the village. Five minutes later, however, all doubts were set at rest by the receipt of an order from the division to " endeavour to push forward towards your objectives supported by the artillery." Everyone knew what this meant. The position was so critical that a sacrifice was now demanded of the cavalry to give time for the arrival of reinforcements. Nothing could be hoped for but, by a daring attack, to delay the impending renewal of the German offensive for a few hours whilst preparations were made to meet it. With none the less ardour did the troops obey the command. It was to be a cavalry ' day,' not in the sense of a clash of arms or of a victorious pursuit, but in the sense that squadrons may often be used to save the situation for their infantry comrades, and in doing so may cover themselves with glory.

The country between Peizière and Villers Guislain is rolling downland, with very few noticeable features to assist direction. A ridge of high ground, starting from a point about a mile to the eastward of Villers Guislain, covers that village from the view of an observer at the northern end of Peizière, then curving round to the southward as far as Peizière itself juts out again to the east, and ends at a point exactly opposite to the end of its northern arm. This northern arm is known as Villers Guislain Ridge, the southern as Lark Spur. Between them is a shallow basin interrupted about its middle by a tongue of lower land, on either side of which are deep ravines known as Targette Ravine and Pigeon Ravine. On the southern side of Lark Spur the ground falls somewhat steeply for a hundred feet into the Catelet Valley, and rises thence less steeply to another ridge, on which stand Malassise Farm and Little Priel Farm, about a mile and a half apart. From Peizière and Epéhy three roads spray out between north and east. Of these, the first leads straight from the northern end of Peizière to Villers Guislain, a couple of miles away, running for part of this distance along the lower ground at the head of the basin, known sometimes as Linnet Valley, and rising to the ridge 600 yards short of a beet factory, the only prominent building on the landscape. The second starts from Epéhy at the head of the Catelet Valley, and runs a little east of north, over Lark Spur, across the basin, up the other side on to the Villers Guislain Ridge, and into the village. This was known as the Fourteen Willows road. At a crucifix in the valley, a quarter of a mile outside the village, another, the third, road forks to the right, runs along the southern slope of Lark Spur for a mile and a quarter, and away over the spur to the north-east. This was known as Fallen Tree road. On this road, a mile from the crucifix, there are four elm-trees, and above them, 200 yards farther on, on the top of the spur, was a strong post, known as 'Limerick Post,' lately occupied by our infantry, but now held by Germans with machine-guns. In front of the villages of Peizière and Epéhy is a line of railway, which passes through a cutting on the high ground opposite Peizière, and on the low ground in front of Epéhy over an embankment. The German line at the commencement of the cavalry attack ran roughly from Catelet Copse, which was not occupied, to the beet factory, which was; but it was neither definite nor continuous.

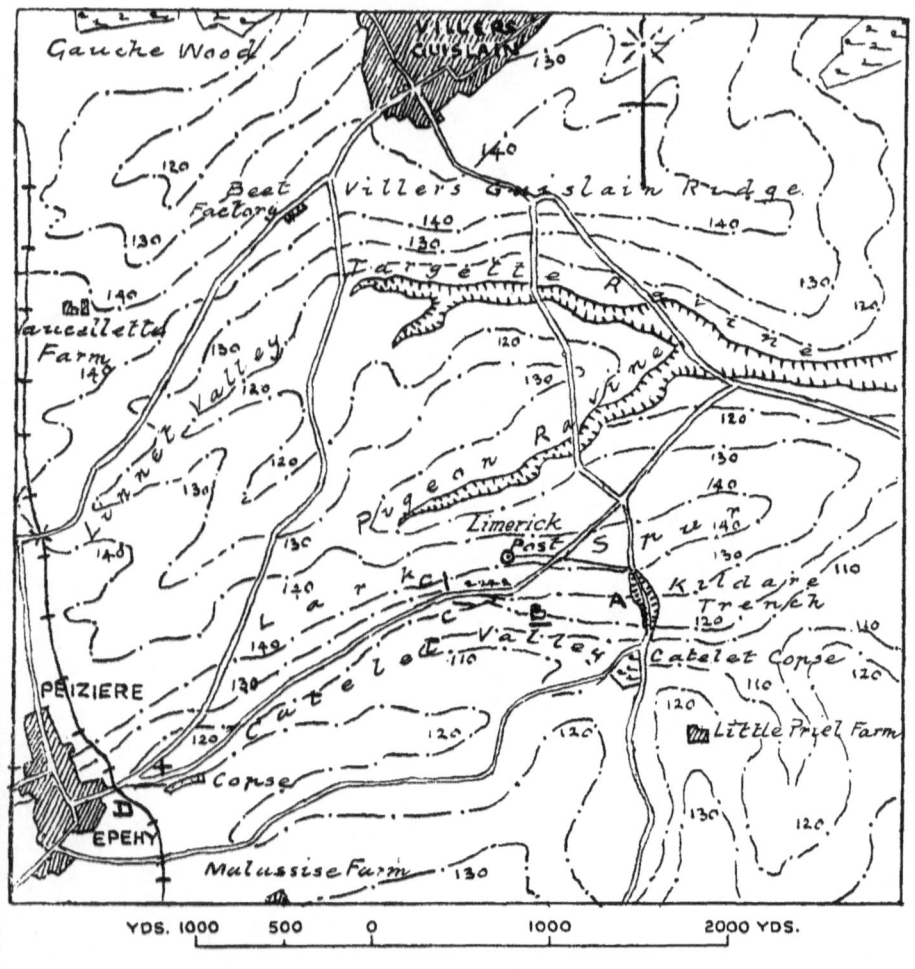

Action of Mhow Cavalry Brigade, 1st December 1917.

Positions at 3 p.m.

    A.   2nd Lancers and one squadron Inniskillings.
    B.   Page's squadron, C.I.H.
    C.   Daunt's two squadrons, C.I.H.
    D.   Brigade Headquarters.

The attack of the Mhow Brigade was made by the Inniskillings and the 2nd Lancers, the Central India Horse being held for the moment in reserve. The 2nd Lancers, with one squadron of the Inniskillings, was ordered to advance from Epéhy village, to gallop Pigeon and Targette ravines, and there to form a defensive flank eastwards whilst the remainder of the Inniskillings, as soon as the 2nd Lancers were seen to be approaching their objective, were to gallop from the northern end of Peizière by the main Peizière-Villers Guislain road, across Linnet Valley to the beet factory, and so to seize the ridge. At 9 o'clock the 2nd Lancers moved down through the two villages, which were at the time being heavily shelled, and set off at once at the gallop. At the crucifix, the leading squadron, instead of following the Fourteen Willows road which leads over Lark Spur to the ravines, took the Fallen Tree road down the Catelet Valley. It was impossible to stop them or to change their direction, for the regiment was now in open column of lines of troop columns extended, and going very fast. Moreover, such a fire greeted their appearance in the open that a halt was out of the question; and so, at a good fifteen miles an hour, this gallant regiment swept down the valley under a storm of bullets from rifles and machine-guns which, properly aimed, should have emptied half the saddles. In point of fact, there were very few casualties. A mile and a half from the crucifix a trench, known as Kildare Trench, full of Germans, seemed to bar the way; but so great is the moral effect of galloping horsemen that the enemy did not wait for them, and the horsemen galloped into the trench, occupied it and held it against heavy odds throughout the day.

As soon as the 2nd Lancers were seen moving down the valley the three squadrons of the Inniskillings at the northern end of Peizière set out on their ride to Villers Guislain Ridge. It was a disastrous ride. They galloped across Linnet Valley and up the hill in front of the beet factory; but here they were stopped, for the factory itself and the ridge in front of Villers Guislain village were very strongly held; the leading squadron was surrounded and completely lost, and Colonel Paterson was obliged, with great difficulty, to withdraw the remnants of the two others to the shelter of Peizière. It was now nearly 10 o'clock, and the Brigadier decided to send help to the 2nd Lancers, who were indeed in a precarious position. They were far behind the enemy's front line of attack, which was now so irregular that definition is impossible. That the hills were alive with Germans is practically all that can be said. Kildare Trench was actually the sunken part of a lane, called Kildare Lane, running from the south over Lark Spur, and across the basin to Villers Guislain. The portion occupied extended from the edge of the spur almost to the bottom of Catelet Valley, and the principal danger arose from the fact that from the left flank held by the Inniskillings squadron a communication trench ran back at right angles into Limerick Post some 600 yards to the Lancers' rear. This trench, as well as Limerick Post, was occupied by Germans.

'D' Squadron of the Central India Horse, under Lieutenant Page, with whom was Lieutenant Milner, was selected to go to the rescue. A patrol had reported that the intensity of the fire in front precluded any further mounted action. Page, therefore, was ordered to leave his horses behind the railway embankment east of Epéhy village; and shortly after 10 o'clock he began his advance on foot down the Catelet Valley on the south side of Fallen Tree road. To cover his movement from the fire of machine-guns on Lark Spur he posted three Hotchkiss guns, under the command of Jemadar Hazura Singh, in a small coppice on the rising ground south of the valley. Hazura Singh did his work splendidly, with the result that the casualties, though many, were far fewer than might have been expected. During the first ten minutes few men were hit; but now a German aeroplane, flying low, dropped a Verey light over the squadron, and a few minutes afterwards the advance was checked by a hail of shrapnel from guns far away to the front. Page then formed his men into two lines, himself leading the first with Rissaidar Jawant Singh as his second-in-command, and Milner, with Jemadar Ram Singh, commanding the second. As he renewed the advance he received a message from the Adjutant at Epéhy that the remainder of the brigade with some infantry would attack the enemy's trenches at 1 o'clock. He decided, nevertheless, to continue his mission. The two lines went on by rushes, the men taking such cover as could be found—a few shell-holes, a bush or two, some dead horses—until, passing the four elm-trees, the first line found itself abreast of Limerick Post; and here it was subjected to an intense fire of rifles and machine-guns from the post itself and from the trench connecting it with Kildare Lane. Many men dropped: Page was hit on the thigh; the N.C.O. in charge of the fourth Hotckhiss gun of the squadron was very severely wounded, and the squadron was ordered to lie prone. This decision was obvious and very fortunate, for, owing to the convex formation of the chalk hills, the men, flat on their bellies, were now invisible from the enemy on the top of Lark Spur, and, since the artillery fire had slackened, they suffered very little, though they were unable to move. Jawant Singh then proposed to continue the advance, and was only prevented from actually doing so by a peremptory order to lie still. Page had with him at this time not more than thirty unwounded men, including the second line, which had now come up to reinforce him. It had suffered severely from the shrapnel. The gallant Ram Singh had been killed by a direct hit from a shell; four sowars had also been killed and several wounded; Milner had been hit on the arm, and was faint from loss of blood. To advance further was to court destruction to no purpose. Page sent a message, describing his position, to the Adjutant by the hand of Lance Dafadar Indar Singh, who was wounded on the way and did not reach Epéhy, and decided to hold his ground until darkness should enable him to withdraw.

The attack of the 2nd Lancers had, by its very boldness, stemmed the enemy's advance in this part of the field. The Germans seemed now to devote themselves solely to an attempt to surround the horsemen in Kildare Trench, and might possibly have succeeded had not Page's squadron appeared in the valley below them. Time, in fact, had been gained; but as the morning wore on it became obvious at Headquarters that new efforts must be made lest the Lancers should be overwhelmed, and the enemy thus set free to surge forward on to our weakly manned trenches. Reinforcements were indeed approaching, but could not arrive for some hours. General Neil Haig therefore conferred with the General Officer Commanding the 166th Brigade; and it was decided to make an infantry attack, supported by two dismounted squadrons of the Central India Horse, in the direction of Kildare Lane. 'A' and 'C' Squadrons, commanded by Captain Daunt and Lieutenant Woodhouse respectively, were told off for this duty, and at 11.30 these two leaders were summoned to a conference at the Headquarters of the 166th Infantry Brigade in a dug-out on the Fourteen Willows road near the crucifix. From here a small patrol, led by Lance Dafadar Dost Mahomed Khan of 'C' Squadron, was sent out to ascertain whether Limerick Post was still held by the enemy. The patrol went out at full gallop. About a mile onward it reached a trench—which may have been Limerick Post, but probably was not,—jumped or scrambled across it, observing meanwhile that it was occupied by Germans, who let them pass on, then turned about and made for home, pursued by a torrent of bullets which nevertheless left them unscathed, and reported that, besides the Germans, they had seen at least one machine-gun and what looked like automatic rifles.

The attack was then ordered to commence at 1

o'clock. It was to be preceded by a short artillery bombardment and supported by a barrage, the infantry, of whom there were but a few tattered remnants of two battalions, on the left; and the two squadrons on the right, directed on the position held by the 2nd Lancers. The Headquarters of the regiment and of the Mhow Brigade were now behind the railway embankment, where Page had left his horses. Here the two squadrons fell in, with Daunt being Dickie Cameron, with Woodhouse Johnnie Pinney. Officers and men knew well that an ordeal was in front of them, and they faced it with all the pride and ceremony that a soldier can command. They set out with the utmost formality, the young leaders insisting on a rigid maintenance of alignment and 'step'; and they marched off down the valley as if on a ceremonial parade. Our guns seemed at this time to be engaged with the enemy on the left; they were giving little help to the dismounted squadrons. Bullets soon began to fall, and Daunt, as the senior officer, spread out his two squadrons in two lines at a distance of 150 yards, 'C' Squadron on the left, in touch with the infantry, and 'A' on the right, with Fallen Tree road between them, the men extended at five yards interval, and Pinney and Cameron leading the first line. The advance continued by rushes, the second line gradually merging into the first. The fire became much hotter, especially on the higher ground, where 'C' was now making a direct attack on German trenches, suffering heavily. Men were sensible of a resistance in the air from the number of bullets streaming past. Woodhouse described the sensation as that of wading. Two hundred yards from the elm-trees, and about four hundred from Limerick Post, a hollow lane runs up from the road over the spur. This was in German hands, but ' C ' Squadron rushed it, sending its occupants running back to the post. Meanwhile, on the low ground, Cameron had been wounded, and as he was being carried by Dafadar Sherjan Khan to a place of shelter, was hit again on the head and killed. As ' C ' Squadron rushed the lane, ' A ' Squadron, now much reduced in numbers, swung half left towards the road, and Daunt got them under cover of a bank and called a halt whilst he surveyed the situation. At this moment Woodhouse went forward to reconnoitre. As he emerged from the lane every machine-gun on the hill seemed to open on him. He advanced a few paces and fell mortally wounded in the chest. Germans were now seen all over the hillside. Daunt, nevertheless, decided to make a converging attack on Limerick Post, and, as a preliminary, got two Hotchkiss guns into action against some men on the slope between the post and the elms. He was standing now at the angle between the two squadrons, where he was joined by Pinney and a sergeant commanding a platoon on our left, who told him that the infantry attack had been held up. A few minutes later some Germans were seen falling back along the top of the hill. Daunt ordered Pinney and the sergeant to get their men forward at once, and, turning to his own men, shouted to them to advance, when a sudden burst of machine-gun fire was put down from Limerick Post, and Pinney, shot in the mouth, fell forward into a shell-hole dead.

'C' Squadron being now deprived of its leaders, Daunt went up to the hollow lane to tell Dilawar Khan to take command, and, returning to 'A' Squadron, sent his batman, Private Saye, and an English-speaking Dafadar, Faiz Mahomed Khan, back with the sergeant to maintain connection with the infantry. For the next half-hour the fight continued, our men trying to work forward along the road, but the machine-gun fire was now continuous and very heavy, and no further advance was possible. At about 3.30 P.M. a message came through by runner from Brigade Headquarters ordering the squadrons to fall back upon our infantry trenches, and at the same time Faiz Mahomed Khan and Saye returned with the information that the infantry had retired and that the enemy was working round our left flank. Daunt then ordered a retirement by alternate squadrons, 'A' going back first under cover of fire from 'C' in the hollow lane. It was then 'C's' turn to withdraw; but their intrepid and defiant leader, Dilawar Khan, who was working a Hotchkiss gun, would not move, and Daunt had to step across to him. "Ham kabhi nahin retire karenge,"[1] he said, "Ham kabhi nahin retire karenge," until Daunt had to take him by the scruff of the neck and shove him to the rear.

The men were wonderful on this day. The gallantry of their British officers, the fighting ardour of Dilawar Khan, and the extraordinary coolness of Lihaz Gal, who, armed only with a walking-stick, moved about directing the operations of his half-squadron as if no bullets were flying, gave them

[1] "I will never retire."

confidence, and the retirement was carried out in good order without many further casualties. Jawant Singh, with the remains of Page's squadron, for Page himself had been taken to the dressing-station and Milner could barely struggle along, joined the others on the way, and at dusk they reached the trenches in front of Epéhy. The 2nd Lancers were able to retire under cover of darkness. After nightfall our wounded and some of our dead were brought in. The bodies of Cameron and Pinney, great favourites in the regiment, were laid side by side in a hut in the village, where Colonel Browne's bearer, Ahmad, kept watch throughout the night: a remarkable instance of the fidelity of the Indian servant. Ahmad had been in the service of Pinney's father, and was the special attendant of the son when a child. In spite of the incessant shelling he refused to leave his young master until the ambulance removed the bodies in the morning. The shock was too much for him, and six weeks later he died by his own hand.

The squadrons were not long in the trenches. At 8 o'clock a fresh division, turned back on its journey to the Italian front, took over the line, and an hour later the regiment was withdrawn. It had suffered much. Of the six British officers who went into action only one, Captain Daunt, remained untouched. Two were killed and three were wounded, of whom Woodhouse died in hospital ten days later. One Indian officer was killed and one (Jemadar Nadir Khan) wounded, and amongst the other ranks there were fifty-one casualties, a large proportion being killed. But they had ' delivered the goods': the Germans had not gained an inch of ground all day. Colonel Browne received the Distinguished Service Order, and both Daunt and Page an immediate award of the Military Cross; but perhaps the most satisfying reward to the regiment as a whole came in the shape of a message from the Commander of the 2nd Lancers, whose Colonel had been killed, which said: "If it hadn't been for the way the C.I.H. attacked, and stuck to it, we should have been surrounded, and none of us would ever have got back." Next day the Mhow Brigade moved a few miles farther towards Athies, and on the evening of the 3rd December the Central India Horse rode back to its old quarters at Ennemain, a decimated but contented regiment.

CHAPTER XX.

THE GREAT WAR—PALESTINE.

THE battle of Cambrai was the last battle on European soil in which Indian troops were engaged. Early in January 1918 all Indian regiments received an official warning that their withdrawal from France was imminent; and rumour, of course, flew round the lines that India was their destination. For three years the men had been absent from their homes. To the English officer or soldier accustomed to living abroad such a period may seem short; to the untravelled Indian it is an age. His news, moreover, had been scanty, and some of it very discouraging. The agitator had been at work, and, to create unrest amongst the soldiers, had spread stories of famine and pestilence in their villages. British officers of the regiment knew something about this. Indian officers knew everything; but with their sturdy loyalty and common-sense, under the guidance of their unruffled leader, Risaldar Major Amar Singh, they kept the men contented. With the prospect of early departure these private troubles vanished. India was in sight. The sunshine and the chatter, the byre and the hearth, the little plot of land outside the village seemed now so close. For all their military ardour and devotion it was no wonder that the men were elated. They were doomed, however, to partial disappointment. The warning notice was soon followed by another, this time more explicit. The Indian cavalry was to be transferred to another theatre of operations. This, however, could only mean a journey eastward; the new theatre would be a little nearer to India at any rate, and, whatever may have been the men's feelings, no disappointment was shown. They had seen their English comrades take leave to England. Surely it would be their turn now to get an occasional respite from the strain of active service. Their destination was Palestine, though they did not know it yet, and in due time their hopes were fulfilled.

The Mhow Brigade was now broken up, though the 2nd Lancers and the Central India Horse remained together for the rest of the war. Before the regiment left France several changes took place amongst the British officers. Colonel Browne, always known affectionately by his father's name of 'Sam Browne,' had completed his tenure of command, and was ordered to report himself at the India Office. Bell was the next senior officer, but had passed the age limit and so could not succeed him. Unlike others, however—Abbott, Hutchison, Lewis, and Wickham, for instance,—who had been seized by the India Office for duty in India, he remained in France, and finished the war in command of a Labour Corps. Lawson-Tancred, having retired from the service, was ineligible. He was transferred to the artillery as an adviser in stable management; and the new Commandant was therefore Colonel James Gourlie.

The brigade marched out of Ennemain on the 2nd February 1918, and went to Fricamps near Amiens. Here the Inniskillings left to join their new brigade, whilst the 2nd Lancers and the Central India Horse made preparations for their coming journey. Before the end of March they found themselves at Marseilles, two regiments of well-tried veterans, to whom nothing now was strange.

His Majesty's transports *Minominee*, *Huanchaco*, and *Maryland* took them to Alexandria. There were other units in other ships, the whole forming a convoy escorted by Japanese destroyers. The voyage was uneventful, though not free from anxiety or discomfort, for German submarines were in the Mediterranean, and every conceivable precaution had to be taken against attack. A zigzag course was followed, no lights were lit, stable accumulations were put overboard after dark so as to leave as little track as possible, and life-belts were worn by night as well as by day. From Alexandria the regiment railed to Tel-el-Kebir, whence they marched together to Kantara, on the Suez Canal, which was reached on the 28th April.

At Kantara they were equipped for desert warfare, and were railed thence to Belah on the Palestine coast, fourteen miles south of Gaza. It was now learnt that both regiments were to form part of the 10th Brigade of the 4th Cavalry Division of the Desert Mounted Corps, and that their destination was the Jordan Valley. The Desert Mounted Corps consisted of the 4th and 5th Cavalry Divisions and the Australian Mounted Division. The other units of the 10th Brigade, which was commanded by

Brigadier-General Godwin, a former Brigade-Major of the Mhow Brigade, were the Dorset Yeomanry, the Berkshire Battery of Horse Artillery, and the 17th Machine-gun Squadron. Major-General George Barrow, once the Brigadier of the Mhow Brigade, now commanded the 4th Cavalry Division.

On the 4th May the two regiments, much refreshed by a few days' halt by the sea, set out from Belah, and, marching along the coast through Gaza and Mejdel, turned eastward to Enab, which was reached on the 8th. They were now on the Jaffa-Jerusalem road, in the heart of the Judæan hills. From Enab the road descends 1000 feet to a narrow valley, and rises thence, less steeply, to Jerusalem, from which point onwards it could be watched by Turkish outposts on the other side of the Jordan. The remaining marches, therefore, were made by night. On the night of the 8th-9th the march was continued to Talaat ed Dumm, half-way between Jerusalem and Jericho, described by the historian of the 2nd Lancers as "an almost indescribably desolate spot." The following night took the regiments to their camp in the Wadi Nueiameh, some two miles north of Jericho, where they arrived at 4 o'clock on the morning of the 10th in a blinding dust-storm. This was the Jordan Valley, here 1250 feet below the level of the sea, a dreary place during eight months of the year, and during the remaining four uninhabitable. Three of these latter months were in store for the 10th Brigade. The remainder of the month of May was spent in the Wadi Nueiameh, chiefly in fatigue duties. It was an exceedingly unpleasant time, for to the discomfort of the

heat and dust were added the stench of dead camels
and a plague of flies such as Egypt herself had
hardly known.

The brigade was in reserve, four miles behind the
line. On the 31st it went forward. The British
trench line at this period extended from the coast,
some ten miles north of Jaffa, due eastward to the
Jordan, where it bent back along the river to the
Dead Sea. In front, between the Jordan and the
Mediterranean Sea, were the 7th and 8th Turkish
Armies, whilst east of the Jordan, along the Hedjaz
railway, was the 4th. After his victories at Gaza
and Beersheba in the winter of 1917-18, and his
occupation of Jerusalem, Allenby was now elaborating his plans for his advance through Palestine into
Syria ; and it was important not only that the
enemy should be kept in darkness as to the line of
this advance but that he should be persuaded, if
possible, to think that it would be made on the left
bank of the Jordan rather than on the right. With
this intent two raids, on a large scale, were made
from the bridge-heads during the months of March
and May in the direction of Es Salt and Amman.
These bridge-heads were held in some strength,
since it was always possible that the 4th Turkish
Army might itself take the offensive in the direction
of Jerusalem.

There were three bridges over the Jordan between
the Dead Sea and the north-east corner of our trench
line. The northernmost, at Ghoraniye, eight miles
north of the Dead Sea, carried the road from Jericho
to Es Salt. Four miles to the southward was the
bridge of Makhadet Hajla, whilst half-way between

this and the Dead Sea was the bridge at El Henu. The Jordan here flows in a tortuous stream between straight banks half a mile across and nearly 100 feet high. Beyond are the hills of Moab, and here, four miles away, were the outposts of the 4th Turkish Army. From the river the plain, covered with low scrub jungle and intersected by numerous deep ravines, rises gently to the foothills, and was to become during the next few months the scene of much ' scrapping ' between the outposts.

On the 31st May the 2nd Lancers and the Central India Horse were sent to the Ghoraniye bridge-head, which was held by a brigade of Imperial Service Infantry. Their task was now that of ' observation.' During the daytime reconnoitring and fighting patrols scoured the plain, whilst at night pickets were posted in front of the infantry trenches. It was on the night of the 1st-2nd June that our first encounter took place. A strong Turkish raiding party, estimated at 100 men, with some machine-guns, attacked our left picket south of the Wadi Nimrin, which here runs into the Jordan up-stream of the Ghoraniye bridge. The picket, held by ' B ' Squadron under Lieutenant T. D. Wilson, suffered the loss of one man killed and repulsed the attack without difficulty. The enemy renewed his attack on the following night, and was again driven back with considerable loss, three of our men being wounded. A week later we lost a very valuable officer. Major Prichard, who had been appointed regimental Intelligence Officer, rode out on the morning of the 7th June, accompanied only by his orderly and a horse-holder, to reconnoitre the ground in front of the outpost line.

LOSS OF A GALLANT OFFICER

Always gallant to the point of indiscretion, he rode farther than prudence dictated, and suddenly found himself face to face with a strong Turkish patrol. All three men were instantly shot down. The sound of the firing was heard by Risaldar Mir Zaman Khan, who was out with a patrol of 'C' Squadron. Galloping to some rising ground he could just see three men unhorsed, with the enemy closing round them. He called up his patrol and charged, and the Turks fled back towards their refuge in the hills. They rallied, however, and opened a heavy fire on Mir Zaman and his men, who suffered further casualties, including the loss of several good horses, before they could bring their wounded comrades to a place of safety. But both Prichard and his orderly died that night.

On the 17th June a demonstration was made against a point in the Turkish outpost line at Tel er Rame. The 2nd Lancers did a notable piece of work during this action, Lieutenant Ranking, with half a squadron, getting home with the lance and inflicting heavy losses. The Central India Horse was, however, in reserve, and was not called upon to fight. A few days later the regiment was withdrawn to the Wadi Nueiameh for a short period, but returned to the outposts on the 3rd July, when it relieved the Dorset Yeomanry at the bridge-heads at Makhadet Hajla and El Henu, with headquarters at the former. Little happened during the next ten days, our casualties during this period being one N.C.O. and five men missing; and on the 13th the whole brigade was moved out of the Jordan Valley for a month's rest at Ras Deiran, near the coast.

Here Brigadier-General Howard-Vyse, the Brigadier-General, General Staff, of the Desert Mounted Corps, took over the command of the 10th Brigade from General Godwin, the two exchanging appointments.

At Ras Deiran officers and men recovered to some extent from the fever and the Jordan sores with which many were afflicted; but there was still work to be done. To begin with, the regiment was called upon to supply a complete squadron of Sikhs and Panjabi Mahomedans to form the nucleus of a new regiment to be raised at Quetta, a somewhat singular demand to be made upon a regiment in touch with the enemy; but whether or no he selected his best and fittest men the commanding officer has not placed on record. The men, however, were despatched to India on the 3rd August under the command of Lieutenants Hirst and Williams. They were replaced by reinforcements from the base who needed training. Horses and men, too, needed preparation for the strenuous work which all knew must begin with the coming of winter, and the 'rest' was thus modified by a good deal of exercise.

The 17th August found the regiment again at the bridge-heads, sending a squadron out to the front day by day alternately with the 2nd Lancers. Before the end of the month it became known that the Turks were concentrating in the hills with the apparent object of making a reconnaissance in force of the crossings near the Dead Sea. From the 1st September onwards two squadrons, therefore, went out daily towards the Moab hills. In front of Makhadet Hajla, and some three and a half miles from it, was an old tomb, known as Kabr el Fendi el Faiz, situated at the junction of two converging nullahs. This was a very convenient spot for the Turks to lie in wait, as they often did, for thick bushes covered the banks of the nullahs, the tomb itself was hidden by trees, and from its roof was a commanding view over the plain. Consequently it was always approached with caution. Other units had had brushes with the enemy here. It was now our turn. On the 6th September, ' A ' and ' C ' Squadrons, under the command respectively of Lieutenants Dalrymple-Hay and Walter, moved out on the usual tour of duty. Unfortunately, there was a thick haze over the valley that morning, and the two squadrons lost touch with one another. At 5 o'clock Walter located an enemy force near the tomb. To attack it at once was his only thought. Making a long but rapid detour he crossed into the terrain between the two nullahs and charged the Turkish detachment from the rear. He rode well home, himself killing two of the enemy with the sword, and his men many others with the lance ; but he soon found that he had encountered a force too strong for him. It was, in fact, the advanced guard of a mixed brigade, with a battery of artillery. Collecting his men as quickly as he could, he withdrew to a flank, and there renewed and continued the action, dismounted, until the arrival of hostile reinforcements, including the guns, compelled him to retire towards the river. Meanwhile Dalrymple-Hay was held up by the mist, which was still heavy on the low ground. It took him an hour to find Walter, who was then on the point of retiring ; but his arrival, welcome though late, not only enabled ' C ' Squadron to withdraw without undue losses, though Walter himself, whose horse had been killed under him, was wounded during this movement, but had also the effect of alarming the Turks, who had seen enough and quickly disappeared. The haze lifted as they went about, and they fired a few shells into regimental Headquarters at El Henu, killing two followers in the horse lines. Five men and twelve horses were killed during this action, one man was wounded, as well as Lieutenant Walter, and two men were reported missing. Walter received an immediate award of the Military Cross for this exploit, and Risaldar Mir Zaman Khan was decorated with the Indian Order of Merit.

This engagement ended the fighting at the Dead Sea end of the Jordan Valley. The Commander-in-Chief had now completed his arrangements for his attack upon the 7th and 8th Turkish Armies. He had two Army Corps in the line, the Twentieth and Twenty-first, led by Sir Philip Chetwode and General Bulfin respectively; but he had something else besides. He had an enormously preponderating force of mounted men. It was for this reason that he decided to make his main attack on the left, on the low ground between the coast and the hills. Here the infantry was to break through, then to swing north-eastward, leaving room for the cavalry to follow and go forward with all speed over the ridge that runs north-westward from the neighbourhood of Nablus to the sea and ends at Mount Carmel, and so down to the Plain of Esdraelon and the railway system, by which alone the enemy could hope to escape. But the cavalry was at this time on the right. The difficult problem of moving it to its positions of readiness in rear of the left, without the movement being known or even suspected by the enemy, had therefore to be considered. Nor was the problem confined to the cavalry. To conceal the movements of a large army, its transport, its ammunition trains, all the impedimenta of war, to its jumping-off positions on the eve of a great battle from the people of the country, as well as from the eyes of a watchful enemy, might have been thought impossible ; but it was done. The most elaborate system of deception ever known in war was put in practice for weeks before the battle. All marches westward were made, of course, by night, but 'make-believe' marches were made eastward by day. Empty camps were left standing, and their horse lines too, with dummy horses made of blankets slung on poles. Dummy bridges and dummy roads were made where such conveniences were not required. A large hotel at Jerusalem was commandeered for Army Headquarters, and every room assigned to its particular use, and labelled accordingly. Allenby never went near Jerusalem. Indignant civilians in other towns were turned out of their houses to make room for Commanders and Staffs, who never occupied them. The troops bivouacked in orange groves, where they could be seen neither from the land nor from the air ; and to complete their seclusion, lest smoke should announce their presence to the inquisitive aeroplane, their food was cooked by solidified alcohol. The army rested by day. There was 'nothing doing.' By night it was as busy as a hive of bees. For all the Turks or the people knew, the lethargy of the hot weather was completely undisturbed; and so, on the day before the battle opened, the Intelligence Branch was able, confidently and quite correctly, to report that the enemy knew nothing.

Thus the three divisions of the Desert Mounted Corps appeared as if by magic in their positions in rear of the left of the line on the morning of the 17th September, the 4th and 5th Cavalry Divisions in the orange groves round Sarona, and the Australian Mounted Division at Ramleh, some ten miles behind them. On this day all commanding officers were called to Divisional Headquarters, where Allenby's great Force Order No. 68, beginning " The Commander-in-Chief intends to take the offensive " was read to them, and his plan of action was disclosed. Lord Allenby himself addressed them; photographs of his opponent, General Liman von Sanders, were circulated; and every officer left the meeting with full knowledge of what he was expected to do. The Desert Mounted Corps was to await information from the infantry in front that the Nahr el Falik and the Zarkiyeh marsh, difficult obstacles on the coast four miles behind the Turkish front line, had been secured and the crossings made passable, and then to make straight for the Beisan-Haifa railway, forty miles farther on. The Desert Corps Commander, General Chauvel, was ordered to cut, at El Afuleh, the lines from Haifa and Jenin, and to send a sufficient body of men to the eastward to close the two roads from the south which converge at Beisan. On the night of the 18th-19th September the two divisions were moved forward to the north of the Wadi Auja. In

front of them now, on the extreme left, was Sir
John Shea's 60th Division, which had been transferred from the Twentieth to the Twenty-first Corps
for this battle, and next to it the 7th Meerut Division,
commanded by Sir Vere Bonamy Fane. Zero hour
was 4.30 A.M.

There was no preliminary bombardment. One
shot from a gun was the signal for the infantry to
advance, and then the battle opened with a roar.
The surprise was as complete as that at Cambrai,
and much more effectual, for the end was victory.
In the first ten minutes the infantry were over the
Turkish front line trenches; within the next half-
hour they were over the second, and by seven o'clock
in the morning they were able to send back word to
the waiting cavalry that the marsh and the nullah
were not the formidable obstacles they were feared
to be. Forward then the cavalry, the 5th Division
following the 60th along the coast, and the 4th
farther inland in the wake of the 7th. The Central
India Horse, now commanded by Major Hutchison,
who had lately been recalled from India, Gourlie
having fallen sick on the march from the Jordan,
was on this morning the rear regiment of the division; but it was through our front trench line by
half-past ten. The infantry had by this time swung
half-right, driving the enemy before them. The
cavalry then pushed on, and for the remainder of
the day the plain was covered by streams of horsemen pressing northward towards El Afuleh and
Nazareth, the noise of the great battle to the eastward ever in their ears. No opposition was encountered, though many stray bodies of weary and

depressed Turkish soldiers were taken and despatched to the rear. At half-past seven in the evening the 4th Cavalry Division halted round Kerkur Beidus, five miles to the south-west of the Musmus Pass, which here pierces the Carmel Ridge, to water and feed and rest a while. The 2nd Lancers found the outposts during this short period, and were then sent forward into the pass, reinforced by the 11th Light Armoured Motor Battery, with orders to secure the cross-roads at Khurbet Arah. The main body of the division left Kerkur Beidus at 11 o'clock, the 10th Brigade leading, followed by the 11th, the 12th bringing up the rear. Unfortunately, the head of the division was guided in the wrong direction, being led along a track to the north-west instead of by the correct road which runs north-eastward into the defile. The divisional commander, who had driven to Khurbet Arah and ordered the 2nd Lancers to push on to Lejjun, without waiting to hold the cross-roads, now returned to his division to find it going the wrong way. He turned the 12th and 11th Brigades about, putting them in the right direction, whilst the 10th, wheeling its head, found its own way by stony tracks to the correct road, and eventually, after much discomfort, borne as stoically as might be, fell into the column between the other two. At Lejjun the road descends sharply into the Plain of Esdraelon. The 2nd Lancers arrived here at 3 o'clock in the morning, and found a hundred Turks sitting round their fires. These made no resistance. The regiment went on towards El Afuleh, but at half-past five found its way barred by a Turkish battalion, obviously sent out from El Afuleh to hold the pass.

It was the 2nd Lancers ' day.' They had taken 500 prisoners in the pass itself, they had surprised an advanced guard at Lejjun, and now, with a dismounted attack in front, strengthened by the L.A.M. Battery, and a gallop round the enemy's left flank and into him, they destroyed or captured a whole battalion with the loss of one man and twelve horses wounded. By 8 o'clock on the morning of the 20th they were in El Afuleh, where they captured 100 German air mechanics as well as three aeroplanes and a considerable amount of rolling stock. Before noon the 4th Cavalry Division was concentrated at El Afuleh. Its rest was short. In pursuance of his orders, General Chauvel had now to send a force to the eastward to complete the ' round up.' The 5th Cavalry Division had by this time reached Nazareth, where they nearly caught Liman von Sanders; and the Australians were not far behind. The whole of the 4th Division could, therefore, be spared for this duty. The railway lines were destroyed, and at half-past one the division set out again for Beisan, seventeen miles distant. Here the railway turns northward along the Jordan Valley, crossing the river at Jisr Mujamieh, to Semakh on the southern shore of the Sea of Galilee, and thence goes east to Deraa, where it joins the Hedjaz railway. The march down the valley of Jezreel was done mostly at the trot, the 10th Brigade leading, with the Dorset Yeomanry as advanced guard; and Beisan was seized without much opposition at half-past four in the afternoon. The division went into bivouac between the village and the railway station, the Central India Horse and the 2nd Lancers finding the outposts which, seeing that there was now no definite 'front' or 'rear,' but that each was either, completely surrounded the bivouac.

The cavalry had now got behind the 7th and 8th Turkish Armies, who were thus completely cut off from their railways between the Jordan and the sea, and unless they could reach the Hedjaz railway by the Jordan fords, had no alternative but to surrender to the horsemen who were lying in wait. As a matter of fact they knew nothing of the trap prepared for them, and during the next few days great numbers of prisoners were swept into the cages at Beisan. Some units did indeed attempt to cross the river, but were forestalled by the 11th Brigade, which was sent down along both banks for this purpose. Some stiff fighting occurred near the ford of Abu Naj, where the enemy fought hard to cover the escape of the commander of the 7th Army, which our troops were unable to prevent; but the brigade returned to Beisan with 3000 captives.

The 2nd Lancers, who had had a very hard time, were relieved from outpost duty on the 21st by the Dorset Yeomanry, who took over the southern half of the circle. Aeroplanes now reported large enemy forces retiring northwards by the Nablus-Beisan road. That evening, therefore, the Central India Horse was ordered to reinforce the Dorsets with a squadron. At 10 o'clock the head of the Turkish column appeared, and immediately attacked the Dorsets' positions. At one point, indeed, the picket line was pierced, when Risaldar Dyal Singh with a troop of 'D' Squadron made a dashing charge in the moonlight, routing the intruders completely. A bunch of 158 prisoners fell into his hands. The enemy meanwhile continued his attack; but there was little spirit in it; he had had enough fighting, and at dawn 3000 men surrendered, including the whole of the 1st Turkish Cavalry Regiment, in the ranks of which were found three women, the wives of Turkish officers.

On the 23rd the Central India Horse was sent to Jisr Mujamieh to relieve the 19th Lancers. This regiment had been sent thither from El Afuleh across the hills with orders to prepare the railway bridge for demolition. They had accomplished a difficult march extraordinarily well, and now that there was no possibility of the Turks escaping by that way they were ordered to withdraw the charges and return to the Twelfth Brigade, to which they belonged. The Central India Horse was ordered to hold this bridge at all costs. On the following day 'A' Squadron, under Captain Filose, reconnoitred the town of Semakh, finding it strongly held; and an attempt was made to cut the railway on the east of the town to delay the possible arrival of Turkish reinforcements from the direction of Damascus. The attempt was opposed and was unsuccessful, for just as preparations were on the point of completion the mule carrying the guncotton broke loose from his driver and disappeared into the blue. Lieutenant Coster, who had been attached to the squadron for this operation, and one Indian soldier were killed. Semakh was taken on the 25th by a brigade of Australian Light Horse after a very gallant fight.

During the three days, from the 22nd to the

24th, the 2nd Lancers were employed at Beisan in guarding and providing escorts for prisoners ; and a difficult job they had, for the defeated Turks came in by the thousand, and our resources were strained to the utmost. The 4th Cavalry Division had, in fact, taken 16,000 out of the 40,000 prisoners reported to have been captured by the whole force up to the 25th September, and it had covered a distance of over eighty miles in thirty-five hours with the loss of very little horseflesh ; but its work was not yet over. On the 25th the other units of the Tenth Brigade joined the Central India Horse at Jisr Mujamieh, and next morning the whole brigade was again on the move.

On the evening of the 25th the Brigadier was warned that the Tenth Brigade would be required to cross the Jordan on the 26th and to move in the direction of Deraa, whither the 4th Turkish Army was now retreating, well harassed by Lawrence's Arabs. At 7.57 A.M. on the 26th the following order was issued by Divisional Headquarters by wire from Beisan: "4th Turkish Army Headquarters is reported moving *via* Remte to Deraa. 4th Cavalry Division will move on Deraa. Lawrence's Arab force is in area and will operate with us. Following moves will take place to-day. 10th Cavalry Brigade will move from Jisr Mujamieh to Irbid and endeavour to get touch with Lawrence. Twelfth Cavalry Brigade will leave Beisan at 10.00 and move to a position covering bridge south of Es Shuni. Divisional Headquarters and Eleventh Cavalry Brigade will leave Beisan at 13.00 and move to Jisr Mujamieh." At 8 o'clock the Central

STIFF FIGHTING ROUND IRBID

India Horse, with a subsection of machine-guns, forming the advanced guard of the brigade, was in position ready for the move. Irbid is but sixteen miles from Jisr Mujamieh ; but the going was very bad and the maps inaccurate, and it was not until 4 o'clock in the afternoon that the leading troop of the 2nd Lancers, who had relieved the Central India Horse on advanced guard duty at mid-day, found itself on the bank of a deep gorge, known as the Wadi el Ghafr, some three miles short of its objective. At this point it was fired on from the village of El Bariha, about half a mile beyond the gorge. The troop scrambled across and galloped this village, and the Commander of the regiment, Major Gould, went forward to see what was in front. He had been warned early in the afternoon by a friendly Arab sheikh, who had met him on the road, that there were about 2000 Turks in Irbid, but that they would probably be willing to surrender. The large village, or town, of Irbid lies on the southern slope of a stony ridge running north and south, parallel to the El Ghafr gorge. Major Gould sent two squadrons, ' B ' and ' D,' to the left to attack the place from the north, whilst a third, ' C,' was ordered to sweep round to the right and attack it from the south, the fourth squadron, ' A,' with the machine-gun subsection, being held in reserve behind a low hill on the south side of El Bariha. The attack was launched at once, but the Turks were found to be much more numerous than the sheikh had reported. The western outskirts were held very strongly, and as the action proceeded the enemy spread out along the ridge and checked the advancing squadrons with a heavy fire. Captain Vaughan's squadron, 'D,' did actually gallop into the town; but his leading troop was annihilated, he himself was very severely wounded, his horse was killed, and it was with the utmost difficulty that he rallied the few men left to him and withdrew towards the village of El Bariha. The main body of the brigade was some way behind. Not till 5 o'clock did the Central India Horse, the leading regiment, and the remainder of the machine-guns, cross the El Ghafr gorge. The Brigadier now sent an order to the three squadrons of the regiment to join its fourth squadron, which as flank guard of the brigade had just ridden through the village of Zebda, a mile south of El Bariha, driving some Turks before it, so as to engage the enemy from the south-east. The galloper, however, repeated the order as "Follow the 2nd Lancers along that valley," pointing to a nullah running down from the southern extremity of the Irbid ridge towards El Bariha and into the gorge. The three squadrons were at this moment behind the latter village. They started at a gallop, but the leading squadron, 'C,' mistaking El Bariha for Irbid and attracted possibly by the sound of firing on his left front, went to the north instead of to the south, and joined a squadron of the 2nd Lancers in action opposite the northern end of the ridge. The other two squadrons, 'A' and 'D,' galloped up the nullah, and soon came under fire from Irbid. Major Hutchison, with his trumpeter, rode to some high ground to obtain a view. Both their horses were shot under them. The two squadrons, meanwhile, reached the head of the nullah, where the ground, strewn with large boulders, made progress faster than a walk impossible. They were now 600 yards to the south of Irbid, and were able to open a fire attack on the southern outskirts, supported to some extent by the flank guard squadron, 'B,' which had come up from Zebda. A few Turks were seen to be leaving the village; but it was late, the sun had gone down, and, before advantage could be taken of the demoralisation which had obviously set in, inky darkness put an end to the fight. The 2nd Lancers lost during this action one British officer wounded, one Indian officer killed and two wounded, and thirty-nine Indian other ranks killed, wounded, and missing. The Central India Horse had only three casualties. It was unfortunate that the Berkshire Battery, being behind the Central India Horse and the Machine-Gun Squadron on the march, could not come into action until too late to support the cavalry attack; but they fired a few disturbing shells into Irbid before nightfall, and the enemy, whose numbers were estimated by local inhabitants at anything between 5000 and 10,000 men, fled eastwards during the night.

Next morning the march was continued to Remte, the Ramoth Gilead of the Bible, the Dorset Yeomanry being the advanced guard of the brigade, and the Central India Horse at the head of the main body. No hostile force was seen until the advanced guard approached Remte, when it was fired on from the village, and a force of some 300 Turkish infantry, with machine-guns, moved out to bar its further progress. The leading squadron commander met this attack with one troop dismounted, the other three hovering, mounted, on the flanks. The remainder of the regiment quickly reinforced him, and the attack dissolved. The Turks, in fact, retired at the double, losing fifty men, and one squadron pursued them into the village, where the white flag was then hoisted. In spite of this the leaders were fired on as they entered. One officer was shot dead at close range, one was wounded, and several men were hit. This treacherous behaviour entailed the systematic clearance of every house in the village, the leading squadron of the Central India Horse being sent forward to assist in the work, whilst the other three galloped round to pursue the Turks as they retired to Deraa. The pursuing squadrons did good work. 'B' and 'D' charged a body of the enemy on the march, slew many of them, and brought back 100 prisoners as well as four machine-guns. Meanwhile another Turkish body, which had retired earlier in the day, had occupied a previously prepared position on a hill overlooking Deraa, which from Remte is only five miles distant. The position was galloped by 'C' Squadron, and again four machine-guns and 100 prisoners were taken. Very few men of the garrison of Remte escaped, and these must have met a worse fate at the hands of the Shereefian Arabs, for that night the Shereefian army entered Deraa, and the result of their conquest made one of the most unpleasant scenes of the war.

The Headquarters of the 4th Cavalry Division, with the 12th Brigade, had meanwhile marched from Jisr Mujamieh and Es Shuni. They joined the 10th Brigade at Remte on the 27th; and early in the morning of the 28th the division marched into Deraa. Only a small portion of the 4th Turkish Army had been accounted for in the operations which have just been described; the rest had retired farther northward. These, however, were encountered by the other two units of the Desert Mounted Corps, which, marching along the western shore of the Sea of Galilee and under the slopes of Mount Hermon, had come down upon Kiswe and Damascus, and completed the final stage in the overthrow of Turkish military power, begun only ten days earlier.

On the 29th the 4th Cavalry Division left Deraa for Damascus, and on the night of the 1st October the 10th Brigade went into bivouac in a vineyard on the outskirts of that ancient city. The fighting here was over. The Australians and the 5th Cavalry Division had done their work. There only remained the formal entry into Damascus, which was made on the 2nd by a column of small detachments from each regiment and battery of the corps, Captain Daunt, with his squadron, representing the Central India Horse on this occasion.

Four days later the march was continued to Baalbek. Colonel Gourlie, released from hospital, now took command of the regiment; but after three anxious weeks, during which the 4th Cavalry Division was swept by an epidemic, called at the time 'Spanish influenza,' he was again taken ill and returned to Egypt. It was a dismal march. Officers and men had been made, no doubt, especially susceptible to this form of disease by their sojourn in the Jordan Valley. Men went down suddenly, on the march and in bivouac alike, and before the epidemic subsided the division lost 3600 men, of whom 400 died. At Zebdani on the 8th October Lieutenant Wilson was sent to hospital, where he died five days later. Lieutenant Evers was stricken on the 12th, and died next day. On the 13th Captain A. H. Williams went down. Captain Daunt was ' evacuated sick ' a week after the arrival of the division at Baalbek ; and by this time the division was so crippled that it was ordered to remain here, whilst the major part of the Desert Mounted Corps went on to Aleppo.

At Baalbek accordingly it remained until the end of November. The regiment was now commanded by Colonel Hewlett, who had come out from India for the purpose. On the 31st October an armistice was signed with Turkey, and the regiment went into the Turkish barracks in the town. The ranks were still woefully attenuated. Squadrons could hardly muster twenty lances on parade. On the 25th November the 4th Cavalry Division moved to Beirut, where it was joined by the 5th Cavalry Division. The troops now reverted to cantonment conditions. The camps were near the sea, of which every advantage was taken ; invalids returned to duty ; the strength was thus gradually made up ; some of the Mahomedans were allowed to make the pilgrimage to Mecca, and with training and sports, both mounted and dismounted, all officers and men spent six very pleasant months.

At the end of May 1919 the Tenth Brigade marched over the Lebanon to Homs, where it remained during the next five months. In the autumn there was a recurrence of the fever, which, however, affected the Central India Horse very little. Syria was now handed over to the French, and our troops were consequently withdrawn. The Tenth Brigade marched back to Beirut and down the coast to Haifa, whence it was railed to Ludd, and finally came to rest on the 23rd December at its original starting-point at Sarona.

In the spring of 1920 the brigade, minus the Dorset Yeomanry, which was now demobilised, was again sent up to the upper waters of the Jordan, where the Arab tribes of Syria, restless since our evacuation, were now pushing their raids into Palestine. The 2nd Lancers went to Beisan, and the Central India Horse to Semakh. Both regiments were subjected to fierce attacks by very large numbers of Arabs, and both successfully withstood them. The Central India Horse was fortunate in having the assistance of four bombing aeroplanes. Against these and the machine-guns the Arabs could do nothing. They came on again and again, only to be mown down, and were finally compelled to retreat to their hills across the border, whither it was forbidden to pursue them. Their losses were very heavy. The regiment had but seven casualties.

The summer and autumn were spent at Semakh patrolling the border, and this was the last of the ' active service ' duties which the men were called upon to perform. The regiment returned to Sarona in November, and here it became known that our ever-cheerful sowars, after crossing the once dreaded ' Kala Pani ' and enduring thereafter six years' experience of the actualities of war in foreign countries, were for home at last. On the 2nd February the regiment embarked at Suez, and reached Agar before the end of the month. Of the 600 men who left Goonah on the 10th November 1914, only 150 returned with the regiment to Central India, and only one British officer, Captain Daunt. All those who had not recently had leave from Palestine were allowed to go to their homes at once. The rest were moved by rail to Goonah, whence the 39th had already departed. A few months later the 38th followed them to Quetta, and here, reduced in numbers and deprived of our special character as a local corps, we were amalgamated into one regiment of Regular cavalry.

CHAPTER XXI.

WE LEAVE CENTRAL INDIA.

DURING the six years covered by the four preceding chapters, whilst the 38th was fighting in France and Palestine, the 39th was employed on the unenviable but not unimportant duty of 'internal security.' Douglas was in command at the outbreak of war, but was sent immediately to Bombay as Embarkation Commandant. His successor, Colonel Walter Daunt, was at home on leave, and, like every other officer similarly situated, had sought employment under the War Office. He had not, however, crossed to France when the permanent command fell vacant, and was therefore recalled to India to take up his new duties. There were other officers in England also, but these were left alone. Of those present with the regiment at the time Major Capper was appointed D.A.Q.M.G. of the Lahore Divisional Area, under the 'internal security' scheme, and Major Kettlewell was sent to the Poona Divisional Area as G.S.O. 2. During the interim between Douglas's departure and Daunt's arrival at the end of October 1914 the command of the regiment thus fell to Brevet Lieut.-Colonel H. B. Birdwood.

Before the end of 1914 the regiment received a

warning, which in normal times would have been deemed exceedingly unpleasant, to be prepared for delocalisation. Seeing, however, that 'internal security' was now the appointed rôle, during such time as the war might last, it was not unexpected and created no despondency. Obviously there was no danger to British rule in Gwalior territory, or in any of the native States. There were no 'agitators' there; and although there might, and possibly would, be a recrudescence of dacoity if the regiment were removed, this could be of little consequence in comparison with disturbances in British India, where a handful of 'literati' can inflame the passions of a mob, and could do much, perhaps more than they themselves intended, to hamper the Government in the prosecution of the war. The regiment was, therefore, prepared without warning to be sent out of Central India at any moment. It was a case of being sent on service—though not 'active service' —a temporary absence only. The war might last a year or two, and at the end of that time there would be a return to normal conditions. That it would last four years and change everything, including our situation as a local corps in Central India, was as yet unforeseen.

The regiment was now at Agar, forty miles from a railway station, where it could be of little use in a sudden emergency. In February, therefore, it was ordered to Goonah, marching up the old road and past the old familiar landmarks, without realising it, for the last time. In April the first act of delocalisation took place. Two squadrons were detached to Poona, where they were quartered for the next two years. Meanwhile it had become very clear that a larger effort would be required from India than any living man had anticipated or would perhaps have considered possible. The entrance of Turkey into the war had increased her responsibilities enormously. She might be called upon to resist Turkish power in more places than one, in Mesopotamia and Egypt in particular, or even to defend her own borders; and so it became imperative to call upon her martial races to produce every available man. An intensive recruiting campaign was initiated, and the strength of all non-mobilised regiments was increased, to begin with, by 12 per cent. In the case of the cavalry the new establishment was fixed at 700 Indian ranks. It was quickly raised to 750, and before the end of the war had reached the high figure of 850, the intention being that each regiment, whilst retaining intact its normal establishment of 625 so as to be ready for effective action if required, should assume also the duties of a large recruiting and training depot, and so keep the regiments at the front up to strength. These duties called for great exertions. Indian officers, pensioners as well as those on the active list, were, as was only to be expected, indefatigable and very successful in obtaining recruits. Several were rewarded for their work. Risaldar Malik Sher Bahadur Khan, one of the toughest sirdars[1] we ever had, who came into the regiment on its augmentation in 1885, was presented with a Sword of Honour and a gold watch by the Viceroy at a Durbar at Lahore. Risaldar Ghulam Ali Khan of Kahnaur, a pensioner and a remarkable

[1] Officers.

man who was never afraid to express an honest opinion, was granted the honorary rank of Risaldar Major. Others received various token of recognition. British officers also made occasional tours round the villages in the Panjab, where they were received with marked enthusiasm; and so it very rarely happened that the regiment was below the mark in point of numbers. Training, however, was carried on with difficulty by reason of the paucity of experienced British officers. Many men from the Indian Army Reserve of Officers, and from Sandhurst, were posted to the regiment—there were, in fact, over fifty such appointments during the war,—but the older hands were absent employed, as Appendix IV. shows, on various duties in almost every quarter of the globe. Nevertheless, during the four years 1914 to 1917, the regiment was able to despatch 734 trained soldiers, and as many horses, to the regiments in the field.

Colonel Daunt had held his command for barely eight months when he had a bad accident at polo, and was invalided to England. Major Capper was recalled from Staff duty to take his place. On the 16th March 1916 Daunt returned to duty, and Capper went on field service to Mesopotamia, where he remained until October 1918. Meanwhile, however, whilst remaining seconded, he was appointed permanent Commandant on the expiry of Daunt's tenure in February 1917, when Major Hewlett, who had returned from remount duty in France a few months previously, took over the reins from him. When Capper rejoined Hewlett was appointed to the command of the 38th, and went, as we have seen, to Syria.

Hewlett's first duty, irrespective of the daily routine, was to raise a fifth squadron, to be mounted on country-bred horses or ponies, and to be armed with swords and rifles only. Before he went to Syria he was ordered to raise a sixth. The latter was sent, as soon as it was formed, to Baleli, near Quetta, where it was incorporated in the 41st Cavalry, one of four regiments of a new mounted brigade under Brigadier-General H. B. Birdwood, who had, in the meantime, left the regiment to command the 27th Light Cavalry.

In the short period during which he held command of the 39th Hewlett had the unusual experience of appointing three Risaldar Majors. Bakshi Jaswant Singh, a very bright officer with some knowledge of English, who had succeeded Risaldar Major Malik Ghulam Mahomed Khan in 1913, retired on his pension on the 15th July 1917 after thirty-two years' service. Risaldar Mumtaz Ali Khan of Kalanaur, a quiet dignified old sirdar with great influence in the Rohtak villages, was selected to fill his place, but retired within a year of his appointment. He was succeeded by Risaldar Malik Sher Bahadur Khan, who remained a couple of months, and was followed by Risaldar Natha Singh. The latter was not, however, the last Risaldar Major of the 39th. He retired in September 1920, when Risaldar Bachan Singh took over the appointment, and held it until the two regiments were amalgamated. The last Risaldar Major of the 38th, and the first of the combined regiment, was Jawand Singh, who was appointed three months before the amalgamation took place, in succession to Bostan Khan, the successor of the great Amar Singh. Capper left the regiment on the 14th February 1921, and no successor was appointed, though Colonel Giles, C.M.G., D.S.O., who had been brought in from the 35th Sindh Horse, and Colonel Kettlewell officiated for short periods; and thus the first Commandant of the combined regiment was Colonel Hewlett.

After the return of the two squadrons from Poona there was no call upon the regiment for special services until April 1919, when two squadrons were moved to Ahmedabad in aid of the Civil Power, one squadron returning almost immediately. The other remained absent from Headquarters until the end of the year, going from Ahmedabad to Bombay and thence to Devlali. Headquarters, with two squadrons, went to Jhelum in May 1919, and the whole regiment was not concentrated again at Goonah until the autumn of the year 1920.

Meanwhile it had become known that our days in Central India were numbered. The war being over, the military policy of the Government of India was reviewed, and it was judged no longer expedient to maintain so large a force of cavalry. The number of regiments was therefore reduced by half, two regiments throughout the force being amalgamated into one, with a combined strength of only 530 all ranks. In this respect we were lucky, for instead of being called by a double number, such as the '17th-37th Cavalry' for instance, in the endeavour to retain the old distinctions of both, we simply became one regiment of Central India Horse. In other respects, however, we were less fortunate. Agar and Goonah were abolished as cavalry stations, and we ceased to be a local corps. But before this could happen certain negotiations had to be concluded with the Gwalior Durbar. It will be remembered that the old Contingents were provided by the chiefs in whose territories they were quartered. In the case of Gwalior the management and revenues of certain districts were assigned to the Honourable East India Company for the upkeep of the Contingent; but after the Mutiny, in recognition of the Maharajah's loyalty and service, some of these territories were restored to him, whilst others were ceded by him in full sovereignty to the British Government. It was stipulated, however, that in place of the old Contingent a 'subsidiary force' should be constantly stationed in Gwalior territory. We were that 'subsidiary force'; and when our removal was contemplated, it became necessary to consult the Gwalior Durbar upon the effect which the terms of the Treaty might have upon the proposal. The Durbar replied that the removal of the regiments would not be considered an infraction of the Treaty, provided that the British Government retained the obligation to defend Gwalior from foreign invasion or serious disturbances.

And so, in the spring of 1921, we bade farewell to Central India. What effect the change, combined as it was with the abolition of the Silladar System, will have upon the character of the regiment the future alone can show. We shall probably lose some of that 'individuality' stamped upon us by our isolation in the jungles. The sowar may lose some of that self-reliance which he gained from his hunting experiences and from frequent service in small bodies amongst the villages of Malwa, where he was always a very important person. We shall become, perhaps, better disciplined, though not better trained. There can be no more of those delightful irregularities, when it was possible to spend weeks in a shikar camp or even at the Indore Residency without the word 'leave' being mentioned, or when news of a panther in a neighbouring beat was enough to cause the abandonment of an important ceremonial parade; but whether we shall be a more useful regiment, except in the strategic sense, is open to question. And as to the districts we have left behind, it is permissible to wonder whether the same tranquillity will endure without us. The Gwalior State forces which have replaced us are no doubt very efficient. They will, perhaps, be a little less watchful and a a little less feared. The march of civilisation may have swept away that sense of insecurity which permeated the lives of dwellers in those remote territories; but the criminal tribes are still criminal, there are still banias to be looted in the villages and cattle to be lifted from the hills, and it will not be surprising if, in the absence of the restraining hand of the British Government, made manifest by the presence of the British officer and his sowars, the jungles revert to their primitive condition, and the dacoit and the tiger come back to their own.

APPENDIX I.

MAKING A 'CAVALRY TRACK.'

By Lieut.-Colonel R. C. Bell, D.S.O., O.B.E.

In November 1917 a plan for a surprise attack on the German positions in front of Cambrai had been worked out, and the extensive preparations had been practically completed. The general idea, put very roughly, was an attack by six infantry divisions supported by some 300 tanks. A cavalry corps was to be held in readiness to dash through the breach made by the infantry and to cut the German communications north and south of Cambrai. Success depended on surprise, surprise on secrecy of preparation. As events turned out the secret was well kept and the surprise complete. The country behind the German front line was undulating and open, but the various trench systems and the great obstacle of the Hindenburg Line prevented the possibility of a rapid advance by the cavalry. It was clear, therefore, that a track must be made along which the cavalry could advance without delay until they emerged into the open country behind the trench systems. With this object in view a 'Cavalry Track Battalion' was formed, consisting of dismounted officers and men of the 4th Cavalry Division. The strength was about 20 British officers and 500 Indian other ranks, including Roxburgh and 100 other ranks of the Central India Horse. I was given command, sent for to Corps Headquarters, sworn to secrecy, and told what we had to do. We assembled at the aptly named village of Misery near Chaulnes Junction. It was a dismal and uncomfortable spot, a ruined chateau situated in what had once been beautiful grounds. The chateau was now a mere rubbish heap in the midst of smashed and torn trees, remains of trenches and heaps of debris of all descriptions from domestic furniture to gas cylinders. However, the cellars of the chateau served for a Headquarter office and officers' mess, and the personnel were accommodated in tents, concealed as far as possible to avoid the attentions of bombing planes. Having thoroughly digested the scheme we started serious training. I was given aerial photographs of the ground behind the German front line. From those I was able to work out a track from near Gouzeacourt up to and beyond the Hindenburg Line. The photographs were fairly clear. The track would be over five miles in length, and would cross twenty-six visible lines of trenches. We then proceeded to construct a replica of the German trench system near our camp. The twenty-six individual trenches or systems of trenches were numbered, and squads told off permanently to each particular trench. The work consisted of clearing ground, cutting wire, filling in or bridging trenches. The bridging work was, of course, the most important, and this would have to be accomplished with material found on the ground. 'Collecting parties' were told off, and they quickly learned what they would require for their particular bridge. The general scheme was as follows: a 'track leader,' a British officer, would go over with the infantry attack. With him would be twenty-six men with notice-boards bearing the numbers of the trenches from 1 (our front line) to 26 (the Hindenburg Line). As the leader identified each trench he would place the notice-board in position so that squads could recognise their positions and get on to their work at once.

We practised daily for about three weeks, and by that time all ranks understood what they had to do.

Finally we had a trial run before the Corps Commander and other red-hats, who were inclined to be critical; but as they had no suggestions of any value to make, things were left as they were.

The night before the attack we were conveyed in lorries through Fins to the neighbourhood of Gouzeacourt, where we debussed. I was taken to see the Cavalry Corps Commander, who remarked, "If you don't do your job I can't do mine." On arrival at Gouzeacourt my command received the addition of a dozen tanks. These were to be used in removing the formidable barrier of barbed wire (said to be 100 yards deep) in front of the Hindenburg Line. We had a meal in Gouzeacourt (shortly afterwards the scene of hand-to-hand fighting in the brilliant counter-attack of the Guards Division), and then proceeded to get the men into convenient positions for their advance in the morning. This was none too easy, as most of the places I had previously selected as suitable were now occupied by other troops, who expressed strong disapproval when batches of sowars fell over them in the dark! By about 1 A.M. they were satisfactorily disposed of. I then accompanied the tanks, which were stealthily moving up, trying not to breathe hard or snort! They were doing about a mile an hour. When we got close to the front line the one in front of me suddenly burst into flame. Everyone in the vicinity fled for cover, expecting a shower of shells!

The burning tank was on a slight rise, and must have been visible for miles. However, nothing happened, and in about twenty minutes the flames died away and we breathed again. Everything was now 'en train,' so we lay down and slept until 5 A.M., when we were wakened by a sudden burst of fire away on our left. The general impression was that the show had been 'blown on.' However, the firing ceased after a while, and by 5.45 A.M. all was calm. When it began to get light I could dimly see the features of the undulating ground around; everything looked brown and khaki-coloured, not a sound or movement anywhere. Zero hour was 6.10 A.M. I had (like hundreds of others) my watch in my hand and counted the minutes, then the seconds. '6.10 A.M.' Our 1200 guns crashed out simultaneously. The hills around seemed suddenly to move bodily, and through the dim light line after line of khaki infantry, bayonets fixed and arms sloped, appeared from everywhere moving steadily forward, and tanks, to the right and left as far as one could see.

The surprise was so complete that tanks and troops were over the German front line and beyond almost without a check. Then began a firework display that put the Crystal Palace in the shade. Up and down the German line for miles rose showers of rockets—red, green, white, every colour known to rockets, simply screaming for help.

It was a wonderful sight, and the attack was, as far as one could see, succeeding all along the line. I had been told to ask the nearest Brigadier for permission to advance, but knowing what infantry Brigadiers feel like when their brigades are going 'over the top' I refrained from troubling any of them, and told my track leader to be off with the leading infantry, an instruction which he faithfully carried out. There was no check and no enemy shelling to speak of, so my parties started off at once. As our knowledge of the ground had been gained from photographs only I was extremely anxious as to whether the track leader would find his bearings and recognise the lines of trenches on the actual ground. After picking up the first few notice-boards I could see that he was on the right line, and as a matter of fact he marked the positions of the squads correctly from start to finish. I moved on with Roxburgh and the C.I.H. party across the sunken road and through the village of La Vacquerie. We dropped the squads as each arrived at its appointed place until only the Hindenburg Line party remained. This was the strongest and most important of all, and was accompanied by the tanks. I sent them on and fixed my reporting station on the low hill known as 'Welsh Ridge.' From this vantage point I had a splendid view of the battle. Infantry and tanks were approaching the Hindenburg Line; behind both flanks batteries were limbering up and galloping forward, a rare sight at this period of the war. There was heavy fighting at the Hindenburg Line, and our party was held up. We got shelled a bit here, but the well-made German trenches afforded good cover. Before long we saw our infantry emerging beyond the Line, and the advance was at once resumed.

The Hindenburg Line party, commanded by Major Wheatley, 27th Cavalry, with his tanks, now reached their objective. They found wire defences over 100 yards deep formed of tangled wire heaped up several feet high, and securely anchored to the ground. The wire-cutting parties got to work and cut lines through it; the tanks followed, hauling anchors behind them and dragging the wire away in great tangled masses. Meanwhile the bridging parties were hard at work, and they had a heavy job on hand. The Hindenburg Line was deep and broad, but within a couple of hours practical hands had completed capital bridges fit for artillery to cross. After seeing this work I returned to Welsh Ridge and awaited my reports. The battle had rolled on towards Marcoign, the Canal, and Cambrai. Long columns of German prisoners passed us on their way to the rear. There were still tanks visible everywhere: some were advancing, many were on fire, others broken down or stuck in trenches. One after another came in the reports, "Track ready." By 10.45 A.M. I was able to send the same message, thrice repeated, to Corps Headquarters. I got no acknowledgment, and no cavalry appeared! 12 o'clock, still no sign; 1 o'clock—two messages, one from a distracted officer: "Tank crossed my bridge and broke it, did all I could but he would not stop, am repairing as quickly as possible." The second from the C.I.H. near La Vacquerie: "Cavalry

APPENDIX I. 419

advancing along track." A few minutes later our spirits were raised by the sight of a body of cavalry trotting gaily along our track. I dashed down the hill to ask who they were. "General Seeley's Canadian Brigade," was the answer. This was a surprise, as I was expecting our 2nd Cavalry Division, and had no information about the Canadians. They trotted past, making a gallant show, across our bridges over the Hindenburg Line and out beyond it. I could see them forming up on the slopes facing the canal. There was only one bridge here, and it was blocked by an adventurous tank, which had tried to cross, and stuck fast in the middle. There was just room for the cavalry to lead their horses past it in single file. One squadron crossed after a lot of trouble. Their story is well known. They charged the enemy, capturing prisoners and guns, but they had taken on too much, and what remained of them recrossed the canal at night, minus their horses and prisoners. We now began to suffer from reaction. The thrills of the morning were over, the battle was dying away in the distance, no signs of our cavalry, and last but not least, it was beginning to rain. Eventually at about 3 P.M. the head of the 2nd Cavalry Division in column of sections (miles long) appeared near Gouzeacourt. It was obvious that it was too late for any serious action before nightfall. The division halted on the track as soon as it got dark, and bivouacked there that night. By the following morning the idea of a cavalry advance in this direction was abandoned, and they were withdrawn. We were also recalled, and returned to Gouzeacourt, where we embussed, and were taken back to Misery. The Corps Commander sent for me, and congratulated all ranks for their work on the cavalry track, which he said could not have been better done.

We were naturally very disappointed that our work had been in vain, the more so as the magnificent and spectacular success of the attack in the morning had led us to believe that we were preparing the way to show that cavalry might yet prove their usefulness in modern war.

Our gallant track leader, 2nd Lieutenant L. J. Peck of the 2nd Lancers, was awarded the Military Cross.

APPENDIX II.

LETTERS TO THE COMMANDING OFFICER ON THE DEPARTURE OF THE REGIMENT FROM FRANCE.

COPY OF LETTER FROM BRIGADIER-GENERAL NEIL HAIG, COMMANDING MHOW CAVALRY BRIGADE.

> 4TH CAVALRY DIVISION,
> *9th March* 1918.

MY DEAR GOURLIE,—This brigade has now been broken up, but before it is entirely dispersed I wish to offer to you personally, also your predecessor Colonel Browne, my best thanks for the loyal support and assistance which you have both given me throughout the entire period of my command. I also beg that you will convey to all the officers, N.C.O.'s, and men of the 38th C.I. Horse my gratitude for the loyalty, courage, and cheerful devotion to duty which they have ever displayed and their magnificent behaviour, which has been consistently so, under often the most trying circumstances. I know that wherever they may be they will gain fresh laurels, and add further lustre to the already splendid records of a distinguished regiment. I only hope that they may have the good fortune to take a leading part in the real cavalry work which must complete the final victories of this war before a favourable peace can be signed. I can only say that no man has ever commanded a finer brigade than I have, and of this I shall always feel justly proud. It is with the deepest feeling of regret that I bid you all farewell and God-speed. I wish you all good luck in the future and a safe return to your homes.—Yours sincerely,

> (Sd.)   NEIL HAIG.

APPENDIX II.

Copy of a Letter from the Officer Commanding Inniskilling Dragoons, 3rd March 1918.

To O.C. 38TH C.I. HORSE.

MY DEAR BELL,—On the breaking up of the old Mhow Brigade after our being together for $3\frac{1}{2}$ years on active service, I wish to place on record the high appreciation of all ranks of the Inniskilling Dragoons of the good fortune we have had in having been brigaded with such a magnificent regiment as yours. During the whole period your officers, Indian officers, N.C.O.'s, and men have been true comrades to us all at all times, whether fighting hard in the field, in the trenches, or training in the back areas. Personally I have had the honour on several occasions to command your men in trenches, and never do I wish for braver, harder fighters or harder workers; never have I heard a grumble from any during any of the periods, however hard and uncomfortable the circumstances. They have been magnificent throughout, and I have always felt it an honour to have had so many opportunities to have had them with me. The Inniskillings as a whole would have liked to come and wished you all God-speed, good luck, and good-bye before your departure, but owing to the distance we are away from each other this is impossible, but I hope you will inform all ranks of the good wishes we send you all. We know well you will carry on the magnificent work in the new battle area to which you are moving, and we all hope that some day our regiments may again be brigaded together when we have finished and won this great war. God-speed, best of luck, and good-bye to you all from all ranks of the Inniskilling Dragoons.—Yours sincerely,

(Sd.) E. PATTERSON, *Lt.-Col.*

APPENDIX III.

BRITISH OFFICERS WHO SERVED WITH THE REGIMENT DURING THE GREAT WAR.

Lieut.-Colonel A. P. Browne, D.S.O., Commanding, 1914-18. (Russian Order of St Anne.)
Lieut.-Colonel A. Hewlett, 1918.
Lieut.-Colonel R. C. Bell, D.S.O., O.B.E., 1914-18. (One year with Royal Welsh Fusiliers.)
Lieut.-Colonel S. A. Cooke, 1914-17. Invalided and died in England.
Major Sir T. S. Lawson-Tancred, Bt. (Retired List), 1915-18.
Major H. K. Barr, 1914-16. Invalided and died in England.
Major R. C. Goodfellow, 1914-16.
Major (Temp. Lieut.-Colonel) J. Gourlie, D.S.O., 1915-18. (16th Q.O. Lancers, 1914-15.)
Major G. Lewis, 1915-17.
Major R. J. Macnabb, 1915-18.
Major J. R. Hutchison, D.S.O., 1914-17.
Major G. Henderson, 1914-16. With R.F.C., 1916-18. (Belgian Order of Leopold and Croix de Guerre.)
Captain and Bt.-Major R. S. Abbott, M.C., 1914-17.
Captain (Temp. Major) C. O'B. Daunt, M.C., 1914-18.
Captain and Bt.-Major Sir N. R. A. D. Leslie, Bt., C.B.E., 1914-16. (Transferred R.F.C. 1916.)
Captain A. H. Williams, M.C., 1915-18. (12th R. Lancers, 1914-15.)
Lieutenant G. B. Lucas, 1915, with R.F.C. Killed in action.
Lieutenant N. M. Martin, 1915. (Transferred to R.F.C.)
Lieutenant R. H. M. Durand, 1914-17. Died of wounds received in action.
Risaldar (afterwards 2nd Lieutenant) Mohamed Kamaluddin Khan, M.C., 1914-18.
Lieutenant E. T. R. Wickham, 1915. Invalided to India.
Captain H. Keighley (retired), 1915. Invalided 1917.
Colonel H.H. The Maharaja of Rutlam, 1916-17.

The above belonged to the regiment before the war. The following joined during the war.

APPENDIX III. 423

Captain W. W. K. Page, M.C., 1915-18.
Major R. G. M. Prichard, Glamorgan Yeomanry, 1915-18. Died of wounds received in action, Palestine.
Lieutenant Leslie Wilson, Cheshire Yeomanry, 1915-16.
Lieutenant Price Jones, Welsh Horse, 1915-16.
Major T. H. Westmacott, Calcutta Light Horse, 1915-18.
Lieutenant E. Woodhouse, I.A.R.O. Died of wounds received in action, 1917.
Captain C. L. Leslie, 35th Scinde Horse, 1916-17.
2nd Lieutenant Wynyard-Wright, I.A.R.O., 1916.
Lieutenant C. L. Reid, I.A.R.O., 1917.
Lieutenant T. D. Wilson, M.C., 10th Royal Hussars (S.R.), 1916-18. Died in Palestine.
Lieutenant G. B. Walter, I.A.R.O., 1916-18.
Lieutenant W. F. Skene, 16th (W.O.) Lancers (S.R.), 1916-18.
Lieutenant P. C. Mangin, I.A.R.O., 1916-17.
Lieutenant C. E. Milner, I.A.R.O., 1916-18.
Lieutenant D. A. Cameron, M.C., Q.O. Corps of Guides, 1917. Killed in action.
Lieutenant J. C. D. Pinney. Killed in action, 1917.
Lieutenant Hirst, I.A.R.O., 1917-18.
Captain R. Westmacott, Calcutta Light Horse, 1917.
Lieutenant G. Roxburgh, I.A.R.O., 1916-18.
Lieutenant H. Pigot, 1917.
Lieutenant S. E. Good, 1917.
Lieutenant A. E. Swann, 1917-18.
Lieutenant T. R. Marshall, 1917.
Lieutenant G. W. Doudney, 1917-18.
Lieutenant B. F. Williams, 1917-18.
Lieutenant S. D. Majoribanks, 1918.
Lieutenant A. A. E. Filose, 1917-18.
Lieutenant R. George, 1917-18.
Lieutenant M. Cox, 1917-18.
Lieutenant B. G. Dalrymple-Hay, 1918.
Lieutenant N. S. Alington, M.C., 1918.
Lieutenant T. G. Evers, Calcutta Light Horse, 1918. Died in Syria.
Lieutenant L. S. C. Skinner, 1919. Died in Palestine.

APPENDIX IV.

RECORDS OF EXTRA-REGIMENTAL SERVICES OF BRITISH OFFICERS DURING THE GREAT WAR.

The following records of the services of British officers, whilst away from the regiment during the Great War, have been collated by Brigadier-General C. G. Hoare. Though they do not, strictly speaking, form part of regimental history, they are included here as a matter of interest, showing what a variety of military experience can sometimes be found in one regiment. It has always been a characteristic of the Central India Horse that its officers are prone to seek service outside its ranks, which is far from being a regimental disadvantage; and in the Great War, whilst the 38th, or 1st Regiment, had the honour of fighting regimentally, the 39th, or 2nd, although regimentally a Training Depot, had officers of its own serving the King in four continents and against almost every foe.

The officers have, in most instances, told their own story. Colonel Bell's description of an infantry officer's experience in the trenches is, like his account of 'The Cavalry Track at Cambrai,' particularly interesting. So also are the stories of the fighting in the air. Pitcher and Hoare were both Adjutants of the 2nd Regiment, the latter succeeding the former. They entered the war as Captains, and came out of it as Brigadier-Generals.

W. A. W.

A.—SERVICES ON LAND.

Major-General J. A. Douglas, C.M.G., C.I.E.

When war was declared I was still commanding the C.I.H. at Agar, and was immediately ordered to Bombay as Embarkation Commandant. I remained in this post till December 1914, when the embarkation work was put under the G.O.C. Bombay,

APPENDIX IV. 425

and I was transferred to Peshawar as A.Q.M.G. In March 1915 I was appointed A.Q.M.G. on the Staff of Sir John Nixon, commanding the Army Corps then being sent to Mesopotamia, and left with him on 1st April. I remained in this appointment till the middle of September 1916, taking part in the action at Kurnah (Townshend's regatta) on the 31st May and the subsequent advance to Amarah.

I was then appointed to command the 31st Infantry Brigade, which formed part of the 2nd Division under General Gorringe. This gave me the rank of Brigadier-General. Townshend was then at Kut preparing for a further advance, and my brigade was sent up to Amarah, and later a portion was detached and sent up to Kut.

Early in December 1915, when Townshend had been obliged to retire on Kut and was invested there, the 3rd and 7th Indian Divisions from France were sent to Mesopotamia, and General Aylmer came from India to take command of this force operating to relieve Townshend. As he had no staff with him it was necessary to improvise one, and I with the whole of my brigade staff was transferred to the Headquarters of his Army Corps, where I held the appointment of Brigadier-General (Administrative). I was with General Aylmer throughout his attempt to break through the Turkish positions on the river below Kut.

In the spring of 1916 Aylmer was relieved by Gorringe, and returned to India.

I was then appointed to command at Bushire, where the Tangistanis and other tribes on the mainland had been giving trouble, and this command was later extended to include all the garrisons in the Persian Gulf and Muscat.

In the summer of 1918 Sir P. Sykes, with the South Persian Rifles, which he had raised, and some Indian troops, was attacked at Shiraz by the Kashgai tribes under Saulat-ud-Dowleh, and there was a good deal of fighting.

It was then decided that a force should be sent from India in the autumn to open up the road to Shiraz, and permit of the withdrawal of the troops there.

I was given command of this force, which consisted of about two brigades with some cavalry and mountain guns. These operations, which consisted mostly of road-making and the construction of a railway as far as Borasjun, with no serious fighting, were practically completed by January 1919, but it was April before the troops were withdrawn and the force broken up.

Immediately on my return to India at the beginning of May 1919 I was sent up to Peshawar as I.G. Communications on the northern line, and remained there till June, when an armistice was arranged with the Afghans. I was then allowed to go.

Brigadier-General H. B. Birdwood, D.S.O.
I was stuck with C.I.H. in India with Daunt and Capper sitting over my head. Accepted command of 27th, but we were shot off to D.I.K. and the N.W.F., where we stayed. In 1918 I got command of the 12th Mounted Brigade, and formed part of the Baluchistan Field Force in the Afghan War of 1919, but we only sat at Chaman in the Frontier towards Kandahar and looked at Afghan patrols.

Lieut.-Colonel A. Hewlett.
He was sent to France in November 1914 to be Second-in-Command of the Indian Remount Depot at Marseilles, where he remained until 15th January 1916. He then served for a short time with the 12th Cavalry in Mesopotamia, but, being appointed G.S.O. 1 of the Mhow Division, returned to India in March. He commanded the Central India Horse in Syria from 15th October 1918 until the end of the war.

Lieut.-Colonel A. M. Kettlewell.
After serving as G.S.O. 1 of the Poona Divisional Area during the first two years of the war he was appointed D.A.A.G. of the 7th Division at Sannaiyat, below Kut. Shortly afterwards he became G.S.O. 2 of the newly formed Cavalry Division, with which he served during the capture of Kut from the Turks and the advance on Baghdad.

Later he was G.S.O. Line of Communications for a while, and in April 1919 was appointed to command the 5th Cavalry.

Lieut.-Colonel J. Gourlie, D.S.O.
A few days after war was declared orders were received by all officers of the Indian Army at home, on leave or furlough, to hold themselves in readiness to embark at Southampton for India at an early date, much to the consternation of all concerned. Many of us, however, were reprieved, and I for one was ordered to join the 8th Cavalry Reserve Regiment at the Curragh as a reinforcement officer for the 16th (Q.O.) Lancers.

APPENDIX IV.   427

Durand was posted in like capacity to the 4th Hussars, and Williams to the 12th Royal Lancers.

I joined at the Curragh some time in August, and was soon sent off in charge of a large draft of reservists to Windsor to make up the strength of the Household Cavalry. I was then ordered to Woolwich to collect another draft of civilians and conduct them back to the Curragh. At Woolwich I was handed over a hundred civilians of every conceivable walk of life. One I remember in a frock-coat, tweed cap, and tennis shoes, whose sole kit seemed to consist of a banjo (in case), which he hugged lovingly; another, a lion tamer with a large flowing moustache, so overcome with sorrow at leaving his pets that he had to be carried to the station. A third was a professor of some kind from one of the 'Varsities. His reason for wishing to join the cavalry was that owing to bad corns he did not think he could walk well enough for the infantry.

I was beginning to despair of ever getting to the war, when one day I was sent for and told that I was first reinforcement officer for the 16th Q.O. Lancers, and to be ready to start for France on twelve hours' notice. I received orders about the middle of September to proceed to Southampton for embarkation, and sailed at once for St Nazaire.

I picked up the 16th Lancers at Braisne on the Aisne River, where the fighting was in full swing. About the 25th September we were ordered to move off with the rest of the cavalry to try to relieve Antwerp. We marched pretty well night and day till we got to Hazbrouke, which place the Germans had just vacated that morning.

The first engagement of any importance was at Mont des Cats, where the Germans were holding the monastery. The 3rd Cavalry Brigade were told off to clear them out, and this we did in great style: galloped to the foot of the hill under cover of our horse battery fire, and, dismounting, rushed the monastery, killing about fifty of the enemy with few casualties to ourselves. After this we pushed on without further opposition to Messines and Warneton, but here we were checked, and had to withdraw to Hollebeke. This was the commencement of the first battle of Ypres. I had been posted to 'D' Squadron, 16th Lancers. Onslow, who commanded the squadron, was killed on the 5th November, and I was given command. We had some very stiff fighting outside Ypres until the cavalry were ultimately relieved by infantry and withdrawn to rest. I rejoined the

APPENDIX IV.

Central India Horse on their arrival in the war area in January 1915.

Lieut.-Colonel C. O. Harvey, M.C.
September 1914.—Appointed Special Service Officer with Mysore Lancers, and sent to Bangalore to mobilise them as quickly as possible.
October 1914.—Joined Imperial Service Cavalry Brigade at Deolali, and appointed Orderly Officer to Brigadier-General W. A. Watson, Commanding.
Sailed for Egypt.
November 1914.—Arrived Suez Canal, and encamped at Moascar on west bank.
1915.—Brigade employed along the whole length of the canal in patrolling and minor skirmishes with Turks.
1916.—Appointed Staff Captain I.S. Cavalry Brigade, and then D.A.Q.M.G. Delta District, with Headquarters at Cairo.
January 1917.—Appointed Brigade-Major I.S. Cavalry Brigade under Brigadier-General Henderson.
Moved up to Palestine.
General Harbord succeeded General Henderson.
Brigade took part in operations ending in capture of Gaza and subsequent pursuit.
1918.—I.S. Cavalry Brigade became 15th I.S. Cavalry Brigade in 5th Cavalry Division, and I remained as Brigade-Major until the end of the war.
Brigade took part in operations in Jordan Valley and Allenby's final drive, being the advance brigade up to Aleppo.
I was wounded in the final battle just outside Aleppo, and then went on leave to England, after which I returned to India in September 1919.

Lieut.-Colonel R. C. Bell, D.S.O., O.B.E.
In addition to his service in command of the detachment which made the 'Cavalry Track' at Cambrai, Colonel Bell served for a year in command of the 15th Battalion, Royal Welsh Fusiliers, and describes his experiences as follows :—
In September 1915 I was commanding a 'Cavalry School' at Marseilles, where Indian Army reserve officers went through a course of instruction before joining Indian cavalry regiments serving in France. After three very busy months the supply of reserve officers began to fail, and I was ordered to rejoin the

APPENDIX IV. 429

C.I.H. This I did, finding the regiment at a small village inland from Le Treport. On arrival I was greeted with orders to proceed at once to London with a view to taking command of a battalion of ' Kitchener's Army.' I was off next morning and reported to the War Office in London. After a few days' delay I was sent to Winchester, and took over command of the 15th Battalion (London Welsh) Royal Welsh Fusiliers belonging to the 38th Welsh Division. The division was under orders for France. We left Winchester at 3 A.M. one morning in heavy snow, and arrived at Southampton Docks in the afternoon wet to the skin. We crossed to Havre, railed to Blendeques, marched by night in sheets of rain to scattered billets between Aire and Clarques. ' Intensive training' was carried out all day and every day, until, within a few days of our arrival, we were attached to the Guards Division for duty in the trenches near Laventie. My battalion was attached to the 1st Scots Guards, and no more helpful and hospitable instructors could have been found in the Army. My personal introduction to the front line was not encouraging. I was being shown round by the C.O. : the procession consisted of an orderly, a sergeant, the C.O., and myself in single file in the above order. A rifle grenade exploded on my left rear. The three others went down, and I was left standing alone and untouched. We got the C.O. back to Regimental Headquarters, and he left for England a day or two later. This officer had been wounded at Loos and sent home. He had just rejoined when I met him. On recovery from this wound he returned to France once more, and was killed shortly afterwards. The trenches we were in faced the Aubers Ridge. From that vantage point the enemy overlooked our position, and made movement by day almost impossible and very unpleasant by night. The Guards were having a lot of casualties, and we did not escape without our share. After a few days with the Guards we were withdrawn and sent in on our own at Richebourg L'avoué, just south of Neuve Chapelle. We thus began a long spell of duty in the trenches, which was only broken when we were withdrawn at the beginning of June 1916 to take part in the Somme battle. In the trenches we had the usual experiences of this kind of warfare, strafes and counter-strafes, raids and counter-raids, and the never-ending job of keeping the defences in repair. Most of the work had to be done at night. As soon as it was dark repair and construction work began : patrols crept out into ' No Man's Land,' wiring parties went over the parapet to repair and strengthen the entanglements. Both sides laid themselves out to impede the other's work. 'Verey lights' rose and fell all along the line, exposing every movement of patrols or wiring parties. Snipers got busy, while all night long the traversing fire of machine-guns swept No Man's Land and the communicating trenches. An hour before dawn the troops 'stood-to,' and remained in a state of readiness until it was broad daylight, when rifles, &c., were cleaned, breakfast eaten, and, if the circumstances permitted, two or three hours' rest was taken. Whenever we left the line for short periods of so-called 'rest,' 'intensive training' was considered necessary for our health and efficiency.

Our worst experiences were, I think, at Givenchy, in front of La Bassee. The front line here had been frequently mined and the trenches blown to pieces. The result was that there was no regular front-line trench, merely a series of mine craters. We held these craters with small detachments. They were difficult to get at, as there were no communication trenches, and the enemy kept up a constant fire on the approaches. These posts were sometimes within as little as ten yards of the enemy, near enough for conversation to be overheard. Both sides were naturally inclined to be nervous, and any unusual noise or sudden movement was as likely as not to produce a shower of bombs and start a 'scrap.' Mining and counter-mining was in full swing. The R.E. officer would state with pride: "We're well under them now and nearly ready for a 'blow.'" "What about our line?" I would anxiously inquire, though to him this seemed to be of secondary importance. "I think they are under you in one place, anyhow, but you won't go up for a night or two," was the kind of reply one would receive. In addition to the mining, we suffered much from the minnewerfere. These were mounted on trolleys behind the German front line. The missiles known as 'rum-jars' or 'flying pigs' could be seen in the air: they carried a heavy charge, and the explosion was terrific, doing much damage to the trenches, as well as causing many casualties. For a long time we had no effective method of replying, our trench-mortars being beneath contempt. Then came the 'Stokes gun,' and at last we gave them back as good as we got and a little better. I had been told that the Welsh disliked outsiders and were difficult to get on with. I did not find this the case, and I think the battalion was a 'happy family.' When not in the line the few of my own countrymen (Irish) gave more trouble than all the Welsh put together. When there was 'dirty

APPENDIX IV. 431

work' on hand, they were second to none. Father Mac., our Roman Catholic chaplain, looked after them; he was a Sinn Feiner, and, I being Protestant and Unionist, we got on capitally. He did not like the English, he disliked Germans (mostly Protestants), and he hated Welshmen. When we went into the front line he always came with us. On one occasion word came that a Roman Catholic was lying badly wounded in a post beyond our parapet. Father Mac. jumped up. I told him to wait until the man was brought in. "Colonel," said he, "you may give orders to your Welshmen, but I take mine from God Almighty," and out he went. Near Lavantie I had my Regimental Headquarters in the line at a house known as 'Bell Farm,' owing to my long (enforced) residence there. We were having quite a large tea-party one afternoon when a shell burst outside. Now the Germans, who are methodical, always gave us six in quick succession, so I gave the word to retire to the dug-out below. The party took a long time to file out, as the door was narrow. When the last man was out, Father Mac. came dashing back: "Colonel," said he, "I've left me hat." I charged him down the steps, and at the same moment a shell burst in the room behind us, utterly destroying Father Mac.'s hat and our nice tin tea-set.

One of the most unhealthy spots in this line was a strip of breastwork known as the 'Boar's Head.' Why we held on to this spot I could never understand. It lay in No Man's Land at a slightly oblique angle to the German front line, only some fifty yards distant from it at the nearest point. Here, behind a low breastwork in a sodden trench, we had a post of one officer and about fifteen men. There were frequent casualties. It was isolated by day, and to get there at night one had to traverse some hundreds of yards across the open on duckboards. This track was systematically swept by machine-gun fire. 'Verey lights' went up at short intervals, shedding a brilliant illumination, and making the unhappy officer or man feel as if the gaze of the whole German army was fixed on him—in fact progress was made by hurried movement between bursts of machine-gun fire and the flare of 'Verey lights,' the intervals being spent lying flat with one's nose in the mud.

At the end of May we were withdrawn from the trenches and moved to Merville.

Thence we marched by easy stages to the neighbourhood of Bernaville, where we remained until the end of June. We then

moved towards the line once more; the week's bombardment
that preceded the attack on 1st July was in full swing, an awe-
inspiring sight from Forseville, where we found ourselves on
the night of 30th June. The attack took place, and as on this
front it was repulsed with heavy losses, we were not moved.
On the right our troops had penetrated the German line, and
the villages of Fricourt, Mametz, and Montauban had been captured. We moved south by night to Morlancourt, and a day
or two later passed through Carnoy, and took trenches between
Mametz village and the wood of the same name. Here we were
well inside the lately captured German line. My H.Q. was
established in a ravine known as the 'Queen's Nullah.' Between
us and Mametz Wood was a tract of high downland, then an
abrupt drop of 60 or 70 feet into the Caterpiller valley—the
wood was a couple of hundred yards from the cliff. We remained
at the 'Queen's Nullah,' occupying advanced trenches overlooking Mametz Wood and in front of 'Bottom Wood.' We
made a reconnaissance which was meant to develop into an
attack, until it was realised that success was wholly impossible.
We had one unforgetable night in the nullah. Our barrage was
on the wood, and the Germans laid one just in rear of us. We
got the 'Shorts' of both sides. I cleared out all our men except
a few signallers. However, other units wandered in, a company
from another division, some sappers and detached men, and six
officers sent from somewhere to spy out the land. During that
night we had 22 killed and 44 wounded out of about 120 all
told; I believe all the six officers were killed; it was a dreadful
mess in the morning. It rained heavily all day; towards night
I was ordered to withdraw the battalion to rest at Carnoy. They
rested in a wet meadow, and spent next day carrying bombs
and ammunition up to the line. That night we were moved to
trenches near Mametz village. The attack was timed for 3 A.M.,
and I was ordered to move at that hour to the 'Queen's Nullah'
as a reserve under the Brigadier's orders. At 3 A.M. hell was
let loose; the whole earth seemed to be flying round us as we
dashed through the barrage to the nullah. There the battalion
formed up; occasional shells fell in the nullah. A wild-looking
officer suddenly dashed at me. He shouted out, "For God's
sake, don't go on, Colonel; my battalion is wiped out and the
Colonel's killed!" He was pulled away crying and laughing.
Then a message from an officer of the same battalion, "Have
got a footing in the wood, but can't hold on unless reinforced

APPENDIX IV. 433

immediately"; that was definite, anyway (the sender was killed after sending this message). I gave the orders for attack, and with a cheer we went over the bank of the nullah. We dashed over 200 yards of open swept by machine-gun fire; my fieldglasses were shot off and a bullet ripped my sleeve; down the cliff into the valley. Here we were met by heavy rifle fire, and the leading companies sheered off to the left towards a salient jutting out from the wood in that direction. Three companies entered the wood here; I stopped the 4th; the edge on our right was evidently strongly held. We tried to push up the right side of the salient, but could not get on. Here my cane was cut off short by a bullet two inches above my thumb! Suddenly a dramatic change. From the edge of the wood on our right front rose scores of field-grey figures, all with their arms above their heads, advancing towards us. "They've surrendered," shouted the men, and so it was. I think about 300 men came out. We got them out of the way and advanced through the wood. I don't know how long we took to do the next few hundred yards, but it must have been hours. Fallen trees, huge shell-holes, undergrowth, dead and wounded men everywhere. Parties of Germans here and there, some fought, some surrendered. Our line of groups broke and reformed, got lost, struggled on again, making steady but very slow progress. The difficulties were great, the fire was incessant, mostly too high, and the noise was appalling. It was impossible to make anyone hear five yards away. At last we reached a cross ride, and the wood beyond was more open. That was about as much as we could do. I sent a message to the Brigadier reporting progress, and asking for reinforcements. Then we set to work to organise the line, and tried to get the men to dig themselves in. This effort was not very successful; they could not dig standing, and tried to scratch themselves in where they lay. Most of them went to sleep at once! The volume of fire from the enemy suddenly increased in intensity through the trees; I could see field-grey groups pushing towards us; a counter-attack was coming. It was a critical moment, but the men pulled themselves together, and after a few minutes of the rapid fire the groups melted away and the attack fizzled out. Then I became conscious of troops on my right, and was presently joined by Colonel Jack Hayes (3rd D.G.'s) with his battalion of the Welsh Regiment. He had fought his way in from the east. Shortly afterwards our Brigadier, General Price Davis, V.C., D.S.O., arrived; he brought

2 E

up a fresh battalion and ordered us to withdraw and reorganise. I got my men out of the wood, and we spent a couple of hours cleaning rifles, collecting ammunition and bombs from the dead and wounded, and consuming the "unexpended portion of the previous day's ration." At dusk we were ordered back to the wood. The Brigadier had made good progress, and the line had advanced a considerable distance. I was told to prolong our line to the left. We moved up, as I imagined, in rear of our line on the right. We got to a small clearing; I halted the battalion, and proceeded to explain to the officers where they had to go. Suddenly a machine-gun opened on us at point-blank range from the scrub in front; at the same instant a shell burst a few yards away. The effect was staggering. The small group of officers—five, I think—was just out of the line of fire of the machine-gun, and we were intact except for some bruises from fragments of the shell. For some time we could not find any men. They were directly in the line of fire; some were hit, and the remainder plunged into the jungle. It was dark by this time; the din was awful, and it was most difficult to make oneself heard. It took us quite an hour's hard work to collect everyone and to form up again. We then advanced again and took up our position in the line in touch with a battalion on our right. I made my H.Q. in a shell-hole, surrounded by dead and wounded Germans.

The night is hard to describe adequately.

The machine-gun and rifle fire was continuous. It came from all sides. Anyone moving about seemed to be shot at impartially by friend and foe. The safest place was flat on the ground amongst the mud and corpses. There were occasional pauses, and groups of men rushed about in any direction, whether German or British one could not tell. Our front line held firm, I think; at least they were there in the morning. The Brigadier, more regardless of personal safety than anyone I ever met, visited us during the night. Just after dawn there was a violent outbreak of bombing and machine-gunning on our right front. A Brigadier and his Staff Officer came along; both were hit and were carried away. When it became light things quieted down a bit, and one was able to take stock of the situation. As far as could be ascertained we seemed to hold all the wood except a nest of strong-points in the north-east corner. We were not being shelled, as the enemy had not yet appreciated the situation. Our excellent Quartermaster brought us up some rations. We were eventually relieved by another division. We got out of the wood by the way we had come in. Dead and wounded lay everywhere. We broke into groups to get through a nasty barrage of 'heavies' on Caterpillar Valley. We marched to Morlancourt, being heartily cheered by troops as we passed *en route*. The division had been, I think, just under 10,000 strong. Our casualties were—I speak from memory—about 5700. I was the only C.O. of the four in my brigade to come out on my feet. Colonels Flower and Ronny Cardon (17th Lancers) were killed, and Colonel Gwyther severely wounded. We spent one night at Morlancourt, were railed next day to Longpré, marched to a village a few miles to the east, and remained there two days. We were hoping for our second line transport and a change of clothes, but instead of that the well-known London buses arrived. They took us to Bus-en-Artois, where there were baths, which we revelled in. After a few days here we went into the trenches in front of Serre. The front line had been blown to pieces, and every alley-way and side trench was filled with our dead. Looking over the parapet the slopes up to Serre were carpeted with khaki. It was a most depressing spot. We had strong parties out every night burying the dead, dismal and also dangerous work, as there was a good deal of machine-gun fire and shelling.

When we were withdrawn from the trenches the men were very weary. As we marched back it was raining heavily; I had to halt the battalion almost every half-mile. Directly we halted the men threw themselves down regardless of the mud and wet, and went to sleep at once. I think we had only one night in billets and then off by train to an unknown destination. We woke up next morning at Poperinghe. We spent a few days in camp and then went into the trenches in the St Julien sector, and had a long spell of front line. I relieved a battalion of the Irish Fusiliers nearly 900 strong with my 220 'trench rifles.' Reinforcements began to arrive, and in due course we were made up to strength. Speaking from memory, I think we absorbed 25 officers and 700 men. After a few weeks at Ypres I left the Welsh division and returned to duty with the cavalry.

Captain J. F. Todd.

Was in England on leave when war was declared. He was attached to the 2nd Life Guards, and was killed very early in the war.

APPENDIX IV.

Lieut.-Colonel W. A. K. Fraser, C.B.E., D.S.O., M.C.

He was on leave in England when war broke out. Together with other Indian Army officers was retained at home for service with the Expeditionary Force. Joined 9th Lancers on 15th August 1914, and went with them to France. Led a troop of that regiment at Mons, and in all actions fought by the regiment until 20th September, when he was wounded at Paissy on the Aisne. Evacuated to England, and in November joined the reserve regiment of the 9th Lancers at Tidworth, where he was employed to train young cavalry officers. Returned to France in February 1915, joining the 16th Lancers and taking over command of one of their squadrons. Was in all engagements of that regiment up to May 1917, when he was sent as cavalry instructor to mounted troops of the Eighth Corps.

Recalled to India in August 1917, and ordered to join the South Persia Rifles, a Persian force then being raised by British officers with British money to counter German intrigues and restore British prestige in South Persia. Here he held, first, the command of a regiment of cavalry at Kerman, then of a mixed force of cavalry and infantry at Abadeh, then of the Fars Brigade, and in 1919 he became Inspector-General of the force.

He was present at the following battles and engagements:—

France—Mons; Le Cateau; Retreat from Mons; Maine, 1914; Aisne, 1914; Ypres, 1915; St Julien; Bellewaarde; Arras, 1917; Scarpe, 1917; Messines.

South Persia—Siege of Abadeh; Action of Kadarjan; Capture of Feragheh.

After the retreat from Mons he wrote the following letter to his brother:—

Copy of Letter by Captain W. A. K. Fraser.

Friday, September 4th, 1914.
A Safe Spot.

At last I can tell you some of my doings.

To begin at the beginning:

We embarked at Southampton on Saturday, 15th, did not sail till 4 A.M. Sunday morning, not knowing our destination till we were out at sea. We reached Boulogne at 4 P.M. and disembarked immediately, and went out to a rest camp some way outside Boulogne.

The next day, Monday, 17th, we spent in camp at Boulogne,

APPENDIX IV.

and on Tuesday evening, 18th, we entrained and went north through Maubeuge to a place called Toumont across the Belgian frontier. We spent the night there and went on next morning to a place called Orbreckies, round and about which the Cavalry Division concentrated. We were billeted in the village, and were quite comfortable. All the way from Boulogne we have had a tremendous reception, and were laden with presents of wine, fruit, cigars, &c. It was most cheering.

Thursday, 20th, we spent at Orbreckies. Early Friday morning we trekked to the front to a place called Harmignies, near Mons, covering the infantry advance and holding a position till they arrived. A squadron of the brigade came into contact with a small party of the enemy, routed them and made some prisoners—our first prisoners. The next morning, Saturday, 22nd, we saddled up at 3 A.M., and expected to have to fight that day, but were not called upon, though another brigade had some good fighting, driving back the German cavalry. During the day the infantry came up and took the position we had been covering, and we moved off to the left flank that night, a long march to a place called Thulin, west of Mons, getting in about 5 A.M., and dead tired we were—we had had the saddles on for twenty-six hours.

A big infantry battle began at dawn and lasted all day. The artillery fire was terrific. At 6 A.M. we moved out against some German cavalry reported to be working round the flank, but after a detour, seeing no signs of them, we returned to our position of readiness about 9.30 A.M.

At 11 A.M. we were ordered to fall back to cover the infantry retirement by taking up a position farther to the rear. We did not know why they were retiring, as all reports said the battle was going well. However, the order came. We started off about 3 A.M., Monday, 24th. We reached the position we were to occupy; we waited till dawn, and then commenced to entrench it. Our infantry had meanwhile fallen back on the flank. About 8 or 9 A.M. the German infantry came on, and soon there was a merry hail of bullets whistling about our ears, but fired from very long range, and we had few casualties. The Germans came on very slowly, and were very cautious about coming to close quarters, so when we had delayed them long enough to allow the infantry to take up a position farther back we slipped away quietly. We took up another position farther back, where we came under shell fire, but were not heavily engaged and came away soon, going behind and to the flank of our infantry, where we hoped for a little rest. We had, however, soon to make a most desperate charge against the enemy's infantry to save one of our own divisions; we were under an absolute hail of rifle and shrapnel fire. I have never imagined such an inferno; but the charge, though to us it seemed ineffective, achieved its object, as the General commanding the infantry division sent round afterwards to say we had saved his division from annihilation. We rallied under a railway embankment, and stayed there for two hours under the most hellish artillery fire. A battery of our own was about 200 yards away from us, and we saw it being gradually wiped out until not a single man was left to work the guns.

At last three or four German batteries concentrated on it, and the way those gunners died at their posts was worth a lifetime to see. The guns were still being so heavily shelled that there was no earthly chance of our horses getting out to bring the guns into the regiment, or whatever of them there were. Only a few left the *comparative* shelter of the railway embankment and man-handled the guns under cover. It was pretty warm work, but we got them away and the limbers, and the gunners wounded; most of us made three trips—I am glad to say I was there. The horses were able to get where we had brought the guns, and *all* the guns got away. By this time the infantry had got hold of the situation and our job was done, so we quitted; we had to cross ground every inch of which seemed to be beaten with shrapnel bullets, but we got away with remarkably few casualties. As our brigade was absolutely done up and good for nothing further, we went back. I was absolutely too cooked to sit on a horse, and had to travel on a wagon, where I got a little rest; we had been saddled up, off and on, for fifty-six hours, and were quite worn out. I was right again by next evening, and rejoined the regiment at Ligny. There had been fighting all day, we always retiring under orders, not a soul knew why, but it was most difficult and heart-breaking work. It was carried out in a most orderly fashion.

On the morning of Wednesday, 26th, we started off at 3 A.M., hoping to get a little quiet and not to be asked to fight; but before long we were called on to go forward again to protect the infantry right flank in a big engagement that was coming off. We were not called on to do much fighting, being mostly engaged in patrolling and in guarding the right flank. There

APPENDIX IV. 439

was a terrific infantry fight, and artillery again played a great part; the German artillery range extremely well, but their shell are ineffective. The fight seemed to be going well for us, but again there came the order to retire, which was very trying. Our infantry had had a hard time, out of which they came extremely well, and have upheld the reputation of the British fighting man. This continual retiring had been most trying for the men. None of us with the higher officers have understood why it has been, but it is no doubt very wise. Since Wednesday we have been fighting slowly and quietly, the cavalry covering the retirement. We had one nice day's fighting, though it was a rearguard action which started by our almost being surprised in our billets; we diddled the Germans for some miles, and it was very pleasant. Otherwise we have only had small scraps with German cavalry, but it has been a strain the whole time.

I may not tell you what we have been doing lately or are doing now, but the situation is supposed to be very good. Nous verrons. For the last two nights we have had some sleep, but previous to that we have had less than eighteen hours' sleep in six days. It has been exhausting. Last night we had a real hog. We are camped in a wood, and it is beautifully sylvan and seems miles from war. All along we have had at least one decent meal a day. Most of the villages were deserted, but there were always eggs, chickens, &c., left behind which seemed to be more our right than the Germans'. It is most pathetic to see all those homes deserted just as they were lived in. People are going back gradually.

Campaigning in this country is very different to what we prepare for in India. One can buy most things—or borrow them.

The British forces have had a hard time. There is no doubt that for four days they withstood the whole of the German army advancing into France, about seven army corps, 280,000 men, which outnumbered us by 4 to 1. They have earned great praise from those who know.

Major D. B. Edwards.

I was appointed Officer Commanding and Adjutant of the 2nd Regiment in May 1914, when W. A. K. Fraser went on leave, and remained in the appointment till I got on service in 1916.

In September 1916 I proceeded to Mesopotamia to take up the appointment of Staff Captain, Karun Front. The force consisted of one cavalry regiment, one pack battery, three bus with ancillary services.

Its duty was, firstly, to protect the all-important Anglo-Persian oil-fields at Mardan-i-Napthun, north of Ahwaz; and secondly, to act as a regimental flank guard to the expeditionary force in its advance on Baghdad.

In August 1918 I was appointed D.A.Q.M.G. Persian Lines of Communication, with H.Q. at Kirmanshah. This force controlled and protected 400 miles of communications from Mesopotamia rail-head to Kasvin.

In August 1920 I was placed in command of a column to clear up the situation and endeavour to restore communications with Baghdad. The railway had been cut and all communications with Baghdad severed, and we ourselves found ourselves in Kanikin unable to move either forward or back until relieved by another column from Persia some days later.

In November 1920, after the situation in Mesopotamia had become normal, I proceeded to Headquarters North Persian Force at Kasvin as liaison Staff Officer to prepare for the evacuation of North Persia, which was due in the following spring.

In April 1921 I was appointed to command the Persian lines of communication, and remained in command until the evacuation was complete.

Major E. T. R. Wickham.

August 1914 found me at home on leave, and I was one of the unfortunates sent out to India on the troopship *Dongola*, an old tub that chugged along at about eight knots. There were 800 of us aboard, of whom, I remember, 12 were Generals and 192 of and above the rank of Lieut.-Colonel; so the Captains and subalterns had Tommies' accommodation, while the Majors functioned as non-commissioned officers. As the ship was short of personnel we had to handle baggage and stores in the hold—no joke in the Red Sea at the end of August.

Though very disappointed, hot, crowded, and badly fed we soon cheered up, and the strange experience was really rather enjoyable.

I joined the regiment at Agar, and six weeks later a telegram arrived saying I was to be transferred to the S. and T. This filled me with dismay. A few days later, however, I was ordered to embark for France. At Marseilles I was promptly annexed by the Officer Commanding S. and T., and spent a grim week un-

APPENDIX IV. 441

loading ships from dawn until dark. After a week of this servitude I succeeded, by pulling a string or two, in getting ordered up to rail-head.

After cooling our heels at rail-head for a day or two we were pushed back to St Omer, and distributed amongst the reserve parks of the Indian divisions. They were heavy draft transport, and I found myself in charge of a section of fifty pairs of dray horses and about seventy men, rough Yorkshire waggoners, quite untrained and unaccustomed to military discipline, but splendid fellows when there was a job of work to be done. Most of them had in civil life formed the habit of getting drunk every Saturday night, and this used to get them into serious trouble in France, where drunkenness was a court-martial offence.

My sergeant-major and I got bored with seeing our best men sent to gaol, so we evolved a disciplinary scheme of our own. We had a squad of four toughs who received preferential treatment as regards fatigues and guard duties. If anyone got drunk, had dirty harness, or an ungroomed horse, he was seized surreptitiously by the toughs, who dragged him to the nearest ditch, broke the ice, and scrubbed him with dandy-brushes. These highly illegal methods were quite popular with the men, and in due course No. 2 Section acquired the reputation of being the best-disciplined section in the park, with a crime-sheet white as snow.

After four months of this I was transferred to the 1st Regiment, but before I had had a chance of seeing any fighting with the regiment I went down with measles, of the German variety too, and was sent home sick. I was then posted to a reserve cavalry regiment in Dublin.

In October 1915 I sailed for India and rejoined the regiment in Guna, and in the following April was ordered to proceed to Persian Baluchistan to raise a corps of 300 levies in the Sarhad, Persian Baluchistan, under General Dyer of Amritsar fame. I shall never forget the 500 miles' trip across the Chagai desert in the latter half of May and first half of June. The heat was intense, the water brackish and scarce; and of my three followers one died of dysentery before he had gone half-way, while the other two barely escaped with their lives.

In 1916-17 we waged war, of the scallywag type, against the recalcitrant tribes of Sarhad, and gradually brought them all to heel. This guerilla warfare—child's play, of course, compared with France—involved a good deal of hardship, forced marches in hot weather, bad food, and brackish water. In the course of a year our casualties, due to wounds and sickness, amounted to about 30 per cent of our officers, and after fourteen months I returned to India with an inside which kept me on the sick or light duty list for nearly eighteen months. After being failed four times I succeeded in passing an accommodating Medical Board by pretending that I had been wounded, and concealing the fact that Glaxo and Bengers were my staple food. I proceeded to Mesopotamia to join the Civil Administration, and arrived in Basrah shortly after the Armistice. There I had a great stroke of luck, as Colonel Kenyon, Chief Political Officer of North-west Persia, fell sick, and there being no one else who knew Persian and French, I was sent up to relieve him. So instead of being A.P.O. in charge of some obscure village in Mesopotamia, I started my political career as a Political Officer of a division, with six A.P.O.'s under me. During the ensuing nine months we quelled the Jangali rebellion in Gilan, and assisted the Persian Government to regain and maintain control of that Caspian Province. During the operations I had to keep up liaison between the Commander of the British troops, the Russian Commander of the Persian Cossack Division, and the Persian Governor-General. I soon found that this could best be achieved by dining several times a week in the company of the two latter and playing baccarat, not merely until the small hours but well into the following day. During the day there was much to be done : I was bombarded with cypher telegrams and had to keep His Majesty's Minister in Teheran and the Civil Commissioner in Baghdad fully informed of the progress of the operations and of our political manœuvres. The operations were successful, the Jangali power was broken, the Persian Government regained control, and I won £200.

Major E. J. D. Colvin.

He rejoined the regiment from the Political Department. Commanded the Depot at Agar from July 1915 to October 1917. Was then appointed Base Commandant at Bunder Abbas. In January 1918 was given the command of the Bunder Abbas Brigade Area, in addition to his other duties, and in this capacity organised the first relief column sent up to Shiraz. Was invalided to India in June 1918, and in August was posted as D.A.Q.M.G. at Army Headquarters, where he remained until the Armistice, when he returned to the Political Department.

APPENDIX IV. 443

Major D. De M. S. Fraser.
Persia, 1911.
Persia, 1918-19. Despatches.

I received orders to go to Mesopotamia to join the Political Department in November 1917, and left the regiment immediately afterwards. I was first sent to Zorbatha, fifty miles north of Kut-el-amara, as assistant Pol. Officer to establish a new agency. This was on the borders of the territory of the Wali of Pusht-i-Kuh, and had only been visited by one or two Europeans before.

I went off into the blue accompanied by one clerk, a safe, a goodly sum of money, and seven Arab police i/c of a British sergeant; the latter left after a day or two. I remained there only a month, and was then transferred to the Persian side as Pol. Officer Shushtar in Arabistan. A few days after my arrival I was ordered to Dizful as Political Officer, Dizful and Shushtar. I remained alone in Dizful for several months till an Assist. Pol. Officer was appointed in October.

I escorted the Gov.-General of Arabistan, a Persian, to Baghdad.

While in Baghdad I received orders to join the Bushire Field Force, commanded by Major-General J. A. Douglas, as Assist. Pol. Officer. I was one of several A.P.O.'s.

I was appointed to the striking force and attached to the staff of General Elsmie, and accompanied the column from Bushire to Shiraz.

He remained for some months as A.P.O. L. of C. after the greater part of the force had returned to India in March 1919.

Captain D. St V. Gordon, M.C.

When the war broke out I was on my way to South Africa to take part in a shooting trip in Rhodesia with my father, who was already out there.

On arrival in Cape Town I immediately booked a return passage by the next mail steamer, and sailed for home again after a short three days at the Mount Nelson Hotel.

I was then sent to Plymouth to train drafts of the 4th H.L.I. for the two regular battalions. Six months later I joined the 1st H.L.I. in France just after the battle of Neuve Chappelle, and was with this regiment at the first gas attack at Ypres, and immediately afterwards in the Rue du Bois attacks.

The battalion suffered very heavily in both of these shows,

and the men—mostly from the slums of Glasgow and miners from that neighbourhood—were splendid.

In the autumn I was ordered to India, and I joined the 39th C.I.H. in November 1915.

In the hot weather of June 1917 I sailed for Basrah in the position of a Salutri, the telegraph office having mutilated a wire from Mhow, which made this word read something very like ' Subaltern.' On arrival there I was posted to the 12th B.C., then in Nasiriyeh.

From the time I joined them till the end of the war I nearly always had command of a squadron, and as the 12th B.C. was corps cavalry, squadrons were nearly always 'on their own,' attached usually to widely separated infantry brigades.

We moved up to Baghdad at the end of the summer. Here the regiment was attached to the 13th and 14th Divisions as corps cavalry, and we remained on the right flank near the Jebel Hamrus and the Persian foothills for the rest of the war.

A Cossack brigade came down from Persia to co-operate with us in 1917, and actually took part in one attack with us (at Qarak Tappan).

In these operations the Turks, in spite of the fact that they were half-starved, put up a very stout resistance.

On the morning of the Armistice I had taken my squadron out hours before dawn to find out the line of retreat of the division in front of us. I ran into it some twenty-five miles away from our camp, and though I was in helio communication with Headquarters, had no news of the Armistice. The result was a general scrap with the enemy rearguard cavalry, and the return in triumph with about thirty prisoners that night to meet the hilarious derision of the rest of the force, which had been sitting down and celebrating the Armistice all day !

B.—Services in the Air.

It may be of some interest to explain how it came about that so many officers of the C.I.H. came to serve in the Air Force during the Great War.

There were no less than eight who served in some capacity in the old Royal Flying Corps and later the Royal Air Force, as it became in 1917.

APPENDIX IV. 445

The first officer to take up flying seriously was Pitcher, who had qualifications far beyond the average Indian cavalry officer, and incidentally disabilities common to all, amongst the latter the most formidable being a lack of cash. He had, however, a fine technical training, being an expert on engines and a good draughtsman. He had, further, indomitable pluck and perseverance.

Early experiments were first made with a 'glider' at Agar by Henderson, assisted by Pitcher, in 1908-09. This apparatus, having taken control and turned a somersault on Henderson, was abandoned, and Pitcher then set to work on an aeroplane proper.

Henderson gives the following account of this :—

"In 1910 experimented with a 20-foot span biplane glider, made from bamboo lance shafts, and succeeded in leaving the ground and gliding for 20 yards. The above infernal machine wrecked itself by attempting to loop from the ground when I was endeavouring to give a demonstration to Pitcher from the top of the butts at Agar, the only person slightly hurt being my orderly Indar Singh, who with Pitcher rushed in, in an attempt to catch me."

At this time Pitcher was Inspector of Imperial Service Troops at Bhopal, and it was here that he built his first machine in 1910, just four years before the war. This machine was a biplane, and its power unit a 20-H.P. De Dion engine removed bodily from one of the Begum of Bhopal's cars. It had a metal airscrew designed by Pitcher himself. On the first trial this piece of metal detached itself, went straight up in the air to some colossal altitude, and on its return journey earthwards just missed Pitcher in the pilot's seat, passed through the centre section of the machine, and buried itself in the ground. At the next attempt the machine got up a good speed, its wheels just leaving the ground for a short period, and in an effort to cut its way through a telegraph post, piled itself up a wreck. Pitcher came out unscathed, and started to design a new machine. He now rejoined the regiment, and the next machine was built at Goonah ; it was a monoplane resembling the old Bleriot (the first to fly the Channel) with a 30 H.P. radial engine called Lascelles, the only one of its sort built. Incidentally on its trial it blew a cylinder clean off, just missing Pitcher's head. Pitcher now required an assistant and odd job man, so roped in Hoare.

Using the big banyan tree opposite 'The Ant Heap,' adjoining

APPENDIX IV.

the red parade ground, as hangar they worked all through the hot weather on this machine, which was almost completed when they obtained leave. They packed it up and departed to England with the intention of learning to fly on someone else's machine before trying the result of their own handiwork.

On arrival in England they proceeded to the Bristol School on Salisbury Plain, and after about six weeks' training got their pilots' certificates, numbers 125 and 126.

The Bristol machines were 'pusher' biplanes, and the pilot sat out in front with an elevator projecting out beyond. There was nothing to keep the pilot in, but it was the custom to put one arm round a strut and hold the 'joy-stick' with the other hand.

The tests included two figures of eight and an approximate height of 300 feet. A landing had to be made in a circle of 100 yards diameter, and there was a further rule that the engine had to be switched off before touching the ground ! In present times these tests appear not very exacting, but it should be noted that in those days a right-hand turn was considered quite dangerous, and, in fact, few aspirants for certificates attempted one until the final day. There was no limit, however, as to how much country was covered in the figures of eight, so no very sharp turns were attempted.

The cost of this tuition was £125, of which £25 was returned if there were no breakages. Both Pitcher and Hoare received the bonus.

In October of this year, 1911, the regiment was ordered to Persia, and Pitcher and Hoare returned post-haste. The regiment remained in Persia until April 1913, and nothing further was accomplished until its return to India.

On arrival at Bushire, Hoare got a cable asking if he would accept Second-in-Command of an experimental flying establishment to be started in India, and went home at once to do a further course at the Central Flying School, a joint naval and military school at Upavon. This was unfair to Pitcher, who had stood the heat and burden of the day, but subsequent events proved it to be to his advantage. On the outbreak of war Pitcher was doing the course at the C.F.S. which Hoare had done the previous year, and Hoare was at Sitapur, where, with three other officers and some civilian mechanics, they were testing out machines in an Indian climate.

C. G. H.

APPENDIX IV. 447

Brigadier-General D. Le G. Pitcher, C.M.G., C.B.E., D.S.O.

On the outbreak of war Pitcher was at the C.F.S., and was sent at once to No. 4 Squadron, Eastchurch, engaged in anti-Zeppelin patrols. There were at this time only four squadrons in the R.F.C. On 16th August they flew over to Amiens, reaching Maubeuge on the 16th. At that time it was quite a feat flying the Channel, and pilots and observers were festooned with inflated inner tubes ready for their contemplated immersion.

It was only after his arrival at Amiens that Pitcher realised he had come to war with no other weapon than his fists, nor for some time was he able to rectify this defect in his equipment.

The total number of machines available was forty-three, and no other weapons than rifles, Hales' grenades, and revolvers were carried.

Pitcher did his first reconnaissance on 19th August with Mitchell, R.F.C., the route being Maubeuge-Binche-La Louviere-Hal-Mons. They were frequently in clouds, and the observer having no compass, it was none too easy to spot their position, especially as the pilot, as was not uncommon then, was apt to come out of a cloud the opposite way to which he went in. No troops were seen: the whole country seemed deserted. On the 21st another patrol over Mons, when they were greeted by the enemy with shrapnel and H.E., but little was seen. The next day, however, revealed endless columns of German troops between Tournai and Ath, part of the German Army marching on Valenciennes with the object of turning our left flank. They were marching across our front with a flank guard along the Condé-Mons canal.

A few extracts from a rough diary of Pitcher's give an idea of what he was doing during August and September 1914 :—

Aug. 24. Left Maubeuge in tender—arrived Le Cateau—went on reconnaissance with Mitchell to Valenciennes—Ath—Grammont. Found missing German column at Grammont.

Aug. 25. Transport left 10 P.M. Slept on ground, and made an early morning reconnaissance with Soames to Bavai-Condé and Valenciennes. Saw German cavalry advancing S. of Dour with bivouacs on canal and British columns leaving Bavai.

Aug. 25. Reconnaissance early morning with Mitchell to Guise-Fresnoy-Catelet. Saw our own columns retiring in good order, but no Germans.

Aug. 29. Reconnaissance with Soames, Roye-Lassigny. Reported columns marching on Compiegne. In evening chased a German Albatross with Mitchell and Spratt. He was driven down and hit by our artillery.

Aug. 30. Left mid-day for Senlis with Soames. Slept in deserted hotel. Reconnaissance to Roye and back.

Aug. 31. Slept in convent in dormitory.

(The above bare statement of a fact is more amusingly described by Maurice Baring in 'R.F.C. Headquarters': "A pillow fight on a gigantic scale took place. The pilots dressed themselves up in the girls' nightshirts, and one of the dormitories was invaded from the outside by a herd of pilots, and, though valiantly defended, was finally taken.")

Sept. 9. Flew with Mapplebeck to Coulommiers. Reconnaissance to Marigny, &c. Saw Germans massed on line of valley. Second reconnaissance to drop petrol bomb, but found all German columns retreating.

Later Pitcher moved to St Omer, where he saw the first contingent of the Indian Army. The Indian ranks were much interested in aeroplanes, never having seen one before.

It was while at St Omer that Pitcher with a few other R.F.C. officers was watching the efforts of the first anti-aircraft gun. Naturally they gazed at the German machine, the object of its attentions. Seeing no bursts one of them cast his eye around the horizon, and saw, miles from the objective, the bursting shells. "Archibald," he exclaimed, "certainly not."[1] This fatuous remark was the origin of A.A. shells being referred to ever after as 'Archies.'

After the first battle of Ypres, Pitcher was posted home and given the command of a squadron at Brooklands. Later he went to the Central Flying School at Upavon as Second-in-Command to Captain Paine, R.N. (now Sir Godfrey Paine). In December 1915, on the latter relinquishing command, he was made Commandant.

In February 1916, after a brief interval at Catterick, he was posted to the 11th Wing in France, and on 1st April 1916 was promoted Brigadier-General to command the 1st Brigade R.F.C. with the 1st Army. James Gourlie was his Staff Captain.

In February 1917 he was appointed Controller of the Technical Dept. to the newly formed Air Board.

In February 1918 his successor to the 1st Brigade in France

[1] The refrain of a well-known comic song of the day.

APPENDIX IV. 449

was killed, and Pitcher was reappointed to the command, remaining with it until he was demobilised in February 1919.

He received a personal wire from Haig congratulating him on the number of Germans brought down by his brigade.

In October 1919 Pitcher made a tour of all Near East stations in connection with demobilisation.

In August 1919 he accepted a permanent commission in the R.A.F., and left the Indian Army for good.

Brigadier-General C. G. Hoare, C.M.G., C.B.E.

In August 1914 Hoare was Second-in-Command at Sitapur of the so-called Indian Central Flying School. This was merely an experimental establishment with a view to becoming one day a flying school for India.

On the outbreak of war the services of the four officers in this establishment were offered to the W.O., and they departed for England on 19th August. On arrival they were posted to new squadrons of the R.F.C. in progress of formation.

Hoare was posted to No. 7, the first absolutely new squadron to go to France. With the exception of two flight commanders, the sergeant-major, and a few other ranks, there were none of the old R.F.C. personnel. The officers were a mixed lot, including one ex-regular cavalry officer who had been farming in East Africa (now Kenia), a South African, a medical student, one Australian rancher, an assistant to a quack dentist in the East End, an odd Canadian, a mercantile marine officer, and a regular infantry officer from West Africa. The latter two were ground officers, having been turned down as incompetent pilots. Hoare, on their urgent request, took a chance, and allowed them to fly. One became a star test pilot, and was killed in France; the other got the V.C.

In April 1915 the squadron left for France, and became the Headquarters long distance reconnaissance squadron at St Omer. Normal reconnaissance work was carried out, and nothing of special interest occurred except that Martin of the C.I.H. joined. He showed great gallantry on one occasion, crossing the line at 2500 feet and returning with his machine riddled with bullets; and this in spite of orders not to cross at less than 5000 feet.

In December 1915 Hoare was promoted Second-in-Command to the Central Flying School, Upavon, and promoted Lieut.-Colonel. He remained at the C.F.S. till April 1916.

2 F

He then returned to France to form the 14th Army Wing (4th Army) for the Somme offensive. Headquarters were at Bertangles, near Amiens. The main work of the squadron was protection, carried out by fighting patrols, keeping the Germans busy well behind their own lines, reconnaissance up to Bapaume, photography, &c.

Some description of the bombardment at the commencement of the Somme offensive in July may be of interest. Hoare, who had orders to remain in his office, took a machine and flew over to see what would happen when zero arrived and the massed artillery should simultaneously open fire. There was a ground mist over the German lines, but on one side it was clear. All seemed quiet until, when zero hour struck, thousands of guns of all calibres opened. The blanket of mist over the German lines shot up in countless pyramids of vapour, the morning sun turning them to every colour of the rainbow. A marvellous and beautiful effect. The mist soon cleared, but Hoare was unable to remain longer. The succeeding months were a period of intense activity, but nothing particular occurred of purely regimental interest.

Up to the beginning of 1917 we had very much the best of it in the air. During the Somme offensive on only two occasions were German machines seen from Hoare's Headquarters at Bertangles, whereas British machines were daily and continuously over the German side as far as Cambrai and farther, though Bapaume was the 14th Wing limit.

Early in 1917 Hoare was recalled, and told to proceed at once to Canada and raise twenty squadrons for training purposes in the Dominion.

Within a couple of years he had built and equipped the great aerodrome near Toronto, as well as four others, had turned out 2900 aeroplanes and 30 flying-boats, and had trained 3905 pilots, 370 of whom were for the United States.

When America entered the war he was sent to Washington as an adviser to the U.S. Government. As he had no instructions as to his action there, he cabled to the Air Ministry in England, who replied, "Do not commit yourself."

He was now made an honorary member of the U.S. Aircraft Production Board, which was then the equivalent to our Air Ministry, and assisted in creating the organisation for the U.S. Air Force, dividing his time between Canada, Washington, and Texas. These somewhat varied duties occupied him up to the

APPENDIX IV. 451

Armistice, when he left the R.A.F. and returned once more to his regiment.

It is interesting to note that the discipline of both Canadians and Americans was extraordinarily high. There was practically no crime. The Canadians seemed to take special pride in being an Imperial unit, and both were exceptionally smart in turn-out and on parade. Personal relations between Hoare and both the Canadian and American authorities remained cordial to the end.

In contrast to the average Britisher's idea of Americans, Hoare found them generous in the extreme, hospitable, and modest, always ready to listen to advice, and keenly appreciative of anything we did for them.

Wing-Commander Sir Norman Leslie, Bt., C.B.E.

I left the regiment in March 1916, and after learning to fly at the C.F.S. was posted as a Flight-Commander to No. 17 Squadron, Salonika. Here there was nothing of interest to record, as the work of the squadron followed the normal course.

I believe I was the first British pilot to carry out a reconnaissance over the Struma Valley [possibly a previous flight by officers of the R.N.A.S. (C. G. H.).] Anyhow, it was not marked by any incidents of importance. Shortly afterwards I was invalided home with dysentery, and spent the last part of the war at the Air Ministry. Here life was certainly hectic, but without any interest from the point of view of the regiment.

Lieut.-Colonel G. Henderson.

1914.—On outbreak of war I applied to be appointed to the R.F.C., but Government of India refused permission, and I proceeded with regiment to France in command of ' D ' Squadron.

September 1915.—As a memo. asking for officers with flying experience had been sent out to all units, I applied again, and was sent direct to C.F.S., Upavon. About 15th December completed training, and was posted to No. 15 Squadron (B.E.2E.) forming under Major H. Le M. Brock at Dover.

16th January 1916.—My first patrol on the line over Ypres, 25th December. On escort with two more machines to Captain Maltby, doing reconnaissance to Courtrai, about five miles north of Lille. Immelman dived and shot down Wilson, 10th Hussars and R.F.C., one of the escort. Observer Brooking killed ; Wilson, shot in three places and unconscious, crashed from 9000 feet, but recovered.

(This was an extraordinary escape. 'Narcissus' Wilson was a friend of Hoare's, and wrote to him when a prisoner in Germany. He was flying about 9000 feet. His observer killed, and finding himself losing consciousness, he shut off his petrol and switched off the engine. His machine came down out of control, but apparently flattened out near the ground, and Narcissus received no further injury. The Germans took a photograph, and sent it with an account of what happened to his mother, and treated him well.—C. G. H.)

Over Courtrai my observer, Corporal Nott, was engaged at firing at a German machine at about 300 yards range, when an 'Archie' burst almost on machine, wounding him in seven places and taking out an eye, at the same time breaking several wires and hitting machine in many places. Enemy's machine followed, and, seeing we were disabled, opened fire at point-blank range. Nott fortunately recovered consciousness and opened fire, sending enemy's machine down in steep spiral. Attacked twice on way home, but each time Nott worked his gun and drove off attack.

Recrossed line over Ypres at 1500 feet, and just got back to aerodrome. Corporal Nott was unconscious on return; he was awarded the D.C.M. the following day. The carburetter was found to have been pierced by a machine-gun bullet; which smashed the needle in two pieces.

26th Jan. Was promoted to Flight-Commander in place of Captain Wodham, who had been killed on the northern reconnaissance on the previous day.

Continued on reconnaissance and photography till end of March, when squadron flew to Marieux on the Somme to prepare for the battle of the Somme on the Beaumont-Hamel section.

About 20th May crashed into Marieux Wood from 300 feet when taking off in the early morning in the dusk. In hospital ten days and given three weeks' leave.

Posted to 16 Squadron at Merville; found my nerves shaken up, and was given a ground job in charge of a liaison party attached to the H.Q., 2nd Indian Cavalry Division (M'Andrew).

Served with division through the three phases of the battle of the Somme.

APPENDIX IV.

Nov. 1917. Posted to command No. 53 Squadron (R.E. 8) attached to Ninth Corps, and stationed at Bailleul, doing artillery and infantry co-operation and photography.

Feb. 1918. Squadron ordered to Villeselve opposite La Fere with Ninth Corps, who were preparing to take over an extension of the British line south of La Fere from the French.

21st-26th March 1918. Took part against the German attack, losing many machines in bombing and low machine-gunning. Ordered to proceed and refit at St Omer.

April. St Omer to Abeele with Ninth Corps, who were taking over the Kemmel front. Took part against German attack on Kemmel-Armentières front, moving back to Marie Capal and Clairmarais as the Germans advanced.

On relief of Ninth Corps by 2nd French Cavalry Division was attached to the latter, and continued to work with the French troops on that front until they were relieved by the Tenth Corps, to which my squadron was then attached. The squadron was personally congratulated by the 2nd Army commander on its work and co-operation with the French during this phase of German attack.

I continued with Tenth Corps during German retreat up to the Armistice, which found the squadron at Swevelghem, S.E. of Courtrai.

Squadron moved to 4th Army near Namur.

Returned home Feb. 1919, and commanded Crail Air Station till October 1919, when I returned to Indian establishment, rejoining the regiment at Agar in Jan. 1920.

Hon. Brigadier-General R. E. T. Hogg, C.M.G., C.I.E.

At outbreak of war was at home on furlough. Ordered to embark for India; order cancelled at last moment, and posted as Adjutant 2nd K.E. Horse, a colonial corps in process of formation at the White City.

In Feb. 1915 services lent to R.F.C. for duty as observer, and after a short training at Fort Grange ordered to Gallipoli.

Arrived at Truedos by destroyer *Grasshopper* from Imbros on 10th April, being attached to Commander Samson's Naval Flying Squadron, or 'party,' as it was called. This was about a fortnight before the first landing by 29th Division.

Orders to carry out reconnaissance of all Turkish dispositions and gun positions on the Peninsula and Asiatic side.

APPENDIX IV.

Took part in landing of 25th April. Only two army observers at that time; all flying operations were carried out from Truedos, sixteen miles from Peninsula, and one had to do from five hours to seven hours a day in the air.

On 22nd June, in a pusher machine (I think a Brequet with Canton Unée engine), pilot Captain Collett, R.M.L.I., brought down a German 'Albatross.' This was the beginning of aerial combats, and the first enemy aircraft to be brought down in Gallipoli. Weapon a service rifle. We learnt afterwards enemy's engine was shot and observer wounded.

Sent home at end of July to take ticket (*i.e.*, pilot's certificate). After taking ticket at Upavon, posted to No. 8 Squadron as Flight-Commander, Nov. 1915. Promoted Squadron Commander to 17 T.S. forming at Croydon, and made the aerodrome there, now grown into the air port. At that time the first London defence units came under my command, and took the air against the first German Zeppelin night raid in London.

In spring of 1916 posted to command F.E. Squadron mobilising at Gosport for France, and went out to Le Hameau.

Promoted Wing-Commander at Newcastle.

1917. Brigade Commander, Eastern Training Brigade. Brevet-Lieutenant-Colonel.

1918. Posted to command 9th Brigade in France, Headquarters near Therouane, with one wing at Villers Bretonneux when the German attack on Gough's Army was launched. This wing got clear, and the whole brigade was employed continuously with bombs and machine-guns attacking enemy's advancing columns.

During subsequent fighting, till the Armistice, this brigade was sent to reinforce each sector where fighting took place. We were also sent to support the French when the Germans made their thrust first at Montdidier in June, and again on the Marne at Chateau Thierry and at Soissons.

Temporary commission as full Colonel, R.A.F.

In October 1918 transferred to command of 1st Brigade, Plumer's Army, and after the Armistice accompanied the army's advance through Belgium to Cologne.

Retired July 1919.

N.B.—The 9th Brigade did splendid work, which was acknowledged by Marshal Foch himself in the following letter to Field-Marshal Lord Haig. W. A. W.

APPENDIX IV.

Commandement en Chef
des Armée Alliées.

G.Q.G.A. *le* 30 *Juillet* 1918.

Etat Major Général.

1°
No. 2555 A.

Le Général Foch, Commandant en Chef les Armées Alliées,

à Monsieur le Maréchal Haig, Commandant en Chef les Forces Britanniques en France.

Monsieur le Maréchal,—

Au moment où la 9° Brigade, R.A.F. quitte la zone française, je tiens à vous dire qu'elle a apporté dans la bataille un appui dont la valeur et la puissance ont été très hautement appréciées.

Cette collaboration a été tout particulierement précieuse aux troupes Alliées dont la 9° Brigade a soutenu l'action offensive, en attaquant sans relâche à la bombe et à la mitrailleuse les colonnes ennemies en retraite.

L'importance des résultats, obtenus (plus de 60 victoires sur l'aviation ennemie, quarante tonnes de projectiles lancés) et les pertes généreusement consenties, ont prouvé une fois de plus d'une maniere éclatante, l'ardeur, la vaillance et la ténacité de l'Aviation Britannique.

Bien sincerement a vous,

(Sd.) J. FOCH.

APPENDIX V.

REWARDS GAINED DURING THE GREAT WAR.

ORDER OF ST MICHAEL AND ST GEORGE. (C.M.G.)

Brigadier-General R. E. T. Hogg.
Brigadier-General D. Le G. Pitcher.
Brigadier-General C. G. Hoare.

ORDER OF THE BRITISH EMPIRE. (C.B.E.)

Brigadier-General D. Le G. Pitcher.
Brigadier-General C. G. Hoare.
Major Sir Norman Leslie, Bart.

ORDER OF THE BRITISH EMPIRE. (O.B.E.)

Lieut.-Colonel R. C. Bell.
Lieut.-Colonel W. B. White.

ORDER OF THE BRITISH EMPIRE. (M.B.E.)

Rissaidar Malik Khan Mahommed Khan.

DISTINGUISHED SERVICE ORDER.

Lieut.-Colonel A. P. Browne.
Lieut.-Colonel A. S. Capper.
Lieut.-Colonel R. C. Bell.
Major J. Gourlie.
Major W. A. K. Fraser.
Major J. R. Hutchison.

MILITARY CROSS.

Major W. A. K. Fraser.
Captain C. O. Harvey.
Captain R. S. Abbott.
Captain C. O'B. Daunt.
Captain D. St V. Gordon.
Captain C. F. Aitken.
Captain A. H. Williams.
Lieutenant D. A. Cameron.
Lieutenant W. A. K. Page.
Lieutenant N. S. Alington.
Lieutenant G. B. Walter.
Lieutenant J. D. Wilson.
Lieutenant Mahomed Kamaluddin Khan.

ORDER OF BRITISH INDIA, 2nd Class, with the title of Bahadur.

Risaldar Major Amar Singh.
Risaldar Dilawar Khan.
Risaldar Mahomed Kamaluddin Khan.

INDIAN ORDER OF MERIT, 2nd Class.

Risaldar Dilawar Khan, Bahadur.
Risaldar Lihaz Gul Khan..
Risaldar Jawand Singh.
Jemadar Mir Zaman Khan.
3116 Dafadar Faiz Mohammed Khan.
Risaldar Dial Singh.
Risaldar Kartar Singh.
2870 Sowar Dalip Singh.
2370 Sowar Indar Singh.

APPENDIX V. 457

THE INDIAN DISTINGUISHED SERVICE MEDAL.

2143 Kote Dafadar Ghilzai Khan.
2613 Dafadar Lal Khan.
2421 Dafadar Sher Jan Khan.
2749 Lance Dafadar Mehar Singh.
2896 Lance Dafadar Hastam Khan.
2486 A.L.D. Nur Mohammed.
Jemadar Juma Khan.
2595 Dafadar Fateh Mohammed Khan.
2637 Sowar Dost Mohammed Khan.
2562 Dafadar Pertab Singh.
2183 Dafadar Sher Singh.
2673 Lance Dafadar Shahnawaz Khan.
2950 Sowar Aslam Khan.
3187 A.L.D. Ujagar Singh.
2477 Dafadar Labh Singh.
2783 A.L.D. Arjan Singh.
2499 A.L.D. Nand Singh.
2788 Lance Dafadar Tara Singh.
Risaldar Natha Singh.
Risaldar Bostan Khan.
2975 Dafadar Fateh Khan.
3089 Trumpeter Sattar Khan.
3161 Dafadar Aslam Khan.
2828 A.L.D. Bishan Singh.
Risaldar Major Amar Singh, Bahadur.
2012 Dafadar Sham Singh.
2588 Sowar Ali Mohammed Khan.
2784 Sowar Mahmud Khan.
Jemadar Moti Singh.
2421 Sowar Harbant Singh.
2588 Sowar Ali Mohammed.
2784 Mahmud Khan.

MERITORIOUS SERVICE MEDALS.

2202 Kote Dafadar Shahmadar Khan.
2503 Kote Dafadar Mal Singh.
2669 Kote Dafadar Mir Zaman Khan.
2095 Kote Dafadar Mangal Singh.
2666 Kote Dafadar Kehar Singh.
2158 Kote Dafadar Kishan Singh.
2170 Dafadar Natha Singh.
2265 Dafadar Shahwali Khan.
2350 Kote Dafadar Bhagat Singh.
2489 Dafadar Balwant Singh.
2588 Dafadar Ali Mardan Khan.
2509 Lance Dafadar Teja Singh.
2162 Tr. Maj. Abdul Rehman Khan.
2329 Dafadar Azad Gul Khan.
2560 Kote Dafadar Mir Zaman Khan.
2381 Dafadar Kapur Singh.
2324 Kote Dafadar Yakub Khan.
2650 Kote Dafadar Khem Singh.
2301 Dafadar Hari Singh.
2317 Kote Dafadar Hassan Khan.
2430 Dafadar Narain Singh.
2359 Ar. Dafadar Shah Mohammed.
2475 Dafadar Kishan Singh.
2485 Dafadar Ibrahim Khan.
2497 Dafadar Phoola Singh.
2502 Dafadar Hayat Khan.
2519 Dafadar Achchar Singh.
2522 Dafadar Kamal Khan.
2574 Fr. Maj. Chanan Singh.
2590 Dafadar Gopal Singh.
2614 Kote Dafadar Mohammed Ghazan Khan.
2616 Dafadar Lal Khan.
2634 Sowar Pahilwan Khan.
2639 Dafadar Diwan Ali Khan.
2662 Kote Dafadar Ata Mohammed Khan.
2664 Dafadar Bostan Khan.
2683 Lance Dafadar Mardan Ali Khan.
2749 Dafadar Mehar Singh.
2806 Dafadar Jagat Singh.
2890 Lance Dafadar Saifoor Khan.
2903 Lance Dafadar Ratan Singh.
2935 Dafadar Amar Singh.
2944 Dafadar Bahadur Khan.
2970 Lance Dafadar Hazar Singh.

APPENDIX V.

2974 Lance Dafadar Ali Akber Khan.
2981 Lance Dafadar Sohawa Singh.
2993 Kote Dafadar Karam Singh.
2994 Dafadar Sher Bahadur Khan.
2997 Sowar Inder Singh.
3011 Dafadar Assa Singh.
3012 Lance Dafadar Mira Khan.
3073 Dafadar Nazir Khan.
3095 Kote Dafadar Jehandad Khan.
2114 Dafadar Mohammed Yakub Khan.
2603 A.L.D. Chand Khan.
2030 A.L.D. Ibrahim Khan.
2301 Sowar Indar Singh.
2235 Sowar Lachman Singh.
1948 Lance Dafadar Jagat Singh.
2150 Dafadar Ahmad Yar Khan.
2262 Lance Dafadar Manchar Singh.
2486 Sowar Nazar Singh.
2506 Dafadar Mahommed Latif Khan.
2065 Dafadar Udham Singh.

MISCELLANEOUS REWARDS.

Risaldar Mahomed Kamaluddin Khan was, in recognition of his distinguished service in the field, promoted to the rank of 2nd Lieutenant, with a view to his appointment to the Indian Army in that rank.

Risaldar Dilawar Khan was granted an assignment of land of the annual value of Rs. 600.

Risaldar Major Amar Singh was granted an assignment of land of the annual value of Rs. 400.

Risaldar Malik Sher Bahadur Khan was presented with a Sword of Honour and a gold watch in recognition of his services in obtaining recruits.

Pensioned Risaldar Ghulam Ali Khan was granted the honorary rank of Risaldar Major for similar services.

Rissaidars Malik Mahomed Bahadar Khan and Surain Singh also received Swords of Honour.

Lance Dafadar Abdul Sattar and Sowar Mansab Ali each received a Sanad and a gift of a hundred rupees.

FOREIGN ORDERS AND DECORATIONS.

ORDER OF ST ANNE, 3rd Class, with swords. (Russia.)

Lieut.-Colonel A. P. Browne.

LEGION D'HONNEUR, CROIX D'OFFICIER. (France.)

Brigadier-General R. E. T. Hogg.

APPENDIX V.

ORDER OF THE LION AND SUN, 3rd Class. (Persia.)

Major D. B. Edwards.
Captain E. T. R. Wickham.

ORDER OF ST MAURICE AND ST LAZARUS. (Italy.)

Brigadier-General D. Le G. Pitcher.

CROIX DE GUERRE. (Belgium.)

Jemadar Shah Wali Khan.

APPENDIX VI.

BRITISH OFFICERS WHO WERE POSTED TO THE 39TH, OR SECOND REGIMENT, DURING THE GREAT WAR.

2nd Lieut. G. N. Vansittart.
2nd Lieut. T. H. Allen.
2nd Lieut. G. A. Roxburgh.
2nd Lieut. G. A. Murphey.
2nd Lieut. E. M. Silverton.
2nd Lieut. H. R. Landale.
2nd Lieut. F. R. Blackwood.
2nd Lieut. A. A. E. Filose.
2nd Lieut. D. St V. Gordon.
2nd Lieut. A. T. M. Parker.
2nd Lieut. B. C. Waller.
2nd Lieut. A. K. Smith.
2nd Lieut. P. G. Morrison.
2nd Lieut. E. J. R. Corin.
2nd Lieut. W. D. Liston.
2nd Lieut. F. W. Rawlins.
2nd Lieut. J. W. Nicholson.
2nd Lieut. H. E. Horsfield.
2nd Lieut. C. C. Wilson.
2nd Lieut. R. H. Rogers.
2nd Lieut. S. Brabant Smith.
2nd Lieut. C. M. Cornell.
2nd Lieut. R. E. G. George.
2nd Lieut. C. F. Aitken.
2nd Lieut. A. H. K. Williams.
2nd Lieut. Morris-Jones.
2nd Lieut. R. P. N. Swayne.
2nd Lieut. H. G. Monks.
2nd Lieut. R. Matthews.
2nd Lieut. C. E. King.
2nd Lieut. A. L. Bettles.
2nd Lieut. D. W. Cockrane.

2nd Lieut. J. F. Lawson.
2nd Lieut. J. H. Michell.
2nd Lieut. D. C. Lalor.
2nd Lieut. H. F. Pearson.
2nd Lieut. L. C. S. Skinner.
2nd Lieut. T. D. Aylward.
2nd Lieut. E. L. Peniston-Bird.
2nd Lieut. H. H. Stable.
2nd Lieut. A. A. S. Alexander.
2nd Lieut. E. J. Johnson.
2nd Lieut. E. B. Tapsell.
2nd Lieut. H. Wallis.
2nd Lieut. A. E. Sanson.
2nd Lieut. A. C. Sherriff.
2nd Lieut. C. J. Tucker.
2nd Lieut. W. H. Everett.
2nd Lieut. C. E. L. Bates.
2nd Lieut. L. A. Bagnall-Oakeley.
2nd Lieut. W. J. Bagg.
Major P. de L. Temple, 37th Lancers.

The following officers of the Indian Medical Service were attached for short periods :—

Lieut. B. N. Burjorjee.
Lieut. F. B. Ambler.
Lieut. R. B. Spencer.
Lieut. G. S. Banker.
Lieut. Teja Singh Uberoi.
Lieut. Jagat Ram Kochar.

INDEX.

Note.—In this index the abbreviation C.I.H. is used for Central India Horse.

ABADEH, 288, 290, 291
Abbott, Capt. R. S., 281, 309, 326, 331, 382
Abdul Hakim Khan, Lance Dafadar, 347
Abdul Rahman, Dafadar, 148
Abdul Rahman, Jemadar, 295, 296, 298
Abdul Wahad, 262
Abdurrahman Khan, Amir of Afghanistan, 152, 155, 242, 266
Achar Singh, Lance Dafadar, 354
Afghan Boundary Commission, 1884-5, 181, 185, 242
Afghan, War, the second, 39, 139, 141, 193, 205, 214, 216, 219, 230, 231; history of, by Colonel Sir N. Chamberlain, 142 *sqq.*
Afseran Committee, the, 101, 102, 103
Agar (or Augur) cantonment, 224, 225 *et passim;* abolition of, as cavalry station, 412-13
Agra, 19, 20, 21, 38, 40, 41, 59, 126-7, 166, 234, 266
Ahmad, 379
Ahmad Yar Khan, Lance Dafadar, 347
Ahmed Khel, action at, 157-8
Ainsworth, Surg.-Capt., 274
Aisne, river, 358
  Battle of the, 312
Ajit Singh, 22, 23
Ajmere, Lord Mayo's Durbar at, 131
Ala Singh, Jemadar, 131
Aleppo, 404
Alexandra, Queen, 132
Ali Haidar Khan, Rissaldar Major, 187, 282, 283-4
Ali Rajpur State, rebels in, quelled by Isri Parsad, 180-1
Aligarh, 41, 72, 209; action at, 126
Alington, Lieut., 356
Alizai, 253
Allenby, F.-M. Viscount, Palestine campaign of, 388 *sqq.*

Alpin, Surg.-Lieut.-Colonel W. G., 274, 282
Amar Ali, Jemadar, 295
Amar Singh, Risaldar Major, 283, 318, 381
Amman, raid towards, 385
Amettes, 324, 325, 331-2
Arab forces and tribes, 390, 400, 403
Arab horses, Bombay, C.I.H., 46, 47, 99, 169; used in polo, 263-4
Arghandab river, 161, 163
Arhanga Pass, carried, 245
Aron jungles, 36, 63
Arras, battle of, 342
Asirgarh, 52, 53
Assami, the, 94, 95
Athies, 362, 364, 365
Atma Singh, shikari, 203
Aurangabad, 9, 10, 11, 48, 54
Australian horses, *see* Walers
Australian Mounted Division, 385, 392, 395, 403
Authuille, 326, 327, 331, 340, 343
Ayub Khan, 153, 159, 161, 162, 163

BAALBEK, 403-4
Baba Wali Pass, 161, 163
Babar Khan, Rissaidar, 50
Bachan Singh, Sowar, 356
Bachan Singh, last Risaldar Major 39th C.I.H., 411
Badaora, 36 *n.*, 239
Badarwas, 36 *n.*
Bagrode, 32; action at, 33 *sqq.*
Bahauddin Khan, Risaldar Major, 181, 217, 354
Bajrangarh, 235
Baker, Surg.-Major, 218
Bakshi Jaswant Singh, Risaldar Major, 283, 411
Bala Hissar, the, 143, 154
Baldeo Singh, Thakur, of Jarreh, 39, 40
Bands of the C.I.H., 262, 276

Banias, regimental, 102-3
Bankaji, dacoit, 181-2, 196
Bannerman, Colonel P., 206
Bannerman, Colonel Sir A. d'A., 206
Bannerman, Major A. J., 116, 170, 175, 177, 206, 231
Barclay, Dr. 137, 141
Bareilly Police, the, 56, 57
Bargirs, 94, 95; abolition of, 96
Barmadin, Risaldar, 57-8, 74, 77, 121-2, 190
Barod, action at, 36, 63
Barr, Colonel Sir David, 253
Barr, Major H. K., 247, 250, 252, 310, 334, 335
Barrow, Major-Gen., 320, 326, 384
Basoda Column, the, 65
Bateson, Assist.-Surg., 71
Baynes, Capt. C. E., 218-19, 253
Bazar Valley Expedition, 170, 171
Beadon, Lieut. C., 71, 85, 91
Beatson, Lieut.-Colonel W. F., and Beatson's Horse, 33-4, 45 *sqq.*, 52, 53, 55 *n.*, 70, 74; organisation of the force, 47-8; uniforms and weapons of, 48; incorporation of, in Mayne's Horse, 58, 69, 70, 89
Beaumont, Assist.-Surg. T., 49, 50, 58, 71, 116, 117, 137
Becher, Colonel C., 36, 48-9, 51, 54
Beirut, 404, 405
Beisan, 392, 395, 396, 405
Belgians, King and Queen of the, 325
Bell, Lieut.-Colonel R. C., 217, 218, 247, 357, 360, 367, 382
Bengal Army, C.I.H. made a unit of, 221 *sqq.*
Bengal Cavalry (Lancers), Irregular Horse regiments becoming, 69; glamour attached to, 257-8, *see also* Lancers, 2nd
5th (Light), 48
6th, 251
9th, lances issued to, 270
Beni Hissar, 154, 156
Be-nokar Silladars, 95
Bersia, 26, 34, 49, 54, 55, 57, 61, 77
Besud, 146; action near, 147 *&n.*, 148, 219
Besud Expedition, the, 169, 171
Betwa river, 26, 31, 64, 236
Bhaggat Singh, Jemadar, 296, 298
Bhagwan Singh, Dafadar, shikari, 203
Bhawar Khan, Risaldar, 50
Bhils, quelled by Isri Parsad, 180
Bhopal Battalion, the, 175
Bhopal Contingent, the, 2, 4, 5, 60, 141
Cavalry of, 6, 7, 17
Bhopal Polo Team, 262
Bhopawar Levy, the, 44
Bhowan, outlaw, 87
Biaora, 26, 61, 75, 77, 84, 93, 118, 181-2, 271, 275
Bijapur, action near, 23, 43, 44

Bird, Lieut. A. C., 280-1
Birdwood, Brig.-Gen. H. B., 247, 248, 253, 291, 293, 294, 298, 407
Bishan Singh, Dafadar, 136
Blair, Lieut. J. J., 62, 63, 64, 71, 85, 112, 116-17
Bolan Pass, the, 164
Bombay, 231-2, 260, 310, 348, 412
Arab horses of, 46, 47, 49
Bombay Cavalry Regiment, new numbers of, 259
Bombs, 327, 346-7, 352
Borasjun, Khan of, 291, 292
Bostan Khan, Risaldar Major, 317, 411
Bourlon Ridge, village and Wood, 361-2, 365, 366
Bradford, Colonel Sir E., 30 *&n.*, 54, 61, 62, 64, 66, 67, 69, 76, 84, 85, 92, 112, 115-16, 131, 184
Braganza, Duke of, 238, 239
Brahmins in Beatson's Horse, 48, 58, in C.I.H., 44, 86, in Meade's Horse, 39, 40, 89; Mayne's exclusion of, 74
Brett, Major De Renzie, 53, 58
British other ranks enrolled in C.I.H., 314-15
Brodrick, Assist.-Surg. H. C., 18, 60, 71, 130
Browne, Gen. Sir S., 122, 123-4, 125, 206
Browne, Lieut.-Colone lA. P., 206, 247, 250, 252, 279, 309, 330, 351, 379, 380, 382
Brydon, Dr, 153
Bulfin, General, 390
Buller, Lieut.-Colonel H. M., 131, 138, 146, 154, 163, 170, 195 *sqq.*, 211
Bundi, Maharajah of, 23
Buner Field Force, the, 178 *n.*
Burlton, Capt. H. M. B., 43, 109, 122, 234
Burmah Military Police, 217, 273
Burnes, Sir Alexander, 143
Burton, Lieut. R. C., 273
Bushire, and the Bushire-Shiraz road, 286-7, 289-90, 291, 304

CADELL, Lieut. J. D., 217
Caldecott, Dr R., 137, 184, 202, 206, 218, 231
Cambrai, battle of, 357, 358 *sqq.*, 381
Cambridge, F.-M. H.R.H. the Duke of, C.-in-C., 23 *n.*, 139
Cameron, Colonel D. H., 210, 253, 261, 268
Cameron, Lieut. R., 343, 347-8, 353, 376, 377, 379
Campbell, General Sir Colin, 127, 128-9
Campbell, Major C., 185, 190, 209, 226-7, 240, 247, 250, 261
Candy, Surg.-Lieut. R. H., 282
Canning, Viscount, Viceroy, 10, 66, 70, 72, 73
Caporetto, 359

INDEX 463

Capper, Major A. S., 217, 218, 240, 291, 292, 302, 407, 410, 412
Carnac, Lieut. E. S. R., 71, 85
Carwithen, Lieut. G. T., 210
Case, Lieut., 43
Cavagnari, Sir L., 142-3, 181
Cavalry, the battle of Cambrai planned to employ, 358
Galloping, moral effect of, 371
Native, mobility of, in the monsoon, 26
Cavalry Brigades
Australian Light Horse, 397
Canadian, Fort Garry Horse, B Squadron, 354
Lucknow, of 4th Cavalry Division, 368
Mhow, 362, 368, 384, break-up of, 382-3
Sialkote, 340
5th, 284
10th, 383-4, 388, 394, 395, 398, 404-5
11th, 394, 398
12th, 394, 397, 398
Cavalry, 4th Indian, 266
Central India, the mutiny in, 3 *sqq.*, 19 *sqq.*, 49
Farewell to, of C.I.H., with a glance at the future, 413-14
Central India, Local Corps in, 208-9
Central India Field Force, campaign of (1858), 19, 23 *n.*
Central India Horse, bands of, 262, 276
Colonel - in - Chief of, H.M. King George, 277
Commandants of, political duties of, 67, 109-10, 117, 222-3; title of, 70
Equipment and weapons of, 48, 100-1, 166 *sqq.*, 179, 189, 205-6, 208, 269-70, 327, 331-2, 335-6
History of, evolution of, *see* Beatson's Horse, Mayne's Horse, *and* Meade's Horse, *see also* Mir Amjad Ali, Risaldar; birth of, nucleus and formation of, 1, 14, 17, 18, 67 *sqq.*, 70 *sqq.*, 107 *sqq.*; classification of, 67, 70-1, 74, 186-7, 222-3, 254-5, 256, 412-13; first Regimental Dinner of, at Delhi, 1903, 272
Honours of, Regimental, 166, 174
Horses of, 46, 47, 99, 100, 169; use of, by officers, 83-4
a Local Corps, 258, delocalisation feared by, and effected, 223, 406, 408, 412 *sqq.*
New system of drill introduced into, 207-8
Officers of, the first, 18, 70, 71
War Services of, 2nd Afghan War, 169 *sqq.*
Polo-playing by, 176, 180, 207, 217, 230 *sqq.*, 258, 260 *sqq.*

Central India Horse *contd.*
Reductions and augmentations of, 87, 91, 92, 186-7 *et alibi*
Silladar System on which concluded, 93 *sqq.*, 413
Sowars of, dismounted and digging, 316, 321-2, 325, 327, 332, 334, 335, 338, 355, 367
Uniform of, 59, 189, 190, 211 *sqq.*, 335-6
War Services of, in order of date
(*a*) Second Afghan War, 142 *sqq.*, 169 *sqq.*
(*b*) Tirah Campaign, 241 *sqq.*
(*c*) Persia, 285 *sqq.*
(*d*) Great War, 308 *sqq.*
Chaman Singh, 56-7
'Chambal Horse,' the, 39, 131
Chambal river, 14, 24, 38, 39, 199 *sqq.*
Chamberlain, Field-Marshal Sir Neville, 69-70, 140
Chamberlain, Colonel Sir N., 139 140, 142, 155 *&n.*, 163, 164, 171; chapter by on the Second Afghan War, 142 *sqq.*
Chamberlain, Major C., 119
Chanda Fund, the, 97, 100
Charasiab, battle of, 143, 171, 172, 175
Charles, Surg.-Capt., 274
Chauvel, General, 392
Chetwode, General Sir P., 390
Chitoo (Cheetoo), outlaw, 87, 233
Chitral, 220 ; defence of, 85
Chitral Relief Force, 177, 178
Christians, *see* Eurasians
Clarke, Lieut. Stanley, 52, 53, 56, 58, 70, 72, 80, 85, 91
Clay, Lieut. H. C., 34 *&n.*, 49, 52, 54
Clothing, C.I.H., Gerard's Orders on, 211 *sqq.*
Cobbe, Captain, 7
Cockburn, Capt. H. A., 20, 41, 44, 82, 88
Coke, Colonel, 125
Colledge, Major J., 116, 148, 154, 155, 170, 177
Colvin, Major E. J. D., 280
Commandant, title of O.C., C.I.H., 70
Connaught, F.-M. H.R.H. the Duke of, 178
Conolly, Lieut. W. P., 82, 85, 91
Cooke, Major S. A., 210, 247, 248, 311, 320, 330, 331
Coper, Surg.-Lieut. D. G., 282
Cooverjee, Merwanjee, Jemadar, 141
Coronation ceremonies, C.I.H. represented at, in India and London, 271-2, 283, 284
Cosserat, Capt., 129
Coster, Lieut., 397
Cotgrave, Colonel E. C. B., 190, 192, 240, 261, 262, 263, 279, 284
Cox, Lieut., 356
Craigie, Capt., 160 *n.*
Croly, Surg.-Capt. R. G. G., 282
Crump, Surg.-Lieut. S. T., 282

464 INDEX

Cumming, Lieut. F. H. T., 112-13
Cunningham, Capt., 2
Curtis, Captain, 32, 115
Curzon of Kedleston, Marquis, 178

DACOIT-HUNTING, 44, 87, 110, 114, 121, 136-7, 179 sqq., 219
Dacoity, 260, 414
Dalhousie, Earl of, Viceroy, 10
Daliki, Khan of, 291, 292
Dalrymple-Hay, Lieut., 356, 389
Daly, Colonel Sir H., 84, 118 &n.
Daly, General Sir H., 111 sqq., 117, 118, 119, 125, 130, 135, 137, 175, 176, 184
Daly, Lieut. E. D. H., 137
Daly, Lieut., G. K., 155 &n., 172, 175-6
Dalzell, Assist. Surg., 43, 90, 112, 117
Damascus, 335, 397, 403
Dandotia Thakurs, the, 39, 40, 89
Daoran Khan, outlaw, 87, 121
Dargai, 250 ; action at, 244
Daunt, Lieut. C. O'B., 281, 309, 330, 351, 375-80, 400, 404, 406
Daunt, Colonel W., 206, 267, 284, 407, 410
Davy Singh, Sowar, 33, 35
Dawson, Colonel, 255, 271, 277
Dayal Singh, Dafadar, 317
de Burgh, Lieut. J., 135
Deh Sarak, action at, 170-1
De Kantzow, Lieut., 72, 76, 79 sqq., 81, 82
Delaney, Surg.-Lieut., 274
Delhi, Camps of Exercise at, 138, 186, 187, 213; Coronation Durbars at, 264, 271-2, 273, 275, 284; a costly Review at, 188 sqq.; Imperial Assemblage at to proclaim the Empress of India, 140 ; Siege of, 46, 110, 111, 112, 119, 120, 125, 126, 133-4
Deraa, 395, 398, 402, 403
Desert Mounted Corps, the, 383, 392, 403, 404
Dewa Singh, Dafadar, 43
Dewa Singh, shikari, 203
Dewas State, and its Rajah, 4, 117
Dhakoni, 27
Dhalip Singh, Sowar, 356
Dhar, and its Rajah, 12, 14
Dhokal Singh of Jodhpore, 262, 265
Dholpur, 19 ; Chiefs of, 39, 189
Dilawar Khan, Risaldar, 353, 354, 378
Disa Singh, Naeb Dafadar, 137
Doing Duty officers, C.I.H., 71, 72, 122
Doran, Brig.-Gen. J., 147 &n., 148, 149, 150
Dorset Yeomanry, 384, 387, 395, 396-7, 401
Dost Mahomed Khan, Lance Dafadar, 375

Dost Mahomed Khan, Sowar, 346
Douglas, Major-General J. A., 279 sqq., 289, 293, 296, 298, 299, 301, 302, 304, 407
Dressner, Lieut. C. J. B. H., 141
Drew, Lieut., 15
Drummond, Major-General Sir F. H. F., 219, 221, 255, 271, 278
Dufferin and Ava, Marquess of, Viceroy, 152, 188
Dun, Capt., 58
Durand, Colonel A. G. A., 139, 150, 155, 157 n., 171
Durand, Colonel Sir H. M., 4 sqq., 139, 157 n.; and the formation of Mayne's Horse, 17-18, 59, 66, 91
Durand, Lieut. R. H. M., 310, 315, 330, 334, 343 sqq., 346, 347, 351, 352-3
Durand, Sir Mortimer, 220
Dysart, Lieut., 13

ECKFORD, Capt. A. B., 264, 267, 273, 288, 290, 291, 303, 304
Edis, Dr, 137
Edward VII., 132
  Coronation of
    Durbar at Delhi, 264, 271, 272
    Indian Contingent at, in London, 271
  Death of, change of style of C.I.H. on, 283
  Indian tour of, 138, 139, 213
Edwards, Brig-General J. B., 172, 177, 238, 239
Edwards, Major D. B., 287, 289
Egypt, 281, 351, 383, 403, 409
El Afuleh, 392, 393, 394, 395
El Henu, bridgehead, 386, 387, 390
Elgin, 8th Earl of, Viceroy, 140, 222
Elphinstone, General, 153
Elphinstone, Lord, 5
Ennemain, 342, 354, 355, 362, 365, 367, 383
Epéhy, 368, 370, 373, 374, 379
Es Salt, 385
Esdraelon, Plain of, 390, 394
Eurasians in Meade's Horse, 40, 42-3, 89
Evans-Gordon, Lieut. K. A. G., 281
Evans-Gordon, Sir W. E., M.P., 184 &n., 221
Evers, Lieut., 404

FAHIM KHAN, Jemadar, 148 n., 219
Faiz Mahomed Khan, Dafadar, 378
Fane, General Sir V. B., 393
Fane's Horse, 69
Fars, Governor-General of, 302, 303
Fateh Khan, Lance-Dafadar, 346
Fenwick, Lieut.-Colonel, 151
Ferris, Lieut. J. F., 272
Festubert, battle of, 312, 315, 325
Filose, Capt., 351, 397

INDEX 465

Fins Wood, 364, 365
Firozeshah, 12 *sqq.*, 16-17, 36 &*n.*, 54, 64
Fisher, Surg.-Capt. J., 274
Fitzgerald, Colonel C. J. O., 86 &*n.*
Forbes, Major H., 85, 112
Forge Fund, the, 100
Foord, Lieut. H. H., 49
Fraser, Lieut., 58
Fraser, Lieut.-Colonel W. A. K., 280, 288, 289, 301
Fraser, Major D. De M., 267, 281, 291, 293, 296, 297

GALILEE, Sea of, 395, 403
Ganda Singh, 6 *n.*
Ganoni, action at, 55
Garbha Singh, Jemadar, 217
Garder Choki, 233
Gardner's Horse, *see* 2nd Lancers, *under* Lancers
Garja Singh, Jemadar, 6 *n.*, 18, 32, 60, 141
Gas and gas-masks, 323, 331-2
Gaselee, General Sir A., 250, 252, 272
Gatacre, General, 178
Gaza, 383, 384; victory at, 385
George V., H.M., Colonel-in-Chief, C.I.H., 277
  Coronation of, Indian Contingent at, 283-4
  Durbar held by, in 1911, 273
  Indian tour of, before accession, with Queen Mary, 277
  Sportsmanship of, 277
George, Lieut., 268, 356
Gerard, Lieut.-General Sir M. G., 46, 131, 155 &*n.*, 157, 162, 163, 164, 168, 170-1, 182 *sqq.*, 195, 204-5, 211, 212, 216, 219, 220
Ghakkars in C.I.H., 187, 256, 309
Ghoraniye, 385, 386
Ghulam Ali Khan, Risaldar, 409-10
Ghulam Mahomed Khan, orderly, 346
Ghulam Mahomed Khan, Risaldar Major, 187, 265, 271
Gibbon, Lieut. W. M., 41
Gibson, Lieut. E. E., 116
Giles, Colonel, 412
Gimlette, Surg., 206-7
Givenchy, 315; battle of, 312
'Godoo,' 262
Godwin, Brig.-General, 384, 388
Gokal Parsad, Rissaidar, 50
Goodenough, Lieut. H. L., 198, 199
Goodfellow, Major R. C., 273, 309, 320, 334
Goonah, H.Q., 83 *sqq.*, *et passim*, 224 *sqq.*; review at, by H.M. Queen Mary, 83, 233-4; the ride to, 83, 233-4; the whole C.I.H. at, for the last time, 412
'Goonah Freebooters' polo team, 263

Gopal Singh, Risaldar Major, 39-40, 42, 43, 94, 95, 96, 131, 151-2, 191
Gopal Swamy, office babu, 269
Gordon, Colonel, 251
Gordon, Sir William, 28 *sqq.*, 32
Gough, Brig.-General Sir H., 156, 163, 170
Gough, Major - General Sir Charles, 188
Gould, Surg.-Major J., 282
Gourlie, Lieut.-Colonel J., 280, 315, 319, 330, 341 &*n.*, 342, 382, 393, 403
Gouzeaucourt, 366-7
Grand Trunk Road, the, 3, 26, 62, 75, 83, 109-10, 113, 114, 129 *sqq.*, 179, 181-2, 196, 233 *sqq.*, 259-60; a last march up, 408
Grant, Colonel F. C., 177, 178, 208, 247, 248, 250, 277-8, 279
Grant, Dr P. M., 141, 184
Greathed, Colonel, 20, 127
Greaves, Major-Gen. Sir G., 188
Gueudecourt, 336, 337
Guides, The, 45, 59, 111, 112, 119, 142-3, 172, 259, 343
Gujar Singh, 6 *n.*
Gulam Nur Khan, Dafadar, 180
Gundi Mulla Sahibdad, action near, 161
Gundigan, action near, 161
Gurmak Singh, shikari, 203
Gussa Khan, mess khitmatgar, 314
Gwalior, 20 *sqq.*, 44, 62, 75, 166, 190, 218, 222, 224, 274, 277
Gwalior, battle of, 19, 21
Gwalior Contingent, the, 3, 5, 23, 38, 41, 43, 225
  Cavalry, 3, 13, 17, 18, 20, 60
Gwalior, Maharajah of (Scindia), 3, 19-20, 21, 23 *n.*, 38, 103, 235, 238-9, 413
Gwalior State, 117, 118, 166, 240
Gwatkin, Lieut., 170-1

HABIB GUL KHAN, Sowar, 346
Hackett, Major, 48
Hadda Mullah, the, 243
Haig, Brig.-General N., 326, 375
Haig, F.-M. Earl, 326 : object of, in the battle of Cambrai, 358, 359
Hall, Colonel J. D., 116, 175
Hamilton, Lieut., 142
Hamilton, Sir Robert, 2, 3-4, 17
Hanuman Tekri, 234, 235
Hanza-Nagar Expedition, the, 139
Happy Valley, Agar, 227
Hargicourt, 342, 353, 367
  Trenches in front of, 343 *sqq.* (*plan*, 344)
Harna Mal, bania, 102-3
Harnam Singh, Jemadar, 284

INDEX

Harsa Singh, Dafadar, 8, 182 *sqq.*, 201, 202, 238
Hart, Captain, 289
Hartigan, Sergt., V.C., 20, 42
Harvey, Capt. C. O., 281, 310
Harvey, Dr, 135, 137
Hawkins, Lieut. H. L., 66
Hazara Singh, Wardi Major, 348
Hazura Singh, Jemadar, 373
Henderson, Lieut.-Colonel L. G., 280, 309, 328
Herati regiments, mutiny of, at Kabul, 143
Herbert, Major-General L., 177, 178 *&n.*
Hewlett, Lieut.-Colonel A., 247, 248, 254, 263, 264, 266, 267, 268, 291, 404, 411
Hidayat Ali, Sowar, 14
Hill, Colonel, 246 *sqq.*
Hindenburg Line, the, 339, 361, 363
Hira Singh, Dafadar, 261
Hirst, Lieut., 388
Hoare, Brig.-General C. G., 203-4, 280, 289
Hodgson, Surg.-Major, 282
Hodson and Hodson's Horse, 69, 112, 119
Hogg, Hon. Brig.-General R. E. T., 273, 310
Holdich-Leicester, Surg.-Lieut., 274
Homs, 404
Hood, Lieut. A. N., 254, 274
Hood, Lieut. G. P., 273, 274
Horsburgh, Lieut. C. B., 116, 139
Horses for Silladar Regiments, sources of, 99-100
Horses of C.I.H., 42, 46, 47, 99, 160, 162, 169, 263-4
Horses of Meade's Horse, 45
Horsford, Lieut. N. D., 273
Howard-Vyse, Brig.-General, 388
Hughes, General Sir W. Templer, 119 *sqq.*, 176
Hughes-Buller, Lieutenant H., 175, 176, 178, 203
Humayun, Shahzada, *see* Firozeshah
Humphrys, Lady, 155-6
Hungerford, Major, 4, 6, 7, 8, 16, 182
Hunter, Surg.-Lieut., 274
Hurnam Singh, Sowar, 148
Hutchison, Major J. R., 268, 280, 309, 323, 330, 382, 393, 400
Hyderabad, 45, 46, 47-8, 50, 253
  Nizam of, 261
  Cavalry of, 46 *n.*
Hyderabad Contingent, the, 5, 9 *sqq.*, 49, 50, 220; renumbered, 259
  Cavalry of, 59
Hyena Hill, Agar, 226
Hyland, Rissaldar, 422

IBRAHIM KHAN, Rissaidar, 240, 262, 263, 265, 293, 296
Imam Khan, Risaldar, 50
Imperial Assembly, Delhi, 140, 213

Imperial Cadet Corps, 170, 178, 210, 277
Imperial Service Cavalry, 178, 310
Imperial Service Troops, 199, 210, 218, 298, 386
Inayat Ali, Sowar, 13
Indar Singh, Lance Dafadar, 374
Indar Singh, Naeb Risaldar, 6 *n.*, 18, 32, 60, 65
Indar Singh, Sowar, 348
Indian Army Corps, the, in France, 307 *sqq.*, 312, 328-9
Indian Army Reserve of Officers, 327, 328, 329, 334, 356
Indian Cavalry, Reconstitution of, after the Great War, 257; Squadron System introduced throughout, 256; three distinct bodies of, 257; Polo Tournaments, 264, 265, 267
Indian Cavalry Corps in France, 322-3, 326, 332
Indian Cavalry Divisions in
  France, 307 *sqq.*, 329, 364, 365
  Palestine and Syria, 382-3 *sqq.*
  2nd, 318-19
  4th, 332, 336, 339-40, 342, 360, 362, 367, 368 *sqq.*, 383, 384, 385, 392, 394, 395, 398, 402-3, 404
  5th, 332, 364, 365, 385, 392, 393, 403, 404
Indian Cavalry Regiments, *see also* Lancers
  27th Light, 411
  41st, 6th Squadron C.I.H. incorporated in, 411
Indian Contingent on duty in London at the Coronation of Edward VII., 271, and at the Coronation of His present Majesty George V., 284
Indian Mutiny, the, 1, 3 *sqq.*, *passim.*, 111, 181, 225, 234, 258, 413; closing events and end of, 19 *sqq.*, 37
Indian officer, the, fine character of, seen in the Great War, 316-17
Indian officers at Queen Victoria Jubilee, 1887, 217; and at the two Coronations, 271-2, 283, 284
Indian Princes, devotion of, in the Great War, 307; Polo playing of, 261, 282
Indian regiments, renumbering of, 258-9
Indian troops armed with ·303 Lee-Metford (1901), 270
  in the Great War, 307 *sqq.*
  Sent to Europe by Disraeli, 141, 270, 306
Indore, 24, 139
  Maharajah of (Holkar), 4, 5, 6, 11, 17, 18 *n.*, 24
  Army of, 4, 6

INDEX

Indore *contd.*
  Polo Tournaments at, 265, 266
  Residency at, 3, 118, 135, 222, 224, 278
  Siege of, 4 *sqq.*, 24, 44, 139, 141, 217
  Indore Durbar, the, 190
  Indore State, 117
  Indore-Fatebad-Ujjain Railway, 225, 226
Inniskilling Dragoons, the, 310, 315, 334, 337, 342, 351, 367, 371, 372, 383
Irbid, 398, 399, 400
Irbid ridge, 406
Irles, 339, 340
Irregular Horse, Mutiny Regiments, later names of, 69
Irvine, Lieut. J. S., 113, 118
Irvine, Surg. G., 207
Isagarh, 27, 28
Ispahan, 288, 290, 291, 292
Isri Parsad, Risaldar Major, 44, 74, 86; dacoit-hunting skill of, 87, 121, 132, 137, 180-1, 190

JACKETS, C.I.H., the Doggie Coat, Patrol, Service, and Undress, 214-15
Jacob, General J., 61
Jacob, Lieut. J., 85
Jacob's Horse, 315, 327, 335
Jagdalak Pass, 143, 154
Jaipur, 23, 62, 66, 131
Jalna, 33, 51, 52
Jalna Field Force, the, 52, 53
James, Dr and Mrs, 3
James, Lieut. C., 85, 91
James, Mr, 287
Jamieson, Lieut. L. F., 118
Jamieson, Surg.-Capt. J. B., 218
Jamonia, 209, 226
Jaora, State of, 117; Ghaus Mahomed, Nawab of, 4, 5, 12, 14, 189; Nawab of, son of Ghaus Mahomed, 189; Nawab of, present day, 281, 282
Jaora Alipur, action near, 21, 23
Jats in C.I.H., 74, 89, 168, 187; in Mayne's Horse, 65; in Meade's Horse, 40, 89
Jawant Singh, Risaldar Major, 373, 374, 379, 411
Jellalabad, 39, 142, 145, 146, 150, 151, 153, 154, 160, 162, 169
Ford, 147
Jenkyns, Mr, 142
Jennings, Lieut. W. N., 72, 76, 77, 80-1
Jennings, Rev. —, 76
Jerusalem, 391; Allenby's occupation of, 385
Jezreel, Valley of, 395
Jhalra Patan, 17, 24, 26, 115, 184, 200, 221
  Maharajah of (1858), 24, 26; (1888), 200; (1896), 221

Jhanda Singh, Sowar, 192
Jhansi, 22, 46, 60, 271, 276
  Rani of, 19, 21;n.
Jhelum, 412
Jisr Mujamieh, 395, 398, 399, 402
Jiwan Singh, Risaldar, 114-15
Jodhpore, 217
  Maharajah of (1887), 191, 261
Jodhpore Cup, the, 268
Johnstone, Lieut. R., 52-3
Jones, Capt. Pryce, 325-6, 330
Jones, Lieut. M. H. S., 281
Jones, Surg.-Lieut. S. W., 274
Jordan River and Valley, 325, 383 *sqq.*, 387, 388, 390, 393, 396, 397, 403
Jubbulpore, 311
  District, 64
Jumrood, 142, 145
Juri, the, 98-9

KABUL, 142-3, 152, 153, 220, *see also* Afghan War
Kabul, march from, to Kandahar, 156 *sqq.*, 166, 169
Kabul river, 151; crossings of, 39, 145 &n., 146, 149 &n., 150, 151
Kach, 164, 165
Kadir Baksh, Dafadar, 200, 203, 204
Kadir Cup, the, 268
Kadir Khan, Wardi Major, 51
Kala Nag, the elephant, 200-1
Kalanaur, 191, 262
Kali Naddi, the, action near, 127
Kama Expedition, the, 150, 169, 171
Kamaluddin Khan, Risaldar, 335, 353-4
Kan Singh, Jemadar, 65
Kanar, 83, 275
Kandahar, 142; battle of, 160 *sqq.*, 169, 170, 171, 172; relief of, 153-4, 160
Kankar-ki-Baori, 226
Kankraoli, action at, 24
Kantara, 383
Kapur Singh, Dafadar, shikari, 203
Kapurthala picket, the, 249-50
Kariakal, 204-5
Kashguli robbers, 288, 294, 295 *sqq.*
Kawass, 164, 165
Kaye, Lieut. J. L., 198
Kazerun, 290, 292, 293, 294, 296; fight near, 297-8
Keegan, Surg.-Major D. F., 130, 137, 172
Keighley, Capt. H. D. S., 273, 274, 326, 330
Kelly, Surg.-Capt. T. B., 143, 274
Kennion, Lieut. R. L., 210
Kerkur Beidus, 394
Kesar Singh, Sowar, 356
Kettlewell, Lieut.-Colonel A. M., 273, 288, 290, 407, 412
Khadi Khan, Jemadar, 148

Khaim Khanis in C.I.H., 74, 76 ; in Mayne's Horse, 65
Khairulla Khan, Sowar, 180
Khalil, Mulla, 146-7, 148
Khan-i-Zinian, 303
Khanki Valley, 244
Khargaon, 34
Khelat-i-Ghilzai, 160 &n.
Khemlasa, 31
Kher Mahomed Khan, Rissaidar, 50
Khudaspa, the, and his horse, 96 sqq.
Khudiar Khan, 14
Khurbet Arah, 394
Khurd Kabul Pass, 143
Khurmana Darra, 248 sqq., 250
Khurmana river, 245
Khushab Singh, Dafadar, 136
Khyber Field Force, the, 145, 170
Khyber Pass, the, 142 ; Mohmand attacks in, 243
Kila Abdulla, 164
Kildare Trench and Lane, 371, 372, 374, 375
King George's Own Central India Horse, new style of C.I.H., 283
Kitchener of Khartoum, F.-M. Earl, 86 &n., 223, 276, 278-9, 326
Koer Singh, Dafadar, 32
Kohat, 142, 244, 245, 246, 247
Kohistan, 152
Kokeran, ford at, 161, 162, 163, 164
Kotah, 279 ; Maharao of, 204
Kotrah, action near, 24
Kunu river, 36, 113, 182
Kurai, 31-2, 34 ; action at, 62
Kurram Moveable Column, the, 246 sqq., 252
Kurram Singh, Rissaidar, 42
Kurram Valley and River, 142, 171, 243, 245, 247
Kurram Valley Field Force, the, 170, 171
Kursi, charge at, 123
Kushalgarh, 253
Kutabuddin Khan, Sowar, 346
Kutal-i-Dukhtar, 294, 299

LA BARASSE, 310, 313
Lachman Jharia, outlaw, 87, 137
Lachman Singh, 6 n.
Lachman Singh, Lance Dafadar, 297
Lahore, 129, 172, 409
Lahore Light Horse, the, 90-1
Lal Khan, Risaldar, 284
Lala Tikha Ram, Munshi, 55
Lalitpur, 3, 26, 28, 109
Lancers
 2nd (Gardner's Horse), 278, 279, 310, 315, 324, 332, 337, 367, 371, 372, 375, 376, 380, 382 sqq., 387, 394 sqq., 398, 399
 13th, 246
 17th, 340
 18th (Bengal), 69, 264, 265, 317

Lancers contd.
 19th, 397
 30th, 327
 32nd, 278
Lancers of the C.I.H., 48, 101, 167 168, 208
Lark Spur, 369, 370, 371, 373, 375
Lash, Lieut. H. A., 210
Latabund Kotal, 154
Lawrence, Colonel T., and his Arabs, 398
Lawrence, Lieut. G. H., 217
Lawrence, Lord (John), 111, 119
Lawson-Tancred, Major Sir T. H., 217, 218, 327, 330, 382
Lehna Singh, Risaldar Major, 217, 275
Lejjun, 394, 395
L'Empire - Malassise Farm - Vaucelette Farm Line, 367
Le Marchand, Major, 25
Lennox, Lieut. C. E., 49, 52
Les Bœufs, 336
Les Plantins, 315, 316, 319
Leslie, Capt. C. L., 327, 330, 335
Leslie, Wing-Commdr. Sir N., 281, 309, 325, 330, 333, 354
Lewis, Major G., 280, 309, 328, 330, 331
Lightfoot, Major, 21
Lihaz Gul, Risaldar, 335, 353, 378
Liman von Sanders, General, 392, 395
Limerick Post, attack at, 370, 372 sqq.
Lions, last in Central India, 114
Lloyd Lindsay Competition, the, 209
Lockhart, General Sir W., 244 sqq.
Loos, battle of, 328, 330
Low, Cornet J., 85
Lowdell, Dr, 184, 192, 193, 206, 210
Lozinghem, 320, 325
Luard, Capt. P., 116
Lucas, Lieut. G. B., 281, 309, 333
Luck, General Sir G., 197, 198, 209, 273
Lucknow, 262-3 ; siege and relief of, 10, 46, 110, 112, 122, 126, 127, 128
Ludhiana lungees, worn by C.I.H., 213, 216
Lumbago, a cure for, 202-3
Lumsden, General Sir Peter, 185
Lwara Mela, 250, 251, 252
Lyons, Lieut. J. G., 272
Lytton, 1st Earl of, Viceroy, 140, 213

MACARDLE, Surg.-Lieut. A. F. F., 254, 274
M'Cowen, Surg.-Capt., 274, 282, 289, 295, 297
Macgregor, Brig.-General C., 163
Mackie, Surg.-Lieut. F. P., 274
MacIvor, Lieut. Ivor, 141
MacIvor, Lieut. Ivor, son of above, 280
Macnabb, Capt. R. J., 280, 315, 330, 335, 345 sqq., 348 sqq., 351
Macnaghten, Sir W., 143
Macpherson, Brig.-General H. T., 171

INDEX

Macpherson, Major, 38
Madhoo Singh, rebel, 77
Madras Cavalry Regiments, renumbering of, 259
Mæuvres, 361, 365, 366
Magar Singh, Risaldar Major, 148 &n., 275
Magniac, Captain, 7
Mahadeo Singh, Naeb Risaldar, 65
Mahmud Khan, Dafadar, 199, 204-5
Mahoiuddin Khan, Dafadar, 180
Mahomed Ali Khan, Chief of the Kashgulis, 299
Mahomed Ali, Shah of Persia, deposed, 285-6
Mahomed Bahadur Khan, Jemadar, 265, 266, 267
Mahomed Sharif Khan, Sowar, 346
Mahomed Zaman, Dafadar, 303
Mahomedans in C.I.H., 89, 187, 247, 256
Mahratta Chaoni, the, 235-6
Mahratta Horse, the (18th Bengal Lancers), 69, 265
Mahtab Singh, Dafadar, head shikari, 136, 148, 200, 201 sqq.
Maidan Valley, 245
Mainpuri Levy, the, transferred to Mayne's Horse, 69, 70, 73
Maison Ponthieu, 333, 334
Maiwand, battle of, 153, 161, 162
Makhadet Hajla, 385, 387, 388
Maksud Ali, Dafadar, 262
Maksudangarh, 26, 37, 66, 114, 181
Malakand, the, 241
Malakand Fort, 243
Malassise Farm, 367, 369
Malcolmson, Surg.-Lieut. G. E., 274
Malik Ghulam Mahomed Khan, Risaldar Major, 275, 283, 291, 411
Malik Sher Bahadur Khan, Risaldar, 409
Malwa Bhil Corps, the, 185, 206
Malwa Contingent, the, 4, 5, 7, 13, 17, 18
Mandesore, battle of, 14, 15, 36 n.
Mangauli, action at, 27-8
Manifold, Surg. C. C., 207
Maniruddin, Babu, 269
Mardan Khan, Lance Dafadar, 148
Marne, battle of the, 312
Marquion-Beaurevoir Line, 364
Marseilles, 310-11, 320, 354, 383
Martin, Colonel Cunliffe, 9, 16, 60, 61, 82, 85, 92, 112, 115, 135, 141 sqq., 147, 148, 169, 175 sqq., 191, 195, 229-30, 281
Martin, Lieut. R. H. M., 281, 309
Martini-Henry carbines issued to C.I.H., 205
Marwari ponies, 100
Mary, H.M. Queen, at Indore, 277
 Christmas gift of, to the Mhow Brigade, problems caused by, 319-20
 Review by, of C.I.H. at Goonah, 284

Masnières, 361, 363, 364, 365, 366
Masters, Colonel A., 40, 137, 139, 155, 170, 191, 211, 221, 223, 253, 254, 255
Masuzai, the, 248 sqq., 250
Maxwell, Capt. F., V.C., 266-7
Mayne, Brig.-General W., 71
Mayne, Major A. B., 190, 191, 261 sqq.
Mayne, Major A. G., 70, 71, 85, 91, 112, 122, 136
Mayne, Major H. O., and Mayne's Horse, 9, 10, 17, 18, 19, 26 sqq., 32, 48, 54, 58 sqq., 66, 67 sqq., 70, 74-5, 76, 79 sqq., 81, 84, 85, 86, 109-10, 115, 129, 269
Mayo, 6th Earl of, Viceroy, 131
Mazar Ali, Sowar, 191 sqq.
Meade, Colonel Sir R., and Meade's Horse, 19, 20 &n., 22, 35 sqq., 39 sqq., 63, 69; the regiment incorporated in Mayne's Horse, 75, 82, 88 sqq., 91
Meerut, 3, 240
Meerut Brigade, the, 320
Mehidpur, 4, 5, 12, 13, 62, 70, 85, 222, 225, 269
'Melrose Abbey,' Goonah, 234
Mesopotamia, 281, 409, 410
Mhow, 4, 5, 6, 8, 9, 11, 12, 16, 17, 115, 177, 191, 224, 234, 309
Mhow Battalion, the, 338 sqq., 342, 351, 354, 355, 356, 357, 367
Mhow Brigade, the, 310, 312 sqq., 317 sqq., 323, 326 sqq., 332-3, 334, 337
Mian Kutal, 294, 299
Michel, General, 24 sqq., 61
Mignon, Lieut. M. J., 112, 118
Military Ranks, English, Indian equivalents for, 18 n.
Miller, Lieut. J., 118
Mills grenade, the, 331
Milner, Lieut. C. E., 334, 372 sqq., 379
Mir Al Rasul, Wardi Major, 13, 14 &n., 136
Mir Amjad Ali, Risaldar Major, 13, 14, 18, 25, 27, 60, 61, 62, 65, 71, 112, 135
Mir Bunyad Ali, Naeb Risaldar, 65
Mir Ghulam Ali, Rissaidar, 50
Mir Kasim Ali, Naeb Risaldar, 32, 62, 65
Mir Kurshed Ali, Jemadar, 60
Mir Tajmal Hosein, Risaldar, 50
Mir Zaman Khan, Jemadar, 387, 390
Mirza Hatim Beg, Wardi Major, 50, 51
Mitchell, Forbes, 193-4
Moab, hills of, 386, 388
Mobin, 251
Mohmands, the (see also Tirah Campaign), 242, 243
Money, Colonel G. E., 136, 171, 180, 209, 211, 221, 223, 247, 254, 255

INDEX

Montauban, 337, 338
Montgomery, General, 226
Moore, Surg.-Capt. M., 218, 247, 252, 254
Morar, 3, 22, 38, 122
   Battle of, 21
Morlancourt, 336, 337, 338
Morris, Lieut. J. G., 141
Morris, Lieut. W. G., 71, 85
Morval, 336
Mory Valley, 339, 340
'Mousquetaire', winner of the Kadir Cup, 268
Multan, 111, 119-20; storming of, 125
Mumtaz Ali Khan of Kalanaur, Risaldar, 411
Murad Ali Khan, Risaldar Major, 136, 191, 217
Muscroft, Lieut. W. St C., 254
Musmus Pass, Carmel Ridge, 394
Muster Parade of the C.I.H., 113-14
Muzaffar Ali, Jemadar, 32

NABLUS, 390
Nadir Khan, Jemadar, 317, 379
Nagars in C.I.H., 74
Nagpur Irregular Force, the, 50
Nahargarh, 63
Nahr-el-Falik, the, 392
Nainwar, action at, 64
Najaf Ali, Jemadar, 32
Nana Rawat, freebooter, 181
Napier, General Sir C., 51
Napier, Lieut. Hon. H. D., 198
Napier, Lieut. Hon. J. P., 137
Napier of Magdala, Field-Marshal Lord, 21 &n., 22, 35, 36, 137, 198, 236-7
Narain Singh, Jemadar, 18
Narayen Singh, Jemadar, 60
Narhat, 28
Narsingarh, 26, 80, 83, 84
   Rajah of, 77 sqq.
Narwar, Man Singh, Rajah of, 22, 23, 27, 35
Nasirabad, 24
Natha Singh, Risaldar Major, 411
Natha Singh, Sowar, 180
Nawabgange, action at, 111-12
Nazar Mahomed Khan, Sowar, 295, 296
Nazareth, 393, 395
Neave, Lieut. K., 86, 225
Nedenchelles, 325
Neemuch, 3, 5, 14, 15, 17, 24, 222
Neill, General, 122, 193-4
Neill, Major A. H. S., 122, 133, 136, 140, 170, 175, 178-9, 182, 186, 191 sqq., 231
Nerbudda river, 31, 32, 33, 34, 35, 52, 53, 54, 135, 196
Neuve Chapelle, battle of, 312, 320
Nibas, 338, 340
Nicholas II., Czar, 177 n., 196
Nicholson, Lieut. C., 122, 125

Nicholson, John, 125
Nimrin, Wadi, action at, 386
North-West Frontier, outbreak on, *see* Tirah Campaign
Northbrook, Rt. Hon. Earl of, Viceroy, 135
Nott, General, 163
Nouguier, Louis, interpreter, 311, 355
Nueiameh, Wadi, 384-5, 387
Nund Singh, Jemadar, 148
Nuriah, 123
Nuthall, Colonel, 200

O'DOWDA, Lieut., 3
Odevaine, Assist. Surgeon, 117, 130
Odlum, Surg.-Capt. W. H., 282
Omignon stream, 354
Oonkar, Bhil dacoit leader, 137
Orakzai, the, 245 sqq., 248, 250
Orcha, 28, 29
   Maharajah of, 28
Orleans, 312
Orr, Major, 11, 13, 14, 15
Oudh, 111, 121, 122-3
Oudh Irregular Cavalry, 1st, 111
Oxus river, 152

PAGE, Lieut., 23, 43
Page, Lieut. W. W. K., 326, 330, 335, 348 sqq., 372 sqq., 380
Paget, Major-General W. H., and the Paget-blade sword, 167-8
Paigahs, 50, 94, 95
Pal Singh, Lance Dafadar, 297
Palestine, 254, 305, 325, 333, 382, 383 sqq., 406
Pamir Delimitation Commission, 185-6, 219 sqq.
Panjab Cavalry
   1st, 111, 119, 125
   2nd, 122, 125
   5th, 125, 167
Panjab Irregular Frontier Force, the (Piffers), 59, 70, 110 &n. sqq., 127, 134, 212, 257, 259
Panjab Singh, Risaldar Major, 86, 130
Panjabi Mahomedans in Meade's Horse, 40
Panjdeh affair, the, 186
Panna, Rajah of, 273
Panthers, 209, 226-7
Paori Fort, 22 &n., 113
Parachinar, 247, 253
Parbati river, action on, 23
Parker, Surg.-Lieut. C. S., 275
Paron, Jungles near, 35 sqq.
Parsee, the only one to enter the Army, 141
Partab Singh, Risaldar Major, 112, 136
Pathans in C.I.H., 187, 256, 309
Paterson, Colonel, 354, 372
Patiala, Maharajah of, and Polo team of, 261, 263
Pearse, Lieut. G., 280
Peart, Lieut. G. R., 113, 116

INDEX

Peiwar Kotal, the capture of, 171, 172
Peizière, 368, 369, 370, 371, 372
Pennell, Lieut. H. L., 184
Persia, 219, 220, 262, 273, 280, 281, 282, 285 *sqq.*
Persian gendarmerie, the, 300
Peshawar, 125, 145, 156, 243, 244
Phayre, General, 163
Philibhit, 123
Picquigny, 326, 327
Pig-mobbing, 228-9
Pig-sticking, 209, 227 *sqq.*, 238
Pigeon Ravine, 369, 371
Pike, Lieut. F., 86
Pinney, Lieut. John, 353, 354, 376, 377, 379
Pinney, Major J. C. D., 209, 210, 351
'Pioneer, The,' on Mayne's services, 81
Pir-i-Zan pass, 294, 298, 299
Pitcher, Brig.-General D. Le G., 266, 267, 273, 274, 279, 291, 298, 299
Platt, Colonel, 6
Pocock, Lieut. M. R., 272-3
Polo playing by the C.I.H., 176, 180, 207, 217, 230 *sqq.*, 258, 260 *sqq.*
Polo ponies, 100, 260, 263-4
Poona, 408-9, 412
Poona Horse, the, 264
Pozière, 333
Prem Singh, Dafadar, 44
Presidential Armies in India, abolition of, 257
Price, Lieut., 151-2
Prichard, Major R. G. M., 325, 330, 335, 386-7
Primrose, Lieut.-General, 153
Probyn, General Rt. Hon. Sir Dighton M., V.C., 96, 124 *sqq.*, 127, 128, 129 *sqq.*, 132, 139, 173, 206
Probyn's Horse, 84, 124, 276 ; renamed, 69
Pula, the, 103-4
Purdah trick, the, 41

QUEENSLAND Horses (Walers), 47, 99
Querrieux, 336
Quetta, 142, 164, 388, 406, 411

RAGOGARH, 63, 76-7, 233
Rahdar caravanserai, 294, 296, 297
Rahim Dad Khan, Rissaidar, 42
Rai Singh, Risaldar, 65
Rajendra Singh, Risaldar, 283
Rajgarh, 24, 25, 61, 63, 83
Rajputana, 21, 34, 49, 61, 130, 131, 139, 191, 196, 198, 221, 284 ; Local Corps in, 208-9
Rajputs in Mayne's Horse, 65 ; in Meade's Horse, 41
Ram Singh, Jemadar, 332, 353, 373, 379
Ram Singh, Sowar, 33, 35

Ramadin, Jemadar, 136, 145
Ramleh, 392
Ramoth Gilead, *see* Remte
Rampur, 195, 220
Rampura-Bhanpura Jungles, 17, 199 *sqq.*
Ramsay, Brig.-General, 3
Randhir Singh, dacoit, 136
'Randullah,' hunting elephant, 238-9
Rangars in C.I.H., 187, 203, 256
Ranking, Lieut., 387
Rao Sahib, the, 54, 63-4, 78
Ras Deiran, 387, 388
Ratlam State, 117 ; Rajah of, 12, present day, 281, 282, 328
Ravenshaw, Lieut. H. E., 141, 155, 164, 171-2
Rawal Pindi, 243
Reaney, Surg.-Lieut. F. M., 282
Rebel-hunting, 55, 56 *sqq.*, 62, 63 *sqq.*, 65, 76, 79, 85, 113
Reid, Lieut. C. L., 334, 335
Remte, 398, 401-2
Rice, Capt., 35-6, 63 &*n.*
Rich, Colonel, 64
Rides between Regiments of C.I.H., 83-4
Rigot, Michael, Nishanbardar, 44
Rimington, General M., 322-3
Ripon, 1st Marquess of, Viceroy, 166
Ritchie, Surg.-Lieut. W. D., 275
Robarts' Horse, renamed, 69, 72
Roberts, Colonel Sir J. R., 218
Roberts, Dr, 135
Roberts, F.-M. Earl, V.C., 140, 176, 188, 197, 208-9 ; *see also* Afghan War, p. 142 *sqq.*
Roberts, General, 23, 24
Robertson, Captain E. E., 172, 177, 253
Robertson, Colonel, 14, 22-3
Roellecourt, 333, 335
Rohilkhand Levy, the, 69, 73
Rohtak, 40, 194, 411
Roome, Capt., 64
Rose, General Sir H., *see* Strathnairn
Ross, Miss, 288, 290, 291
Roxburgh, Lieut., 328, 330
Royal Humane Society's Medal conferred on Pitcher and Keighley, 274
Rumilly, 364, 365
Rupaheli, 196-7
Russell, Lieut. N. F., 280
Russia, 142-3, 152, 153, 185 *sqq.*, 285, 365
Russo-Japanese War, the, 220
Rustam Ali Khan, Risaldar, 50, 55

SADDA, 247, 249, 253
Safdar Jang, 271
Safdar Khan, Risaldar, 50
Saheb Dad Khan, Jemadar, 136, 180, 182
Sailana State, 117 ; Chief of, 12

INDEX

St Acheul, 333
St Ouen, 339
St Petersburg, 196, 198, 211
St Pol area, 331
St Quentin, 342
St Valerie, 338
Salar Masrud, Wardi Major, 51
Sale, Sir Robert, 153
Saledi Singh, Naeb Risaldar, 65
'Sam Browne' belts, 214, 215
Samana Ridge, 243
Samauli, action near, 21-2
Sampagha Pass, 244
Sampson, Lieut. D. T. H., 71, 84
Sanwal Singh, Risaldar Major, 217, 275
Saragheri post, 243
Sarajevo murders, the, 305
Sarangpur, 83
Sarona, 392, 405
Satpura hills and forests, 34, 53
Saugor, 19, 28, 262
Saye, Pte., 378
"Scented Minstrel Horse, The," 210
Scudamore, Colonel, 36
Sedgefield, Dr, 184
Sehore, 4, 9 ; Sikh colony at, 2
Semakh, 395, 397, 405
Senlis, 327
Serias, 28, 233
Seth, the, Regimental Banker, 102
Seton, Surg.-Capt. B., 254, 274, 282
Shabkadr Post, 243, 246
Shadora, 101, 236
Shah Mirza Beg, Rissaidar, 262
Shahabad, 113
Shahpur District, Tiwana Maliks of, 187
Shakespeare, Sir Richmond, 68, 70, 74, 75, 77, 78-9, 80, 81, 86, 88, 109, 110, 196
Shaw, Surg.-Capt. T., 210, 218, 254
Shea, General Sir John, 393
Sheikh Daud, Capt., 60
Sheikh Najaf Ali, Jemadar, 60
Sheikh Shubrati, Risaldar, Bandmaster, and Wardi Major, 262
Sheikh Wazir Ali, Jemadar, 136
Sheppard, Lieut., 56
Sher Ali, Amir, 142, 152, 155
Sher Ali Khan, Rissaidar, 50
Sher Singh, Risaldar, 42
Sherjan Khan, Dafadar, 377
Sherpur cantonment, 143, 144, 155, 156, 171
Shettle, Surg.-Capt. E. B., 282
Shikaris, notable, see Harsa Singh, and Mahtab Singh
Shiraz, 287, 288, 290, 292, 293, 300, 301, 304
"Shiraz Vale Hunt, The," 302
Showers, General, 20
Showers, Lieut. H. F., 122
Shujawalpur, 101
Shutrgurdun Pass, 142
Şibi, 165, 166

Sift Ali Khan, Risaldar, 50
Sigligar, the, 132
Sikh Colony at Sehore, 2
Sikhs, the, 125, 227 *sqq*., 238, 243, 250, in Beatson's Horse, 48, in C.I.H., 74, 75, 89, 187, 247, 256, 309, in Bhopal Cavalry, 17, in Mayne's Horse, 60, 65, in Meade's Horse, 40, 89
Silladar Cavalry Regiments, 96 *sqq*., 100-1, 105
Silladar System, the, 42, 93 *sqq*.; and Eurasian troops, 90-1; pros and cons of, 105-6; abolition of, 276, 413
Silladars, 50, 94 *sqq*.
Simla, 135, 211, 218
Sind, 164
Sindh Horse, 35th, 327
Sindhora, 56, 57 ; action at, 55
Sindwaha, action at, 28, 54, 61, 62, 115
Singram, Jemadar, 14
Singwasa, 276
Sipri, 3, 22, 35, 36, 37 &n., 60, 109, 174
Sirdarpur, 4
Sironj and the Sironj jungles, 23, 26, 27, 28, 37, 54, 63, 66, 67, 109, 114
Sironj Column, the, 65
Sirsi, 36
Sitamao State, 117 ; Chief of, 12
Skene, Lieut. W. F., 333
Smart, Mr, Vice-Consul, 293, 296, 297
Smith, Brig.-General, 22, 27
Smith, Captain Emslie, 274
Smith, Lieut. F. de H., 198, 210
Smith, Lieut. F. S., 282
Smith, Lieut. G. de H., 210
Smith, Lieut.-Colonel R., 151, 152
Snider Carbines, 205-6
Somme, river and area, 326, 342 *sqq*. Battle of the, 336, 339
Souastre, 332
South African War, the (1900), 140, 254, 268, 273, 306
Sowars' Reserve Fund, the, 104-5
Spanish influenza epidemic, 403-4
Specie convoy, the, 288, 293, attack on, 294 *sqq*.
Spence, Lieut. A. H. O., 217, 218, 247, 250, 252, 253, 261
Spencer, Sir Lionel, 130, 135
Spencer, Surg.-Major D. B., 254
Squadron Subalterns substituted for "Doing Duty Officers," 122
Squadrons, Divisions of, at different dates, 207
Steen, Surg.-Lieut. H. B., 275
Stevenson, Surg.-Capt. F. M., 282
Stewart, F.-M, Sir Donald, 153, 155, 157-8, 174-5, 187-8
Stewart, Lieut., 23, 43
Stocker, Surg.-Lieut. C. J., 282

INDEX

Stockley, Lieut.-Colonel, 17
Strathnairn, F.-M. Lord (Sir H. Rose), 19 *sqq.*, 22, 23 *n.*, 35, 46, 52
Stuart, Brig.-General, 11, 12, 14, 15, 17, 19
Subha Singh, orderly, 204-5
Suez Canal, the, 178, 383
Suket river, 233
Surmakh Singh, Jemadar, 65
Susner, 24
Swords of Beatson's Horse, 48; of C.I.H., 132, 167-8, 411; of Meade's Horse, 45
Sylvester, Dr John, 34 &*n.*, 49-50, 52, 54, 58, 70, 71, 80, 84
Syria, 267, 385 *sqq.*, 405, 410, 411
Syud Mohiuddin, Naeb Risaldar, 65

TALAAT ED DUMM, 384
Tancred, Lieut. Sir T. H., *see* Lawson-Tancred
Tanner, Colonel O., 160
Tantia Bhil, dacoit, 87, 190, 196
Tantia Topi, 19 *sqq.*, 36-7, 44, 52, 53, 61, 62, 113
Tapti Valley, 34
Tara Singh, Naeb Dafadar, 136
Targette Ravine, 369, 371
Taylor, Lieut. A. F., 122
Taylor, Mr, 235
Teja Singh, Risaldar, 228
Tel-el-Kebir, 383
Tel er Rame, demonstration at, 387
Temple, Sir Richard, 135-6
Tentpegging, 206, 267
Territorial Horse Artillery, Berkshire Battery, 306, 401
Terrot, Major, 351
Thabai, attack on, 251 *sqq.*
Thal, 247, 253
Therouanne, 312, 313, 317, 318, 319-20
Thiepval, 327
Thompson, Lieut. W., 49, 52
Thomson, Capt., 170-1
Thurburn, Capt. H., 49, 52, 54, 56
Thursday, the Army whole holiday in India, 236-7
Thurston, Lieut. G. O., 274
Tigers and Tiger-shooting, 62, 63 *n.*, 174, 175, 179, 182, 183, 195, 199 *sqq.*, 226, 237 *sqq.*, 271, 277, 414
Timmins, Major, and Mrs, 13
Tincourt Cemetery, 353
Tirah Campaign, the, 178, 210, 218, 241 *sqq.*, 262, 268, 272
Titles of officers of C.I.H., Change in, 1877, 140
Tiwana Lancers, 18th, 264, 265
Tiwanas in C.I.H., 187, 255, 265
Tochi Valley, 241, 243
Todd, Capt. J. F., 266, 267, 280
Tombs, General Sir H., 134
Tonk, State, 117; Nawab of, 23

Townshend, Major-General Sir C. V. (of Kut.), 185, 198-9
Trautmansdorf, Count, 238
Travers, Colonel J., V.C., 4, 6, 7, 8, 18 *n.*, 44, 82, 84, 85, 87 *sqq.*, 107, 182
Trônes Wood, 337
Troop, term explained, 207
Tsappar, 251
Tudor, Lieut. J. B., 49, 54
Tulwar, the, 270; in Beatson's Horse, 48; in Meade's Horse, 45
Tuohy, Surg.-Lieut. W. E. J., 282
Turkey, 241-2, 409
Turkish Armies
    4th, 385, 386, 398, 403
    7th, 385, 390, 396
    8th, 385, 390, 396
Turkish Cavalry Regiment, 1st, 397
Turner, Charles, trumpeter, 91
Turner, John, 91
Turner, William, trumpeter, 91
Turton, Lieut. T. T., 49
Tweedie, Lieut., 53
Tytler, Brig.-General J., 170-1

UDAIPUR, 24 *n.*; hills of, 23, 35; Maharana of, 210
Ujjain, 24, 174, 224, 225, 232
Umar Ali Khan, Risaldar Major, 275
Umbajee, Soondeah Rebel Leader, 44
Umballa, 65, 188, 240, 264, 265, 266
Umballa Brigade, the, 327
Umballa Division, the, 55 *n.*, 121, 196
Uniform of C.I.H., 211 *sqq.*; of Beatson's Horse, 48; of Meade's Horse, 45
Unnamed Farm, 347, 348 *sqq.*
Upen d'Amont, 313
Upen d'Aval, 313

VAUCELETTE FARM, 367, 368
Vaughan, Capt., 400
Vendhuile, 366, 367
Vermelles, 325
Victoria, Queen, Jubilee of (1887), 217; proclaimed Empress of India, 140
Victoria Cross, the, 8, 57, 124, 127, 129; not awarded, originally, to officers of the Indian Army, 111-12
Villers Faucon, 367
Villers Guislain, village and ridge, 366, 368, 369, 370, 372
Villers L'Hôpital, 328
Vincent, Colonel H. A., 131, 195, 211, 220
Vivian, Major, 157

'WALERS' or 'Bounders' (Queensland horses), 47, 99, 263-4

2 H

INDEX

Wales, T.R.H. Prince and Princess of, *see* Alexandra, Queen, Edward VII., H.M. George V., *and* H.M. Queen Mary
Wallis, Mr, 204, 205
Walter, Lieut. G. B., 327, 334, 389, 390
Wano, action at, 242
Ward, Lieut. T. M., 210
Wardi Fund, the, 100
Wardi Major, the, 47 &*n*.
Watson, General Sir J., V.C., and Watson's Horse, 120, 124, 125 *sqq*., 129, 133, 135, 138-9, 140-1, 178, 197, 213; the regiment renamed, 69
Watson, Major-General W. A., 177, 178, 192, 208, 263, 265, 266, 277-8, 279, 280
Watts, Lieut. J. B., 131
Wazir Singh, Jemadar, 136
Wells, Surg.-Lieut. N. S., 274
Westerham (France). 313
Western Malwa, Chiefs in, *see* Jaora, *and* Ratlam
Westmacott, Capt. R., 356
Westmacott, Lieut. T., 320, 333
White, General Sir G., 222
Wickham, Major E. T. R., 281, 288, 320, 382
Wigram, Colonel Sir Clive, 266 &*n*.
Williams, Capt. A. H., 268, 281, 310, 315, 334, 351, 388, 404
Wilson, Capt. T. F., 48, 49
Wilson, Lieut. H. A., 131
Wilson, Lieut. L., 325-6, 330
Wilson, Lieut. T. D., 334, 335, 351, 352, 353, 355-6, 386, 404

Wolseley, Major-General Sir G., 210
Wood, Capt. E. G., 48, 52, 53, 54, 55
Wood, F.-M. Sir Evelyn, V.C., 25 &*n*., 29, 30 *n*., 31, 55 *sqq*., 57, 58, 69, 70, 71, 76, 80, 84, 121 *n*., 194
Wood, Lieut. R. B. M., 273
Woodburn, General, 5, 9, 10, 11
Woodcraft, military value of, 236
Woodhouse, Lieut., 346, 375, 376, 377, 379
Woolcombe, Major, 16
Wrench, Lieut. F. A. C., 273-4
Wright, Mr, 287
Wynyard-Wright, Lieut., 334, 335
Wyllie, Ensign R. J. H., 122

YAKUB KHAN, Amir, 142, 143
Yaucourt-Bussue, 328
Yazd-i-Khast, action at, 291
Younghusband, Lieutenant J., 125
Ypres, battles of, first and second, 312, 323-4
Ypres, F.-M. Earl (Sir John French), 318-19
Yser Spruit, 254

ZAHIDABAD, 156-7, 172
Zaimukht Expedition, the, 170
Zairulla, Khan Bahadur, Risaldar, 148 &*n*., 219-20
Zarkiyeh marsh, the, 392
Zawa, capture of, 170
Zebda, 400
Zebdani, 404
Zergatta, 157
Ziauldin, Dafadar, 32
" Zugs," 207

www.ingramcontent.com/pod-product-compliance
Lightning Source LLC
Chambersburg PA
CBHW021824220426
43663CB00005B/126